THE NEW KI

LUKE PATEY

The New Kings of Crude

*China, India, and the Global Struggle
for Oil in Sudan and South Sudan*

HURST & COMPANY, LONDON

First published in the United Kingdom in paperback in 2014 by
C. Hurst & Co. (Publishers) Ltd.,
41 Great Russell Street, London, WC1B 3PL
© Luke Patey, 2014
All rights reserved.
Printed in the USA

Distributed in the United States, Canada and Latin America
by Oxford University Press, 198 Madison Avenue, New York,
NY 10016, United States of America.

A Cataloguing-in-Publication data record for this book
is available from the British Library.

ISBN: 978-1-84904-294-9

www.hurstpublishers.com

This book is printed on paper from registered sustainable
and managed sources.

To Thea and Victor, for helping me chase oilmen across continents

CONTENTS

ACKNOWLEDGMENTS

The research for this book began seven years ago over several heavily sugared glasses of tea with Sudanese academics at the University of Khartoum. Since then I have conducted well over a hundred interviews with scholars, government officials, activists, executives, and others. Some asked to remain anonymous, but I am grateful to all for offering their time and energy to discuss oil and Sudan.

The guidance of Atta El-Battahani, Safwat Fanous, Mustafa Babiker, Asim El-Moghraby, and others in Sudan was indispensible early on. At the Unviersity of Juba in what is now independent South Sudan, Leben Moro was always willing to enlighten me on sides of the story that I would not see.

In Beijing, Wang Suolao broadened my horizons on China over many lunches at Peking University. Xing Qizhi provided superb translation assistance. In India, I could not have been more fortunate than to receive the guidance of Gulshan Dietl; invoking her name opened the heaviest of closed doors. Shebonti Ray Dadwal and Ruchita Beri at the Institute for Defence Studies and Analyses and Ajay Dubey at Jawaharlal Nehru University were kind enough to answer my questions hour after hour in New Delhi.

During an intensive writing period in New York, Tatiana Carayannis was a welcoming host to an overly preoccupied guest at the Social Science Research Council. Among many colleagues at the Danish Institute for International Studies who gave their support to me over nearly a decade in Denmark, I thank Nanna Hvidt for getting me to Sudan in the first place and Peter Albrecht for telling me when enough was enough.

Strangely, it was a recommendation from a New Zealander in a Parisian restaurant that was most decisive in this book seeing the light of day.

ACKNOWLEDGMENTS

In taking the advice to have Dietrich Jung as my supervisor for the dissertation that later evolved into this book, I would benefit immensely from his scholarly, professional and personal support. Daniel Large was a constant source of encouragement and feedback. From Copenhagen, Khartoum, Beijing and New Delhi, both Dietrich and Dan very much shared the journey of this book with me. But I alone take responsibility for any errors.

I am indebted to my publisher, Michael Dwyer, for taking on a book that was seemingly trapped between two worlds. Susan Michael offered thorough editing and plenty of enthusiasm to push me through the final stretch.

Finally, I would like to thank family and friends close and far for their confidence and understanding. This book is dedicated to my wife, Thea Christensen, and our son, Victor. Thea stuck with me over one abbreviated weekend after another in a long writing process. I love her for always distracting me towards the more important things in life.

ABBREVIATIONS

ABC	Abyei Boundaries Commission
AGI	Arab Group International
APM	Administered Pricing Mechanism
AU	African Union
BGP	Bureau of Geophysical Prospecting Ltd.
BHEL	Bharat Heavy Electricals Ltd.
BJP	Bharatiya Janata Party
bpd	barrels per day
CNOOC	China National Offshore Oil Corporation
CNPC	China National Petroleum Corporation
CPA	Comprehensive Peace Agreement
CPECC	China Petroleum Engineering and Construction Corporation
CRN	Conflict Risk Network
ECOS	European Coalition on Oil in Sudan
EU	European Union
EXIM	Export-Import
GNPOC	Greater Nile Petroleum Operating Company
GOSS	Government of Southern Sudan
GWDC	Great Wall Drilling Company
ICC	International Criminal Court
ICG	International Crisis Group
IGAD	Intergovernmental Authority on Development
IMF	International Monetary Fund
IPO	Initial Public Offering
JEM	Justice and Equality Movement

JNOC	Japan National Oil Corporation
LAPSSET	Lamu Port and South Sudan Ethiopia Transport
LPG	Liquefied Petroleum Gas
MEA	Ministry of External Affairs (India)
MEM	Ministry of Energy and Mining (Sudan)
MFA	Ministry of Foreign Affairs (China)
MPI	Ministry of Petroleum Industry (China)
MPNG	Ministry of Petroleum and Natural Gas (India)
NASA	National Aeronautics and Space Administration
NCP	National Congress party
NDRC	National Development and Reform Commission
NELP	New Exploration and Licensing Policy
NGO	non-governmental organisation
NIF	National Islamic Front
NYSE	New York Stock Exchange
ONGC	Oil and Natural Gas Corporation
ONLF	Ogaden National Liberation Front
OVL	ONGC Videsh Ltd.
PCA	Permanent Court of Arbitration
PDOC	Petrodar Operating Company
PLA	People's Liberation Army
PLO	Palestine Liberation Organisation
SASAC	State-owned Assets Supervision and Administration Commission
Sinopec	China Petroleum and Chemical Corporation
SPLA/M	Sudan People's Liberation Army/Movement
SSDF	South Sudan Defence Forces
UN	United Nations
US	United States of America
WNPOC	White Nile Petroleum Operating Company
ZPEB	Zhongyuan Petroleum Engineering Co. Ltd.

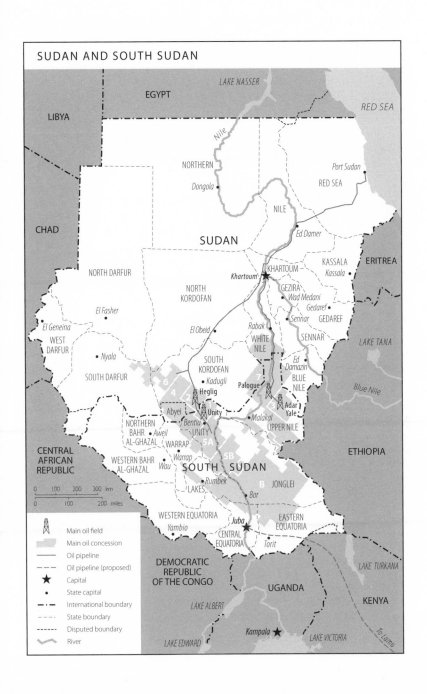

SUDAN AND SOUTH SUDAN

LIBYA

EGYPT

LAKE NASSER

RED SEA

CHAD

NORTHERN

Dongola

Port Sudan

RED SEA

NILE

Ed Damer

SUDAN

KASSALA

ERITREA

NORTH DARFUR

El Fasher

NORTH KORDOFAN

KHARTOUM

Khartoum

Kassala

GEZIRA

El Geneina

WEST DARFUR

Nyala

El Obeid

Rabak

Wad Medani

Gedaref

GEDAREF

SOUTH DARFUR

SOUTH KORDOFAN

Kadugli

Heglig

WHITE NILE

Sennar

SENNAR

LAKE TANA

6

4 2

Abyei

Unity

Palogue

7

Ed Damazin

BLUE NILE

Blue Nile

NORTHERN BAHR AL-GHAZAL

Aweil

Bentiu

UNITY

3

Adar Yale

Malakal

UPPER NILE

CENTRAL AFRICAN REPUBLIC

WESTERN BAHR AL-GHAZAL

Wau

Warrap

WARRAP

5A

5B

ETHIOPIA

SOUTH SUDAN

0   100   200   300 km

0   100   200 miles

LAKES

Rumbek

Bor

B

JONGLEI

WESTERN EQUATORIA

Yambio

Juba

CENTRAL EQUATORIA

EASTERN EQUATORIA

Torit

LAKE TURKANA

Main oil field

Main oil concession

Oil pipeline

Oil pipeline (proposed)

Capital

State capital

International boundary

State boundary

Disputed boundary

River

DEMOCRATIC REPUBLIC OF THE CONGO

UGANDA

KENYA

LAKE ALBERT

Kampala

LAKE VICTORIA

To Lamu

LAKE EDWARD

INTRODUCTION

THREE MINUTES IN FEBRUARY

In a little known corner of the world, everything was about to change. In early February 1984, a group of southern Sudanese rebels, under the cover of darkness and with automatic weapons in hand, approached the base camp of the American oil company Chevron. Hundreds of kilometres south of Sudan's capital of Khartoum, Chevron had set up shop at Rubkona on the Bahr-el-Ghazal river, a tributary of the White Nile, near the town of Bentiu. After years of extensive exploration, the oilmen had discovered oil in the isolated region and now intended to reap the rewards of their hard work. But the armed rebels heading into the camp were intent on something altogether different.

The southern Sudanese rebels saw Chevron as an arm of their sworn enemy, the regime under Sudan's President Jaafar Mohammed Nimeiri in Khartoum. Twelve years earlier, a civil war between the Sudanese government and the southern rebel group known as Anyanya had ended. But, over time, Nimeiri continued the same neglect of development of the south and exploitation of its resources that had led his predecessors into war in the first place. He planned to pipe the freshly-discovered oil north and cut out southern Sudan from the hundreds of millions, if not billions of dollars that it would generate. Under no circumstances did the guerrilla fighters want to see Sudan's northern rulers benefit from the oil wealth that lay beneath southern soil. If they could put a halt to Chevron's activities, they could also put a stop to Nimeiri's oil ambitions.

Chevron's base camp at Rubkona consisted of a double-storey barge resting at the riverside, including a number of container houses, and an airstrip nearby. When the first group of rebels entered the camp, they were startled to find members of the kitchen staff still at work late at night. A shot was fired. Unaware of the source of the gunfire, the other rebels instinctively opened fire. The bullets from their automatic weapons easily cut through the thin walls of the camp's sleeping quarters. The unsuspecting workers, already in their beds for the night, escaped unscathed as gunfire tore through the quarters at chest height. But those who were standing suffered a different fate.

In the end three contractors workers—a British national, a Kenyan and a Filipino—were killed; seven others were badly wounded. Rumours swirled after the attack that the rebels were only looking to take Chevron oilmen hostage, that the violence that unfolded was not premeditated.[1] But the attack led Chevron to immediately suspend its operations in southern Sudan.

This was a devastating turn of events for Chevron. Over a period of nine years the company had invested a billion dollars in Sudan, and it was just beginning to set into motion plans to build a pipeline to Port Sudan on the Red Sea to bring the oil to international markets. The American oilmen had first arrived in Khartoum a decade earlier, their cowboy hats and boots offering a sharp contrast to the traditional *jellabiya* of long white robes worn by locals. Their subsequent discovery of oil gave promise to the impoverished country that after emerging from a bitter and long civil war, it would achieve an economic miracle.

News of the Rubkona attack dogged George Keller, Chairman of Standard Oil of California, Chevron's parent company, as he and other company executives headed to Khartoum a week after the attack for a meeting with President Nimeiri and his oil minister Sharif al-Tuhami. At first Keller was not interested in coming to Sudan; he was busy trying to close the biggest deal in the history of the international oil industry at the time by merging Chevron with Gulf Oil. But the Sudanese would not accept anyone else but the head boss.

When Chevron's executives arrived in Khartoum, they found little sympathy from Sudan's leaders. The Sudanese urged the American oilmen to continue their activities in the south and insisted that adequate security would be provided by the Sudanese military. President Nimeiri wanted to get the oil flowing in order to ramp up the government's finances to repair Sudan's crumbling economy and respond to what was evolving into a renewed civil war with southern rebels. But Keller and his executives implored the Sudanese president to find a political solution with the rebels before the company resumed its work. They suggested that the company could invoke *force majeure* in the south, which would free it from its contractual obligations to develop the oil fields until it could operate again with reasonable security.

The situation was tense. Sudan was one of the American oil major's largest international investments. 'It is not so much that Chevron does not want to work in the South, indeed they have well over a billion investment which they have to justify to their shareholders,' wrote Robert O. Collins, a Sudan scholar and personal adviser to Chevron at the time.[2] 'But they will not as a matter of principle, and their employees will not as a matter of practice, go to the South if they are going to get their heads shot off.'

The suggestion of a prolonged suspension of oil production frustrated Sudan's oil minister Tuhami. Rather than give in to Chevron's demands, he asked the executives present at the meeting how many employees they were willing to lose in southern Sudan, callously explaining that 'everyone has to die at some time'.[3] In response, the American oilmen shut their briefcases, left the meeting, and maintained their suspension of operations in the south.[4] Chevron would struggle with the Sudanese government to hold on to its assets in the years to come, but as the civil war continued, the company finally decided to leave Sudan completely in 1992.

Many Sudanese officials felt that Chevron had acted too hastily by suspending operations in the wake of the attack at Rubkona. Sudan's oil ministry in Khartoum dubbed Chevron's decision to suspend its operations the 'three-minute *force majeure*', referring to what was believed to be the span of time of the attack.[5] But regardless of its brevity, the attack by the southern rebels had altered the course of Sudan's future. In a blaze of gunfire, they had ushered in the winds of a changing world. A new chapter in Sudan's history was beginning with the outbreak of the country's second civil war and the withdrawal of Chevron. The oil was left beneath the ground, ready for taking by those with the means to pump it out and the daring to face the dangers above ground.

Asia's oil giants and Sudan

This book is about the Chinese and Indian national oil companies that came to replace Chevron and later other Western oil companies in Sudan. It tells the stories of oilmen, politicians, rebels, and human rights activists, in Sudan, South Sudan, and around the world, who have struggled to control the flow of Sudanese oil since it was first discovered over thirty years ago. It shows how the violent and unstable politics of oil in Sudan and South Sudan came to both empower and restrict the wider international expansion of Chinese and Indian national oil companies. Investing in Sudan during one of Africa's longest and deadliest civil wars galvanised the international rise of Asian national oil companies for over a decade, but the political turmoil leading up to the birth of South Sudan in 2011 would prove to be a daunting challenge for Asia's oil giants.

The attention this book devotes to the role of oil in Sudan, and later South Sudan, serves a wider purpose.[6] China's and India's relations with Africa have blossomed over the past decade from an astonishing growth in trade and foreign investment. Intense debates have explored the character and motivations of Chinese and Indian engagement and the impact that China and India have on development, economics, and politics in Africa.[7] But to a large extent, the influence of Africa on China and India has been neglected.[8]

This book explores in depth a case of Chinese and Indian engagement in the pursuit of oil in Africa. It disentangles the web of interactions spun between the politics and civil war of Sudan, and later South Sudan, and the politics and business of oil in China and India.[9] From this close examination, it reveals how Sudanese politics, civil wars, and foreign relations influenced Asian national oil companies not only in these countries, but also in their wider international operations.[10] Just as Chinese and Indian engagement is having a growing economic and political influence in Africa, the experiences of Asian national oil companies in Sudan and South Sudan demonstrate how Africa can shape China and India as rising powers in the world.

It did not take long for Sudan to find replacements for the departing Chevron oilmen. The China National Petroleum Corporation (CNPC) first invested in Sudan in 1995. CNPC was the largest oil company in China but relatively unknown in the international oil industry at the time. It was not deterred by Sudan's civil war. In the coming years, Chinese oilmen endured the harsh climate and difficult working conditions, faced down assaults by the southern rebels, and gradually came to play a leading role in building Sudan's oil industry.

CNPC was not the only oil company to come to Sudan in the wake of Chevron's departure. A handful of small- and mid-sized oil companies from North America and Europe and the Malaysian national oil company Petronas were also instrumental in rejuvenating the oil industry in the late 1990s.[11] The foreign arm of India's national oil company, the Oil and Natural Gas Corporation Videsh, also entered Sudan in 2003. Just as the Chinese oil giant stepped in for Chevron, ONGC Videsh (OVL for short), replaced departing Canadian and European oil companies which were facing pressure from human rights activists in their home countries.

China and India are distinct rising powers in the world. The Chinese one-party political system contrasts sharply with India's democracy. While this book may at times group together Chinese and Indian national oil companies for the purpose of demonstrating the influence of Sudan, and later South Sudan, on their international expansion, they should not be seen as monolithic. Each Chinese and Indian national oil company has its own corporate history and follows its individual strategy, so that each one invests and competes both with its national counterparts and with international oil companies. Many of these characteristics come through upon examination of the history of their investments in Sudan and South Sudan. After the exodus of Chevron and other Western oil companies, Sudan became central to the quest of Asian national oil companies to build international oil empires, but later also presented a fair number of challenges to their continual expansion overseas.

Oil and war in Sudan

Before heading north to Egypt and the Mediterranean Sea, the White and Blue Nile rivers meet at Khartoum. But their confluence did not represented a symbol of unity and peace for Sudan. Rather, Sudanese governments built on the legacy left by their Anglo-Egyptian colonial rulers between 1899 and 1956 and exploited and manipulated populations in the country's periphery for their own political power and personal enrichment.[12] The denial of economic opportunities and political freedoms to the people of southern Sudan led the country into decades of civil war, and eventually, the birth of South Sudan.

Even before Sudan won independence in 1956, unrest was bubbling to the surface in the south. Later, the harsh imposition of the Arabic language and Islam in southern Sudan, where indigenous and Christian beliefs were most prevalent, and the marginalisation of southerners in the national government created the perfect recipe for insurrection. The southern rebel group Anyanya, named after a type of poison, was founded in the early 1960s to fight for the independence of southern Sudan.[13] But after over a decade of conflict between the Sudanese government and southern rebels, the two sides were locked in a military stalemate. Anyanya was not able to capture and secure key southern towns and the Sudanese military was unable to expel the rebels from the bush of the southern interior.[14] In 1972, the Addis Ababa Agreement was signed to bring an end to a civil war that had left an estimated half million people dead.

But peace would not last. Eleven years after bringing Sudan's first civil war to a halt, the Sudanese President Jaafar Nimeiri fanned the flames of political animosity in southern Sudan again, which led to the outbreak of a second civil war in 1983. The new rebellion was fought under the banner of the Sudan People's Liberation Army/Movement (SPLA/M). Rather than a war to secure outright independence for southern Sudan, the second civil war was one aimed at forming a new Sudan in which inclusive governance would replace the neglect and oppression served by Khartoum in the past.

Oil alone was not responsible for the outbreak of Sudan's second civil war, but the Sudanese government's plans to exploit the resource for its own narrow purposes reinforced the wider grievance of regional marginalisation in southern Sudan. During the fighting, oil fields became hotly contested areas of strategic control and sites of horrendous human rights violations against southern Sudanese communities by the Sudanese army and its militias. The multiple civil wars that emerged from the north-south conflict devastated the country, particularly the south, leaving an estimated two million people dead and four million internally displaced.

In January 2005 the signing of the Comprehensive Peace Agreement (CPA) marked the formal end of Sudan's second civil war. In contrast to the destructive influence of oil during the conflict, revenue generated from the industry was shared between the Sudanese government, now led by President Omar Hassan Ahmad al-Bashir and the ruling National Congress party, and the former rebels of the SPLM, which ruled a semi-autonomous southern Sudan. The CPA gave the south the chance to vote to separate from Sudan and become an independent country after a six-year interim period. But the celebration surrounding the peace agreement was marred by another outbreak of violence in Sudan's western region of Darfur.

Sudan could not escape from its tragic history of civil war. Grievances against Khartoum reverberated across the country to spark the Darfur civil war in 2003. As it did in the south, the Sudanese government exploited its oil revenue to wage war in Darfur and again committed horrendous abuses against civilians.[15] The conflict captured the world's attention and left 300,000 dead and millions internally displaced.[16] But as the Darfur civil war simmered, with sporadic bursts of violence, the southern Sudanese voted nearly unanimously for independence. South Sudan became the world's newest country on 9 July 2011.

The breakup of Sudan and South Sudan was anything but straightforward. The majority of the oil was now located in the independent South Sudan, but the main pipelines and infrastructure necessary to transport it to international markets were in Sudan. In 2012, as officials from the two sides negotiated to seek an agreement on shipment of South Sudanese oil northward through Sudan, the armies of Sudan and South Sudan clashed on the battlefield of a disputed border. Even if short-term solutions to the oil dispute and conflicts in border areas between the two Sudans can be found, prospects for a problem-free future remain doubtful. A half-century of political animosity and armed conflict will be hard to overcome and reverse into a lasting peace.

Chinese and Indian national companies had replaced Chevron and other Western oil companies in Sudan in the 1990s and 2000s; now they were firmly entrenched within the turbulent and often violent politics of Sudan and South Sudan. The Rubkona attack on Chevron in February 1984 set in motion a chain of events that helped shape the rise of Chinese and Indian national oil companies as major players in the international oil industry. But the Asian oilmen would later come to better appreciate why their American counterparts had left Sudan in the first place.

PART I

SUDAN

1

AMERICAN DREAMING

November 2007: El Gamhuriya Avenue was teeming with activity. The daily grind of central Khartoum was a slow moving mass of cars, buses, and three-wheeled auto-rickshaws. The tall brown stone minarets of the al-Kabir mosque presided over the congested avenue, its call to prayer trumpeting over speakers placed around the city centre. At the nearby central bus station and the Souq al-Arabi market, Sudanese men in *jellabiya*, the traditional garb of long white robes, and women in brightly-coloured dresses streamed in and out of buses and vans as vendors shouted their wares. At the edge of the market, a line of men waited their turn to receive the services of a street-side barber, whose shop consisted of a plastic lawn chair, a small mirror fastened to a brick wall, and a pair of scissors.

Wealthy suburbs were developing outside Khartoum's city centre with villas and restaurants catering to an increasingly prosperous middle and upper class. At new cafés, young and affluent Sudanese men and women chatted over frothy lattes and chilled juices. While most people in Sudan's capital were still poor, the buzz of commercial activity was a sign of a growing economy. Khartoum was looking to become the 'Dubai of Africa', eager to repeat the path to riches of its Middle Eastern neighbours. An oil boom was in progress.

Petrodollars began to flood into Sudan in 1999. In less than a decade, oil-energised business activity filled the government's coffers as never before and reshaped the skyline of the city on the Nile. Chinese trade and investment were behind much of the boom; Chinese national oil companies were essential in fuelling the engine of Sudan's oil-powered economy in the late 1990s. China had become Sudan's largest foreign investor and trading partner as its economic presence spread across the African continent. China was not new to Sudan, but its presence, which had once been characterised by the rattling sounds of a wok in the dim lighting of a dilapidated Chinese restaurant in Khartoum's Riyadh district, was now represented by groups of Chinese geologists stepping out of white shuttle vans and large numbers of Chinese construction workers at building sites around the city.

But China was fuelling more than Sudan's economy. If anything, Khartoum was a thriving oasis in what was otherwise a desert of war and poverty in Sudan. Beginning in 2003, a civil war escalated in Sudan's western region of Darfur. In the years to follow, the Sudan Armed Forces and pro-government militias carried out a brutal counterinsurgency campaign that targeted civilian populations. China was accused of financing the Sudanese government through its oil investments and providing diplomatic protection against international sanctions through its veto on the United Nations Security Council.[1] This was in marked contrast to the role of the US. From the late 1990s, Washington had isolated and sanctioned Sudan because of its support for international terrorism and human rights abuses against its own people during the previous civil war between the government and the Sudan People's Liberation Army. Whereas China's role in Sudan was business-driven, the US position was intensely political.

But there had been a time when things were different, when an oil boom was coming to Sudan and China's presence was barely audible. It was a time when American, not Chinese companies were making a bid for Sudan's oil, when America played a very similar role in Sudan to that of China today. In the late 1970s, the discovery of oil in southern Sudan by Chevron offered to take Sudan's struggling economy to once unimaginable heights. Khartoum was described at that time as a flower blossoming in a vast and barren landscape, but talk was of the capital becoming the 'Paris of the Arab World', rather than an Abu Dhabi or Dubai. American businessmen of Chase Manhattan bank and Ford Motors descended on Khartoum to capitalise on the oil rush. While enjoying the air-conditioned confines of Khartoum's new Hilton Hotel, they acted as 'scouts of capitalism', seeking to infuse Sudan with capital, technology and the liberal ideology of a market-driven economy.[2] Chevron was at the head of the pack. After years of intense exploration in the massive and imposing virgin territory of southern Sudan, it was eager to build a pipeline north to Sudan's Red Sea coast in order to cash in on its costly investment.

But oil was only one part of the warming relationship between the US and Sudan in the 1970s. When the first Sudanese civil war ended in 1972, Sudan's military regime under then President Jaafar Nimeiri wanted to find foreign partners. The US fitted perfectly as its relationship with Sudan helped fulfil Washington's regional interests in the Middle East and countered Soviet intervention in the Horn of Africa during the Cold War. The political ground was ripe for Chevron to flourish.

The African frontier

Discovering Sudan's oil did not come easily for the oilmen of Chevron. Brian Kay was one of them. A graduate of the prestigious St. Andrews University in Scotland, Kay was a veteran of over two decades in the oil business. His overseas work had already taken him to Nigeria before the Biafra war and later to the jungles of Indonesia. He was looking for new challenges in Sudan. 'I volunteered for Sudan because I realised that it was a huge focus area for Chevron, and would be a very busy operation and a place I could grow,' Kay recalled.

Arriving in 1980 to lead a geophysical team of three exploration crews, Kay helped Chevron explore what began as a massive concession area of over 500,000 square kilometres. 'When I landed, in forty degrees and extremely dry conditions, and saw the dusty streets, plastic bags and flies of Khartoum for the first time, I wondered if I had made a mistake,' Kay remembered.[3] 'Within a month I settled down and I knew I had made the correct decision.'

For Kay, Chevron's Sudan operations were breaking new ground in the international oil industry. In the early 1970s, Chevron was drawn to Sudan after taking advantage of new technologies, concepts and tools that had recently become available for oil exploration. In particular, after the National Aeronautics and Space Administration (NASA) launched its Landsat satellite in July 1972, which brought back images of much of the earth's surface, the Chevron geologist John B. Miller used this new information to help the company search for oil in East Africa. 'Many other companies were doing work like Miller's, but Chevron was the first to act on it,' said John Sutherland, Chevron's first country manager in Sudan.[4] Miller was exploring how to use the Landsat images to steer

Chevron's work programme in Kenya, where it had signed an exploration license in June 1972, when his research pointed towards the possible presence of a large sedimentary basin where oil might be found in southern Sudan.[5] On the basis of his study of Kenya's geology and the satellite images, Miller wrote a memo in February 1973 to Bill Chapman, the Chevron country manager in Kenya, suggesting that Chapman visit Khartoum and look into the possibilities for investment in Sudan.

A year later, Chapman travelled to Khartoum to look for further geological data. He was impressed with the Sudanese capital and its people. 'Khartoum is very interesting. Its residents make up a representative cross-section of the various ethnic groups in the Sudan. Most are Moslem, with Egyptian Coptic Christians, and animist tribes. The people are handsome, well-built, and Arabic in behavior,' Chapman wrote in a report to the President of Chevron Overseas in San Francisco after his visit.[6] Met with open arms at the Ministry of Industry and Mining, Chapman found what he was looking for. A 1973 United Nations geophysical survey gave further indication that there was a major sedimentary basin in southern Sudan. He also found that the Sudanese government was very friendly and helpful, open to reasonable economic terms, and that there was little competition to speak of. Chevron signed an exploration agreement with the Sudanese government on 23 November 1974. The combination of Sudanese regulations and the enormity of the exploration concession resulted in the contract documents weighing 990 pounds.[7] After the contract was vetted and finalised in San Francisco and airfreighted to Khartoum, it took an entire night of signing to finish the job, but the deal was done.[8] The company also demonstrated its good will in Sudan by devoting $200,000 a year to scholarships for Sudanese students and gave Nimeiri a bonus cheque for $100,000 'for the beautification of Khartoum'.[9] It then began the momentous task of exploration in the great African frontier of southern Sudan in early 1975.

In most areas of the world, oil companies are able to refer to data produced by previous exploration efforts. However, there were almost no data available on the interior of Sudan; the American oilmen were starting from scratch, basing themselves on what was still considered at the time 'a geologically educated guess'.[10] 'No one thought oil could be found in Sudan's non-marine sedimentary basins,' said one former Sudanese oil official.[11] The immense territory available to Chevron reflected not only the lack of oil exploration in the past, but also the sheer size of Sudan.

This was, after all, Africa's largest country; at 2.5 million square kilometres, Sudan was one-quarter the size of the US.

Chevron did some exploration work near the sweltering seaside town of Port Sudan on the Red Sea, where other oil companies had been active in the past. It was able to make several non-commercial natural gas discoveries there, but shortly afterwards the company decided to focus its efforts on the interior. Moving from the northeastern coast to southern Sudan meant a shift in culture and ethnicity. Sudan's population was of African-Arab decent with scores of languages and ethnic groups. Largely Arabic-speaking Muslims lived in the north of Sudan, while the south was characterised by African roots and dominated by the Dinka and Nuer peoples.

The physical geography of northern and southern Sudan was equally diverse. From the burning coast and deserts of the north, Chevron was entering the great savanna and the dense marshland and lush rainforests of the south. The only geographical constant was the Nile river. The many tributaries of the White Nile stretch over southern Sudan. The isolation of this region was staggering. For Brian Kay, the main problem with operating in Sudan was that 'wherever you are, you are a long way from anywhere'. Southern Sudan was essentially landlocked except for the Nile. Chevron's first challenge was to move the necessary personnel and machinery to explore for oil so far inland.

With half a million square kilometres at its disposal (a territory as big as Spain), Chevron's first task was to narrow down where it should focus its search.[12] After completing a barrage of aeromagnetic and gravity surveys in 1975, it mapped out not one but two sedimentary basins, the Muglad and Melut basins, named after nearby towns.[13] By early 1976, the first exploration crew hit the ground and began to carry out controlled explosions, called seismic surveys, to measure the geological qualities of the ground beneath. A year later, in October 1977, the bit of an oil drill pierced the ground of Sudan's interior for the first time.

In May 1978, Chevron found the first signs of oil in the Muglad basin. It was near the town of Bentiu in southern Sudan, where mud cuttings from a drill showed that oil lay beneath.[14] Less than a year later, in March 1979, Chevron made the first commercial discovery of oil at Abu Gabra in north Sudan.[15] The oil well was located west of the town of Muglad, near the border of the provinces of Kordofan and Darfur, an area that is home to the various ethnic groups of the Arabic-speaking Misseriya nomads. While it was not a large discovery, and Chevron was far from impressed, finding oil was a historic event in Sudan. In a rally attended by over 10,000 people in June 1979, President Nimeiri jumped over sacrificial bulls to celebrate the discovery.[16] But Abu Gabra was just the beginning. Much more was waiting for Chevron farther south.

In April 1980, the company made its first significant oil find north of Bentiu in Upper Nile province. It was dubbed the Unity oil field by the Sudanese government. A year later, Chevron found the Adar and Yale oil fields in the Khor Adar valley in the eastern Upper Nile region. Later, it struck oil again between Kordofan and Upper Nile, discovering what came to be known as the Heglig oil field. Altogether, Chevron made a dozen discoveries in both Upper Nile and Kordofan by the end of 1983. Because it was clear that most of the oil was in southern Sudan, the company elected to establish its main camp at Bentiu in the south to exploit the Unity and Heglig fields. Secondary camps were set up in Muglad to the north in Kordofan, in the town of Melut in eastern Upper Nile, and in Adok farther south, in the hope of making further discoveries. Chevron was on a roll now.

Into the Sudd

The climate and terrain of the south were intimidating even to the most seasoned oilman. Chevron hired a few foreign contractors who had experience in the African bush and could stay in the field for long periods without supervision to help establish base camps and run logistics.[17] These hardened men were of varying ages, nationalities and personalities, and were invaluable for getting Chevron started. Still, when Brian Kay first came to Sudan in 1980, Chevron had already tried but failed to conduct a successful year-round exploration of the south.

Half of the year in southern Sudan is dominated by the rainy season. Typically from April to September, heavy rains turn the ground into a vast, sticky clay surface that makes much of the oil region inaccessible for heavy machinery. Sudan's infrastructure provided little help, simply because there was very little of it. Before any work could get underway, roads and airstrips would have to be laid, temporary housing set up, and power generators brought in. The dilapidated railway did not even go into southern oil regions. The ever-industrious oilmen brought in four fixed-wing aircraft, ten helicopters, a large variety of road vehicles, construction equipment and a fleet of tugs and barges to move down the Nile.

Kay knew that the main bottleneck to Chevron's activities was the problem of learning how to operate efficiently during the short and scorching hot dry season, and the even more daunting long and humid rainy season. Before he arrived in Sudan, Kay had worked for a year at Chevron's San Francisco headquarters as an operations geophysicist for worldwide operations, a position which included developing equipment for some of the most difficult parts of Sudan.[18] 'The clue to working year round in Sudan was to understand the wet and dry seasons,' Kay explained.[19] 'We equipped exploration crews with large-tire buggies and specially designed camp units that were heliportable. We had three Bell 212 helicopters designed for the wet weather crews and these moved personnel and equipment to otherwise inaccessible operational areas. This went a long way in managing the rainy season.'

There were still setbacks. At one point, Chevron had to turn to the manpower of the local Dinka ethnic group when it needed to replace a faulty drill line that was too heavy for helicopters to move and trucks could not access the area because of mud. Three hundred labourers were hired to carry the drill line over their shoulders.[20] Yet thanks to the changes in its operations to account for Sudan's challenging climate and terrain, Chevron was able to double seismic production and drill wells at any time, anywhere. But there were even more imposing natural challenges awaiting Chevron farther south.

Southern Sudan is transformed into a great marshland near the village of Adok. When the White Nile hits the plains of southern Sudan, it scatters like a delta to form one of the largest wetlands in the world. Known as the Sudd, a word for 'barrier' in Arabic, the swampland expands and contracts depending on the level of rainfall during the wet season. It was in the Sudd that Kay organised a fourth exploration crew.

I first saw the Sudd from the back of a Vertol Twin Rotor Helicopter, flying slowly about 10 feet above the ground. I realized what a challenge this would be to record seismic in such a difficult environment. It was clear to me for the first time how vast it was and how varied—20-feet high papyrus, open water, acres of water lilies, some, but not much dry land.[21]

At its largest in the rainy season, the Sudd can form up to 30,000 square kilometres of shallow water. On its western side, Kay and his exploration crews marvelled at the hippopotamus and elephants that inhabited the shallow waters. But the danger of giant crocodiles and snakes lurking in the thick vegetation kept the American oilmen on their toes. There were many challenges in the dense marshland.[22] This was, after all, where the great explorers like Samuel Baker had struggled to find the source of the Nile. But there was one big difference between the legendary adventurers and Kay and his crews: the Chevron oilmen were not interested in finding a way through the Sudd, but in drilling deep beneath it.

Water was everywhere in the Sudd. Rolling along on large-tracked buggies with pontoon-mounted drills, the oilmen were fortunate to find occasional grasslands and pushed on through large areas of four-foot deep water. But it was only where the water suddenly dropped to depths of forty feet that the real trouble began. In some places oilmen might as well have been on the open sea. In order to take on the Sudd, every piece of machinery or equipment needed for Kay and his crews had to be able either to float or to be completely amphibious. But even some of the most innovatively designed machinery fell victim to the Sudd's natural force. One was the Lily-chopper, a boat designed to grind up lilies in front of it in order to clear a path; unfortunately, the Sudd produced much thicker vegetation than just lilies, and before long the Lily-chopper broke down. There was also the Ty-Ty Tiger, a huge buggy designed to tow an entire exploration crew on firm ground or in deep water. But it was left to rust in the middle of the marshland after its drive systems gave out.[23] Yet in spite of all these setbacks, the crews managed to map thousands of kilometres of terrain and found promising geological structures along the way.

From the sandy soil where Chevron's concession began in central Sudan to the depths of the Sudd in the south, there was oil to be found. 'At one time I had crews working right on the Chad-Central African Republic borders to the West,' Kay recalled. 'If you stand on the border you are as close to the West African coast as you are to Port Sudan!'[24] Exploration crews also drilled as far east as the Ethiopian border. By the early 1980s Chevron had drilled a total of almost 830,000 feet in eighty-six wells with an estimated 545 million barrels of recoverable oil waiting to be squeezed from the earth.[25]

And Chevron was not even close to finishing its search. Only five wells had been drilled in the Melut basin to the east, and none in the Sudd.[26] Earlier trepidation that Chevron's crew felt about taking on the technical and physical challenge of Sudan became exaltation. 'Most, not all, but most people assigned to the Sudan operation loved it,' Kay recalled. Chevron had a massive presence in Khartoum with some 105 families posted there. 'The work was fascinating. It was a huge virgin area where we were successfully finding oil.'[27] After nearly a decade of painstaking work, the Chevron crews had done their job. It was as if the American oilmen had conquered the great African frontier. Now it was time for Chevron's executives to do their job.

Grand plans

There was a buzz on the sunburned streets of Khartoum when George Keller's corporate jet touched down in 1982. As Chairman and Chief Executive Officer of Chevron, then still under the parent company name of the Standard Oil Company of California, Keller had come to meet with Sharif El-Tuhami, Sudan's Minister of Energy and Mining. The men were to negotiate how to proceed with exploiting the freshly-discovered oil fields in the south. Keller was a veteran of Chevron's overseas operations, and had risen through the company's ranks to the top in May 1981.[28] He was known as a sociable and opinionated leader. During long hauls overseas, the Kansas City native and Massachusetts Institute of Technology graduate was known to insist on a game or two of dominoes with his fellow executives before getting down to work. He was also a lover of foreign cultures. Keller often arrived a day early to meetings abroad in order to savour the local cuisine, take in entertainment, and get a feel for the rhythm of everyday life.[29]

After he became chairman, however, the enormity of Keller's responsibilities took over. 'I can spend four days in Egypt and never see the Pyramids,' he said. 'It would be great to go back to all those places and tour them with the people I've met.' When time came for business, Keller was known as a cold-calculating and aggressive risk-taker. He made the enormous gamble of purchasing one of Chevron's competitors, Gulf Oil, for the price tag of $13.3 billion in 1984,[30] the largest deal in the history of the oil business at the time. When it entered Sudan, Chevron hoped it might make big waves overseas, too.

Chevron and the entire international oil industry were under pressure to find new areas for exploration in the 1970s. In 1973, King Faisal of Saudi Arabia led an Arab oil embargo against the US and the West for their support for Israel in the Yom Kippur War. As a result, international oil prices soared to record heights and the oil producers of the Organisation of Petroleum Exporting Countries (OPEC) began to aggressively nationalise foreign-owned oil and gas assets to reap the profits and break what was essentially a cartel formed by Chevron and six other major American and European oil companies, called the Seven Sisters. In response, international oil companies began in earnest to explore and exploit petroleum resources outside OPEC member countries. They responded to the nationalisation of their assets in the Middle East, North Africa and Latin America by ramping up activities in the more friendly regions of the world, such as Alaska, the North Sea, and the Gulf of Mexico. For Chevron, Kay explained, 'Sudan was a friendly and sufficiently stable country'.[31]

Chevron had originally sought to partner with Texaco, another major American oil company, to help finance the enormous costs of exploring Sudan's interior. But Texaco backed out as Chevron was negotiating its exploration licenses with the Sudanese government; the risks of the vast and unknown terrain of southern Sudan were too big.[32] Later, before Chevron won the license for its Sudan concession, the company got word that Esso, later ExxonMobil, was submitting a competing proposal to the Sudanese government. Chevron was worried about Sudan's Petroleum Resources Act at the time, which provided no terms for production earnings should it be successful in finding oil. But, faced with competition, it elected to drop the concern for the time being, and focus on acquiring exploration rights. This move proved crucial, as Chevron later discovered that Esso was unwilling to consider exploration in Sudan without full exploration and production terms set in stone.[33] Chevron was later able to sign a production sharing agreement with the Sudanese government, bypassing its problem with the Petroleum Resources Act.[34] The discovery of oil was a vindication of Chevron's big gamble in taking on the unexplored terrain and unclear contractual conditions of working in Sudan. Now, in 1982, Chevron's boss Keller needed to make sure it was a gamble that paid off.

The oil minister Tuhami was waiting for Keller to arrive. The two men were to discuss pipelines and refineries. A trained geologist, Tuhami was thoroughly impressed by the American oilmen. 'Chevron geologists are talented and have the ability to smell oil,' he recalled.[35] Chevron, after all, had found the largest oil field in the world, the Ghawar, underneath Saudi Arabia's sands. But Tuhami was to find himself increasingly at odds with Chevron on how to move forward once the company caught that scent of oil.

When Chevron signed its exploration license with the Sudanese government in 1974, company officials recognised that the Sudanese were keen to find oil soon. Allan V. Martini, Chevron's Vice-President of Exploration and Production, recalled the ceremonial signing and celebrations as 'warm and enthusiastic', with one exception. 'Our only problem was in explaining to our impatient hosts how it could possibly take more than six or eight months before we would know whether or not oil was there,' Martini recalled. Sudan pushed Chevron to increase its spending commitments and accelerate its exploration programme with the requirement to drill its first oil well within three years.[36] After oil was discovered, Sudan asked Chevron to satisfy local demand by constructing an oil refinery. The reason for the government's sense of urgency was clear: soaring international oil prices after the 1973 Arab oil embargo, and later from the 1979 revolution in Iran, had raised Sudan's oil import bill from $1 million to $400 million a year. 'There was always an acute shortage of benzene, gasoil and heavy furnace oils for cars, trucks, industry, and electric power stations,' wrote Tuhami.[37] The total cost of imported oil was valued at 95 per cent of the country's total exports in 1980.[38] Burdened by the rising oil import bill and desperate for production to begin on their own soil, frustrated Sudanese officials were beginning to lose their patience.

Along with billions in loans from Arab Gulf states to develop Sudan's agricultural sector into the breadbasket of the Middle East,[39] oil offered to remake the Sudanese economy. In response to the Sudanese oil ministry's request, Chevron proposed that a small refinery processing 5,000 barrels per day (bpd) could be built near the oil fields outside Bentiu. But Sudanese oil officials had another idea. They were keenly interested in the construction of a larger refinery, handling 25,000 bpd, at Kosti in the north. According to Tuhami, Chevron agreed at first, but a few years later changed its mind.[40] Keller and his executives now wanted the Sudanese to focus completely on the construction of an export pipeline to Port Sudan on the Red Sea.

The same reasons that made Sudan want to build an oil refinery pushed Chevron to focus solely on an oil pipeline. After the Iranian revolution drove international oil prices sky high and Chevron discovered more oil reserves in southern Sudan, there was much more money to be made for the company through exports. Company executives in San Francisco also wanted to see some return on the Sudan venture. The exploration programme may have been an impressive feat of man over Mother Nature, but that was not going to pay the bills. Chevron had made a $15 million commitment to the Sudanese government for exploration, but actually ended up spending almost $90 million during its first four years.[41] After the discovery of oil Chevron's operations grew immensely in size. By late 1982, the company was spending a half a million dollars a day in Sudan.[42]

Tuhami was a strong advocate of the oil refinery option. He alleged that Chevron executives were undermining the refinery plans by urging President Nimeiri to agree to the export pipeline. 'Chevron privately whispered in the corridors of the Ministry of Energy and Mining that should the refinery project proceed, Sudan's government would not have enough foreign currency funds to repay its foreign exchange debts, as well the refined products would be assigned for local consumption [sic],' recalled Tuhami.[43] But President Nimeiri did not see eye to eye with Tuhami and sidelined the oil minister. Tuhami was from the Umma party, one of Sudan's main traditional political parties, but became oil minister in Nimeiri's national reconciliation with opposition parties in 1977, a year after an attempted coup d'état against the Sudanese president.[44] Nimeiri did not want a protracted negotiation with Chevron over the refinery, but rather wanted something to happen as soon as possible to help Sudan's economy. 'The regime is at danger if we don't get this done,' said one of Nimeiri's close aides to Chevron executives.[45] In 1982, Nimeiri met George Keller without Tuhami and gave the go-ahead for the company to proceed with the pipeline.

In January 1983, Keller returned to Khartoum. With Omer el-Tayeb, the Sudanese Vice-President, at his side, he announced the construction of an export pipeline from Sudan's southern oil fields to its northeastern Red Sea coast. 'We are optimistic and we will continue to make significant discoveries,' Keller said.[46] Chevron's oil discoveries in Sudan were not going to change the face of the world oil map, but they were surely going to revolutionise the Sudanese economy. It was the largest and most important economic project in the country's history. Oil production from the Unity and Heglig oil fields was slated to produce 50,000 bpd, increasing to 200,000 bpd in the coming years. The resulting petrodollars would represent an unprecedented amount of wealth for the impoverished country. The total cost of Chevron's pipeline project was estimated to be almost $1 billion. It was the company's largest exploration project outside North

America and central to its international growth strategy.[47] A contract was awarded to the Italian firm Snamprogetti to provide over 1,400 kilometres of steel pipes; other Western subcontractors were brought in for facility construction at the oil fields.[48]

But Chevron could no longer finance the Sudan venture on its own. It formed the White Nile Petroleum Company with the Sudanese government to take on the enormous project. Royal Dutch Shell was brought in as a major financial partner with a one-quarter stake in the venture, along with the Arab Petroleum Investments Corporation and the International Finance Corporation of the World Bank, which acquired minority stakes. Loans also came from a number of American commercial banks and the Overseas Private Investment Corporation, the US government's development finance institution.[49] This was proof that despite Sudan's weak financial position, President Nimeiri had friends in Washington.

Uncle Sam

Oil was only one part of the mix of American interests in Sudan. Before George Keller arrived in Khartoum, another George visited Sudan. In February 1972, George Herbert Walker Bush, an oilman turned politician, was US Ambassador to the United Nations under President Richard Nixon when he attended the inaugural African session of the UN Security Council in Ethiopia, going on to visit eight other countries in Africa, including Sudan. The Netherlands arranged the visit since there were no official relations between the US and Sudan at the time. Bush stayed in the guesthouse of George Curtis Moore, an American Foreign Service officer who was stationed at the Dutch embassy.[50] Bush was invited by the Sudanese to see how their efforts to end the decade-long civil war with southern rebels were faring.[51] He was taken aback by the enormity of the development challenge Sudan faced. 'Once one gets out into the countryside of the Sudan, poverty is all around you all the time', he wrote later of the visit.[52]

After visiting Khartoum, Bush became a strong advocate of the US fostering official relations with Sudan, which had followed other Arab states in severing ties with the US after Washington had supported Israel during the Yom Kippur War. After meeting President Nimeiri, Bush thought that Sudan might now play an important role for the US and its interests in the Middle East. In a cable to the then US Secretary of

State William P. Rogers, Bush noted Nimeiri's interest in helping the US win over other Arab states, mainly Egypt and Libya: 'The Sudan could assist any initiative which the US might undertake, provided he (Nimeiri) felt it was serious and genuine and provided that any action he was called on to take would not embarrass or weaken Egypt.'[53] According to the former Sudanese Foreign Minister Mansour Khalid, after his February 1972 visit Bush told the Sudanese government that satellite imagery suggested oil exploration activities should be focused in southern Sudan, and advised the Sudanese which American oil companies could carry out the work.[54] With the future American president setting the stage for a renewal of relations, the US government sought to establish closer ties with Sudan's leader.

Jaafar Nimeiri was a 39-year-old colonel when he took control of Sudan in a bloodless coup in May 1969. The son of a postman, Nimeiri was a skilled soccer player in secondary school. During his formative years, he honed his political skills by leading a strike against Britain's delaying of Sudan's independence, which closed his school for seven months.[55] He attended Sudan's Military College and after graduation studied for two years at the US Army Command College in Fort Leavenworth, Kansas. When he returned home, Nimeiri led a military coup, the so-called 'May Revolution' of 1969. The civil war was in full swing at the time, and after a few years in power Nimeiri sought to make peace with the south. On 27 February 1972, talks between his government and the rebels began at the Hilton Hotel in Addis Ababa, which culminated with the signing of a peace agreement that promised southern Sudan a fair degree of regional autonomy. But Nimeiri's intentions were far from altruistic: he won the political support of southern leaders to make peace in order to counter his political opponents in the north.[56] Nimeiri also sought new international friends.

Sudanese political winds had been blowing in favour of the US before Bush arrived in Sudan. When Nimeiri seized power in 1969, his socialist tendencies and support from the Soviet Union did little to encourage any change in US-Sudan relations. But this phase passed quickly after a failed coup d'état by the Sudanese Communist Party against Nimeiri in July 1971. The coup attempt, together with the Addis Ababa Agreement, encouraged a reorientation of the Sudanese economy away from state intervention towards increased cooperation with foreign governments, companies, and international organisations.[57] Nimeiri declared shortly after signing the peace agreement that he was interested in resuming full diplomatic ties with the US.[58]

In July 1972, Moore, the American Services Officer, left the US section of the Dutch embassy to become the chargé d'affaires at the reopened US embassy in Khartoum. American aid was made available to Sudan once again.[59] That same month, NASA launched its Landsat programme which provided the American oil industry with a new exploration tool. But just as Chevron took an interest in Sudan, the newly-minted political relations between the US and Sudan would receive a violent jolt.

On 1 March 1973, Khartoum was busy celebrating the first anniversary of the signing of the Addis Ababa Peace Agreement. That evening a group of foreign diplomats met at the Saudi embassy for a farewell party for the outgoing American chargé d'affaires George Curtis Moore, who had recently sworn in the incoming US Ambassador Cleo A. Noel Jr., the first ambassador formally assigned to Sudan in nearly six years. As the evening was winding down, a pair of Land Rovers roared up to the embassy's front entrance. Seven armed men stormed out of the vehicles and sent the departing guests scattering. The diplomats were quickly rounded up and ushered back into the embassy at gunpoint.[60] The armed men announced themselves as members of the Palestinian terrorist group Black September, and, after sorting out the guests, held Moore, Ambassador Noel and the Belgian chargé d'affaires. Making their demands known through the Sudanese authorities, Black September demanded that Sirhan Sirhan, the man who assassinated Robert Kennedy in 1968, be released from prison in the US, and Palestinian prisoners in Jordan and Israel also released;[61] if not, the three hostages would be killed.

In Washington, President Nixon rejected the idea of giving in to Black September's demands. What followed was twenty-six hours of negotiations that ended when the three Western diplomats were bound, taken down to the embassy's basement, and shot at point-blank range.[62] In the aftermath of the assassinations, relations between the US and Sudan remained strong. Sudanese officials arrested the Black September members and the US State Department attributed the planning of the assassinations to the Palestinian Liberation Organisation (PLO) and the Fatah leader Yasir Arafat. President Nixon told the Sudanese that in the opinion of the US, Sudan was only 'accidentally involved'.[63] The Sudanese government tried and convicted the Black September members. American economic assistance to Sudan continued with the EXIM Bank of the United States, the Overseas Private Investment Corporation, and American commercial banks making loans available to the Sudanese government for development projects.[64] While these loans were small in scale, the Sudanese hoped that bigger things were to come.

But it did not take long for the blossoming relationship between the US and Sudan to be in jeopardy. In June 1974, under pressure from his Arab neighbours, President Nimeiri released the Black September members convicted of killing Moore and Ambassador Noel to the PLO authority in Cairo. The reaction of the US government was swift: it recalled its new ambassador and suspended economic assistance to Sudan. 'President Nimeiri's decision is offensive in both form and substance,' wrote the American diplomat Donald B. Easum to the US Under Secretary of State Joseph John Sisco.[65]

But the positive momentum George H.W. Bush and other US officials had created in building relations with Sudan proved to be enough to ride out this political storm. In October 1974, US Secretary of State Henry Kissinger reinstated a US ambassador to Khartoum, albeit quietly, in order to avoid any public backlash in the US.[66] American diplomats conceded that Sudan was not of critical importance to wider US foreign policy in the Middle East. 'Admittedly, the Sudan is in a way a half-breed poor boy of the Arab world, and it therefore will never have a loud voice in larger regional events of interest to the US,' an officer at the American embassy in Khartoum wrote at the time. But abandoning the Sudanese would have served very little purpose for the US. US officials felt that isolating Sudan would have only threatened to push it towards Soviet influence and 'the revolutionary siren song of Libya', and away from following the lead of moderate Arab states. The Sudanese government also played an essential role in the release of American hostages working for Tenneco Oil Company who had been seized by rebels in Eritrea in 1974.[67] Nimeiri also made good on his suggestion to Bush during the US diplomat's first visit to Sudan, and became the lone Arab state to back the US-brokered Middle East peace process between Egypt and Israel. The US began to cautiously explore steps towards normalising ties with the Sudanese once again.

While US aid to Sudan froze in 1975, the process of normalising relations was underway; the US State Department was encouraged by President Nimeiri's stance towards supporting private enterprise and avoiding nationalisation of industries, and his vigilance against 'communist machinations'.[68] Beyond the relative geopolitical importance of Sudan to the US, its economic significance was on the rise. The new ambassador, William D. Brewer, was impressed that US exports to Sudan were rising sharply, despite a lack of official military and economic assistance. He urged the State Department to assist US companies by reopening official loan programmes.[69] In June 1976, President Ford received President Nimeiri at the White House and US aid to Sudan resumed. Sudan continued to serve American foreign policy interests in Middle East politics in the coming years.

In 1978–79, President Jimmy Carter brokered the Camp David accords between Israel and Egypt and the Israel-Egypt Peace Treaty. Sudan's ongoing support for this initiative was no small gesture as it earned the Sudanese the ire of many in Arab states and caused Gulf states' investment in the country to dry up.[70] Sudan's drive to become the region's 'breadbasket' failed miserably. By 1978, its debt had risen to $6 billion; it was forced by the International Monetary Fund (IMF) to implement austerity measures and devalue the Sudanese dinar. Fortunately, Nimeiri's favours to Washington, including the establishment of a large Central Intelligence Agency station in Khartoum, softened the stance of Sudan's creditors.[71] The US State Department pressured the US Treasury, and through it the IMF, to grant significant leniency to Sudan on multiple occasions.[72] The Americans were also supplying Nimeiri with arms.

President Ford declared Sudan eligible to purchase US military material and services in November 1976. US military delegations, accompanied by contractors from the weapons manufacturer Lockheed Martin, visited Khartoum looking to sell hundreds of millions of dollars' worth of arms.[73] Gathering speed under President Carter and accelerating under Ronald Reagan, the US sold Sudan military aircraft, tanks, firearms and ammunition, and trained hundreds of Sudanese military personnel.[74] Until 1981, US military aid to Sudan totalled $63 million, but between 1981 and 1985 it shot up to $350 million.[75] Sudan became the largest recipient of US economic and military assistance in all of sub-Saharan Africa.[76] That year, when Libyan aircraft bombed Omdurman, one of the three towns constituting Khartoum, President Reagan sent four surveillance aircraft to monitor Libya's actions in the region and vowed that 'aggression against Sudan would not be tolerated'.[77] During his successful re-election campaign in 1984, Reagan held up Sudan as an example of his protection of foreign countries from Soviet influence.[78] Washington also considered Sudan as a possible staging ground for military operations to protect Middle East oil fields.[79] Military cooperation was the last piece of the puzzle in what were now comprehensive relations between the US and Sudan.

Forging ahead

During the highs and lows of US-Sudan relations in the 1970s, Chevron continued to advance its own interests. The budding relations between Sudan and the US had initially encouraged the oilmen to enter Sudan. When Bill Chapman of Chevron came calling in late March 1974, the Sudanese government was eager to build further cooperation. In his report to headquarters in San Francisco after his trip to Khartoum, Chapman made brief mention of the fact that a civil war had recently ended. 'The Democratic Republic of the Sudan is ruled by the military, who appear to have pulled the various dissenting tribal groups into a peaceful, if not completely harmonious, association,' he wrote. Chapman also noted the 'prevalent friendly, and possibly even pro-American, attitude' of Sudan:[80]

The Russian influence has been reduced since 1971. The American Embassy appears to have a great deal of confidence in the present Sudanese government... and states that relations between the US and Sudan are good...and that foreign investment, particularly American, will be more secure in the Sudan than in many other African and Arabic countries...

The failed communist coup three years earlier in Sudan and the subsequent visit of George H.W. Bush had helped iron out any political bumps the company might have otherwise encountered.[81]

But Chevron's interest in Sudan was driven most of all by its keenness to expand into new territories and its geological evaluations, rather than as a calculated part of the US government's interest in engaging Sudan. 'We talked to the State Department,' said Allan Martini, Vice-President of Exploration and Production when Chevron entered Sudan. 'They had kind of a cheerleader attitude, nothing extensive.' Martini also dismissed the idea that George H.W. Bush had played a large role in Chevron getting involved in Sudan. 'I heard some story about Bush providing satellite mapping to the Sudanese to show that oil was there,' he said. 'That's complete hogwash. It started in my shop, with my geologists.' Bush may have encouraged the investment of American oil companies in Sudan, but any advice he gave to the Sudanese government on satellite imagery was clearly something that Chevron already knew and acted upon.

Chevron was guided by the lure of oil alone, not by the hand of Washington. It did not need the assistance of the US government to foster friendly relations with the Sudanese government. It was putting forward a tantalising prospect to President Nimeiri and his ministers, that oil could invigorate Sudan's impoverished economy. The diplomatic uproar after Nimeiri released members of the Black September group responsible for the assassination of Ambassador Noel and the other diplomats in Khartoum did not slow down the company, or other American oil firms looking to get into Sudan.

In July 1974, as US diplomats were preparing to freeze relations with Sudan, Chevron moved aggressively to win its exploration license from the Sudanese government in the face of competition from Esso. The following rupture in official US-Sudanese government relations did not deter the company from going ahead with its plans. Chevron signed its exploration license with Sudan a month after Ambassador William Brewer quietly returned to his post in Khartoum.

Ambassador Brewer attended Chevron's license signing ceremony in November 1974. But with official relations with Sudan still strained, he declined to have his photo taken with Sudanese officials and company executives.[82] After official aid restarted in June 1976, US diplomats in Khartoum saw the potential discovery of oil as an opportunity to take Sudan's economic importance to the US to new heights.[83]

But Chevron operated quite separately from US diplomats in Sudan. 'I opened the Khartoum office in late 1974 and had good relations with the US Embassy, but received little other than moral support from its staff,' recalled John Sutherland, Chevron's first Sudan country manager.[84] 'The involvement of the US embassy was solely to keep a finger on the pulse of Chevron's activities,' said James Payne, Sutherland's successor. 'Chevron was very independent from the US government.'

As Sudan country manager, Payne fostered a close relationship with President Nimeiri. 'We played tennis about once every six weeks,' he said. 'Nimeiri really stuck with us after we drilled some dry holes; he could have brought in another company.'[85] While Sudan was pursuing closer relations with the US on multiple fronts, Chevron's oil discoveries on their own promised to reshape Sudan's economic landscape.

In November 1983, after agreeing to Chevron's demand for an export pipeline, President Nimeiri went on a whirlwind tour of the US. His first stop was Washington to meet President Reagan. 'It's been an honor and a pleasure to welcome President Nimeiri to Washington once again. President Nimeiri is a friend. Few can match his courage and foresight as a peacemaker in Africa and in the Middle East,' Reagan said, while standing on the South Portico of the White House with the Sudanese president at his side. Reagan went on to affirm further economic and military support to Sudan and applauded Nimeiri's efforts to privatise industry, reform government policies, and thus align the country with Reagan's free-market economic ideals. 'The people of America are proud to stand with the people of the Sudan as friends and partners for peace and progress,' Reagan concluded. Nimeiri, in turn, drummed up support for Sudan in its efforts to avert the Soviet menace. 'Ethiopia and Libya are both playing a very dangerous role and executing policies serving the interests of a superior power,' he said.[86] After his political feting at the White House, the Sudanese president travelled to Chevron's headquarters in San Francisco to get down to business.

During Nimeiri's visit to San Francisco, Chevron executives updated the Sudanese delegation on the status of the pipeline project. On the way back to Khartoum, Nimeiri visited Milan to review the final stages of production of the pipeline by the Italian company Snamprogetti. The pipes were on their way to Port Sudan and the first batch of engineers was about to leave Italy.[87] The grand opening of the pipeline was scheduled for 2 April 1986, after which much-needed petrodollars would flow into the struggling Sudanese economy.[88] The painstaking work of Brian Kay and the rest of the Chevron Sudan crew, the calculating negotiations of George Keller, and the political manoeuvres of Ambassador George H.W. Bush had all come together. Everything was in place. A new page in Sudan's history was ready to be turned. But Chevron was not to enjoy the fruits of its labour. Three months after Nimeiri's trip to the US, gunfire broke the silence of a February night at Chevron's Rubkona base camp. Sudan's American dream was about to become an agonising nightmare.

2

THE LONG GOODBYE

February 1984: As a Sudanese woman, Lillian Skander was a double minority among the largely male and foreign contingent of Chevron's staff and contractors. A well-site geologist, Skander joined the company after working as a researcher on pollution along Sudan's Red Sea coast. 'It was an exciting time,' Skander recalled. 'No one ever thought we would find oil in Sudan.' In early 1984, Skander was working out of Chevron's Rubkona base camp in southern Sudan. But after receiving a three-week assignment at an oil well far away from base camp, she felt sorry for herself—she would have to spend her birthday in the middle of nowhere rather than at Rubkona. It was while she was on this temporary assignment that she heard the news that the base camp had been attacked.

'We heard about it over the radio and shortly after were told to return to collect our belongings for evacuation,' Skander said. 'Women, wounded, and dead were out first.' When she returned to Rubkona, Skander was startled at what she found. 'It was a gory scene,' she remembered. The sleeping quarters of the Chevron workers were covered in blood and her room was riddled with giant metal slugs from so-called elephant bullets. It was on the night of her birthday that the southern rebels had attacked. 'It could have easily been me who was killed,' she said.[1] Skander felt lucky to be alive as she boarded a company plane back to Khartoum with the bodies of her co-workers also on board. When the plane touched down on the dusty runway in Khartoum she saw Gary Connell, Chevron's Sudan country manger, standing waiting for her. Connell offered her a word of comfort and a glass of brandy to numb the shock.

Three members of Chevron's foreign contractor staff died in the attack. Jackson Wythaka, a Kenyan cook, was first to come across the southern rebels. Working in the kitchen, he was shot after coming upon the intruders. After hearing the gunshots, the rebels still surrounding the camp began to open fire. George McFee from Britain and Rudy Miguilino, a Filipino, were killed as bullets flew into their sleeping quarters. Seven others were badly wounded and flown to hospital in Nairobi.[2] 'It was nerve-wracking, hundreds of rounds were ripping through the walls of the sleeping quarters,' said a British worker, Steve Morters, who was shot in the leg. 'They were shooting my friends in the corridor and the bedroom.'[3] The attackers were later identified as members of the southern Sudanese rebel group Anyanya II, which had re-emerged after fighting the government in Sudan's first civil war until 1972. Increasingly a target of these southern Sudanese rebels, Chevron was now, more than ever, caught up in the political storm of an expanding civil war.

In the early 1980s, the political manoeuvres of President Nimeiri to capture future oil wealth had enflamed animosities in southern Sudan. The Anyanya II rebels were players in the uprising, but this time the southern rebellion would be led largely by the Sudan People's Liberation Army (SPLA). After the attack at Rubkona, Chevron suspended most of its Sudan operations; progress in the oil industry in general ground to a halt. Without the hundreds of millions in petrodollars promised by Chevron's production, the Sudanese government was unable to resuscitate its crumbling economy. President Nimeiri turned to Washington for help in 1985, but found the Americans less accommodating after witnessing his divisive politics in the south and his imposition of Islamic law on the entire country.

President Nimeiri struggled to find a way to ensure his political survival as Sudan's economic situation worsened. But in 1985 the strongman's sixteen-year rule came to an end in the wake of popular demonstrations on the streets of Khartoum. The once friendly political environment in Sudan turned upside down for Chevron. The National Islamic Front (NIF) seized power in a 1989 military coup and pressured the American oilmen to either restart operations or face expulsion. The growing southern rebellion threatened to destroy Chevron's $1 billion investment.

Petro-politik

After celebrating the signing of their exploration license with the Sudanese government in late November 1974, visiting Chevron executives insisted upon meeting southern Sudanese political leaders. After all, two-thirds of Chevron's new oil concession was located in the south. Accompanied by Abdel Latif Widatalla, Sudan's Minister of Mining and Industry at the time, the Chevron team travelled south to Juba, capital of the southern regional authority, to visit members of the High Executive Council, the newly-formed southern government established after the 1972 Addis Ababa Agreement. In an informal meeting on the evening they arrived, the Chevron team got a glimpse of the wider cultural and political landscape of Sudan from southern officials while listening to music from a record player in the humid evening air. 'Many of them had fought in the civil war, and I got the feeling that perhaps the war had ended as much from weariness and fatigue as from the resolution of any issues,' remembered Allan Martini, the Vice-President of Exploration and Production for Chevron at the time. The following morning, in a meeting with Abdel Alier, the President of the High Executive Council, the Chevron executives discovered that the southern Sudanese were in the dark about oil.

'The atmosphere could best be described as polite but guarded,' recalled Martini. 'It was soon obvious that they knew an agreement had been made in Khartoum, but they knew little else about the matter.' But the Chevron team felt that explaining their plans and answering questions during the Juba visit went a long way towards fostering good relations in the south.[4] John Sutherland, Chevron's first country manager in Sudan, stayed in touch with southern officials. 'I went down to Juba every month to make a personal report,' said Sutherland. 'The (Sudanese) government did not want me to give formal reports (to southern officials), but we wanted to keep in touch'.[5] As the Chevron team flew back to Khartoum from Juba in 1974, Martini remembers looking over the land the company was about to enter: 'The flight back to Khartoum was made at an altitude of about 3,000 meters, and for more than four hours, from horizon to horizon, over river, swamp, bush, and desert, we looked down on the contract area. The exploration challenge we faced was impressive.'[6] But it was the deep historical divide between northern and southern Sudan that would end up being Chevron's biggest challenge.

Even before Chevron made its first discovery, oil had been a major point of contention between the Sudanese government and the High Executive Council and Regional Assembly of southern Sudan. Abel Alier has claimed that southern authorities had to convince Nimeiri to even allow Chevron to explore the south.[7] Northern politicians feared that oil projects and other large economic projects in the south might stir up ideas of economic independence and separation that the southern Any-anya rebels had fought for in the first civil war. When oil was found, the Nimeiri government did everything it could to make southern oil seem as far away from the south as possible.

Shortly after Chevron discovered the first signs of oil near Bentiu in 1978, Nimeiri and his new oil minister Sharif el-Tuhami travelled to California to meet Chevron. After their deliberations, the Voice of America broadcasted that oil had been found 'in the southern parts of western Sudan' and that a pipeline was under consideration to take the oil to Port Sudan and on to international markets. The notion that freshly-discovered oil would travel north to the Red Sea infuriated the southern Sudanese and protests spread across the south.[8] Demonstrations demanded that the oil be taken to Mombasa in Kenya instead. Nimeiri's reaction to the unrest was to replace southern soldiers stationed in Bentiu with soldiers hailing from western Sudan under the command of northern officers.[9] This only served to raise southern suspicions of his intentions regarding oil. Nimeiri was rapidly encroaching on the political gains he had made in southern Sudan through the 1972 Addis Ababa Agreement.

Since coming to power, Nimeiri was known as a political chameleon in Sudan; he constantly shifted alliances in order to maintain his personal power.[10] In the late 1970s, Sudan's economic instability drove him to search for some sort of political stability. In 1977, he called for a national reconciliation process to consolidate his power by making amends with the political opposition. The Muslim Brotherhood, a group with little power at the time, found its way into government and began to infiltrate large parts of Sudanese society. Hassan al-Turabi, the Brotherhood's outspoken leader, was appointed attorney general by Nimeiri. Turabi and his Brotherhood were keen to establish an Islamic state in Sudan; destroying the political rights won by the southerners after the first civil war was essential to accomplishing that goal.[11] The southern population was already disappointed over the lack of peace dividend. It was evident to them that the Sudanese government was not making good on its promises to invest in the south. 'One does not eat peace' was one popular slogan in the south at the time.[12] The rising political influence of Turabi and the Muslim Brothers was a turning point for Chevron in its relations with Nimeiri and the southern regional government. 'Sudan was one of the best experiences of my life. The Sudanese were very generous and caring people,' said James Payne, who was Chevron's country manager in Sudan for much of the 1970s before he left in 1980, 'but once the fundamentalists started to take over, things got dicey.'

The road to rebellion

William Doh was full of pride on his first day of work. In 1980, as a young man living near Bentiu in western Upper Nile province of southern Sudan, Doh landed a job as an assistant in a storeroom for Chevron. He was responsible for keeping stocks of food and other supplies for Rig 199 of the Oklahoma-based Parker Drilling Company, Chevron's main drilling contractor in Sudan. For young Doh, the arrival of the American companies opened a window to the world. Even in the storeroom, Doh felt he was witnessing a global corporation at work. Goods, equipment, and heavy machinery arrived from overseas and foreigners passed through his town every day.

Born in Kialoui village north of Bentiu town, Doh was of the Nuer people of southern Sudan. When Chevron first arrived in the late 1970s, the company's hiring of locals from the Nuer, Dinka, Shilluk, and other ethnic groups was looked upon favourably. 'Chevron was positively perceived by local communities in southern Sudan,' Doh recalled. Although many of the jobs were menial, there were training possibilities that allowed southern Sudanese to take on more skilled work, 'even as drillers and assistant drillers', Doh said.[13] Each of his four brothers found work with Chevron, too. His brother Riek, a giant of a man, was a security guard and porter. His brother Lang worked with a drilling team on the other side of the Upper Nile province near the town of Melut. Socially, Doh recalled, the southern Sudanese workers saw Americans as an approachable and likeable bunch, who offered gifts of clothes and cowboy boots. One Nuer driller even picked up the southern twang of some of the American drillers.[14]

Chevron felt it had turned a corner in Sudan by engaging local communities in the south. 'Sudan was the first country that I remember us getting serious about community relations,' Brian Kay recalled. 'Before this, we just showed up and did the work on the basis of a contract with the government without much involvement or approval of the local people.'[15] But despite its good relations with its southern Sudanese employees, there was resentment about the company's destruction of agricultural land and property by its exploration activities during its early operations in the south.[16] Recognising these problems, Kay appointed one of his geophysical representatives to act as a community relations manager and the company started to provide water projects and health clinics and compensation for damage to those adversely affected by its operations. The company also provided around a half million dollars in funding for technical education of southern Sudanese.[17] Jim Payne remembers Chevron making its vehicles and facilities available to locals in both northern and southern Sudan for medical emergencies in an effort to maintain good relations: 'Our well-being depended on it,' said Payne.[18] But it only took a few years for Chevron's goodwill efforts to be undermined by Khartoum's political agenda in the south.

Oil may have opened a new world to William Doh in Bentiu, but it also exposed the fractious politics of his country. Every operational move Chevron made in Sudan instantly became political. When Chevron made a major oil discovery outside Bentiu in the spring of 1980, the Sudanese government decided to name the oil field 'Unity'. This drew concern from William Doh and his fellow Nuer. They knew the place as 'Yohnial'. Their doubts grew when Chevron found the 'Heglig' oil field further north. The local Dinka called the area 'Panthou', but the government used the name 'Heglig', a name originating from the nomadic Arab Misseriya of Kordofan who traditionally grazed their cattle southward through the territory. The Sudanese government even proposed redrawing borders in oil-rich areas to create a new province, again called 'Unity', ostensibly to promote north-south cooperation.[19] At that point the Southern Regional Assembly, rightly seeing this as another move to strip away southern rights over the oil, quelled this idea.

As William Doh rose up the ranks at Chevron during the early 1980s, political division between the north and south around the issue of oil was increasing. In 1981, Doh was promoted to manage his own storeroom in Muglad. Soon afterwards he was relocated farther north to Kosti. A year earlier, President Nimeiri had announced the scheduled construction of a refinery in Kosti, dismissing the idea of building a refinery in

Bentiu, where oil had been discovered, and denying the south tax revenue from the refinery's construction and operation. As if the southerners were not already irate, the oil minister Tuhami added, for good measure, that it made no sense for the refinery to be built in Bentiu because it was 'in the middle of nowhere'. Oil policy at the time was the domain of 'a small group comprising of the President, a few palace aides, the Minister of Energy and Mining, Chevron, and a few expatriate mediators.'[20] No southerner was involved in the inner circle. While Nimeiri later scrapped the idea of a Kosti refinery at Chevron's insistence, southerners nonetheless voiced their anger at his calculations to exclude them from the coming oil bonanza.[21]

Some Anyanya rebels never accepted becoming integrated into the Sudanese army after the Addis Ababa Agreement ended the first civil war in 1972. The guerrilla bands, mostly composed of Nuer, operated separately from one another, but were collectively known as Anyanya II. By the early 1980s, they were launching hit-and-run attacks on northern merchants and government representatives in the south. The new Southern Regional Assembly initially resisted the Anyanya II, but when Nimeiri began to whittle away southern rights, southern soldiers and civilians began to support and join the rebels.[22] In June 1983, the evolving political situation in Khartoum led Nimeiri to abrogate the Addis Ababa Agreement by dissolving the Southern Regional Assembly and dividing southern Sudan into three regions, Bahr al-Ghazal, Equatoria, and the oil-rich Upper Nile. He later imposed Islamic *shari'ah* law on all of Sudan in September. The different armed groups of Anyanya II and the thousands of southern defectors from the Sudanese army assembled at Bilpam in southwestern Ethiopia.[23] The southern rebellion was reborn.

Not long after starting work in Kosti, William Doh was transferred to Chevron's main storage facilities in Khartoum. But he was not unaware of what was going on in the south. 'The rules of the game changed,' he recalled. 'More northerners than southerners were finding work with Chevron in the south and the company was now clearly seen as an arm of the Sudanese government.'[24] Doh had befriended Jim Payne, the country manager, and told him that he wished to be released in order attend Rumbek Secondary School. Payne tried to convince Doh to stay with the company, but Doh said he felt a 'national calling' to go back to the south. It was at Rumbek that students protested against a visit by Nimeiri in December 1982, shortly before the dissolution of the peace accords.

Soon enough, southern students made up a large share of rebel recruits.[25] Doh decided to join them. 'As an angry nineteen-year-old man, I could not tolerate such humiliation,' he recalled. He left Rumbek in March 1983 to join the rebellion.

At Bilpam, the gathering place for southern Sudanese rebels, former officers of the Anyanya rebellion congregated to establish a new resistance against the Sudanese government. The man who eventually brought the rebels together as the SPLA was Dr John de Mabior Garang. A Dinka from Twic county with a doctorate in agricultural economics and military training in the US, Garang was a colonel in the Sudanese army when President Nimeiri sent him in May 1983 to Bor to pacify a southern battalion that was refusing to move north. But instead of bringing the southern forces into line, Garang defected with the troops and joined the rebellion. Garang pursued the idea of national unity rather than separation of the south, aiming at a new national union in which Sudan's multicultural and multiethnic society would prosper under an equitable system of government. The veteran fighters of Anyanya wanted nothing less than independence for the south and challenged his leadership.[26] But Garang's stance towards the unity of Sudan pleased the Ethiopian government, which gave him strong support. Outgunned and outnumbered, the remaining Anyanya II could not unseat Garang as leader of the new rebel movement and returned to Sudan from Ethiopia.

Three weeks before the Rubkona attack, a Chevron spokesman in Khartoum said that after making deals with local chiefs, the company had security 'all sewn up' and was 'drilling more water wells than oil wells'.[27] But Chevron had not satisfied the Anyanya II rebels, who orchestrated the attack on the company's base camp in early February 1984. Bul Nyawan, a Nuer, was said to have led the operation, with Paulino Matip serving as his deputy.[28] The SPLA denied involvement in the attack, but still warned Chevron not to restart its operations.[29] Following a meeting between Chevron's George Keller and Nimeiri in Khartoum, the official announcement from Chevron was of a 'temporary suspension of operations'.[30]

Other foreign companies were also experiencing the consequences of the political upheaval in Sudan. Total, the French oil major, had been conducting exploration work since 1980 in a 100,000 square kilometre concession called Block B, south of Chevron's activities. Total, like Chevron, was seeking to diversify its international resources in the Middle

East, hoping that uncharted territories in Sudan would provide a major source of oil.[31] Based in Bor, the company was planning to drill its first well at the end of 1984 when signs of civil war began to appear.[32] A Total manager recalls witnessing firsthand the unrest in Bor after the 105th Battalion of the Sudanese army mutinied and disappeared into the bush with the soon-to-be rebel leader John Garang.[33] Soon afterwards the SPLA demanded that Total cease its operations and leave. Security conditions were not overly bad before 1983, but when two contractors were killed in the wake of Garang's mutiny, and oil field engineer the next year, the French company declared *force majeure* in 1985.[34]

William Doh remained with the SPLA and joined its Jamus battalion. 'I took my stand to fight the ruling cliques in Khartoum until we were no longer second-class citizens in the Sudan,' he recalls. He would soon earn the nickname the 'Young General' for his skills on the battlefield. Just over a week after Anyanya II rebels attacked Chevron's Rubkona camp in February 1984, Jamus of the SPLA launched a strike against the Jonglei Canal, another major project in the south, and chased out the French Compagnie de Constructions Internationales that was digging it.[35] Doh abandoned a promising future with Chevron and instead found himself in the midst of a growing civil war. In the aftermath of the Rubkona attack, the company scrambled to make sense of what had gone wrong.

Hunkering down

Publicly, Chevron initially placed the blame for the Rubkona attack on bandits; the company downplayed the idea that any larger menace was at work.[36] But as time passed, it became harder to deny that the growing rebellion was a major threat to Sudan's oil industry. Chevron may have wanted to balance its relations with the Sudanese government, the regional authorities in southern Sudan, and local populations in oil areas, but as the drums of war became louder, the company was clearly seen as an ally of Khartoum by most people in the south.

'Political instability is a risk for us, just as much as the technical risk of finding oil. But it is a risk we're willing to take based on the potential oil production possibilities in Sudan,' said Chevron's country manager Gary Connell just five months before the deadly attack on the base camp. Connell felt that 'with any luck' Chevron would double its oil reserve finds in Sudan in the coming years. The Sudanese army provided little security for Chevron at its camps and drilling sites. This was actually at Chevron's insistence—it hoped not to be seen as affiliated with the army, and hired only local police for security. 'The last thing in the world that these oilmen want, and in fact they argue that they cannot do it, is to be surrounded by trigger-happy frightened Sudanese paratroopers,' wrote Robert O. Collins, a Chevron adviser in the early 1980s.[37] But the company failed to convince the southerners that it was a neutral party.

After a March 1981 debate in the Southern Regional Assembly, resolutions were adopted against President Nimeiri's decision to build an oil refinery at Kosti in northern Sudan. The assembly chastised the 'attitude of the Chevron Oil Company in blatantly and deliberately taking part or side in a politically-motivated decision which clearly adversely affects the interest of the people of the Southern Region'.[38] The southerners were also unhappy that Chevron's seismic lines had created roads for government troops to use.[39] Collins thought that the company's poor relations in the south was in part due to the behaviour of its British contractors towards local southern Sudanese near the oil fields. 'These are not the Gentlemen from Oxbridge with whom we associate the British,' he wrote home to his parents.[40] 'That is part of Chevron's problem.' While Collins enjoyed playing 'tour guide' for the oilmen, he felt that the travel expenses Chevron incurred to fly him from Khartoum to the south to sort out the company's political and social problems often could have been substituted on the spot by 'an hour's friendly talk with the locals over a beer.'

The Anyanya II rebels said they targeted Chevron as a symbol of US cooperation with the Sudanese government, claiming that company survey planes were feeding Khartoum with intelligence.[41] While this may have seemed far-fetched to most, the view from the ground looked very different. Before the Rubkona attack, a freelance photographer at Chevron's base camp witnessed Sudanese soldiers taking two captured Anyanya II rebels aboard a government military plane bound for Khartoum. The Chevron contractors he spoke to knew very well that the rebels would be tortured when they arrived in the Sudanese capital.[42] The Sudanese army made use of the company's airstrips and infrastructure. 'Chevron wanted to be neutral, but couldn't avoid being seen to side with government,' the photographer said. Chevron was seen as cooperating with the military, even if it was not doing so deliberately.

There were clear warning signs for Chevron executives that security in Sudan was heading in the wrong direction. The Rubkona attack in February 1984 was the culmination of growing resentment and aggression against Chevron. 'During the last six months, a large percentage of my time was spent dealing with security problems and employee and government relations,' said Rob Buglass, a senior employee at the base camp in 1982.[43] That year, Anyanya II rebels kidnapped five Chevron contractors near Bentiu. A local Nuer priest was able to negotiate their release a few weeks later, but with a message for the company and Sudanese government that the oil 'belonged to southerners'.[44] In November 1983, two Chevron workers were held hostage. They were later released, accompanied by demands that Khartoum free political prisoners and end Islamic law in the south and that Chevron halt its activities.[45] A month later, Charles Hubbard, a Chevron employee, was shot and killed in a robbery attempt at the company's base camp at Rubkona.[46]

Despite the security risks, Chevron was driving forward an 'aggressive exploration and evaluation program' in 1982. Four seismic crews and three drilling teams were working full-time, with another rig on its way by late 1983.[47] The company was fixated on finalising its export pipeline by the end of 1985 and seeing a reward for all its hard work over the years. 'Everything has now been transferred to Rub Kona,' wrote Collins. 'An elaborate and very expensive barge and transport system has developed on the White Nile, and they are dropping oil rigs into the sudd like gum drops.'

But Chevron misunderstood the speed of the change in Sudanese politics and the lack of power of local leaders over the rebel activity of Anyanya II.[48] 'The corporate world, particularly someone with the power of Standard Oil (Chevron's parent company), has the best and the brightest and indeed a very impressive group of individuals, but they are woefully ignorant about the land beyond the Sudd,' observed Collins a week after the Rubkona attack.[49]

Chevron was not alone in suffering losses due to its suspended operations in the south. Royal Dutch Shell had been brought on as a major partner with a quarter stake in Chevron's concession and pipeline project only a week before the Rubkona attack. At the time, Chevron was under enormous pressure from Nimeiri to start the pipeline project in 1983, but felt it was a very risky decision because the oil reserves were still not firmly established. By bringing on Shell, Chevron sought to spread the risk and find some financial relief.[50] Shell committed to spending the next $250 million on the project. But after the attack, it was stuck. 'The first time they saw the oil assets was after the raid,' remembered Allan Martini. He flew to the Netherlands to pick up Shell's representatives on the way to Khartoum, but in Bentiu they could only look at equipment lined up row after row rather than at work producing oil.[51] Shell was forced to spend its contribution on drilling in northern Sudan where the prospects for further discoveries were very poor. Chevron had tried to manage political risk in Sudan and took Shell along for the ride.

Chevron did not want the Sudanese army guarding its facilities. Only unarmed Sudanese army trainees and local police were at the Rubkona camp. There were two American security officers also present, but they only handled petty theft by local workers. 'There wasn't a gun in the camp,' said the British worker Steve Morters.[52] After the attack, Sudanese Vice-President Omar el-Tayeb and the Chevron country manager Gary Connell met in Khartoum, 100 Sudanese paratroopers were sent to defend the base camp.[53] The company surrounded its other camps with 40-foot containers and earthworks to protect the people inside and set up a Global Corporate Security Division, but did not go back into the south.[54] 'We have to have access to the south before we can go back to work and we're not going to expose our employees to undue risk. And being in the middle of a civil war zone is an undue risk in our opinion,' said John Silcox, the new president of Chevron's overseas operations in 1984.[55] The majority of the company's expatriate staff was not willing to work in the south, there was very little the company could do, and Washington was of no help. 'In all this conundrum, the American government is frankly rather useless,' wrote Collins.[56] Chevron kept operations going near the town of Muglad in the north, but produced few results.

'It was a terrible mess,' said Allan Martini about the aftermath of the Rubkona attack. 'We just sort of hunkered down and hoped that there was some way of getting the situation sorted out.' Martini visited the southern Sudanese towns of Wau, Malakal and Juba a week after the attack to explain to local officials what the company was doing: 'We wanted to make ourselves desirable citizens.'[57]

In response to these security issues, the Sudanese government produced a plan to secure the oil fields. In early 1984, it started to arm Misseriya nomads living in southern Kordofan to protect the oil areas to the south. Carol Berger, a Canadian journalist who was the first to report the attack on Rubkona and was deported by the Sudanese authorities as a result, claimed that Chevron asked Nimeiri to provide the Misseriya with automatic weapons. She said the company only later decided that a political settlement was needed, after it saw that arming the Misseriya only increased fighting between them and the southern Dinka and Nuer ethnic groups.[58] But Chevron's adviser Collins wrote that the CEO, George Keller, had already requested that Nimeiri find a political settlement with the SPLA, in their 11 February 1984 meeting in Khartoum, just a week after the Rubkona attack:

'Chevron has evacuated its people and there will be a titanic meeting on Saturday, the 11th, between all the great corporate honchos of Chevron and Nimeiri which will basically tell him that he's going to have to make some sort of arrangement to ameliorate and accommodate the Southern grievances or he can forget about having his oil money....'[59]

Later that year, Chevron hired an international security firm made up of Vietnam veterans from the US army. They told the oil company that it was not possible to protect the oil fields in the south. Nonetheless, in the coming years, Sudan's armed forces and militias began to drive Nuer and Dinka inhabitants from their homes around Bentiu and fought the SPLA for control of the region. The Vietnam veterans hired by Chevron never considered the tactic that Nimeiri let loose in depopulating the land to clear the way for oil companies.[60] This was the beginning of a vicious counterinsurgency strategy that became apparent in Sudan's second civil war.

In an effort to control oil areas, Nimeiri also made contact in 1984 with the Anyanya II rebels. He sought to exploit infighting between them and the SPLA as well as ethnic divisions between the Nuer and Dinka, which represented the majority in the Anyanya II and SPLA respectively.[61] Some Anyanya II rebels succumbed to their weakened position and joined the SPLA. But others made contact with Khartoum for arms, ammunition, and uniforms to form a pro-government southern militia. Daniel Matthews, who, as the former point of contact between Chevron's first country manager John Sutherland and the southern regional government, followed instructions from Nimeiri to provide arms to one group of Anyanya II fighters for them to become a government militia.[62] Strategically placed in western Upper Nile to protect the oil fields, Paulino Matip, a Bul Nuer, also became a key Khartoum ally. Matip was reported to have been involved in the Anyanya II attack on Chevron's Rubkona base camp, but was now fighting for Khartoum to secure the oil fields. This would not be the first time that personal ambition blurred political goals in the fast-changing allegiances of the civil war.

Nimeiri did not waste much time pressuring Chevron to continue its work after the Rubkona attack. He made an agreement with the Saudi Arabian financier Adnan Khashoggi to develop Sudan's oil fields in late 1984. The agreement was a not so subtle warning to Chevron that the company needed to restart its activities or face expropriation. 'We need Chevron. We need them to come back and work,' said Khashoggi, who had become close to Nimeiri through a number of financial deals.[63] But Chevron held its ground on the suspension of work in the south. CEO Keller wanted a political solution to southern discontent.[64] Chevron officials urged Nimeiri to follow a conciliatory approach and consider giving at least 25 per cent of future oil revenue to the south to resolve the conflict.[65] But the possibility of the American oilmen returning to the southern oil fields grew increasingly thin with each passing year. As the heat was rising on Sudan's budding oil industry, political temperatures in Khartoum were becoming unbearable for President Nimeiri.

Downfall

The last ounce of Khartoum's formerly easygoing atmosphere was literally thrown into the river in September 1983. The consumption of alcoholic beverages was strictly forbidden under *shari'ah*; to demonstrate his commitment to the new laws, President Nimeiri led the dumping of five million dollars' worth of alcohol into the Nile by emptying a beer can.[66] It was a bold move for the once heavy-drinking, chain-smoking army officer. The party really ended a month later when Chevron announced that it was halting its activities in southern Sudan. The $380 million financial package put together by the International Finance Corporation of the World Bank, which included the participation of a number of American private banks, was put on ice.[67] Royal Dutch Shell, Marathon, Sun Oil, Texas Eastern, and other international oil companies were also eager to cash in on the coming Sudan oil bonanza, but after the Chevron attack everything unravelled. Nimeiri's last chance to rescue a struggling economy with an infusion of petrodollars was snuffed out by the southern rebellion.

Now that Chevron's oil project was going nowhere, the deteriorating economic situation in Sudan, even in Khartoum, was undermining

Nimeiri's rule. The barbaric executions, amputations and floggings enforced under *shari'ah* repelled most Sudanese, and the poor state of the economy threatened them all.[68] In 1973, Sudan had a serviceable debt and a favourable trade balance. Ten years later, it was burdened with an untenable debt of $7 billion and a hefty trade deficit that made the price of imported consumer goods, such as petroleum and sugar, much more difficult for the average Sudanese to afford.[69] The austerity packages invoked under pressure from the IMF only managed to make the situation worse. All manner of disenfranchised Sudanese took to the streets of the capital in protest.

The suspension of Chevron's activities in the south was the last nail in Sudan's economic coffin. Nimeiri blundered miserably by failing to maintain at least some form of manageable ties with the south, where the vast majority of oil was located, and the economic means with which to cement his political power. One of Nimeiri's last political allies in Khartoum, the Muslim Brothers, only encouraged southern marginalisation. A month before his downfall, Nimeiri sought to seize complete control over Sudan when he threw Hassan al-Turabi and hundreds of Muslim Brothers into prison for allegedly plotting to overthrow his government in March 1985.[70] But Nimeiri had backed himself into a corner. He had no political or economic base to uphold his claim to power. His divisive politics at home also began to strain relations with the US.

US military sales to Sudan continued throughout the 1980s. The Reagan administration was fearful of the consequences of an insurgency in Sudan. If Nimeiri were to fall, the possibility of another anti-American government in power in North Africa worried Washington.[71] Two months after Nimeiri introduced *shari'ah* law in Sudan, President Reagan may have seemed naïve in praising the Sudanese president as a 'peacemaker' on the South Portico of the White House in November 1983. But Nimeiri was able to leverage US support because of Libyan aggression against Sudan and the Ethiopian Marxist regime's relations with the SPLA, as well as his support for the US Middle East peace plan. A US Defense Department cable indicated that a Security Evaluation and Assistance team had been sent incognito to Sudan in late 1983 to consider the 'need for an effective Sudanese counterinsurgency capability'.[72] While the US Congress was in the dark about this mission, a Chevron representative was reported to have accompanied plain-clothes US security officials who were to develop plans to protect 'proposed oil facilities in southern Sudan against an insurgent threat'. The Pentagon was considering sending Special Forces to train the Sudanese, but the team was instructed not to give false expectations of US support.[73]

If there was a plan for the US military to provide assistance to the Sudanese to protect Chevron, it was not known widely across the company's top brass or to its people in Sudan. 'There were (US) military missions in and out of Sudan, but they had nothing to do with oil as far as we were concerned,' said Allan Martini.[74] But it mattered little. Sudan's relations with the United States were only souring. It took time for Washington to read the political trends in Sudan, but it was becoming increasingly uneasy with the Sudanese president's policies in the south and his imposition of *shari'ah*.[75] In March 1984, the US position was that the problems of Sudan were best addressed in 'economic terms'.[76] US officials saw military ties as offering purely 'defensive' support.[77]

Before visiting Washington in 1984, shortly after the Rubkona attack, the Sudanese Vice-President Omar el-Tayeb took the opportunity to lash out at Ethiopia's support for the SPLA, in the hope of winning political points. He returned from his US visit saying that the Reagan administration would provide further military assistance to fend off the southern rebels.[78] There were even rumours in the south that US Marines might land and wipe out the SPLA.[79] But not long afterwards, President Reagan sent his envoy General Vernon Walters to Khartoum to meet Nimeiri. The US administration made clear that no promise of such help had been made and that the US aid programme was under review. The following year, in a further test of the extent to which the US government would aid Nimeiri militarily, a Sudanese request for helicopter gunships to eliminate southern guerrillas was declined by Washington.[80]

Vice-President George H.W. Bush received a clear picture of the unfolding political situation in Sudan when he visited in March 1985. The primary reason for his trip this time was humanitarian. A widespread famine caused by drought and desertification struck the western Sudan in 1984 and 1985, resulting in some 100,000 deaths.[81] But Bush was also playing *Realpolitik* behind the scenes. He held meetings with political factions from both the north and the south in secret meetings at the US embassy in Khartoum and was informed by all factions that there was a strong sentiment growing against Nimeiri among large swathes of the population.[82] During the visit, Bush told President Nimeiri that the US sought further political and economic reforms, including the scaling back of *shari'ah*, if US financial support to Sudan was to continue. Clearly,

Nimeiri's political decisions at home had damaged Sudan's relationship with the United States. But with popular protests growing in Khartoum against the deteriorating state of the Sudanese economy, the Sudanese president, now desperate for solutions, flew to Washington in search of help in April 1985.

The reception of President Nimeiri in Washington paled in comparison to his visit two years earlier. Nimeiri wanted the Reagan administration to release $114 million in economic aid earmarked for 1985, but the White House indicated that this aid would be delayed until Sudan made further liberal reforms to its economy. Lifting subsidies and privatising state-owned enterprises were exactly the reforms that were putting the Sudanese president in hot water back home, and yet Washington wanted to see more. The cutting of subsidies on fuel and sugar under pressure from the Americans released another wave of anger among a Sudanese population already suffering under a failing economy. Nimeiri left Washington with a promise of only $67 million in economic aid. The US State Department continued to push for leniency for Sudan's financial woes, but the patience of the US Treasury was running out.[83] The White House also wanted to see 'conciliatory' approaches taken to end the civil war in the south. 'We do not believe there can be a military solution,' said one senior administration official.[84] President Reagan, a close friend of Chevron's CEO Keller, was on the same page as the company: he wanted the civil war to end before engaging further with the Sudanese president.[85]

Popular protests had begun even before Nimeiri left for Washington, and continued after his departure. In Khartoum, some 20,000 demonstrators shouted in Arabic 'Down with one-man rule', demanding Nimeiri's resignation, and 'down, down with the USA' in English.[86] The president was seen as bending to and fro in obedience to Uncle Sam's demands.[87] En route back to Sudan, Nimeiri learned that under the command of his Defence Minister, General Suwar Al Dahab, the army had launched a coup d'état and seized control of the government.[88] The strongman that Chevron and the US government had hoped would provide stability in Sudan was no more.

In the immediate aftermath of the coup, General Dahab promised that national democratic elections would be held after a one-year transition period. In May 1986, Sadiq al-Mahdi was elected prime minister of a coalition government. Sadiq was an Oxford-educated economist and great-grandson of the Mahdi, the nineteenth century Islamic leader who freed Sudan from Turco-Egyptian rule. But the rise of Sadiq to power did little to change the oil scene. He demanded that Chevron continue its operations in the south, while Chevron maintained its position on suspending its operations until the security situation improved.[89] Sudanese oil officials felt the company was using the security issue as a pretext for waiting until international oil prices went up, having plummeted earlier that year.[90] Mass demonstrations and strikes broke out once again.[91]

In the meantime, Washington saw little reason to provide military and economic support to Sudan. The geopolitical dynamics that had first helped forge strong ties between the US and Sudan began to wane with the accession of Mikhail Gorbachev in the Soviet Union and the end of the Cold War.[92] All US non-humanitarian aid was terminated in December 1988; there was no political will left in Washington to provide financial support to Sudan.[93] For Sudan's ruling elite, the exhilaration of the coming of oil was beginning to be replaced by a desperate need to squeeze it out of the ground against all odds.

Sadiq al-Mahdi would not have much time to pressure Chevron to restart its activities in southern Sudan. Like Nimeiri, he was prone to isolating political allies and antagonising political foes. He also failed to relieve Sudan's economic woes. Early in the morning of 30 June 1989, his democratically-elected government was overthrown. A relatively unknown Brigadier named Omar al-Bashir led the military coup with three hundred elite paratroopers, men who as part of the Sudanese army were the beneficiaries of years of American training and equipment.[94] Bashir and a small group of junior military officers called the Revolutionary Command Council for National Salvation took Khartoum in a matter of hours. They rounded up Sadiq and political leaders from all major parties, including Hassan al-Turabi of the NIF, and threw them into the Kobar prison across the Blue Nile in Khartoum North. But within a year, it became apparent that Turabi and the NIF were behind the coup, with the aid of Bashir and his military forces. Over the years, Turabi and the NIF had gradually expanded their political influence in Sudan, and now they were seizing complete power. The NIF had opposed Sadiq's moves to reform *shari'ah* law and make peace with John Garang's SPLA.[95] Now in power, they continued *shari'ah* and the war against the southern rebels. But as with previous governments, economic salvation for the Islamists required that they revive Sudan's oil industry.

After leading Chevron's operations in Somalia for three years, Brian Kay was reassigned to Sudan as country manager in 1989. When Kay returned to Sudan, he immediately noticed that the political climate for Chevron had turned on its head. 'Doing work in Sudan changed from being safe and stable to dangerous and unfriendly', Kay recalls. 'There was huge anti-West and particularly anti-American sentiment in the end.' The NIF gutted the oil ministry and installed a crop of Islamist loyalists. 'All the old hands were kicked out and a new, very difficult breed installed,' Kay remembers.[96]

Chevron made an effort to build relations with the new regime, taking Bashir on a 'show and tell' tour of their operations. Kay and Chevron Overseas President Richard Matzke met the new Sudanese leader in Washington after he had taken control in Sudan.[97] Bashir demanded that the company begin to develop the Unity and Heglig oil fields immediately, and pledged to improve security.[98] Chevron was still unconvinced that the Sudanese army was capable of protecting its base camp and ensuring the safety of supply routes.[99] 'Basically they wanted us to go back to work in the south, without any idea of how they could protect the operations,' recalled Kay. It was the same old bone of contention between the company and the government.

The Islamists in charge in Khartoum were not immune to the dire economic situation that previous governments had faced in Sudan. Oil remained particularly scarce. The majority of fuel imports were guzzled away by the military to wage war against the southern rebels. Khartoum and other Sudanese cities were experiencing fuel shortages and the government was spending $20 million a month to buy oil on international spot markets.[100] Bashir sent emissaries to Libya, Iraq and Iran in search of additional oil but none provided a supply for long. With little to lose, the Sudanese called Chevron back to the negotiating table.

In June 1990, as Sudan's sweltering summer heat descended on Khartoum, government oil officials sat down with visiting Chevron representatives at the Friendship Hotel. They did not want to lose Chevron, but were interested primarily in seeing oil flow. By now, the company knew the lie of the land, and plenty more about what was beneath it. 'There were no better options than Chevron,' said a Sudanese oil official.

The Sudanese government offered Chevron anything it wanted. But the company executives asked for something the Sudanese could not give them: 'They (Chevron) wanted 100 per cent security,' said the official.

'We told Chevron that if they would not return, they should find a third-party to operate the oil fields for them within a year or else we would take the asset.'[101] After these talks, Chevron never sent another senior delegation from the US to Sudan again.

As time passed, the Sudanese became frustrated with what they saw as continual foot-dragging by Chevron and began to make life for its country staff a living nightmare. 'I was busy trying to keep my people out of jail and trying stop the government stealing our assets, and watching my own personal safety,' recalled Brian Kay. It was not too long before the inevitable happened. In June 1992, Chevron sold its oil concessions in Sudan. Omar al-Bashir, the Chairman of the Revolutionary Command Council, went on state television to announce the sale as a 'national achievement' which would now allow the government to proceed with developing the oil fields after so many years of inaction.[102] ConCorp International, a small-sized Sudanese company owned by a Sudanese businessman with ties to Turabi, took over Chevron's oil stakes.[103] The Unity and Heglig oil fields and over 170,000 square kilometres of territory were, it was reported, sold for only $23 million,[104] a fraction of their value and of the $1 billion Chevron had invested in Sudan since the early 1970s. It was baffling to many in the international oil business that Chevron was leaving Sudan with what constituted merely pocket change in the oil business. But just as there were leadership changes in Sudan during the late 1980s, there were also changes under way at Chevron's headquarters in San Francisco.

An executive decision

In January 1989, George Keller retired and Ken Derr took over as Chevron's CEO and Chairman. A tall, stocky Pennsylvanian with a business degree from Cornell University, Derr had started at Chevron as a trainee and had worked his way up through the company's refinery operations in the US.[105] From his stadium-size office at Chevron headquarters, Derr embarked on an aggressive efficiency campaign to turn the company around in the early 1990s. The oil crash of 1986 had devastated the industry, with prices falling by over 60 per cent; many oil companies were forced to slash entire divisions in order to cut costs.[106] Together, the oil majors divested $10 billion in non-core exploration and production assets between 1989 and 1995.[107]

Chevron was faring worse than others. Its lucrative assets in Saudi Arabia were nationalised, its exploration efforts overseas had come up mostly dry, and its gigantic merger with Gulf Oil in 1984 turned out to be a 'cataclysmic event', according to Derr. While Chevron still held $34.5 billion in assets worldwide and was the third largest American oil company behind Exxon and Mobil, it was vulnerable to takeover because its poor performance was pushing down its stock value.[108] Derr was hounded by rumours at the time that the Houston-based company Pennzoil was considering a hostile takeover in December 1989.[109] To rescue the company, he focused on 'return on capital' and 'fixing the finances'.[110] Deer needed an overseas investment that could restore Chevron to its former glory.

Derr's corporate career, spent largely on home soil, did not deter him from making overseas deals. He actually increased Chevron's foreign exploration and production by 50 per cent in his first five years, selling off company assets in the US in response to what he saw as over-zealous government regulation.[111] His biggest overseas gamble was in the former Soviet republic of Kazakhstan. 'People say, "Have you lost your mind, Ken? Why are you willing to spend money in Kazakhstan, with all the political instability?" And I tell 'em, "have you ever tried to do business in Santa Barbara County?"'[112] Notwithstanding the regulatory barriers to offshore drilling in California, the political storm of the dissolution of the Soviet Union hardly presented a smooth ride. But Washington was behind Chevron and the efforts of other American oil companies to invest in Central Asia; the nine billion barrels of untapped oil in Kazakhstan's Tengiz and Korolev oil fields were worth the initial $750 million risk in 1993.[113] Whereas Sudan was a $1 billion stain on Chevron's record, Kazakhstan offered Derr a chance to turn around the company's falling fortunes in one fell swoop.[114] 'This is the kind of opportunity that comes along only once in a generation,' Derr said.[115]

Investing in a country in the midst of civil war was not the only factor that pushed Chevron out of Sudan. Sudanese oil officials argued that the company was not as sensitive to insecurity as it claimed, since it was carrying out operations on the other side of Africa in war-torn Angola.[116] But Chevron saw a difference between the two. In Angola its oil fields were offshore, out of harm's way in the civil war; only the company's onshore camp at Malongo was under threat, and Angolan and Cuban forces were on guard. Derr remarked that the locals in Angola only killed each other and were smart enough to leave the oilmen alone to do their work.[117]

In Sudan, not only were the oil fields onshore, the area of production was spread out and difficult to protect. In addition, in Chevron's view, the protectors, the Sudanese army, were neither trained nor experienced.[118] In Angola the company's involvement with the ruling pro-Soviet People's Liberation Movement of Angola, better known by its Portuguese acronym MPLA, turned heads in the US during the waning years of the Cold War, but Chevron was seen as providing the Republican White House with an 'important informal channel' to the MPLA.[119] In contrast to Sudan, political and security risks in Kazakhstan and Angola were deemed to be worth taking.

John Silcox, President of Chevron Overseas from 1984 to 1990, met the SPLA rebel leader John Garang in Washington in the spring of 1989. 'He was an educated man and the meeting was cordial,' recalled Silcox. 'I told him we would not return to work without adequate security and he admitted he could not provide such in the near term.'[120] Sudan's Prime Minister Sadiq al-Mahdi considered making peace with Garang's SPLA that June, but when the NIF took power in Khartoum, it was clear that the civil war was not ending any time soon.

As if dodging the bullets of southern rebels was not enough, the economics of the Sudan deal did not work for Chevron executives in San Francisco. They judged that Sudan was anything but an efficient investment. Chevron's stated reason for leaving Sudan was to focus on its 'core assets'.[121] 'Sudan ran incredibly over budget,' said former country manager Jim Payne.[122] Chevron had spent $1 billion in Sudan, in large part on George Keller's watch, without a single barrel of oil to show for it. And if Derr wanted to see some return, investment of another billion dollars was needed to build the export pipeline.[123] In addition, the returns from the oil exports would be far below previous estimates. International oil prices averaged only $14 per barrel in 1986, less than half of the predicted price in Chevron's feasibility study for the Sudan export pipeline, and even below the pessimistic forecast of $25 per barrel.[124] This gave some truth to the accusations thrown at Chevron by Sudanese oil officials that the company was waiting until the oil price was right to restart operations. In combination, the persistent physical insecurity and poor economic payoff made Sudan far from attractive. The hostile political environment did little to assuage the company's concerns.

By the beginning of the 1990s, the NIF was keen to get the oil indus-try up and running, with or without Chevron. At the same time, by the end of the NIF's first year in power, US officials began to realise that the new government intended to continue both *shari'ah* law and the civil war. George H.W. Bush, who had travelled to Sudan as UN ambassador in 1972, and as US Vice-President had watched Nimeiri fall in 1985, was now the US President. His administration told Chevron to pack its bags and leave Sudan in 1990.[125] 'Given the situation, it didn't take much of a push,' said Allan Martini.[126] John Silcox, Martini's successor as head of Chevron's overseas operations, had already advised the company to leave Sudan when he retired on 1 January 1990.[127] Again, Washington was fol-lowing rather than leading the company in Sudan.

That year, Hassan al-Turabi proclaimed Sudan's support for Iraq in the Gulf War.[128] A 1991 US State Department report indicated that the US was also becoming worried about Sudan's links with international ter-rorism.[129] Barbara Bodine, a US State Department official, later decried Sudan as a 'Holiday Inn for terrorists'.[130] At this juncture, if Chevron was still pondering what to do in Sudan, accounting may have helped tip the balance in its decision to get out. It was reported, but never confirmed, that Chevron received an impressive $550 million tax write-off from the US government for leaving Sudan.[131] Chevron may have received tax breaks and deductions during the 1980s for its dormant assets in Sudan, but such a sizeable, one-off write-off was a far-fetched notion. 'There was no financial advantage to leaving other than we didn't have to spend more money there anymore,' Martini said.

If Ken Derr was keen on 'fixing the finances' at Chevron, leaving Sudan helped his cause—Sudan was a $1 billion investment that had produced no return. Chevron was no longer a takeover target by the mid-1990s. Derr's strategy of cutting company slack and expanding overseas invest-ments paid off. In his first five years, Chevron shareholders earned on aver-age nearly 19 per cent annually from dividends and stock price appreciation, the highest among the top six US oil companies.[132] But while Chevron executives in San Francisco pushed forward their decision to leave, Chevron's skeleton crew on the ground in Sudan was unconvinced.

'For those of us who worked a long time in the Sudan, it was a bad day when Chevron decided to give away vast concession areas and proven oil,' remembered Kay.[133] He saw the move as too hasty, lacking proper consideration of available alternatives. The company had already managed to hold on to its assets for eight years; Kay felt there was a chance it could continue to wait for a better day when the civil war ended and international oil prices lifted. 'On the surface, the (Sudanese) government made it hard for us, but the higher ups knew that it was the most sensible decision to continue with Chevron.'

Kay believed the Sudanese would have made a deal to allow Chevron to stay until security improved, because the Sudanese government was desperately poor and looking for some kind of finance and support. All the company had to do was agree to give the Sudanese all its equipment on the ground, totalling some $25 million, which Chevron did not take out of the country anyway. 'But top (Chevron) personnel wouldn't come to Sudan, which infuriated the government,' said Kay:[134]

Derr did not visit the area and would not even send a representative during the last two years of our involvement. No attempt was made to speak to people who had lived and worked there who would have offered different opinions. No attempt was made to evaluate the options and preserve the right to a billion barrel project.

Kay also felt that Derr did not want to carry on a project created by his predecessor, Keller: 'He was probably also trying to make a point of changing the "bad" decisions of Chevron's past Chairman.'

Indeed, the 'champions of Sudan' within Chevron had moved on. Swede Nelson, the President of Chevron Overseas when the company entered Sudan, left the company in 1980; his successor, Allan Martini, retired in 1988 along with CEO Keller.[135] Chevron adviser Collins wrote in a letter that Chevron's 'chief officials have a serious case of what I call Sudanitis.'[136] But at the end of the 1980s, a new team of executives was in charge. In 1992, they told Brian Kay to be quiet, close up shop, lay off all the employees, and move on.

Kay was the last remaining Chevron expatriate to leave Sudan. 'The close down of operations and the withdrawal from Sudan must rank as one of the worst decisions ever made by a major oil company,' he argued, especially in the light of the future oil production that CNPC and its partners would bring out of Chevron's former concession.[137] Years of hard work mapping Sudan's oil basins, exploring the southern interior, and conquering the hazards of the Sudd were thrown away for nothing.

Lillian Skander continued to work for Chevron around the world. But as the years passed, the dead and wounded of the February 1984 attack on the company's Rubkona base camp in southern Sudan were mostly forgotten. Chevron's days in Sudan may have been over, but the lure of oil was irresistible for others.

3

BOARDROOMS AND BATTLEFIELDS

November 2008: The wooded banks of Lake Geneva seem as far away as anywhere from Sudan. But in the boardroom of the small but sleek office of Lundin Petroleum, only a short drive from the city's waterfront, Sudan had been on the front burner for years. The Lundin family of Sweden was famous for its successes in the oil and mining industry. The company was first and foremost an explorer. Rather than seeking large payoffs from decades of production as sought by oil majors, Lundin focused on discovering and developing oil fields and then selling the assets to prospective producers.

Lundin Petroleum was just one of several Western and Asian oil companies that moved into Sudan after Chevron's departure in the 1990s. Despite Sudan's continuing civil war, it did not take long for these companies to descend upon the American oil major's abandoned stakes. Decisions made in faraway corporate boardrooms would mix dangerously with those of callous political rulers and impulsive rebel commanders to define the struggle to control Sudan's oil fortunes at the turn of the century.

The chances of Sudan's ruling NIF developing the country's oil industry seemed bleak without the immense financial power and seasoned experience of Chevron. But the NIF was willing to go to great and heinous lengths to ensure the resumption of oil operations. In order to clear the way for oil companies to operate freely, the government sanctioned a scorched-earth campaign by the Sudan Armed Forces and pro-government militias throughout the 1990s that resulted in the death and displacement of thousands of southern Sudanese. At the same time, the division among the SPLA rebels offered the Sudanese government the opportunity to control the southern oil fields outright. Arakis Energy, an obscure Canadian oil company with a few gas wells in Kentucky, struck a deal with the NIF regime to replace Chevron. But whereas the Sudanese government employed devastating means to capture oil areas, Arakis was unable to make much progress without the financial capacity to advance the long sought after $1 billion pipeline project that Chevron had abandoned. Arakis sought to bring in Occidental, a large American oil company, as a partner, but the potential deal fell apart with deteriorating relations between Washington and Khartoum. Instead, the current confrontational US foreign policy towards Sudan, culminating with the imposition of economic sanctions, opened the door for the China National Petroleum Corporation (CNPC) and Malaysia's national oil company Petronas to take the lead role in Sudan's oil industry.

In the late 1990s, the arrival of Asian national oil companies in Sudan made the prospect of large-scale oil production and exports suddenly very possible. After Arakis was bought out by Talisman, its larger Canadian counterpart, and Lundin and other European companies entered the scene, it did not take long for the first oil barrels to find their way to international markets. But the destructive influence of oil on Sudan's civil war led to the rise of civil society activists in North America and Europe, who demanded that oil companies stop their operations. The ability of activists to win political support from the US government was instrumental in leading Talisman to exit Sudan, with European oil companies following shortly after. Asian national oil companies were the least susceptible because they were state-owned and largely off the stock markets, from where activists could otherwise exert downward pressure on a company's share price. Paradoxically, the US sanctions and activist campaigns that drove out Western oil companies allowed Chinese, Malaysian, and later Indian oil companies to dominate Sudan's oil industry.

Wheeling, dealing, and destroying

If the NIF regime wanted a long and prosperous political life in Khartoum, it needed to bring Sudan's dormant oil industry to life. To make this happen, it had to find international oil companies willing to take the plunge. But Chevron's departure had tainted Sudan as a legitimate investment destination. 'We couldn't attract better companies because people asked questions about insecurity and the commercial potential of the oil fields,' said a senior Sudanese oil official.[1] Instead, the NIF relied on a number of personal connections in the US and Canada to push forward the advancement of its oil industry.[2] In 1992, the Vancouver-based State Petroleum Corporation, a company existing more on paper than in reality, began to pursue Chevron's oil concessions.[3] Lutfur Khan, State Petroleum's owner, established the company solely to gain the rights to Sudan's main oil fields through the personal connections he had established with the NIF leadership.[4] Ironically, about a year before Sudan was placed on the US government's list of state sponsors of terrorism, Khan met NIF leader Hassan al-Turabi at the Watergate Hotel in Washington in January 1992 to initiate the deal.[5] State Petroleum later decided to partner with Arakis, which was slightly better positioned to help find the required financing. In August 1993, after Sudan parcelled out Chevron's former oil concession, State and Arakis took over the rights of Blocks 1, 2, and 4, which contained the coveted Unity and Heglig oil fields.

Elsewhere, through its International Petroleum Corporation, the Lundin family gained the rights to oil concessions along the Sudan-Egypt border.[6] Qatar Petroleum also signed an agreement to develop Chevron's oil finds in Block 3 of the eastern Upper Nile in August 1995.[7] The following month, CNPC was awarded the rights to Block 6, which included Chevron's smaller oil finds north of the border near Muglad. But the chances of Arakis successfully completing the $1 billion project to develop Sudan's main oil fields and construct a 1,500 kilometre pipeline to the Red Sea still seemed bleak.

The SPLA rebel leader John Garang did not want to give the oil industry a chance. 'We are very clear about it: we will prevent drilling,' he said at the time.[8] But Garang did not make good on his threat. Rather, the SPLA had its back against the wall during the early 1990s: the fall of Mengistu in Ethiopia left the southern Sudanese rebels short of a key supporter. As he led the rebels with a heavy hand, Garang's vulnerability generated dissension among his commanders. In August 1991, a number of senior SPLA officers sought to seize upon Garang's weakened position and take over the rebel group. Led by Dr. Riek Machar, a Nuer from western Upper Nile, they called for new leadership within the movement and for southern independence, rather than Garang's vision of a reformed but united Sudan.[9] But the coup attempt failed. Instead, Machar formed a splinter group which waged war against the SPLA in a south-

south civil war. As the rebel leaders vied for power, ethnic violence between the Dinka and Nuer, which dominated the rank and file of the SPLA and Machar's splinter group respectively, grew to devastating levels, resulting in some 300,000 deaths.[10]

Southern infighting gave the NIF exactly what it wanted. It pursued a strategy of divide and rule to weaken the SPLA, but also to capture key oil areas. Riek Machar's splinter group happened to hold much of the oil-rich Upper Nile province and was in need of a steady supply of arms and ammunition to battle Garang's SPLA. This was the perfect match for the Islamists. As early as 1991, Machar began to receive military support from the Sudanese government.[11] The NIF already had the Bul Nuer militia, led by the former Anyanya II fighter Paulino Matip, on its side. Together, in a lust for personal power, Matip and Machar handed the NIF regime what its predecessors in Khartoum had failed to achieve for decades: control of the oil regions.

The NIF also continued a military tactic used by former Sudanese governments, by arming local militias from the nomadic Rizeigat and Misseriya ethnic groups of southern Darfur and Kordofan to battle southern rebels. Since few other economic opportunities existed for the impoverished Arab nomads, raiding southern communities, regardless of their affiliation with the SPLA, became widespread.[12] The NIF essentially sanctioned *murahaleen* militias to pillage and destroy the communities of the Dinka and Nuer African pastoralists of the south. In a five-month offensive between November 1992 and April 1993, the Sudan Armed Forces and militias destroyed almost sixty Dinka hamlets in oil areas near Bentiu town, killing hundreds and displacing more than one thousand people. A month later, another offensive took place near Heglig, with rape and abduction for slavery often part of the attacks.[13] Death and destruction were laying the foundation for oil exploration.

James Terence Alexander, the ambitious and fast-talking CEO of Arakis, was aware of the security risks in Sudan. 'This is not West Texas or Alberta. These things happen in new areas ... when dealing with pipelines and oil,' he said.[14] But unlike Chevron, Arakis claimed that it was confident in the Sudanese army's ability to protect oil operations. Alexander said that security 'looks 100 per cent different inside the country than it does outside the country. Whether you like the politics or not, (Sudan) does appear to be relatively stable. The government does appear to have things under control.'[15]

Alexander's testament glossed over the brutal counterinsurgency campaign the NIF was waging in and around oil regions in southern Sudan. But he was certainly not going to give a negative impression of the security situation when trying to attract potential investors. In contrast to Chevron, whose exploration and investments spanned continents, for Arakis Sudan was the only investment of note. If their Sudan venture failed, so did the company.

Arakis made some progress on the ground in 1993 and 1994, but struggled to raise capital to fully carry out its operations. A breakthrough seemed to come in 1995 when Alexander announced that a financier, Arab Group International (AGI), was willing to make a $750 million investment.[16] The news took financial markets by storm and Arakis stock on the Vancouver stock market went from trading at $5.50 in September 1994 to $26.00 in July 1995. At the time, trading volumes from the company's listing on the NASDAQ stock exchange in New York were at the same level as Microsoft during the heyday of the software giant's upcoming Windows 95 operating system.[17]

But the excitement surrounding Arakis did not last long. It was soon clear that AGI was not going to provide the necessary funding. The company's stock crashed and Alexander resigned in December 1995.[18] He blamed US government policy towards Sudan for souring the company's chances to find suitable funders.[19] The World Bank and US commercial banks, which had participated in Chevron's earlier international consortium in Sudan, were not eager to put their trust in the relatively small Arakis when an oil major like Chevron had already failed.

Alexander defended his financing schemes in Sudan: 'Muslim fundamentalists are like everyone else, and those who speak ill of them have a cultural bias.'[20] Beyond his business dealings, if one thing was becoming clear, it was that the task of developing Sudan's petroleum resources was more than one company could handle on its own.

Seeking partners

Arakis did not bow out of Sudan after its fundraising debacle in 1995. Instead, it changed strategy. John McLeod, an experienced oilman who had been working for State Petroleum as a project consultant on Sudan, replaced Alexander as CEO of Arakis. McLeod quickly decided to follow the more conventional path of financing the project through joint venture partners.[21] His efforts were assisted by a series of discoveries made by Arakis in Sudan in 1996. In June, a ceremony was held to mark the delivery of oil by truck from Heglig to a small refinery in the north. 'You had to be there to believe it,' McLeod said. 'The president showed up with most the Cabinet. It was a grand foofaraw. They cut ribbons and pushed buttons and made oil flow and trucks move. There was dancing and singing. It was almost like a Southern Baptist-type participatory religious thing.'[22]

McLeod also tried his best to give a positive spin on the security situation in Sudan. 'There have been no rebel incidents. Period. Full stop. Security seems good.' Thanks to the Sudanese government, McLeod remarked, 'It's as peaceful as ever.'[23] If Sudan did offer Arakis peaceful surroundings, it was the result of the divide and rule strategy towards southern rebels and the displacement and killing of local populations by the Sudanese government.

Still under pressure to fulfil its contractual obligations to develop the oil fields or lose a sizeable portion of its concession area, the new Arakis CEO moved quickly to find partners. Arakis was sitting on hundreds of millions of barrels of oil reserves just waiting to be pumped out of the ground. McLeod called Sudan 'the best oil play in the world', but because of the company's recent shady financial dealings, its stock value remained depressed, making it an obvious takeover target.[24] Hoping to avoid a takeover, Arakis sent its senior geophysicist, George Fulford, armed with data on Sudan, to some forty companies in search of partners.[25] In June 1996, McLeod announced that eighteen companies and groups were interested in joining a venture to construct a pipeline to the Red Sea. CNPC and Malaysia's Petronas were pegged as likely suitors.[26] A month later, the rumour mill continued to spin when representatives of the California-based Occidental Petroleum Corporation appeared at Arakis headquarters in Calgary.[27] Occidental had previously constructed a fast-track oil pipeline in Yemen, where conditions are similar to Sudan.[28] When Occidental entered the Sudan sweepstakes, it became strikingly clear that Arakis had served a purpose for the Sudanese government despite it failings to carry out the project alone.

The line-up of companies wishing to enter Sudan during the 1990s indicated that they were no longer concerned about the reasons for Chevron's departure. These companies included the Asian national oil companies CNPC, Petronas, OVL, and the Japan National Oil Corporation and a number of American and European oil majors and independents, such as Total, Royal Dutch Shell, Occidental, and the International Petroleum Corporation of the Lundin family.[29] The pint-size Arakis progressed just enough with developing its operation in Sudan to demonstrate to the larger companies that the oil reserves were there and they could work in Sudan without major security incidents. 'Arakis was a vehicle,' said a Sudanese oil official. 'They worked without incident for three years, improved reserve amounts with discoveries and were producing 24,000 barrels a day.'[30] Arakis also gave the NIF more time to carry on its destructive military campaign to secure oil regions from excessive rebel incursion. But exactly how and where Arakis would take Sudan into the future was yet to be seen.

Learning from the past, Sudanese oil officials were keen that potential partners for Arakis would need to be able to get the job done. Bidding companies were told that they would need to maintain the same terms as the Arakis contract, as well as demonstrate sufficient funds to develop the oil resources and construct an oil pipeline in a short time. Occidental, Total, Petronas and CNPC were closing in on leading the new joint venture. The Malaysians were looking to take on 50 per cent of the joint venture, but it was the Chinese who stood out, asking for an 80 per cent share with Arakis and Sudapet, the Sudanese national oil company. 'Unlike the other Asian companies, CNPC took decisions on the spot,' said one former Sudanese oil official. 'They were radically different, not having to constantly call home like the others to make their decisions.'[31]

But Sudanese oil officials were very interested in regaining access to the US technology and expertise that Occidental could offer. Arakis, too, leaned towards Occidental, as it provided the opportunity to access long-sought-after funding opportunities with US banks. The entry of Occidental into Sudan would signal an improvement in relations between the US and Sudan which would theoretically encourage US banks to provide the needed financing for the pipeline project.

Relations between the US and Sudan had worsened since Chevron's departure. In 1993, US President Bill Clinton placed Sudan on the list of states sponsoring terrorism. After Khartoum was linked with the 1995 attempted assassination of Egypt's President Hosni Mubarak in Addis Ababa, the US supported UN sanctions against Sudan in 1996. In April that year, Sudan was included in the 'Anti-Terrorism and Effective Death Penalty Act', which banned Americans from engaging in financial transactions with governments on the US terrorism sponsors list. On the face of it, it looked as if Occidental's chances to enter Sudan were slim. But when the US Treasury Department released the actual regulations of the Anti-Terrorism Act, the company discovered it could still engage in Sudan as long as its financial transactions did not support terrorism.[32] The timing of these regulations was preceded, interestingly enough, by Arakis CEO McLeod and Occidental executives visiting Washington to meet the US State Department and other government agencies.[33] It seemed that another US oil company was about to enter Sudan.

In early November 1996, the Sudanese government was considering the composition of the joint venture of companies to operate its coveted oil fields. Occidental looked to be the front-runner, but as negotiations ensued, Khartoum got word that President Clinton was sending a $20 million non-lethal military aid package to Ethiopia, Eritrea and Uganda, which at the time were key allies of the SPLA in Sudan's civil war. Infuriated that Washington was plotting its downfall with its hostile neighbours, the Sudanese government rejected any involvement of Occidental in its country's oil industry.[34] 'In the end, it was decided (by Sudan) that they (Occidental) would not be included. There was a significant political component in the decision,' said the Arakis CEO McLeod.[35] The sudden absence of US competition offered the remaining Asian and European companies an opening. The Chinese leaped at the opportunity.

In late November 1996, Wu Yaowen, CNPC's Vice-President, flew to Khartoum to make the final push to win the leading stake in the Arakis joint venture. 'We built the Chinese oil industry,' Wu told Sudanese oil officials. 'We have the experience and capability to build your oil industry.' Hinting at Sudan's troubles with the US, Wu added, 'China is a nation that honours its commitments. Unlike your previous investors, we will not take out our investment before the end of the project.'[36] The Chinese oilmen were also prepared to go well beyond the other financial offers on the table.

A former Chevron oilman commented after the company left Sudan in 1993 that the infrastructure needed for Sudan's oil fields required a 'virtual re-colonization' of Sudan.[37] CNPC was prepared to go the distance to provide Sudan with the necessary infrastructure. Chinese oil officials promised to construct a large oil refinery outside Khartoum and complete the export pipeline quickly.[38] For decades the Sudanese government had sought an oil refinery to avoid the staggering cost of importing fuel, but Chevron had been reluctant to build one for financial reasons. Remarkably, CNPC was proposing the oil infrastructure at a time when international oil prices were actually lower than when Chevron left. The Chinese oil company was playing by a different set of rules; it demonstrated little concern with the calculated rate of return on its proposed investment.[39] Instead, the Chinese 'incorporated additional benefits to the Sudan government, which essentially got them their participation,' said McLeod.[40] CNPC was in.

The ousting of US competition simplified the decision for Sudan to choose CNPC. But the Sudanese government was unwilling to give the Chinese company the majority of the joint venture. It wanted to diversify the risk involved in the consortium's search for funds for the $1 billion oil pipeline project, and brought Petronas into the deal. Total had been another possibility, but Sudanese officials were not pleased with their proposed pipeline construction schedule. They chose Petronas because they thought the company would work better with CNPC as a fellow nationally-owned company. However, neither company was looking for such a partnership. In fact, Sudan was attempting to blunt the ambitions of both Asian companies. As a senior Sudanese oil official put it, 'it was a forced marriage'.[41]

The Sudanese had long sought Malaysian investment in the oil industry. President Omar al-Bashir visited Kuala Lumpur in June 1991 and met the Prime Minister Dr. Mahathir during a three-day state visit. His delegation prioritised attracting Malaysian investment to Sudan's oil industry.[42] But Petronas turned down its Sudanese suitors. The relative novelty of international operations at the time led the company to keep its focus on its operations in Vietnam and other parts of its neighbourhood in South East Asia.[43] Senior management was not yet united on the idea of expanding overseas.[44] 'Petronas sent a team, but they were not interested,' said a Sudanese oil official. 'They were in a hurry to go on to *Hajj* in Mecca.'[45]

There were considerable political, religious and social links between Sudan and Malaysia that encouraged the Petronas connection.[46] 'We feel very close to Petronas, probably because of the skin colour and same names. My people feel at home with Malaysians,' said Hassan Ali, the Secretary General of Sudan's Ministry of Energy and Mining.[47] In 1996, given the growing confidence in its ability to seek international opportunities amid a clearer commercial and security environment, Petronas was eager to stay in Sudan. In early December 1996, Arakis signed an agreement with its new Asian partners. CNPC took 40 per cent, Petronas 30 per cent, Arakis 25 per cent and Sudapet 5 per cent in the Greater Nile Petroleum Operating Company (GNPOC). Zhou Jiping of CNPC was named the joint venture's first president after formal agreements were signed with the Sudanese government in March 1997.[48] Nearly twenty years after the discovery of oil in Sudan, serious activity was underway again.

Targeting Talisman

Arakis may have brought in Chinese and Malaysian partners to shoulder the majority of the financing needs for Sudan's oil pipeline project, but it was still unable to cover its own share. Takeover rumours that had been dogging Arakis for some time finally came true in October 1998 when its fellow Canadian oil company, Talisman, bought it out. Unlike Arakis, Talisman was hardly a small player in the international oil industry. Seen as Canada's flagship oil company, Talisman was an independent oil company with a major inheritance, having once been the Canadian branch of British Petroleum. Its small but impressive portfolio of projects in Canada, the North Sea and Indonesia produced close to 150,000 bpd of oil in 1998.[49] But Talisman was also eager to find strong growth possibilities at the frontier of the international oil industry, aiming for a 20 per cent increase in production.[50] Talisman saw Sudan as a 'long-life strategic asset with a large exploration and development side'.[51] But while Canadian executives were making plans in their Calgary offices, the Sudanese government was busy continuing to unleash mass violence in southern Sudan.

In April 1997, a month after the GNPOC consortium was established, the Sudanese government signed the Khartoum Peace Agreement with the rebel defector Riek Machar and other armed groups that had broken away from the SPLA.[52] The umbrella group of southern militias was known as the South Sudan Defence Forces (SSDF) and would fall under Machar's leadership. Before it decided to invest in Sudan, Talisman representatives met the pro-government southern leader Machar, who told the company he supported its entry into the country.[53] The Khartoum Peace Agreement did not stop the NIF continuing its divide and rule strategy, even among those southern militias now fighting on its side in the civil war. The NIF was seeking to wear down Machar's power base in oil areas by offering direct military and political support to his commanders.[54] The regime also continued to kill and displace civilians of the south.

Now able to use future oil production as collateral for international loans, the Sudanese government bought arms from a long list of overseas suppliers, particularly Iran and China, in order to wage war and depopulate oil regions.[55] Beginning in May 1999, Sudanese troops and pro-government militias launched an offensive against civilian populations in Ruweng county east of the Unity oil field in Block 1.[56] Russian-built Antonov planes dropped crude bombs and helicopter gunships terrorised helpless villages before armed militias of *murahaleen* arrived on horseback to continue the attacks on the ground.

After the arrival of CNPC, Petronas, and Talisman, it did not take long for crude oil to find its way from the southern oil fields through a newly-built 1,500-kilometre pipeline that emerged at the Bashair terminal on the Red Sea to fill a Singapore-bound tanker. On 30 August 1999, crowds were on hand to watch as President Bashir and other Sudanese and foreign dignitaries commemorated the event.[57] 'We have defeated all the foreign enemies wishing to stop the export of the oil. We must now defeat the internal enemy, who may try to halt the full utilisation of the oil revenue,' Sudanese government radio announced.[58] The war with the SPLA would indeed continue, but the NIF had not vanquished all its enemies abroad. Despite the celebration, not everyone was happy with the oil deal in Sudan. Activists ranging from grassroots church groups to sophisticated international non-governmental organisations in Canada, the US and Europe were calling on international oil companies to halt their operations in Sudan. They saw these companies as complicit in the human rights abuses of the Sudanese government in oil-rich areas, and Talisman was enemy number one.

Before the takeover of Arakis by Talisman, the Toronto-based Inter-Church Coalition on Africa declared, 'Arakis' work in Sudan lends legitimacy to a regime that has been condemned by the UN for genocide, slavery, indiscriminate bombing of civilians, killing of political opponents and forcing an extreme form of Islam on all Sudanese.'[59] Arakis deflected the criticism: 'We're investors here. We're just doing a job,' said CEO John McLeod in April 1997. 'We get a tremendous amount of anti-Sudanese publicity and sentiment.'[60] The company sponsored a multi-million dollar hospital at Heglig to demonstrate its goodwill. But what was a mere spark of activism against Arakis in Sudan spread like wildfire against Talisman, which quickly became the main target of activists.

Intent on shutting down Sudan's oil industry until the civil war ended, activists urged investors in Talisman to divest their stock in order to bring the company to heel. The initial public response of Talisman CEO Jim Buckee to the connection drawn between his company and the civil war was absolute denial. He countered claims about the severity of the violence, saying that accusations of genocide in Sudan were untrue and those of slavery 'grossly misrepresented and possibly manipulated'.[61] He insisted that in fact no displacement had taken place in areas around the oil fields,[62] arguing that fighting and displacement were due to inter-tribal conflicts and not connected to Talisman's operations.[63]

Buckee brashly called activist pressure 'white noise we can live with'.[64] He said that he valued the support of the former rebel leader Riek Machar. 'He will be intimately involved,' said Buckee.[65] In 1998, Machar was also front and centre as a demonstration of Sudan's steps towards peace during the three-day visit of Malaysian Prime Minister Dr. Mahathir bin Mohamad.[66] Time and time again, Machar acted as a tool for the Sudanese government and oil companies in order to legitimise their activities in the south.

In the coming years, numerous investigations by Amnesty International, Human Rights Watch, the European Coalition on Oil in Sudan, and Christian Aid argued that oil was fuelling Sudan's civil war.[67] Talisman would be forced to pay notice. Lloyd Axworthy, Canada's foreign minister and a strong proponent of human security and humanitarianism, warned the company of the potential for 'economic and trade restrictions'.[68] As accusations mounted from Canadian civil society groups, the Canadian government sponsored a study in 1999 to explore the link between oil and Sudan's conflict.[69] Dubbed the Harker Report after its lead investigator, it detailed the connection between oil and displacement in southern Sudan, finding that the Sudan Armed Forces had even refuelled at GNPOC's Heglig facilities in order to carry out attacks on civilian targets.[70] Activists appeared to be gaining momentum; Talisman's depressed stock price demonstrated that investors were feeling increasingly insecure about its Sudan operations.[71] Talisman decided to do a little lobbying of its own in an effort to reduce the pressure.

With the threat of Canadian government action looming, Talisman hired the global public relations firm Hill and Knowlton to develop a communications strategy. It lobbied Canada's International Trade Minister Pierre Pettigrew and Natural Resources Minister Ralph Goodale to support its position in Sudan.[72] Talisman also warned that it might become a takeover target should its stock value fall much more, and that Canada might lose its flagship oil company in the process. Lloyd Axworthy was warned that by threatening Talisman he was doing no favour to his Liberal Party in maintaining a political foothold in western Canada, where the oil and mining industry was well-established and would not look kindly on government pressure damaging its international interests. Axworthy's fellow Cabinet members were also disturbed by the idea of a possible new law to sanction Talisman, determined at 'the whim of the Foreign Minister'.[73]

In the end, Ottawa would not sanction Talisman. Rather, it asked the company to sign the International Code of Ethics for Canadian Business, a set of non-binding codes and practices concerning ethics and human rights. Civil society activists were displeased with the Canadian government's seemingly conciliatory decision to follow a constructive approach with Talisman and Sudan; activists remained determined to force the company out.

Losing the battle

While Talisman had avoided possible sanctions from the Canadian government, it was in trouble south of the border in the US. The company was traded on the New York Stock Exchange and American institutional investors were unloading hundreds of thousands of Talisman shares because of civil society pressure. Talisman scrambled to buy back around $300 million of its own stock in 2000 in an effort to keep its value up.[74] But some analysts still felt the 'Sudan discount' that depressed the share price was as much as 35 per cent.[75] 'We will destroy your share price,' a long-time Sudan activist, Eric Reeves, warned Talisman.[76] As divestment continued to develop, the company began to brand its community development work and self-proclaimed role in promoting peace more actively. It was already running medical facilities, agricultural programmes and schools in areas around its oil fields.[77]

But in the face of mounting pressure, for the first time in company history, and in a path-breaking move in the international oil industry, the company completed an in-house, independently-audited, corporate responsibility report.[78] Although Talisman continued to confront civil society activists about its activities in Sudan, gone was its complete denial of the link between oil and civil war. In 2002, the company admitted that the Sudan Armed Forces had used oil field airstrips and said it was lobbying the Sudanese government to stop doing this for offensive purposes.[79] 'What is in our sphere of influence, what we can do, we will do,' said Talisman's Buckee.[80] But these tactical concessions failed to win over the activists; pressure was heating up on Talisman in the US.

The US government was not finished with Sudan. The religious persecution, slavery, and human rights abuses in Sudan brought a growing chorus of condemnation from US humanitarian, African-American, Christian rights, and human rights organisations that set off alarm bells in the US Congress. In June 1997, there were calls in Congress to impose comprehensive sanctions on Sudan through the Freedom from Religious Persecution Act. In November, President Clinton placed sanctions on Sudan, citing its support for terrorism, destabilisation of its neighbours, and ongoing human rights abuses.[81] The next year, things got even worse for the company.

In August 1998, terrorists linked to Osama bin Laden and Al Qaeda bombed US embassies in Kenya and Tanzania.[82] The US responded with missile strikes on Sudan and Afghanistan in an effort to hit back against the international terrorist network and its state sponsors. Although bin Laden had already been expelled from Sudan in 1996, US Tomahawk missiles destroyed the al-Shifa Pharmaceutical Factory, a suspected chemical weapons plant in Khartoum North. The assault turned out to be a massive intelligence failure. As its name suggested, the plant was only producing pharmaceuticals. Nonetheless, US relations with Sudan were transformed from containment to confrontation.[83] Talisman's investment in Sudan was a particular concern. In 1999, US Secretary of State Madeleine Albright urged her Canadian counterpart Axworthy to 'get Talisman out'.[84] A year later, when President George W. Bush came to power, the US would engage in Sudan as it had never done before.

Sudan was at the top of George W. Bush's Africa agenda. The conservative Christian groups that drove his presidential campaign were now eager to see an end to the conflict. Joining them were Jewish groups and the Black Congressional Caucus, forming an impressive civil society coalition.[85] The sheer clout of activists lobbying the US Congress, not to mention their having the ear of a born-again Christian president, was a real and present danger to Talisman in Sudan.[86] US activists took pressure on the Canadian oil company to a new level by demanding that companies on US financial markets with activities in Sudan be delisted.[87] These restrictions were part of the Sudan Peace Act, which passed the US House of Representatives on 13 June 2001 by a vote of 422 to 2.[88] The results spooked Talisman; its New York Stock Exchange listing was vital to the company to raise capital. 'We want to remain in compliance with laws and we will,' said CEO Buckee. Fortunately for Talisman capital market restrictions had powerful opponents in the US who helped stave off direct market consequences.

Talisman lobbied to turn around the congressional campaign to enact capital market restrictions on US financial markets. It also had several natural allies. Alan Greenspan, Chairman of the Federal Reserve, opposed capital market restrictions; he feared that the precedent of the act would alone weaken the competitiveness of US financial markets, sending companies overseas to raise capital. There was also resistance in the US Senate, which had to pass the Sudan Peace Act before it ended up on Bush's desk to be signed into law. Even President Bush was not fully supportive. One official in his administration said that capital markets restrictions 'would significantly damage our relations with European and African countries that are essential to the peace process in Sudan.'[89] In July 2001, the Senate passed a watered-down version of the Act without the capital market restrictions, and sent the bill back to the House of Representatives.[90] Feeling they were losing the battle to keep the possibility for restrictions alive, a group of leading activists arranged a press conference at the US Congress in September 2001 to launch a national campaign.[91] But before the press conference could get under way, US Capitol police rushed in. Passenger airliners had struck the World Trade Centre in New York and the Pentagon; a new political landscape now confronted the activists.

After the 9/11 attacks, Washington's relationship with Khartoum evolved. The Bush administration maintained a congenial relationship with Sudan's National Intelligence and Security Services agency in order to gather counter-terrorism intelligence on international terrorism.[92] 'Their cooperation was really terrific,' said Deputy of State Richard Armitage, to the disdain of activists.[93] The Bush administration also pushed the UN to lift diplomatic sanctions on Sudan and assured Khartoum that capital market restrictions would not be included in the Sudan Peace Act,[94] a notable expression of Washington's own economic and security limits in responding to the human rights concerns of civil society activists. It might have been a positive sign for Sudan's oil industry in general, but it was too late for Talisman.

The initial passing of the Sudan Peace Act in the US House of Representatives sent Talisman searching for willing buyers for its Sudan assets. The mere threat of capital market restrictions was the last straw; Talisman was wrapping up a deal to sell the assets in the autumn of 2002. 'We learned the power of our stakeholders, not only in Sudan, but also North America,' said Reg Manhas, former Talisman Vice-President of Corporate Affairs. 'The Board of Directors realized our vulnerability to the political process in Washington.'[95] CEO Buckee later remarked that Sudan only represented 10 per cent of Talisman's oil and gas production, but took up well over 10 per cent of his time. According to Buckee, it was not worth the trouble of such a depressing effect on the company's share value.[96] 'I think we had not anticipated how the protests would snowball,' said Buckee.[97] Talisman did reassess its decision to leave Sudan after the capital market restrictions were dropped from the final version of the Sudan Peace Act, but decided to proceed with the sale of its Sudanese assets to India's ONGC Videsh (OVL) on 30 October 2002. Manhas reflected that Talisman 'lost the battle' against activists, but by helping to ensure that the capital market restrictions failed, the company had 'won the war'.

In the end, it was the ability of the activists to translate their social pressure into political consequences that pushed Talisman to leave Sudan. The company made a hefty profit of CAN$296 million from the sale to OVL, but its increasing net income in Sudan of US$184 million (2000), US$210 million (2001), and CAN$310 million (2002) told a different story.[98] Sudan was an international growth vehicle for the company, with output from the Heglig and Unity oil fields still growing when it left. Talisman would certainly have made a higher profit if it had remained— OVL earned €262 million profit in 2004 and €377 million in 2005 from Sudan alone.[99] But despite Talisman's efforts to find a way to continue to work in Sudan, in the end the political risk and consequences of Sudan's civil war had blossomed into an international nightmare for the Canadian oil company and led to the demise of its operations in Sudan.

After it left Sudan, Talisman's strategy revolved around the concept of 'post-Sudan'.[100] According to Reg Manhas, the Sudan experience 'fundamentally changed' the company.[101] Talisman subsequently became a torchbearer of corporate responsibility in the international oil industry. In 2005, it was the first Canadian company to commit to the Extractive Industries Transparency Initiative, a voluntary global multi-stakeholder that strives to ensure transparency of payments from natural resources. It was named one of the leading companies in the field by the anti-corruption watchdog NGO Transparency International in 2008.[102] It also became a member of the UN Global Compact, a voluntary code of conduct on environmental, labour and human rights for corporations. 'The lessons learned from Sudan and the application of those lessons into our policies really put us in a leadership position on the international scale in terms of how we address issues related to human rights, transparency and community relations,' Manhas said.[103]

In essence, activist pressure on Talisman's Sudan operations left it with a corporate responsibility infrastructure that it could exploit elsewhere. 'One of the things we did learn is that you have to have the provision of security very well-stated and documented, who does what, when and why,' remarked Buckee.[104] 'We certainly take care to assess the above-ground risks; to get those issues right is, in fact, a risk-mitigation process.' Driving Talisman out of Sudan was a bittersweet victory for activists. While they were able to draw considerable support from the US government, in reality they merely succeeded in breaking the weakest link in Sudan's oil industry.

The limits of global activism

Activist fury in the US and Canada over the deadly connection between oil development and human rights abuses obfuscated more consequential determinants of the behaviour of oil companies. The contours of Sudan's civil war and the enlarging international strategies of Asian national oil companies had far more influence on Sudan's oil industry than the efforts of activists.

Talisman was not alone in facing pressure from civil society groups. Lundin and OMV, a Swedish and an Austrian company operating in Sudan, were also forced to respond to growing condemnation of their activities. In 1997, Lundin became the operator of Block 5A in a consortium with Petronas, OMV and Sudapet in southern Unity state.[105] In 2001, it also put together the While Nile Petroleum Operating Company with the same partners to explore even further south in Block 5B. Both these concessions were in Chevron's old territory, where Brian Kay had led exploration teams into the vast swampland of the Sudd nearly two decades earlier. The development of the oil pipeline by GNPOC in 1999 encouraged the new exploration activities by providing a means to bring potential new oil to international markets.[106] Like other oil companies, Lundin executives were encouraged by the Khartoum Peace Agreement signed between the Sudanese government and southern rebel factions, including the rebel leader Riek Machar.[107] But the violence of the civil war translated into an international publicity storm for the company.

'Lundin Oil activities are negative for Sweden,' Anna Lindh, the late Swedish foreign minister, said in April 2001. 'We expect Swedish companies to respect an ethical code in line with human rights and the environment in which they operate abroad.'[108] Lundin tried to navigate its way through the human rights mess. It hired a Canadian lawyer, Christine Batruch, as a consultant in 1999 to focus mainly on its growing public relations difficulties in Sudan. The company appointed Batruch as Vice-President of corporate responsibility in 2002.[109] She wrote later that Lundin perceived that exceptional circumstances in Sudan were forcing it to detach itself from its apolitical principles.[110]

Like Talisman, Lundin engaged its shareholders and wider stakeholders head-on in an effort to show it was actually a force for good in Sudan. It welcomed Swedish and foreign journalists to visit its operations and invited the governor of Unity state to Sweden to relate the company's positive influence on local communities through social investments.[111] It also engaged a member of its board of directors, the former Swedish prime minister and UN special envoy Carl Bildt, to promote the opportunity that oil development provided to help build peace in Sudan.[112] Yet despite the verbal battles underway in Europe over the company's activities in Sudan, Lundin and its partners could not help being in the thick of the often violent divide and rule strategy of the Sudanese government to gain control over areas of the country that held the promise of new oil.

In May 1999, Lundin was forced to suspend its activities in Block 5A for eighteen months after rebel forces loyal to Riek Machar attacked an oil rig, killing three government employees. Machar was technically on the government's side at the time, operating as part of the SSDF, but infighting with his fellow pro-government Nuer militia leader Paulino Matip over control of Block 5A led to the attack.[113] Politically exploited and militarily weakened by the Sudanese government, Machar was to abandon the Khartoum Peace Agreement in January 2000 and rejoin the SPLA. Government forces also carried out waves of civilian displacement in Block 5A to secure the area for oil operations.[114]

In early 2001 Lundin discovered the lucrative Thar Jath oil field in southern Unity state. But the shifting allegiances in Sudan's civil war would soon catch up with the company. In January 2002, it halted its operations again after a company helicopter was shot down and the pro-government southern militia defending its operations left the government side to rejoin the SPLA.[115]

European oil companies active in Sudan began to unload their assets shortly after Talisman's departure in 2003. In June, Lundin sold its stake in Blocks 5A to Petronas for $142.5 million and OMV sold its shares in both 5A and 5B to OVL for $115 million.[116] These sales acted as a launching pad to expand the international activities of both companies within the safe and stable confines of Europe. Lundin stated at the time that the sale of Block 5A demonstrated 'the value that could be generated from successful exploration drilling'.[117] It then acquired assets in the North Sea that immediately increased the company's petroleum reserves and production levels.[118] As international oil prices rose, Lundin's earnings went from being in the red in 2001 to making a profit of 993,975 million Swedish kronor ($127,433 million) in 2005.[119] Its Sudan proceeds allowed the company to transform from a frontier company highly reliant on one risky venture to a balanced independent oil company with diverse international assets. In 2004, OMV made the largest acquisition in its history through its Sudan profits, by buying a majority stake in Petrom, a Romanian gas and oil company.[120] Its net income rose from €393 million to €1,495.8 million from 2003 to 2005.[121] Altogether, activists were not as influential in the decision-making of the European oil companies as they had been with Talisman. As much as they were affected by civil society pressure, the general insecurity of both Lundin and OMV operational areas in Sudan was a much more influential factor in their decisions to withdraw from Sudan.

Both Lundin and OMV, companies full of engineers and geologists with their heads focused deep underground looking for oil, were forced to pay attention to security and political issues above ground. A Lundin company representative said that the costs of considerable work stoppage due to insecurity in Block 5A, coupled with the impressive offer from Petronas, led to the selling of its assets.[122] Demonstrating the limits of activists' impact on Lundin, the Swedish company still maintained its Block 5B asset.[123] In general, social pressure from activists generated less political heat for the two European companies than it did for Talisman.[124]

Both Lundin and OMV stood beside the 'constructive engagement' approach followed by the European Union policy on Sudan.[125] 'Every organ of society has its sphere of influence and responsibility,' said Lundin's Christine Batruch,[126] as if reading from the same corporate responsibility playbook as Buckee at Talisman. Batruch felt that Lundin could make a positive difference by investing in social programmes in its operational areas, but it could not be expected to develop the entire country or end the protracted conflict.[127] Talisman, Lundin, and OMV had all sold assets in Sudan, but any celebration by activists in response to this pullout was short-lived. Paradoxically, the end result of human rights pressure was to improve the positions of less susceptible Asian national oil companies.

The Asian replacements

The situation took a turn for the worse for many activists when it became apparent that OVL would simply replace Talisman. 'We wanted them to halt production but not to leave and hand over to someone (such as OVL) who will be harder to bring to account,' said Andrew Pendleton of Christian Aid.[128] Talisman produced few results in improving human rights in Sudan, but the constant dialogue between the company and the Sudanese government on ethical issues, its efforts to ensure that GNPOC facilities were not used offensively by the Sudanese military, and its multiple community development programmes came to an end after it left.[129]

OVL was not unaware of the international political risk of investing in Sudan. Before it bought Talisman's stake in March 2003, the Indian company sold a 10 per cent share in the North Hell Bayou Prospect of Louisiana to its Indian counterpart Oil India Ltd.[130] Learning from Talisman, OVL worried that it might face a class action lawsuit in the US because of its commercial presence in Sudan. CNPC too was not completely unaffected by activist pressure.

In late 1999, CNPC aimed to take a significant step forward in its drive to become a global corporation by listing public shares on the New York and Hong Kong stock exchanges. But its plans to secure capital in the US were in direct opposition to the wishes of Sudan activists. As with

Talisman, it was believed among activists that the ability of CNPC to raise capital through US financial markets helped it finance its Sudan operations, which in turn generated revenue for the Sudanese government to carry out abuses against its own people. 'This is uncharted waters for religious and human rights groups,' said Nina Shea, a leading activist and Commissioner of the US Commission on International Religious Freedom. 'But if American companies can't invest in Sudan, why should we be capitalising foreign companies who do it?'[131]

In early 2000, more than 180 US religious leaders, conservative Republicans, and human rights activists sent a letter to President Clinton imploring him to bar CNPC from US financial markets because of its activities in Sudan.[132] The pressure did not let up as the bid drew closer. US activists who wanted to keep CNPC out of US financial markets did not face much vocal opposition from Chinese oil executives. Rather, they were up against many of their own countrymen and women. Over two thousand bankers, consultants, accountants and lawyers, led by the American investment bank Goldman Sachs, worked on CNPC's bid.[133] After calls for capital market restrictions on foreign companies in Sudan listed on US financial markets grew in early 2000, Goldman Sachs advised CNPC to restructure its initial public offering (IPO) to include a new subsidiary called PetroChina, which would operate only in China and exclude the Sudan operations. This so-called 'Chinese firewall' was hardly convincing, as a close managerial and financial relationship would still exist between CNPC and PetroChina.[134] However, apprehension over how capital market restrictions would influence the competitiveness of US financial markets and wider American foreign policy ultimately cleared the way for CNPC to gain access to US financial markets.

CNPC's Sudan activities did limit the amount of capital raised in the PetroChina IPO. It was believed that the IPO would generate $10 billion initially, but this estimate was downgraded to between $5 and $7 billion by January 2000, after it met fierce political opposition in the US.[135] The final result was still far below what CNPC had hoped. In April 2000, only $2.9 billion was raised, much of it thanks to last-minute purchases by Hong Kong investors and the British oil major BP.[136] CNPC fell flat on its face in its grand entrance on international financial markets.

Some activists overstated the impact the depressed value of PetroChina's IPO had on Sudan. 'If China had raised all the money it wanted, the SPLA would have been toast,' said Dennis Bennett, the co-founder of

Servant's Heart Relief, a Christian organisation active in southern Sudan.[137] The lack of enthusiasm for PetroChina's IPO among investors went well beyond Sudan. AFL-CIO, the largest American trade union federation, voiced concern that massive layoffs would take place in the Chinese oil industry if PetroChina raised enough capital from the IPO. At the same time, the idea that CNPC might use the IPO to help fund severance packages for redundant employees stirred financial concern among would-be investors.[138] They were not interested in funding the company's redundancies.

Sudan activists certainly helped delay and ultimately lower the capital raised by the PetroChina IPO. They were also influential in causing CNPC to change the name of its new subsidiary to PetroChina and its attempt to distance Sudan from the company's wider operations. But they failed to connect their actions with results on the ground in Sudan. Oil production and civil war carried on, despite all the attention activists had created in the US Congress and on Wall Street. The US government had come full circle, from Sudan's most important foreign patron to a powerful antagonist, and as a result, corporate executives in the boardrooms of Western oil companies sought to distance themselves from the battlefields of Sudan—but at the same time, Chinese, Indian and other Asian national oil companies charged forward.

PART II

CHINA

4

OIL FOR THE PARTY

February 2008: On a quiet tree-lined street in the Xicheng district of Beijing stood the unlikely home of the CNPC, the China National Petroleum Corporation. The unassuming off-white, ten-storey building did not fit the picture of a company making enormous investments across the globe. When it first entered Sudan in 1995, CNPC was largely unknown in the international oil industry. But ten years after its entry into Sudan, it paid $4.18 billion for the Canadian oil company PetroKazakhstan in 2005, building on its investments in Central Asia. The following year, it bought a string of exploration blocks in Nigeria to add to its African assets. Back in Beijing, the bland exterior of its headquarters and the stark atmosphere of its red-carpeted hallways did not reflect the high-flying path that CNPC was blazing overseas.

But there was good reason for CNPC to be conducting its business, and that of its better-known subsidiary PetroChina, out of such relatively modest headquarters. The ageing building was once home to the Chinese government's Ministry of Petroleum Industry. CNPC headquarters harkened back to the old China, when the economy was controlled by rigid central government planning, rather than the current fusion of a one-party political system with freewheeling capitalist economics. CNPC was one of many state-owned enterprises brought to life with an ample dose of capitalism during China's reform years of the 1980s. Born in 1988, by the turn of the century it had become an aggressive buyer of international oil and gas stakes.

But the fact that CNPC and its fellow Chinese national oil companies remained under the ownership of the Chinese government stoked political fears around the world. Voices in the US government and oil industry saw Chinese national oil companies as supported by unfair soft loans and diplomatic support from Beijing to 'lock up' oil around the world for China's exclusive use.[1] But, as CNPC's early investment in Sudan demonstrated, political leaders in Beijing were not capitalising on their ownership of Chinese national oil companies to capture oil for China. Rather, CNPC was exploiting its longstanding relations with the Communist Party of China to achieve its own corporate strategy overseas.

After nearly two decades of Sudanese leaders working with American oilmen to achieve their goal of home-grown oil, the arrival of China's premier national oil company stemmed from its deliberate strategy to become a globally-competitive corporation. A long history of Chinese oilmen wielding political power at home gave CNPC the independence to invest in Sudan at a time when few other Chinese companies were going abroad. The importance of oil in driving China's economy during the formative years of the People's Republic of China had forged deep relations between Chinese oilmen and the Communist Party. But when it became evident that China's oil production was stagnating, CNPC began to invest abroad, even before the government urged Chinese companies to 'go out'. CNPC was not striving to lock up oil for China; it was following a corporate agenda to ensure its long-term survival and well-being by acquiring new oil reserves and production. The timing was not right for Sudan to engage China on oil in the past, but with CNPC looking to expand its international operations in a big way in the mid-1990s, the Sudanese government was finally able to draw in Chinese oil investment. Beyond the competitive advantages of soft loans and diplomatic support that Chinese national oil companies gained from their close affiliation with Beijing, it was the political independence of CNPC in China that empowered the company to make its first major overseas investment a bold one—in Sudan.

The rise of the petroleum faction

After gaining steam in the international oil industry in the early 2000s, it was not long before CNPC found a new home. In January 2009, the company moved into its new corporate headquarters in Beijing's

Dongcheng district. Standing ominously over a steady crawl of Beijing's dense, noisy traffic, the four interconnected towers of glass and marble were more fitting for a global corporation. A giant stone pulled from a river in southwest China was placed in front of the new headquarters to bring the company good fortune. If the main lobby was any indication, luck was clearly on the CNPC's side. Guests arrived in an immaculate glass cortile stretching ten storeys high, which seemed big enough to fit the old ministry building inside. Down the street were the headquarters of CNPC's fellow national oil companies, the China Petroleum and Chemical Corporation, or Sinopec for short, and the China National Offshore Oil Corporation, CNOOC.

While CNPC is China's main producer of oil, Sinopec is its leading refiner. The company was established in 1983 to take on the responsibilities of several government ministries to provide the fuel to keep China's economy moving. It is housed in a set of dark towers that resemble the many oil refineries it controls around the country. Known as the 'little brother' among China's big oil companies, CNOOC has its main offices across the street from Sinopec. CNOOC was founded in 1982 as China's main offshore oil producer. Its shapely glass headquarters stands on pillars like an oil rig in high seas.

Together these three national oil companies remain under government ownership, but they have increasingly embraced a profit-seeking rationale, striving to improve efficiency, enhance their competitiveness, and expand overseas. But even though intimidating towers of corporate power have replaced the austere halls of government ministries, CNPC and its fellow national oil companies still have deep roots in the Communist Party.

CNPC's political past is on full display at the new headquarters. Immortalised in a statue in its main lobby is Wang Jinxi, otherwise known as Ironman Wang. The bouquets of flowers at the statue's feet and tall bamboo trees rising above it honour Wang's history as a model worker to promote all Chinese industry and his diligence and determination in helping bring China's oil industry to life against all odds. A large stone plaque nearby is engraved with the lyrics to a song that calls on workers to find oil for the motherland.

The heroics of Wang and his drilling team in the 1950s and 60s came in work on the massive Daqing oil fields on the Songliao Plain of China's northeastern Heilongjiang province. It was said that Wang was filled with a 'fiery passion for self-reliance'; a man so devoted to his profession that he made his bed at night on drill pipes with a drill bit as a pillow.[2] His best-known act was halting an oil gusher at a far-off drilling site. As the story goes, after equipment to mix the cement needed to cap the oil well broke down, Wang jumped into the pit using his own body as a mixer and stopped the blowout.[3] While a fair deal of fiction was mixed with fact in stories about Ironman Wang, the impact of the Daqing oil fields on China's economy was very real. Daqing, meaning 'big celebration', was found just ten days before the tenth anniversary of the People's Republic of China. Over time, the economic impact of Daqing elevated the men who led the drive to find oil to the height of political power in China.

Oil was closely linked to the armed struggle after the birth of the People's Republic of China in 1949. After facing down the invading Japanese army and the nationalists of Chiang Kai-shek, Chairman Mao Zedong launched the search for oil to satisfy the country's needs as a military campaign in the 1950s. In an effort to improve upon China's modest oil finds at the time, Mao redeployed the 57th Division of the People's Liberation Army (PLA) as the 1st Division of Oil.[4] The job of the soldiers-turned-oilmen in developing the fledgling oil industry became even more difficult after the Korean War, when the US led an oil embargo on China. Domestic oil production in 1959 only satisfied around 40 per cent of the country's demand, and, more worryingly for the Party leadership, only 20 per cent of the needs of the PLA.[5]

The Sino-Soviet split a few years later made the situation dire. Moscow was a significant supplier of crude oil and petroleum products as well as technical expertise and material assistance to China's oil industry.[6] Consequently, Chinese government policy in the early 1960s was designed to develop oil fields as quickly as possible to fill the gap without relying on foreign technology, equipment and capital.[7] When Russian oil experts left the country after the Sino-Soviet spilt in the early 1960s, the Chinese continued to follow the Soviet philosophy of focusing on finding and developing large oil fields: 'shoot for the elephants and ignore the mice'.[8] Fortunately for China's oilmen, they bagged a big one in Daqing.

The fantastic stories of Ironman Wang should not overshadow the harsh reality workers faced in developing China's oil industry in the late 1950s and beyond. The winters of China's northeast are bitterly cold and the summers of the Songliao Plain are plagued by mosquitoes. 'When they (Chinese oilmen) arrived at Daqing, there was little food and little accommodation,' a CNPC oil official in Beijing recalled.[9] The oilmen lived under horrible conditions and worked without the aid of modern technology and few vehicles to transport equipment.[10]

But Daqing was a beacon of hope in China's otherwise dismal economy. In 1963, Daqing gave Mao his wish when China became self-reliant in oil. The oil field's production satisfied roughly 40 per cent of China's total oil needs for the next forty years and churned out enough oil to make it one of the world's largest producers.[11] After Beijing's rapprochement with the US in the early 1970s, Daqing generated sizeable government revenue and foreign currency, as oil exports began to flow to Japan.[12] Oil exports rose from $923 million in 1975 to $6.7 billion in 1985.[13]

The living conditions of Chinese oilmen at Daqing also improved. The Daqing Petroleum Administrative Bureau, which managed the oil fields for the Ministry of Petroleum Industry, met all the social needs of its workers, including the provision of farms, housing, hospitals and schools. Daqing was run like a 'little country'; a third of the workforce was engaged in non-oil services to support the Chinese oilmen.[14] The Communist Party was quick to exploit Daqing as a symbol to promote its wider objective of self-reliance for the economy.

During the Spring Festival to celebrate the Chinese New Year in February 1964, Chairman Mao confirmed the political importance of Daqing in China. 'We must study the PLA and study Daqing of the Ministry of Petroleum,' he said to Party cadres.[15] Mao's satisfaction with the oil industry and frustration with his official economic planners led him to name Yu Qiulu, the Minister of Petroleum Industry and First Party Secretary at Daqing, to head his new government planning commission by the end of the year.[16] Known as the 'one-arm general', Yu was a seasoned military man during the war of resistance against Japan and China's civil war, who was said to channel his fighting days into oil work by yelling battle cries during drilling.[17] His lieutenants, Kang Shien, Song Zhenming and Tang Ke, also eventually gained prominent positions in the Chinese government.

This group quickly earned the dubious name of the 'petroleum faction' in Chinese and international circles because of its roots in oil and its general promotion of central planning and exploiting foreign technology to propel China's wider industrialisation.[18] The ability of these oilmen to steer Chinese government policy towards acquiring foreign technology was particularly remarkable. In the 1970s, after it became clear that Daqing's production levels would soon stagnate after years of intense exploitation, acquiring foreign technology was necessary in order to keep the oil industry growing by accessing new offshore resources in the Bohai Bay of China's eastern coast. Even though the Chinese government had trumpeted self-reliance for decades, the petroleum faction was successful in transforming government policy towards engaging the outside world through an exchange of oil exports for new technology in oil and other heavy industries.[19] They were keen to ensure growth and sustainability in the oil industry, as its well-being underpinned their political legitimacy.

Enduring Party politics

China's Cultural Revolution from 1966 to 1976 stalled the rise of the petroleum faction. Leading Chinese oilmen were ridiculed and demoted as distrust for intellectuals and experts prevailed during this tumultuous period in China's history. But in its aftermath China's first oil minister, Yu Qiulu, regained his position at the top of the State Planning Commission. His lieutenants also regained their political footing: Kang Shien became the head of the State Economic Commission and Song Zhenming and Tang Ke became the Ministers of Petroleum and Metallurgy respectively.[20] After the death of Mao in 1976, Hua Guofeng, his hand-picked successor, forged ahead with the same heavy industry-focused economic policies promoted by the petroleum faction.

But Hua's ten-year plan for the economy quickly fell apart. China recorded the largest trading deficit in decades after total imports grew by 85 per cent from 1977 to 1978, owing to a long string of over-ambitious industrial projects.[21] Across the board, Hua's plan grossly overestimated China's ability to produce the resources needed to fund expensive imports, as well as the government's ability to cope with the organisation necessary to achieve these objectives.[22] Exploration efforts in Bohai Bay and later in Xinjiang autonomous region of western China did produce results, but ultimately came up short in reversing the stagnation of China's total oil production.

Re-emerging after the Cultural Revolution, Deng Xiaopeng, then a Vice-Premier, leapt on the opportunity to oust the weakened Hua. Having already established himself as *de facto* leader in 1978, Deng was officially installed at the head of the Party in 1982. Along the way, he had made sure to demote Hua's supporters in the petroleum faction in order to forward his political agenda. Regarded as the architect of China's economic rise, Deng pushed for an increased role of the market in the economy and a shift in focus from heavy to light industries that would empower China's export-led growth in the future.[23] These new policies left little room for the petroleum faction in the government.

In 1979, Deng usurped the power of Yu Qiulu, the Chairman of the State Planning Commission, by elevating his economic czar, Chen Yun.[24] A year later, Deng's supporters reopened an inquiry into the sinking of an offshore oil rig in Bohai Bay that killed seventy-two oil workers in 1979. While the Ministry of Petroleum Industry had blamed poor weather conditions for the disaster,[25] the inquiry authorised by Deng found that it was caused by 'bureaucratic arrogance and complacency'. The Petroleum Minister Song Zhenming and a fellow petroleum faction member, Kang Shien, who had risen all the way to the rank of vice-premier, were demoted.[26]

While to the Chinese public it may have appeared that Deng's new stance on government accountability was producing real consequences for government officials, behind the scenes Deng was in effect doing house-cleaning to remove his political foes.[27] Members of the petroleum faction were to remain dominant in the oil industry, but their wider influence over the economy was diminished. In the 1980s, the Chinese government created CNOOC, Sinopec and finally CNPC, hoping that China's oil and gas resources would be managed in a more efficient manner. Similar transformations took place in other strategic sectors, such as coal, power and telecoms. In essence the Chinese government moved out of the way of industry, but retained ultimate ownership.

Deng's economic reforms ignited high levels of growth in China's economy for decades to come, but the consequent rising energy needs brought on the beginning of the end of China's tenure as an oil exporter. Economic growth drove oil consumption to overtake stagnating production by 1993. China was still the world's fifth largest oil producer at slightly over 4 million bpd in 2011, but its oil consumption had increased more than fivefold since 1980 to over 9.7 million bpd, second only to the 18.8 million barrels guzzled daily in the United States.[28] China surpassed the US to become the world's largest consumer of energy in 2010.[29]

Ironically, Deng's economic reforms also paved the way for the re-emergence of the oilmen on the political scene. After Jiang Zemin took the reigns of Party leadership in the early 1990s and solidified his position following Deng's death in 1997, Chinese oilmen found their way back to high-level government positions. Premier Zhu Rongji's 1998 Cabinet included the former Sinopec general manager Sheng Huaren as head of the State Economic and Trade Commission. Zhu prized the knowledge of executives in transforming former government ministries into corporations as he pursued the wider marketisation of China's economy. Bringing corporate leaders like Sheng into the fold gave the Party key allies in the business world and fused political interests with those of industry.[30]

Over time, a long line of political figures continued to come from the oil industry. The Vice-President and Politburo Standing Committee member Zeng Qinghing, and the Vice-Premier and Politburo member Wu Yi, spent time in the oil patch. Wu worked her way up through the refinery business and later into key government positions. She was ranked behind only Germany's Chancellor Angela Merkel in *Time Magazine's* 2007 'World's 100 Most Powerful Women' list.

At the turn of the century, Chinese national oil companies were also important to Party leaders on account of China's growing energy security concerns. President Jiang first voiced concern for energy security at an economic working meeting of the central government in 2000. 'We must closely watch the trend of international oil prices and their impact on the economic and social development of our country. We must take precautions and earnestly work out our strategy,' he said.[31] During the 1990s, oil consumption in China grew almost five times faster than production.[32] In 2000 alone, oil imports doubled and China's import bill tripled, having already risen at the steady pace of 60 per cent per year throughout the 1990s.[33] In 2010, oil imports constituted 55 per cent of China's total consumption.[34]

The Middle East has played a central role as China's main oil supplier, meeting around fifty per cent of its foreign oil needs on average over the past two decades.[35] China has been successful in replacing declining production by Asian oil exporters, mainly Indonesia, with African producers.[36] Angola was China's second largest supplier after Saudi Arabia; it has also been able to acquire increasing amounts of oil from Russia and Kazakhstan. However, despite its success in diversifying sources, more and more foreign oil will be needed in the years to come. The International Energy Agency estimates that China will need 15 million bpd by 2035.[37] Expectations are that by that year, China will import over 75 per cent of its crude oil.[38] Certainly, the role of Chinese national oil companies as the gatekeepers to China's energy markets has ensured their political importance into the foreseeable future.

After Hu Jintao became General Secretary of the Communist Party and the country's President in 2003, Chinese national oil companies maintained their political power and autonomy due to rising energy concerns in China and their growing profits, corporate tax payments, and internationalization through stock market listings.[39] In October 2007 Jiang Jiemin and Su Shulin, the respective heads of CNPC and Sinopec, were named alternate members of the Central Committee of the Communist Party. Su later was made deputy Party secretary and Governor of Fujian Province, a powerful posting in China's political world. The former CNOOC President Fu Chengyu replaced Su at Sinopec, but was also elected as a member of the Central Commission for Discipline Inspection.[40] Fu was known as a 'good communist' in the oil industry, a contrast on paper to his daily work as a top oil executive, but a sign of how the Party was continuing to nurture corporate leaders in the political world.[41] In turn, Chinese national oil companies have exploited their longstanding ties with the Party leadership to advance their own corporate strategies. Sudan was an early example of the political history of CNPC working in favour of its corporate interests to expand overseas.

The oil boss

The most influential man in fostering the relationship between China and Sudan around oil was Zhou Yongkang. If Chevron had its CEO George Keller finalising agreements greased by the political calculations of the then American Ambassador and future US President George H.W. Bush, then Zhou was the two Georges wrapped into one. He was a product of the oil industry's political power in China. Educated in geology at the Beijing Petroleum Institute, the cradle of future oil industry talent, Zhou joined the Communist Party as a student in 1964. Thanks to the political support of former oilmen at the pinnacle of government, Zhou would climb the corporate ladder of the oil industry as he rose through the political ranks of the Party.

Zhou began his career as an oil technician in the midst of the Daqing oil boom. He was stationed in Liaoning province on the border with North Korea during the 1970s. At the Liaohe Oil Exploration Bureau, where the Ministry of Petroleum Industry was developing oil fields in the Bohai Bay basin, Zhou served as deputy secretary of the Party committee and mayor of Panjin City in the early 1980s. It was at Liaohe that he gained the patronage of Zeng Qinghong, the power-broker of future Chinese President Jiang Zemin and Vice-President during Hu Jintao's first term.[42] Zeng was serving as secretary for the famed Chinese oilman Yu Qiulu in 1981 when both men visited the Liaohe oil field and met Zhou. Yu was influential in kick-starting Zeng's political career. After their meeting at Liaohe, Zeng was instrumental in promoting Zhou through Party ranks in the years to come. From 1999 to 2002, Zeng served as director of the Organization Department of the Party, the institution responsible for overseeing all senior appointments in government, business, academia and the media, and from 2002 to 2007 as executive secretary of the Politburo secretariat, which approved the Organization Department's decisions.[43] Zhou could not have found a better patron.

After rising through the ranks of the Ministry of Petroleum Industry, Zhou became vice-minister to Wang Tao in 1985. Three years later, he was number two in the newly-christened CNPC when the oil ministry was abolished. Zhou remained in the Bohai Bay region and became Party secretary at Shengli, China's second largest oil field, and an alternate member of the CPC Central Committee in 1992. He was involved in the ministry's transformation into a corporation and the push to improve company-wide efficiency.

One of Zhou's most pressing tasks was to keep China's oil industry alive. By the 1990s, production at the coveted Daqing and Bohai Bay oil fields was stagnating; Chinese oilmen saw the writing on the wall if they did not find more oil soon. They pinned their hopes on the Tarim basin located in the vast Taklimakan Desert of China's Xinjiang Uyghur Autonomous Region. Zhou was active in the campaign to replenish the company's production and reserves in China's Wild West.

In the language of the Uyghur people of Xinjiang, Taklimakan means 'you can get in but not out', but the Chinese oilmen did not seem to believe in local myth. Keen to exploit Xinjiang oil, they built a road through the desert to facilitate transport. Zhou was Party Secretary of the Tarim Oil Exploration Campaign, which was the first time CNPC implemented its new management system. Rather than carry out all oil services on its own, the Tarim Campaign contracted the best-suited companies under CNPC to do the work and outsourced the social service needs of its employees, as opposed to creating its own companies to support oil operations.[44] While the new reserves were not nearly enough to replace Daqing,[45] Tarim was an important trial run for CNPC to conduct operations aimed at efficiency rather than self-sufficiency, and Zhou was at the forefront of these efforts. These experiences shaped his leadership of the company when he became CNPC General Manager in late 1996.

Zhou took over a company undergoing immense change. China's oil resources were stagnating and CNPC was haemorrhaging cash trying to stabilise its ageing oil fields in the east and discover new ones in the west. It had to borrow money from domestic and foreign sources to simply maintain current production levels.[46] But the oil industry underwent significant restructuring in line with ongoing economic reforms in government and industry during the 1990s. In 1993–94 the government relaxed controls on crude oil prices, which gave a tremendous revenue boost to national oil companies. As the major oil producer, after shouldering deficits in previous years, CNPC benefited immensely from the new pricing regime. The company produced revenue of $6 billion in 1993; the figure rose to $21 billion in 1997 because of rationalised prices.[47] The official government owner of the national oil companies, the State-owned Assets Supervision and Administration Commission (SASAC), did not even collect profits from the companies in the form of dividends to protect their fragile financial position.[48]

With the national oil companies on a better financial track, major government restructuring would shake up China's oil industry in 1998. Both CNPC and Sinopec became vertically-integrated companies, with activities in exploration and production as well as refining and retail, in order to enhance the efficiency of their operations. Rather than each company maintaining a monopoly over oil production and refining respectively, the Chinese government created an oligopoly. But this did not change the fact that there was no easy oil left in China to exploit.

At a meeting in February 1991, the CNPC General Manager Wang Tao first suggested that the company include overseas expansion in its corporate strategy.[49] CNPC made small investments in Canada, Thailand and Peru in the early 1990s to get its feet wet.[50] In 1995, as Wang's right-hand man, Zhou Yongkang announced the company's ambitious plans to expand overseas oil production to 20 million tonnes by 2010.[51] Two years later, as CNPC General Manager, Zhou advocated that China should expand its overseas exploration and development investments rather than rely on oil imports.[52] 'Zhou is far more outward-looking than Wang, and he realized that China was going to need guaranteed supplies from overseas long before—if ever—Xinjiang finally came good,' said one Chinese oilman.[53]

CNPC had its share of international critics when it first began to invest overseas. And there was reason to be sceptical. The company had only a handful of people with the management expertise to work abroad in a foreign environment. Its oil field development equipment was a decade behind that of international oil companies; experts regarded China's ability for technological innovation at the level of a 'third world country'.[54] 'CNPC has basically been under the government's thumb for years and told to punch holes in the ground and produce oil at a loss,' said one American oil executive.[55] 'They're babes in the woods.'

But there were also compelling reasons for the company to go overseas. Better oil discovery rates and lower production costs could be found abroad, and it was cheaper to ship oil to China's main cities in the east and southeast from overseas than bring it from the newly-discovered Xinjiang oil fields in far western China. Recognising the need to improve CNPC management practices and experiencing the deflated expectations of Xinjiang oil, Zhou certainly understood the need to go overseas. While he served for only two years as CNPC General Manager, he oversaw important changes in the company. Together with the new Vice-Presidents Ma Fucai and Wu Yaowen, Zhou sought to intensify the pace of market-orientated reforms in the company by breaking down the company's many self-sufficient petroleum administration bureaus into a smaller number of specialised subsidiaries.[56] 'National oil companies are no longer fat organisations,' Zhou told a gathering of international oil executives and government officials in Houston in 1998. 'We have been forced to become competitive as business globalises.'[57] Going after major investments overseas was the only answer for CNPC, and Zhou's position in the Party gave him the power to make that goal a reality.

Getting the timing right

CNPC's expanding global interests warmed up political relations between China and Sudan in the 1990s after several false starts. Formal relations between China and Sudan were established in 1959. China gradually became a main buyer of Sudanese cotton in the 1960s, but otherwise trade, aid and cultural ties were of no major significance to Sudan's domestic politics or foreign relations. After President Nimeiri broke with the Soviets in the early 1970s, China, which was also at odds with Moscow,[58] provided soft loans to Sudan and built Khartoum's Friendship Hall and Friendship Hospital, along with roads and bridges in and around the capital.[59]

By the mid-1970s, President Nimeiri became interested in improving ties with China and attracting Chinese assistance to Sudan's oil industry. In one of the rare international activities of China's Ministry of Petroleum Industry, it carried out a six-month initial survey in South Yemen in 1973.[60] In January 1976, when relations between Sudan and the US were suspended, after meeting the Yemenis and hearing about the cooperation Nimeiri broached the idea with the Chinese that they should engage in Sudan's oil industry as well.[61] The Chinese, it was reported, advised Nimeiri to stay with US oil companies, which had the technology necessary for the major exploration work Sudan needed.[62] CNPC was not yet in existence and the idea of going global was still far away for the Chinese oil industry.

China-Sudan relations did not take-off until after the NIF seized power in 1989. Brian Kay, Chevron's former country manager, remembers that when Sudan was putting the company under pressure to resume its oil operations, the NIF tried to leverage the company with the threat of bringing in the Chinese. 'We were just told by the Sudan (oil) ministry in about 1989/90 that China was ready to operate the southern fields and that they would accept the level of insecurity there.'[63] This was likely just a bluff on the part of the Sudanese; at the time, CNPC was still not ready to take on the size of commitment required in Sudan.

In November 1990, Sudan's new leader, Omar al-Bashir, paid a state visit to the new Communist Party Chairman Jiang Zemin in Beijing. As on his visit to Malaysia that June, Bashir was looking to build stronger ties with China and for alternatives to develop its oil industry, as relations with Chevron and the US government were deteriorating fast. China was open to expanding economic ties with the Sudanese and it moved forward with an Iranian-funded arms deal that sent Chinese weapons worth $300 million to Sudan. But Jiang was also uncertain about the Islamist politics of the new Sudanese regime.[64] Where oil was concerned CNPC, like its Malaysian counterpart Petronas, was still easing its way into the international oil industry during the early 1990s. The company was not yet at the point where it was ready to commit to such a large endeavour overseas.

Sudan continued to press the Chinese on oil. In January 1994, during the Sudan leg of a six-nation Africa tour, the Chinese Foreign Minister and Vice-premier Qian Qichen again found the Sudanese government offering investment opportunities in oil, mining, and other sectors.[65] In December of that year, a seventeen-member Sudanese trade delegation arrived in Beijing for a meeting of the Sino-Sudanese Economic and Trade Joint Commission.[66] The Sudanese met Wu Yi, China's Minister of the Foreign Trade and Economic Co-operation, who had her roots in the oil refining industry. Wu was not overly optimistic about trade and economic cooperation with Sudan—'China is mainly a capital recipient, not an investor in the world,' she said.[67] The head of the Sudanese delegation, the Minister for Industry and Trade Dr. Tag Elsir Mustafa, nonetheless encouraged Chinese companies to invest in Sudan's oil industry. Unlike Wu, Zhou Yongkang and CNPC would soon enough take notice. By the mid-1990s CNPC's expanding global interests began to coincide with Sudan's longstanding quest to find new oil partners to replace Chevron.

CNPC geologists took their first look at the geological data of Sudan's oil fields in late 1994 and liked what they saw.[68] In July 1995 CNPC President Wang Tao met the visiting Sudanese oil minister Major General Salah al-Din Muhammad Ahmad Karrar in Beijing.[69] Karrar also met the Foreign Minister and Vice-premier Qian Qichen, but China's oilmen were ultimately the group that played the pivotal role in advancing oil relations with Sudan. Zhou Yongkang and his patron Zeng Qinghong were instrumental in pushing the Sudan deal through with President Jiang.[70] Zeng was serving as director of the General Office of the Communist Party at the time, managing communications and administrative matters of Party leadership. He was also a confidant of the President, having served as Jiang's chief of staff while he was Party secretary in Shanghai.[71] For Zhou, investing in Sudan was a straightforward decision to promote the international expansion of CNPC and support the growth of China's oil industry.

At the Great Hall of the People in Beijing in September 1995, President Jiang hosted President Omar al-Bashir and promised to push China-Sudan relations to 'greater heights'.[72] During the Sudanese leader's visit, CNPC signed an agreement with Sudan to explore and develop

Block 6 in Sudan, a former section of Chevron's oil concession along the Darfur-Kordofan border. The earlier reluctance of Jiang to engage the Sudanese had disappeared. CNPC's evolving corporate strategy of expanding its international assets and enlarging its revenue base after reforms to oil pricing at home brought China and Sudan closer together.

Serve the servant

International investments were a strategic necessity to replace CNPC's stagnating domestic oil production and reserves and ensure its long-term survival. The Chinese government supported the Sudan investment, but it was CNPC that steered the process forward. After Party leadership approved the investment of CNPC in Sudan, the Chinese government got to work serving the company's needs. CNPC's investments in Sudan helped launch wider collaboration between government ministries and newly-established policy banks in China to support Chinese companies abroad.

In late September 1995, China signed a framework agreement with Sudan for a concessional loan of 11.5 billion Chinese yuan, roughly worth $1.84 billion at the time, to help develop its oil industry and presumably other sectors of the economy.[73] A few months later, the Ministry of Foreign Trade and Economic Cooperation, later restructured into the Ministry of Commerce, approved a 100 million yuan loan (roughly $12 million) for CNPC in Sudan, to be provided by the China Export-Import (EXIM) Bank.[74] The loan was made at CNPC's request to finance test exploration in Sudan.[75] While that amount of money was minuscule in the international oil industry, CNPC was still heavily indebted in the mid-1990s; it needed the financial support to cover its initial risk. In the years to come, the company would spend billions in Sudan.

Agreed at a ceremony in Beijing's Diaoyutai State Guesthouse, the loan to Sudan was one of the first concessional loans provided by the EXIM Bank. Founded a year earlier, the bank's initial focus was on promoting Chinese exports overseas rather than foreign investment in itself. The Sudanese finance ministry and the Central Bank of Sudan would be accountable for the loan repayment, but they never actually touched the funds, which went straight to CNPC. An EXIM Bank official said that giving the loan directly to the company would 'simplify the procedures and reduce the cost of lending'. The EXIM Bank Chairman, Tong Zhiguang, praised the loan as both helping a cash-strapped Sudanese government and helping a Chinese national oil company to enter international markets.[76] For Sudan, these initial Chinese loan agreements required that 70 per cent of all contracts go to Chinese companies.[77] By the end of 2009, Sudan still owed $1.69 billion of outstanding debt to China, which had become one of its largest lenders since the first loan in 1995.[78] The political strength of CNPC and the Party connections of its Vice-President Zhou Yongkang gained the company a unique independence among Chinese companies for investment in Sudan and elsewhere. These were unprecedented loans for China, granted before its policy banks would become some of the largest lenders in the world.

When CNPC was expanding its investment in Sudan, it was also making a bold move into Kazakhstan, beating competition from Amoco and other international oil companies for control of the country's oil fields. During negotiations with the former Soviet state, Premier Li Peng was brought in to lobby CNPC's case with Kazakh officials.[79] Such high-level political negotiations were not uniquely Chinese; US President Clinton lobbied for American oil companies to win investments in Central Asia in the 1990s.[80] But CNPC was paying a hefty price to win assets in Kazakhstan, Venezuela and Iraq. 'They're acquiring a lot of crude-oil resources and they're certainly very liberal in what they're paying. From that point of view, they're a formidable competitor,' said John Imle, President of Unocal.[81] Aggressive over-bidding for overseas oil fields would be a label that would dog Chinese national oil companies in the years to come. But the Chinese were consciously pursuing this strategy in order to gain the necessary technical and managerial experience in international oil projects.[82] Moreover, the Chinese national oil companies were in an advantageous position overseas thanks to their strong political standing at home.

The Chinese government's support for CNPC helped the company establish a dominant position in Sudan's oil industry through preferential loans and development assistance. Loans from state-owned banks, such as the EXIM Bank and the China Development Bank, provided CNPC with a competitive advantage in acquiring overseas oil and gas assets. After the global economic downturn in 2008 and 2009, the China Development Bank signed an agreement with CNPC to provide $30 billion to support its overseas ventures.[83]

But the willingness of Chinese oil companies to accept higher levels of political risk and lower rates of return than most international oil companies investing abroad has been even more influential in their expansion than government support.[84] At the same time, as CNPC and other Chinese national oil companies continue to invest abroad, they have more often drawn from retained earnings and profits in order to make mergers and acquisitions. The benefits of loans to oil-rich countries to support the investments of Chinese national oil companies have also not been so clear-cut. Since Chinese national oil companies rarely compete head-to-head against oil majors in overseas bids, it is hard to fully measure the competitive advantages Chinese policy banks offer.[85] In addition, oil-rich governments in recent years have become increasingly more cautious of conditions in loans that require heavy involvement of Chinese companies and the opening up of domestic markets to Chinese suppliers.[86] Nonetheless, loans from Chinese policy banks did help kick-start the international expansion of Chinese national oil companies.

After a thirty-year career on the oil patch, Zhou Yongkang left CNPC in 1998. Along with Sinopec's Sheng Huaren, Zhou was brought into Zhu Rongji's State Council as China's Minister of Land and Natural Resources. He was benefiting from the Party's creation of a revolving door between government and business in China, through which corporate leaders are vetted for senior political positions because of their management skills and knowledge of the global economy.[87] This trend in China also established key supporters for the corporations in powerful positions. Sheng went on to grant Sinopec the right to issue permits for fuel imports into China after he entered the government, basically giving his former company a stranglehold on the refining market.[88] Zhou came to CNPC's aid in his new government post by appealing to Zhu for the company to be awarded a project for a gas pipeline from Xinjiang to Shanghai.[89] A year later, marking his ascent in the Party, Zhou was concurrently named Party secretary of Sichuan province. But he never forgot his political power base in the oil industry.

The strength of Chinese national oil companies reflected the strength of Zhou Yongkang and other political leaders with a background in oil. Support from the provincial Party cadres of the vast Chinese oil industry, stretching from the Daqing oil fields in the northeast and Xinjiang autonomous region in the northwest to the refineries of the southeast, translated into political power in Beijing.[90] Just as Zeng Qinghong advanced Zhou's career, Zhou remained keen to support his own people in the oil sector. Zhou's protégés were Ma Fucai and Jiang Jiemin, who both worked at the Shengli oil field with him and followed his path to the post of CNPC General Manager.[91] Naturally, Zhou wanted his people to succeed and to ensure that the oil industry maintained its influence on policymaking in China.

The transformation of Chinese national oil companies from ministries to corporations in the 1980s did not take them out of the government hierarchy. When ministers became general managers in the 1980s, they all lobbied hard to maintain their influence on government.[92] 'CNPC is a former ministry, but it still thinks like one,' said one former Chinese diplomat in Beijing. 'The company has influence in government decision-making alongside current ministries.'[93] In fact, CNPC and Sinopec continue to hold the same ministerial rank as ministries under the State Council, the highest government administrative body in China. On the bureaucratic side, over a dozen government bodies hold responsibilities for energy; but none have the autonomy and authority to govern the energy sector effectively, and national oil companies maintain significant power to shape policy.[94]

Since its establishment in 2003, the National Development and Reform Commission (NDRC) has been the largest body governing the energy sector. Among a host of responsibilities, the NDRC sets fuel prices and provides the required approval for large domestic and international investments. Overseas expenditures exceeding $200 million, essentially every project in the oil industry, are reviewed by the NDRC and passed on to the State Council for final approval.[95] The NDRC oversees the National Energy Administration, which is in charge of long-term energy security and development strategy. But the companies have technical advantages over the energy bureaucracy. Much of the technical expertise on energy issues remained within the companies after their transformation from ministries; government officials often consult the companies on the establishment of new policies and laws.[96]

Despite the bureaucratic and technical strengths of the national oil companies, the Party maintains control over the oil giants through its top personnel. Executives in each company are appointed, promoted, and dismissed by the Organisation Department of the Communist Party, with all decisions requiring ratification by China's ruling Politburo. All large Chinese state-owned enterprises fall under a longstanding *nomenklatura* system, and executives must learn to balance corporate and Party interests.[97] Becoming the head of a national oil company is not the end of the line for Chinese oilmen; each seeks a longer political career.

Yet, while China's Party leadership wishes to build world-class national champions in oil and other strategic sectors, its national oil companies have also upset the wider political goal of maintaining stability in China. After a major blowout from a gas well near the city of Chongqing that killed 243 people in 2003, the Party's Organization Department announced that the CNPC boss Ma Fucai was stepping down. Ma shouldered the blame for the accident, as public outrage grew over negligence by the company and local government officials in responding to the disaster.[98] Ma's chance of rising further in the government hierarchy fizzled out after the blowout.[99] In response to an industrial accident or social protest, the Party generally uses the system of *wei wen*—stability maintenance—to remove political leaders in hopes of pacifying the situation.

While CNPC's poor environmental track record continued, its counterpart Sinopec had a more calculated and deliberate negative impact on social stability that upset Party leaders. In 2007, the Sinopec boss Chen Tonghai resigned in face of a corruption probe, but rather than graft, it was the displeasure of senior Party leaders at Chen's earlier mothballing of refineries during fuel shortages in southern China in 2005 that led to his ousting. Fuel shortages during the harvest season typically bring about consumer anger, and Chen's brash move to shut down refineries to pressure the government to raise fuel price ceilings only made the situation worse.[100]

For all the political power of the national oil companies, corporate interests did not always sit well with the Party's goal of maintaining social stability. Chinese oil executives may not be immune from political punishment, but the ongoing tradition of Chinese oilmen crossing over to Party leadership, and at times back to the corporate world, has still allowed national oil companies to shape government policy in their favour.

Major changes in the oil industry over the past two decades have demonstrated the enduring power of the national oil companies. Building on CNPC's initiative, Jiang Zemin made 'going out' an official policy for all other sectors to expand overseas in October 2000.[101] But NDRC officials have complained that the corporate heads of national oil companies exploit their direct access to Party leaders.[102] They argue that the ability of the oil companies to win high-level political backing for domestic and international overseas investments dampens potential bureaucratic resistance. At times, the companies have gone ahead with projects before official state approval is granted.[103] Owing to the embedded political power of the oil industry in the Party, when national oil companies seek favours from political allies in Party leadership for overseas investment it is not just an issue of energy policy or foreign affairs, but also a matter of domestic politics.[104] In 2007, after SASAC, the official government owner of all state-owned enterprises, began to demand 10 per cent of after-tax dividend profits from leading national companies, the government also lowered corporate income tax to nullify the loss.[105] Similarly, after years of delay, the Chinese government finally imposed a resource tax on domestic sales of crude oil and natural gas in late 2011. But at the same time, it reduced the level of windfall tax that companies paid.[106] More tellingly, while the establishment of Wen Jiabao's Energy Leading Group, and later the National Energy Administration, were steps taken by the Chinese government to coordinate energy strategy, the much needed step of reestablishing a Ministry of Energy to balance the power of the national oil companies did not occur. Oil executives successfully resisted the move, as it would restrict their access to the Party leadership.[107]

After CNPC moved into its new headquarters in the Dongcheng district of Beijing in 2009, it did not abandon the hallowed halls of China's oil ministry. Divisions of the company still worked out of the old ministry, even though the two wings of the building were falling into disrepair. Underneath a gold-painted company sign, employees still lined up in straight rows outside in the parking lot for morning exercises. Instructions for air circles, knee bends, and jumping jacks were yelled out through a bullhorn, while music more fit for a military parade than for a global corporation exercise routine played in the background. Such communal exercises are traditional in small and large Chinese businesses alike. But the slow movements and hand clapping of the CNPC workers seemed stuck in the past, a symbol of fading government influence that was becoming less and less a part of the everyday life of a company surging forward overseas.

5

A CHINESE MIRACLE

July 1999: Someone needed to turn on the taps in Sudan after the oil pipeline from southern oil fields to the Red Sea was finished. There was no better person to do so than the square-jawed former Chinese oilman Zhou Yongkang, who joined Sudanese Vice-President Ali Osman Mohamed Taha to start the flow of oil into the new pipeline from the Heglig oil field. Sweat soaking his light blue shirt, Zhou stood beside a gap-tooth smiling Taha as each man rested a hand on a valve wheel.

Zhou was no longer General Manager at CNPC, but China's Minister of Land and Natural Resources, and he was acting as China's special envoy at festivities marking ten years since Sudan's ruling regime, the NIF, seized power. Similar to the legendary Chinese oilman Yu Qiulu, who led the development of China's Daqing field, Zhou compared the operations of CNPC in Sudan to battle. In a speech to the CNPC employees during his visit, he said:[1]

This is a fight, you have conquered difficulties that no one can imagine. You are the backbone of China and heroes of our nation. You have made miracles happen and set great examples for friendship between China and Sudan. Our country will never forget your sacrifice. The Sudanese people will never forget your sacrifice.

Two decades after oil was first discovered in Sudan, the NIF certainly appreciated the Chinese oil company's 'sacrifice'. CNPC investment allowed the NIF to finally cash in on an oil prize coveted by a long line of Sudanese governments. Sudan's evolving civil war and the violence unleashed by the NIF in Sudan's oil regions brought pressure from human rights activists and the US government to push out Canadian and European oil companies. But neither activist campaigns nor the conflict deterred the Chinese oilmen.

CNPC had not been working from scratch since it first came to Sudan in 1995. Rather, it benefited immensely from Chevron's previous exploration work. Chinese oilmen were not alone in developing the oil industry: Western service companies provided key technical and managerial support. But Sudan held strategic importance for CNPC and its subsidiaries, as it gave them valuable new experience in international operations. Sudan acted as a launching pad for the careers of many Chinese oilmen. Oil executives may have been demoted or fired from their posts after social and environmental disasters occurring under their leadership in China, but for success in Sudan, where the company's investments helped spawn so much death and destruction, such executives were promoted. Sudan also became an international symbol for the Communist Party and demonstrated the developmental benefits that Chinese companies could provide to Africa. With Zhou Yongkang leading the way, Chinese political leaders made Khartoum a must-stop on diplomatic visits to Africa in order to revel in the company's success.

Rediscovery

A little more than a month before Zhou Yongkang and Sudan's Vice-president Taha arrived at Heglig to turn on the taps, thousands of Sudanese gathered at the oil field to witness the inauguration of the new 1,500-kilometre pipeline heading northeast to the new Masra al Bashair terminal on the Red Sea.[2] The mound of sand and earth covering the pipeline protruded out of the flat and barren landscape like a bulging vein carrying the lifeblood of Sudan's economy. It was the one piece of an extensive billion-dollar infrastructure puzzle that would in the coming months start to generate petrodollars for the NIF.

His signature walking stick in hand, President Omar al-Bashir stood on the podium witnessing the occasion. On one side of Bashir was Hassan al-Turabi, the founder and spiritual leader of the NIF. Turabi was regarded as the Sudanese president's puppeteer, but his power over Bashir would soon enough reach its end. In December 1999, just months after celebrating the tenth anniversary of the National Salvation Revolution that brought the NIF to power, the Sudanese president put Turabi in a prison cell. Ousting Turabi in a palace power struggle, Bashir would continue to rule Sudan, but the National Islamic Front was now known as the National Congress party. In bringing oil to Sudan, Bashir succeeded where his predecessors had failed; now the incoming petrodollars would help ensure his political longevity. Jaafar Nimeiri, who was standing on Bashir's other side at Heglig, knew very well the consequences of failing to start up the oil industry.

Nimeiri must have felt humbled at Heglig. The former Sudanese president had recently been granted amnesty and returned from fourteen years of exile in Egypt just in time for the pipeline inauguration.[3] The completion of the pipeline had been a goal he had coveted dearly as president. His failure to realise Sudan's oil dream had helped bring about his fall from power in 1985, as Sudan's economy crumbled without the desperately-needed injection of petrodollars. Nimeiri had pinned his hopes on Chevron, but the American oil company had left him empty handed when it refused to restart its operations in face of a growing civil war. Now Sudanese oil was about to churn through a steel pipeline towards the Red Sea and international markets. Amid the singing and dancing at Heglig, the red hard hats worn by the men standing behind the political leaders indicated who had succeeded where the Americans had failed.

Sudan may have been in far away Africa, but for CNPC it was the new Daqing. When the CNPC General Manager Ma Fucai visited Sudan in 2000, he said that the oilmen showed the 'kind of spirit of dedication and hard work demonstrated by the workers in the Daqing oil fields decades ago', proving that the 'Daqing spirit' was alive overseas.[4] While Sudan would not provide the same amount of petroleum as the legendary oil area in China, it produced plenty of pomp and glory for CNPC's international expansion. It had all the ingredients of a hard-won project: an unforgiving terrain and climate, the insurmountable odds of bringing oil from the frontier to the market, and the need to build the oil infrastructure from the ground up. Sudan, like Daqing with Ironman Wang, also had its heroes.

The cowboy boots of the oilmen of Chevron were long gone from Sudan. From the scorching grasslands of the south to the dusty streets of Khartoum on the Nile, thousands of Chinese oilmen and labourers made Sudan their home in the late 1990s. They dubbed Sudan 'the stove of the world'.[5] Together, they would develop Sudan's oil industry rapidly in the years to come.

By December 1995, CNPC had opened an office in Khartoum.[6] Su Yongdi, a CNPC geologist, arrived in the Sudanese capital in July 1997 and soon became a well-known name in the Chinese oil industry. Su was from the class of 1985 at the prestigious China University of Petroleum, which had evolved out of the Beijing Petroleum Institute where the later CNPC boss Zhou Yongkang graduated in the 1960s.

Su had done his homework before coming to Sudan. Soon after CNPC won the bid to lead the Greater Nile Petroleum Operating Company (GNPOC) in March 1997, Su and other geologists at the Zhongyuan oil field in Henan province in central China were instructed to focus their attention on the biggest prize in the newly-won Sudan concessions, the Unity oil field. Su and the geological team at Zhongyuan needed to provide locations for the drilling of exploratory wells within two months. Anticipating the coming of the rainy season, CNPC construction teams needed to lay all-weather roads to the sites beforehand, or else it would be almost impossible to conduct the drilling. 'It was a great opportunity for me and my colleagues to show CNPC's technical strength,' Su said later.[7] Su and his colleagues worked day and night going over data at the company's offices during what was a bitter winter in China, while construction crews began work in the heat of Sudan thousands of kilometres away. Barely pausing to enjoy the Spring Festival to celebrate the Chinese New Year, Su recommended that nine wildcat wells should be drilled at the Unity oil field.[8] The drilling crews in Sudan then went to work and, to the excitement of oil executives back in Beijing, they struck oil at each site that Su had recommended.

The feats of Su Yongdi in Sudan became a legend back home. He received a host of industry accolades from his work, and was compared to the Chinese oil geologist Li Siguang, who had discovered the Daqing oil fields in 1959.[9] Su was the Ironman Wang of a new era in which his technical expertise and knowhow stood side by side with the sheer physical strength of Chinese oilmen in the field. Su spent eight intense years working in Sudan.

When he arrived in Khartoum, Su moved into a rented building that served as both CNPC country headquarters and accommodation for its employees. Over the coming years he witnessed little of Sudan's civil war or political turmoil. Like most geologists around the world, Su had his head firmly stuck underneath the ground. He spent most of his time inside his office hunched over maps and poring over data on his computer screen. During his few moments of relaxation, Su went downstairs to join his colleagues to sing songs in the lobby of CNPC's building or upstairs to walk on the roof for exercise. They rarely ventured outside; when they did, it was always in groups. Not only did they fear for their safety, they also did not really know what they should do in the foreign city. The one regular stop outside the office was the restaurant at the Hilton Hotel where American businessmen once enjoyed cold drinks at the Sunset Bar decades earlier. But while Su only occasionally travelled to southern Sudan, his achievements in Khartoum were making quite a stir in Sudan's faraway oil fields.

CNPC was not granted the rights to explore and develop Sudan's prized oil assets overnight. Rather, both the Sudanese government and the company exercised caution before jumping into any major commitments.[10] The initial rights for the Chinese oil giant to develop Block 6 of Chevron's former concession along the border between Southern Kordofan and Southern Darfur acted as a test case. Chevron had discovered and developed oil in the concession beginning in 1979 and smaller, less experienced oil companies did some work later. When CNPC won the rights to the concession, it needed to demonstrate to the Sudanese government that it could get the oil out of the ground. At the same time, it wanted to gauge the potential of Sudan's oil reserves and test its own capacity to work with foreign geological structures underground and a harsh desert climate above. After an initial field survey, company geologists were pleased to discover that the Muglad Basin had faulted depressions similar to the oil fields in Bohai Bay in China.[11] By early 1996, CNPC proved it could get the job done by striking oil at its first exploration well.[12] This early success was critical leverage in winning the bigger stake with GNPOC a year later.

It was not long after Chinese oilmen hit the ground in Unity state that the 1997 Asian financial crisis hit. While China was not as badly affected as much of Southeast Asia, economic growth nonetheless slowed. Zhou Jiping, the President of GNPOC, was forced to keep costs low in the face of CNPC's shortage of foreign currency.[13] In 1998, the company even suspended new overseas investments to account for its financial constraints.[14] But after riding out the crisis, CNPC found out just how big an oil play it had in Sudan.

By the time President Bashir inaugurated the oil pipeline at Heglig in 1999, GNPOC had added new oil finds to Chevron's discoveries.[15] Sudan's oil production averaged close to 180,000 bpd in 2000, making it sub-Saharan Africa's fifth largest producer.[16] CNPC's continual success helped it maintain a strong position with the Sudanese government. That year, it established the Petrodar Operating Company with Petronas and a number of minority stakeholders, which later included CNPC's national counterpart Sinopec. Petrodar held the rights to Blocks 3 and 7 in the Melut Basin of Upper Nile, where Chevron had set up one of its secondary camps two decades earlier. After restudying the geological features of the basin and launching a major exploration campaign, CNPC discovered the Great Palogue oil field in 2003.[17] A 1,370-kilometre pipeline from the Upper Nile oil fields to a new oil terminal near Port Sudan was finished in 2006, adding yet another major achievement to CNPC's work.

But the Chinese oil company's discoveries were not made on an unknown frontier. Chevron had started the search for oil in Sudan, carried out the first risky geological surveys on the massive virgin terrain in the late 1970s, and mapped out the Muglad and Melut basins and discovered the Unity, Heglig and other oil fields. After investing $1 billion, the US company was only just getting started when it halted its activities at the onset of the civil war in the early 1980s.

Two decades later, CNPC made its finds close to those of Chevron, where it was expected that more oil would be found. A 1992 preliminary report on Sudan's oil potential written by John McCleod, later the CEO of Arakis, found that existing wells of 280 million barrels were 'ready to produce' at the Unity, Heglig and Adar-Yale fields, and that the Palogue discovery was made in an oil basin where Chevron had once planned to drill thirteen more prospects.[18] When Talisman took over from Arakis, CEO Jim Buckee recalled that 'Chevron did excellent work and we still use some of their seismic and core data'.[19] A Sudanese oil official put it more simply, 'The Americans did everything except turn on the taps'.[20]

Chevron's work further south in the concessions of the White Nile Petroleum Operating Company (WNPOC) was also instrumental in the future operations of European and Asian companies in Blocks 5A and 5B. 'We did not conduct any seismic studies, relying totally on the data we received from Chevron,' said a Sudanese oil company manager. 'Without Chevron, these areas would never have been discovered.'[21]

Not only was CNPC building on the already significant work of Chevron, it was also not alone in developing Sudan's oil industry. The oil revenue produced for the NIF and later the National Congress party to fund the war against the south was not produced by Chinese oil companies, but rather by a shared enterprise between Asian and Western oil companies. Although CNPC held a leading stake in the GNPOC consortium, its Malaysian and Canadian partners managed exploration and development as well as the pipeline and marine terminal project. A German company, Mannesmann, supplied several hundred kilometres of sophisticated pipes designed to endure the extreme heat of certain sections of the route to Port Sudan; Weir Pumps of Scotland sold the pumps and drivers to get the oil flowing.[22] Fittingly for a company with over 1.6 million employees in China, CNPC was put in charge of administration of human resources.[23] CNPC's Zhou Jiping stressed that the company gained valuable experience in international bidding, production sharing agreements, oil service contracts, and the business management skills needed in large-scale projects from their international partners.[24] But he also praised his CNPC's advantage in offering comprehensive and low-cost oil services. What was missing in Sudan when the Chinese arrived were oil field surface facilities, a pipeline, refinery, and an export terminal to bring the oil to international markets. This is where CNPC made its biggest contribution.

Learning under fire

Chinese oil executives made good on their promise to Sudanese officials to construct the necessary infrastructure for a functioning oil industry. The ability of CNPC to put infrastructure together in a relatively short period of time made the company the perfect partner for the internationally-isolated NIF, which was craving oil revenue to fund its brutal war machine. The southern Sudanese rebels of the SPLA, however, held an altogether very different opinion about China's presence in Sudan. The rebel leader John Garang saw all oil companies as 'legitimate targets,' saying, 'We consider them mercenaries working for the Islamist regime.'[25]

CNPC managers were not oblivious to the ongoing civil war. Unlike Chevron before them, they were willing to take the chance that the Sudan Armed Forces and the pro-government militias could provide the security necessary in and around the oil fields. CNPC was not the only company drawn in by the Sudanese government's promises of security. Like its Canadian and European counterparts, CNPC was encouraged by the signing of the Khartoum Peace Agreement in 1997 that brought southern militias into closer collaboration with the Sudanese government, which would presumably ensure better security.

The Chinese company was confident that the defensive line of the Sudanese army and its militias along the Bahr el Arab river south of GNPOC's main operations would hold. In particular, the Chinese saw the South Sudan Defence Forces (SSDF) of Riek Machar and the Nuer militia of Paulino Matip, a Major General in the Sudanese army, as vital for protection.[26] It was a peculiar situation for CNPC. When Chinese oilmen were working north of the border, the Sudan Armed Forces were on guard, but when they travelled south, pro-government southern militias provided protection.[27] Claims that thousands of Chinese soldiers were protecting the oil facilities were 'pure fantasy', according to Nicholas Coghlan, a Canadian diplomat stationed in Sudan.[28] The Sudanese government did not allow foreign forces to be brought in during the civil war. According to one Chinese oil industry consultant, CNPC actually had to pay both the Sudanese army and pro-government southern militias for security.[29]

During the dry season, the government was able to bolster its defences in the oil regions. But when the rainy season arrived, opportunities for crack teams of rebels to strike opened up, particularly after key militia allies of the government in oil areas went back to the SPLA. On the night of 25 January 2001 a CNPC exploration rig came under attack by rebel forces at Tamur, the most southerly point of GNPOC oil operations during the civil war. Led by the Nuer commander Peter Gadet, who had recently defected from the government back to the SPLA, the rebels crossed the Bahr el Arab river, CNPC's envisioned defence line, to make the assault on the oil rig. Chinese oilmen, who were asleep in their Portakabins, scampered under their beds as the rebels pounded government defences. Hundreds of Sudanese soldiers were on guard along with several 'technicals', machine-gun mounted pickup trucks. They had cleared scrub from four hundred metres, dug a ditch, and erected a three-metre-high earth wall around the rig to provide protection. Outnumbered by the soldiers, the rebels were pushed back, but a dozen soldiers were killed. In the morning, the Chinese oilmen discovered they had been lucky to survive: an unexploded rocket-propelled grenade lay at the foot of the rig near their sleeping quarters.[30] The Chinese oilmen would not venture so far south again until the civil war came to an end, but SPLA rebels were still determined to push north.

In August 2001, SPLA fighters surprised the Sudanese army and oil-men from around the world in a pre-dawn attack on the Heglig oil field. It had been thought that the rebels could not strike so deep into govern-ment-controlled oil territory, especially where the GNPOC consortium of Chinese, Canadian, Malaysian and Sudanese oilmen were hard at work developing one of Sudan's largest oil fields. Heglig was known as 'the biggest hotel in Sudan', with row after row of Canadian-imported Por-takabins housing the international oilmen.[31] In the cafeteria each eve-ning at dinner, each nationality of the GNPOC consortium sat separately; the Canadian oilmen of Talisman ate their meat and potatoes, the Malay-sians fried rice, and the Chinese chow mein. But while food may have failed to bring the oilmen together, mortar rounds from the SPLA did.

When the shelling began, alarms sounded and over five hundred per-sonnel rushed to the assembly point on the east side of the workers' quar-ters. But luck was on the side of the oil companies again. The mortars fell narrowly short of their targets during the attack and government forces successfully intercepted an SPLA ground force the day before. After the attack, oil pumps were shut down for twelve hours as a precau-tionary measure, and the lights of the facilities were turned off for sev-eral days, but regular activities resumed shortly thereafter.[32]

In general, sabotage and bombing of the oil pipeline during the civil war only caused minimal damage.[33] Under the protection of the Sudan Armed Forces, the Chinese and their foreign colleagues at GNPOC were able to evade several potentially devastating attacks. They felt the worst fighting was taking place south of their oil concessions in Block 5A oper-ated by Sweden's Lundin,[34] but they also became increasingly wary of pro-government militias. 'One day they were in the army, the next day they were rebels,' said one Chinese oil industry consultant.[35] The rapidly changing alliances in Sudanese politics were a growing threat, but in the meantime, oil companies in Sudan had to worry about more than rebel mortar rounds falling from the skies.

CNPC was busy laying the 1,500-kilometre pipeline from southern oil fields to Port Sudan when the US military struck alleged terrorist tar-gets in Sudan and Afghanistan. The August 1998 cruise missile strike on the al-Shifa plant in Khartoum North did not go unnoticed by CNPC. Company officials were worried at first that there might be a larger US attack on Sudan, but felt that since the pipeline was not finished and the oil fields were relatively small and spread out, the situation would not warrant an attack on their assets.[36]

Four years later, when the oil pipeline was complete, there was a clear threat made by the US. Months after the 9/11 al-Qaeda terrorist attacks on New York and Washington, senior CIA officials gave a stern warning to the Sudanese intelligence chief Salah Gosh and Vice-President Ali Osman Muhammad Taha during a meeting at a London hotel. Sudan had started to slowly share intelligence with the CIA about al-Qaeda from Osama bin Laden's time in the country, but US officials were not overly impressed with the information they had received, and after the 9/11 attacks they had little patience.

In London, Gosh and Taha were told that if the quality of their counter-terrorism intelligence did not improve soon, the US military would hit Sudan's oil pipeline and related infrastructure. It could 'be done in an afternoon with cruise missiles or a few aircraft,' said one official to the Sudanese leaders.[37] The idea of an oil sector that took Sudan over two decades to achieve being wiped off the map by US warplanes in a matter of hours got the men's attention. They had already witnessed the quick ousting of the Taliban in Afghanistan by the US just months earlier. After this threat, cooperation between the CIA and Sudanese intelligence authorities reached new heights. Although diplomatic ties with the US were still largely broken, Sudan had 'a complete normalization of our relations with the CIA,' as Sudanese Maj. Gen. Yahia Hussein Babiker put it.[38] For CNPC, the political manoeuvring of the Sudanese to satisfy American counter-terrorism interests provided a signal that its oil infrastructure was secure from US attack.[39] Another bullet dodged.

CNPC did not get through the civil war without losing men. Kidnappings and killings did occur before the peace process between the Sudanese government and southern rebels began to gain traction with the 2002 Machakos protocol and a meeting between President Bashir and John Garang. In May 1999, a Chinese oil engineer was kidnapped with a four-man Sudanese exploration crew in Block 1 near the Munga oil field in Unity state.[40] Later that month, twenty-three CNPC oil workers were held captive in the Bentiu area by a breakaway unit of the pro-government SSDF, but released a few days later.[41] While there were probably other unreported incidents, CNPC's operations moved forward at a steady pace during the civil war. In fact, the combination of Sudan's harsh climate and the high-paced demands of CNPC executives and Sudanese oil officials constituted more of a constant 'threat' to the oilmen than an armed attack.

The international oil industry has seen its fair share of accidents due to negligence in enforcing safety measures, but CNPC brought its particularly low safety standards from China to Sudan. During the civil war, more lives of Chinese oil workers were lost to disease and traffic accidents on Sudan's hazardous roads than to the bullets of southern Sudanese rebels.[42] Zhang Lifu, a pipeline manager, died after suffering a cerebral haemorrhage while conducting a gruelling review of Sudan's pipeline route. Diseases such as malaria, cholera, yellow fever and meningitis all dogged overworked Chinese oilmen.[43] Five workers died during the construction of the pipeline. One manager at an international service company working for CNPC complained that he spent too much of his time reminding Chinese oil workers to fasten their seatbelts, and constantly needed to demand that the company observe its own health, safety, and environmental measures.[44]

Chinese oilmen did face tremendous hardships from the insecurity and harsh environment of Sudan. But their sacrifice was praised in China. At Heglig, Chinese workers were said to have stayed calm when SPLA rebels attacked, instructing Sudanese employees to turn off the oil production to lessen any possible damage to the wells. In the aftermath of the US missile strike on Khartoum, 'all the employees of CNPC stayed at their positions, waiting for orders and believing that China would make the best arrangement for its people'.[45] Regardless of the accuracy of these claims, it was clear that CNPC, or at least its executives tucked away in Beijing, were willing to face the risk of Sudan's civil war and challenging environment. Sudan was more than just another investment on the company's portfolio: it was a venture of crucial strategic importance for CNPC's international expansion.

Training ground

By 2007, Sudan was sub-Saharan Africa's third largest producer (nearly 470,000 bpd) and reserve holder (6.7 billion barrels), behind only the African oil juggernauts Nigeria and Angola.[46] That year, it was estimated that CNPC had invested $7 billion since it first arrived in Sudan twelve years earlier.[47] But the payoffs were well worth it. Sudan was easily CNPC's largest overseas revenue earner for the better part of a decade. Between 2003 and 2007, Sudan represented over 40 per cent of CNPC's overseas oil production, averaging 6.7 per cent of the company's total domestic and international oil production.[48] But Sudan was not only about acquiring oil reserves and production for the company; it was at the centre of CNPC's internationalisation strategy. The first barrel of Sudanese oil was also the first that CNPC sold on international markets.[49] It was where CNPC and the many oil service companies launched their first major overseas projects in order to gain crucial experience for further expansion.

CNPC had a long line of subsidiary companies to draw from in China, particularly in oil services and construction, to bolster its international operations. The Zhongyuan Petroleum Engineering Co. Ltd. (ZPEB) was the first company under CNPC to perform geophysical surveying and drilling work in Sudan.[50] Later, the Bureau of Geophysical Prospecting Ltd. (BGP), sent three exploration crews to conduct seismic surveys in Unity state shortly after CNPC won the GNPOC stake. BGP was regarded as a pioneer as it went abroad before most other service companies and broke into the African and later the international marketplace by way of its work in Sudan.[51] Following in its footsteps, the Great Wall Drilling Company (GWDC) began its international work in Sudan in 1997, investing $700 million and drilling fifty-seven oil wells over the next three years.[52]

It did not take long for Chinese oil service companies to dominate Sudan's oil industry. CNPC used its leading stake in the GNPOC consortium to stimulate the international expansion of its oil service companies, products and labour. Where it could, Petronas was also active in promoting Malaysian oil service companies, but CNPC took much of the cake. 'CNPC has been championing its service companies and pushing its own products in joint ventures. There is little competitive bidding,' said an official at Sudan's Ministry of Energy and Mining.[53] 'The Chinese want to do everything on their own. That's their international business model,' added a Sudanese oil company manager.[54] His counterpart at an Asian national oil company echoed this comment: 'The Chinese bring the whole package'.[55] Soluxe International and the Sunny International Group, two CNPC subsidiaries, even provided the food, accommodation and logistics for the Sudan operations. CNPC was, after all, a company that had a long tradition of supplying all its needs, and building quasi-societies around its oil fields in China. In Sudan, CNPC found an international training ground to operate in for its elite subsidiaries. It did not take long for Chinese oil service companies, such as BGP and GWDC, to start working for international oil companies across the globe after their experience in Sudan, and often without the need for CNPC contracts.

If there was one example that reflects CNPC's capacity to construct oil infrastructure quickly, it was Sudan's first oil pipeline from the southern oil fields to Red Sea terminals. The China Petroleum Engineering and Construction Corporation (CPECC), CNPC's main construction service company, was contracted to carry out the brunt of the work. The brute strength and endurance of 6,000 Chinese labourers finished the pipeline in a mere eleven months.[56] By 2007, a decade after CNPC won a leading stake in GNPOC, there were almost 12,500 Chinese workers in Sudan, working in oil, construction, and the service industries.[57] 'Our workers are used to eating bitterness. They can work thirteen or fourteen hours a day for very little. The quality isn't high, but we charge less,' said Wang Guoqing, a CPECC Vice-President. 'A Western company couldn't have done what we did.' He claimed that CPECC made no profit on the Sudan pipeline, but completed it to gain critical experience of working overseas.[58] The massive organisation of Chinese labour for the pipeline would become the infamous but often misunderstood calling card of China in Africa.

As China's presence on the African continent expanded at the turn of the century, Chinese companies were widely criticised by both African and international observers for not hiring enough local labour. But Chinese companies often brought many of their own workers for practical reasons such as the limited skills of local labourers and the ease of communication in language and culture between Chinese managers and workers. The level of foreign work permit allowances offered to Chinese companies by African governments also dictated the amount of Chinese labour brought from abroad.[59] In Sudan, CNPC also had its own corporate goals for bringing in thousands of Chinese workers.

During the construction of the GNPOC pipeline, rumours spread that Chinese convicts had been brought in to carry out the painstaking job in such a short time.[60] But CNPC did not need to reach into China's prison system to find the manpower to lay the Sudan pipeline. The company was beginning to lay off hundreds of thousands of redundant employees over the coming decade, a decision that Party leadership was nervous about, given the ramifications of mass layoffs on social stability. Company executives jumped at the opportunity to deploy thousands of workers to a new project in Sudan as a chance to demonstrate their sensitivity to the social tensions the company's reorganisation was creating at home.[61] After all, their tasks included corporate and political goals; Sudan would help them fulfil both.

In the early 2000s, Chinese oil executives started to demonstrate the wider benefit of their Sudan investment to Chinese government and party officials. Zhou Jiping, who became head of CNPC International after serving with GNPOC, wrote that the influx of Chinese exports of machinery, equipment and other products into Sudan to cater to CNPC's needs constituted 135 per cent of the company's initial investment in the GNPOC consortium.[62] This 'knock-on effect' not only helped reduce the risk of recovering its investment, but also invigorated other Chinese companies. The Shanghai-based Baosteel produced 200,000 tons of steel for the Sudan pipeline.[63] While Chevron's pipelines had long rusted away in Italy, this was the first time Chinese oil pipelines were exported abroad. CNPC was not only helping to internationalise many of its own subsidiaries, it was also helping other Chinese companies, and opening the door for Chinese goods and investment to flood into Sudan.

During the height of the oil boom, Sudan bought increasing amounts of Chinese exports, from textiles to motor vehicles. Chinese construction companies arrived to support the oil industry, and to do extensive work on roads, bridges and railways in northern Sudan.[64] The development of hydroelectric dams along the cataracts of the Nile represented the second major investment drive by Chinese national companies in Sudan, this time by Sinohydro and others in the power industry.[65] There was also a noticeable influx of small-sized Chinese companies and entrepreneurs into Khartoum. American diplomats dubbed the capital's eastern suburbs 'Chinatown on the Nile', referring to the Chinese company compounds, hotels, travel agencies, supermarkets and restaurants, some selling pork and alcohol openly despite Sudan's *Shar'ia* law. There were opportunities in Sudan that many Chinese could not find at home, particularly in rural areas. 'I came here for the money,' one Chinese waitress told the American officials. 'It was better than staying at home in Yantai.'[66] For these Chinese, Sudan offered a way out of a dead-end life in rural China; for the Communist Party, CNPC's expanding operations in Sudan were a beacon of China's growing influence in the world.

A promotional tool

When the oil came on in Sudan, life changed for Su Yongdi and his colleagues in Khartoum. In 2000, they moved out of their rented apartment building and into the more sizeable and accommodating confines of the Sudan Hotel on the Nile River. At this picturesque locale, they had a garden to tend during their free time, as well as a swimming pool, a basketball court, and other recreational facilities. Both the joint venture companies led by CNPC, GNPOC and Petrodar moved into sparkling new headquarters near the Nile near the new sail-shaped Burj Al-Fateh Hotel, which stood out on the otherwise dreary Khartoum skyline. On weekends, the CNPC staff ate out at an expanding list of new restaurants, visited the upscale Afra mall, walked on the nearby Tuti Island, and shopped at Chinese markets springing up in the city.[67]

But similar to the 'life in the bubble' of their international colleagues across the globe, CNPC staff did not become immersed in local life; they remained elusive figures on the city streets and rarely strolled along the broken promenade on the Nile in front of their headquarters. Most were not fond of living overseas. On weekends, they played cards in the hotel until the small hours.[68] While they longed for the chance to return home, working conditions had improved. Those at the oil fields worked one month on, one month off; those at the Khartoum headquarters worked three months on and one month off. This was a considerable improvement from the initial years, when leave was only granted every six months.[69] Families of the staff were often able to stay in the Sudan Hotel for extended visits; some even made Khartoum their permanent home. Like officials at the Ministry of Petroleum Industry in Beijing during the glory days of Daqing, CNPC oilmen were envied by their counterparts working for other national companies—Chinese workers at the Merowe dam and other hydroelectric dams only received leave after eight months. Sudan was coveted by CNPC as a symbol of its accomplishments overseas.

When CNPC started to invest overseas in the 1990s, some Western oil executives suggested that Chinese national oil companies were 'babes in the woods'. This criticism stung Chinese oil executives. But while the assessment was strictly correct—the Chinese had little experience overseas—CNPC was no minnow. It was running one of the world's largest oil industries at home, and controlled the vast majority of China's production of 2.8 million bpd.[70] In 1997, the year when CNPC won the rights to exploit Sudan's main oil fields, China was the seventh largest oil producer in the world.[71]

Only the best of the best of Chinese oilmen went to Sudan. Getting work for CNPC International or in one of its joint ventures in Sudan was no easy task. The initial team sent to Sudan were the elite of China's behemoth oil industry. They were put through strict examinations to measure their business skills and foreign language proficiency.[72] Operations on the scale of the Heglig and Unity oil fields in China would have normally been carried out by 100,000 workers in China, but CNPC did it all with 1,000 oilmen in Sudan.[73] For the future CEO Zhou Jiping, Sudan put CNPC on the map. Its operations in Sudan cultivated an international work force to manage CNPC's overseas activities in the future, and broke the belief that Chinese national oil companies could not compete overseas.[74]

If Chinese oil managers wanted to move up to the executive level of the oil industry, going to Sudan was a step in the right direction. The careers of a growing line of CNPC oilmen were born in Sudan. While Canadian and European oil executives were preoccupied with countering claims at home that oil was fuelling conflict in Sudan, Chinese political leaders praised the work of their oilmen for excelling overseas while under fire. 'Sudan was a fostering ground for the development of the company's next leaders,' said an oil industry consultant in Beijing.[75]

Su Yongdi is perhaps the most well-known employee in Sudan who went on to greater glory. He became Chief Geologist in the Africa department at a CNPC research institute in Beijing. Wang Shali, known as the 'Iron Lady', was CNPC Country Manager in Sudan in the early 2000s before rising to be Africa General Manager, and later Vice-President and Middle East chief. Zhou Jiping ascended from President of GNPOC in the late 1990s to head of CNPC International and later CNPC CEO in 2011. Certainly Sudan alone did not lead to Zhou Jiping's climb up the corporate ladder, but it was instrumental in offering he and others the opportunity to demonstrate their managerial skills in an international environment that was crucial to the company's long-term survival. The other Zhou, Zhou Yongkang, rose even further.

After Zeng Qinghong became China's Vice-President under President and General Secretary Hu Jintao in 2002, Zhou Yongkang took on a combination of Party and government posts. But he stayed close to Sudan even after he entered the highest ranks of the Chinese government and Communist Party. When the Sudanese First Vice-President Ali Osman Taha visited China in 2001, he visited Zhou in Sichuan, where he was serving as party secretary.[76] In 2004, as a Politburo member and Minister of Public Security, Zhou met a high-level Sudanese delegation including oil minister Awad Al-Jaz in 2004.[77] Zhou's political ascent would take him to the top of the Party, when he joined the Politburo Standing Committee of the Communist Party in 2007.

As the ninth highest-ranking member of the Politburo, Zhou was head of the Party's Politics and Law Commission. Underlining the rising importance of domestic stability under Hu, in 2010 Zhou commanded the biggest budget in the Chinese government when public security expenditure, rising to $111 billion in 2012, overtook China's military spending.[78] He was a formidable figure in Chinese politics and was regarded as 'the embodiment of the old communist system' and a fierce opponent of liberal thinkers inside and outside the Party.[79] Zhou also became a key figure in China's relations with North Korea when he entered the Politburo after previously spending a good decade near the China-North Korea border during his oil industry days in Liaoning province. Having had experience in Xinjiang, Zhou was also instrumental in quelling domestic instability in the regional capital Urumqi after clashes between Muslim Uyghurs and Han Chinese in July 2009 killed nearly 200 people.[80] Sudan was a foreign gem in the political career of Zhou Yongkang. It was also portrayed as a shining achievement of China in Africa.

The pearl of Africa

The main stop on the Sudan pipeline's route was seventy kilometres north of the capital at the Khartoum Refinery Complex. CNPC calls the refinery its 'pearl on the African continent'.[81] From the roadside restaurants nearby serving the traditional Sudanese dish *foul*, a mixture of beans and onions, the sprawling site of towers and pipes juts out of the emptiness of the desert, an island of modernity amid the impoverished communities north of Khartoum. The refinery was a key bargaining chip of CNPC in its effort to win the leading stake in Sudan's main oil fields. CNPC finished the expansion of the existing refinery to a production level of 50,000 bpd in May 2000. In June 2006 it revamped the refinery further to handle 100,000 bpd and connected it to oil fields in Southern Kordofan with a 750 kilometre pipeline.[82] This was not only the first overseas refinery built by CNPC,[83] it was big enough to essentially eliminate the need for the Sudanese government to import fuel for its domestic economy, a key constraint on its pre-oil budget and a point of friction in the past with Chevron.

Before the CNPC refinery was completed, there were often major shortages of fuel in Sudan, even in Khartoum and northern towns. Line-ups stretched far out of filling stations and cars and trucks sometimes waited days to tank up. The wait was so long that young boys were paid to watch over cars and move them forward as the line crept ahead. Once at the front of the line, customers were often limited by fuel stamp allowances, and could rarely drive with a full tank. Almost everyone carried long rubber hoses in their cars and trucks in order to flag down a passing motorist to siphon fuel. 'We had to beg, borrow and steal for fuel,' said a Sudanese businessman.[84]

Even for CNPC, the absence of quality fuel stung. In its first years in Sudan, jet fuel was so hard to come by that when its chartered Air China planes arrived at Khartoum International Airport, they often had to wait for days for fuel to be specially flown in from Kuwait and other Gulf states before making the return flight to China.[85] But once the refinery opened, fuel became readily available, meeting much of the new demand for the oil company and the new cars and trucks on the streets of the city centre.

Sudan also became a notable oil supplier to China. It provided on average 5.5 per cent of China's total oil imports between 1999 and 2011, making Sudan China's sixth largest supplier. But usually this amounted to roughly 2.6 per cent of China's total oil consumption. It is Angola that has been by far China's largest African source of crude oil, providing 12.2 per cent of total imports in 2011, ranking second only behind Saudi Arabia.[86] Sudan was an important supplier of oil, but expendable among many producers in the global oil market. CNPC usually sent most of its share of crude oil production back to China, but the oil coming home from its equity deals in Sudan and elsewhere did not necessarily enhance China's energy security.

Equity deals only provide price security if the future oil prices are high enough to cover the investment; besides it was CNPC, not China, that was gaining from any profits. But China's leadership has little trust in the supply security of buying oil from international markets and sees equity deals by Chinese national oil companies as a means to ensure that oil will come to China in times of crisis. However, the supply security of equity deals depends on the nature of the crisis; equity oil can just as easily be militarily blocked from reaching China as imported oil bought from the market.[87]

CNPC and other Chinese national oil companies were not the only supporters of equity oil deals abroad. For instance, the National Development and Reform Commission, the key Chinese government institution governing the energy sector, determined in 2006 that, where China's energy security was concerned, it preferred oil and gas to be acquired from the wellhead through overseas investments rather than bought from international oil markets.[88] But there has been little evidence of Chinese national oil companies deliberately 'locking up' oil for China. CNPC actually sold more of its Sudan equity oil to Japan than to China in 2006.[89] The following year, more than half of the overseas oil produced by Chinese national oil companies was sold outside China.[90] Its practice of selling oil to the highest bidder on open seas markets, which were often Chinese refineries, matched those of international oil companies. Worries in Washington that Chinese national oil companies were 'locking up' oil for the motherland were not only unfounded but also, more importantly, irrelevant. Even when CNPC sells oil from Sudan and other overseas ventures in China, it means that Chinese refineries will have to purchase less oil from other producers, freeing up that production on international oil markets for other consumers.[91] CNPC was helping to ease tight global supply and demand flows by bringing more oil onto the market. But because it was a Chinese corporate success story overseas, there was still a strong political connotation to CNPC's investment in Sudan as an important symbol for the Party.

Sudan was proof that Chinese national oil companies could compete in the international oil industry. It also became the centrepiece in China's growing engagement in Africa: the Khartoum refinery was a frequent stop for visiting Chinese government and Party officials. It demonstrated what China could do for an African economy by not only helping Sudan become an oil producer, but also breaking its dependency on expensive fuel imports. The Khartoum refinery was central in depicting what CNPC could bring to oil-rich but poor countries.

When the Vice-premier and Politburo member Wang Bannguo visited Khartoum in November 2000, he wrote that CNPC's operation in Sudan was 'a Model of Diligent and Pioneering Spirit, a monument to Sino-Sudanese Friendship'. Five years later, when a Politburo standing committee member, Li Changchun, visited Sudan, he called it a 'model for South-South cooperation'.[92] Zhou Jiping wrote that CNPC's success in Sudan was crucial to Chinese national oil companies winning investments in other African countries, including Chad, Niger and Uganda, which wanted to 'realize their oil dream' as the Sudanese had.[93]

Sudan's President Omar al-Bashir praised the creativity of the Chinese oilmen and honoured the hardships they faced in bringing the oil industry to life after Western companies had abandoned Sudan.[94] 'We express our gratitude to CNPC, to the Chinese government, and to the Chinese people,' he said.[95] CNPC was behind each oil industry inauguration the Sudanese President would preside over in 1999 as Sudan's oil industry came to life. The Chinese company brought the main oil fields into large-scale production, laid down the pipeline, and constructed an oil refinery outside Khartoum. No one would dispute that Chinese oilmen were responsible for industrial miracles in the desert of Sudan. But after witnessing CNPC's accomplishments in Sudan, newcomers began to make their plans to follow aggressively in the Chinese oil giant's footsteps.

PART III

INDIA

6

KEEPING THE LIGHTS ON

December 2008: The rickshaw driver was shaking his head in dismay. Pulling into a filling station along one of New Delhi's many bustling motorways, he noticed that the price of fuel had still not budged from its summer high. It was a time of heightened tension in India. A week earlier, ten heavily-armed men went on a rampage in India's commercial and entertainment capital of Mumbai, leaving nearly 200 people dead and hundreds more injured. At the Taj Mahal hotel and other high pro-file locations in the city, the lifeless bodies sprawled out in the sudden shock of violent death were a gruesome reminder of the threat of Islamic terrorism in India.

His hand now running through his hair, the rickshaw driver brushed off news of the attack. 'Bombs,' he muttered dismissively. Filling up his green and yellow three-wheeled rickshaw, a vehicle synonymous with India and South Asia, he continued to shake his head as he watched the dashes on the meter rise. What was on his mind was not the Mumbai massacre, but the price at the pump.

The rickshaw driver in New Delhi may have been upset, but he was still enjoying relatively low fuel prices. Despite the steady rise of inter-national oil prices over the past decade, the Indian government was still shouldering a heavy burden by keeping fuel prices artificially low through a massive subsidy programme. In recent years the Indian Prime Minis-ter, Manmohan Singh, had struggled to find the right balance between the economics of taming the long-term effects of a growing debt brought on by such subsidies and the short-term political demands of the Indian population for affordable prices.

How to handle fuel subsidies was just one piece of India's growing energy security challenge. Oil was vital in driving the economic growth needed to battle widespread poverty and maintain social stability. The importance of energy security to New Delhi at the turn of the century empowered India's once dormant international oil company, the Oil and Natural Gas Corporation Videsh Limited, or OVL for short, to invest overseas as never before.

For decades, Indian political leaders had pushed ONGC, OVL's corporate parent, to meet rising oil demand and stem the tide of the country's growing dependency on foreign oil imports. By and large, however, this had been unsuccessful. Whereas the China National Petroleum Corporation was politically strong at home, India's ONGC was traditionally weak.

But the combination of liberal reforms to India's economy and the Indian government's growing energy security concerns in the late 1990s dramatically changed ONGC's fortunes. The Indian government began to develop a comprehensive plan to bolster India's energy security, including strong support for the overseas investments of its national oil companies. ONGC's international arm, OVL, would be thrown into the limelight. Bureaucratic controls that had hindered OVL's international investments in the past were eased, and—more importantly—New Delhi put its diplomatic weight behind the company as never before. Just when Canadian and European oil companies were looking for a way out of Sudan, OVL was gearing to make its mark in the international oil industry.

High and dry

ONGC was born out of the idea that India could survive on its own in the world. Impressed by the Soviet Union's rapid economic growth in the 1930s, India's first Prime Minister, Jawaharlal Nehru, pushed forward an agenda of self-reliance and state control over the economy after winning independence from the British Empire in 1947. Consequently Shri K.D. Malaviya, Nehru's Minister for Mines and Oil, drove the British oil companies out of India and established national control over the oil industry.[1]

ONGC was established as a commission under the government in 1956, converted into a statutory body through an act of parliament three years later, and finally christened as a corporation in 1994. Despite several public offerings on Indian stock exchanges since then, the Indian government retains majority ownership. In return, ONGC maintains the rights to the majority of India's oil and natural gas wealth. But over time, the company has been unable to meet India's growing energy security challenge.

A series of early successes for ONGC offered hope that Nehru's plans for self-reliance in oil might actually work. It made discoveries in the Cambay basin of Gujarat in 1958, and in the years to come continued to find black gold in Assam, where oil production dates back to the late nineteenth century.[2] In 1974, ONGC found the massive Bombay High oil fields off India's southwestern coast. Bombay High reached a peak production of 400,000 bpd by the end of the 1980s, comprising over 60 per cent of domestic crude production during much of the decade.[3] With little inclination to push ONGC and its other national oil companies to search for oil abroad, the Indian government instigated a four-tier strategy in the early 1980s that called for maximisation of indigenous oil resources, promotion of energy conservation, exploitation of renewable resources, and acceleration of other domestic energy resources.[4] Regardless of size and potential, every strike of oil was cheered across India.

Despite its insistence on going it alone, the Indian oil industry would receive some outside assistance. While India generally shunned US and European oil company assistance during the Cold War, it turned to Soviet expertise for guidance. Offshore geological work from the Soviet ship *Akademic Arkhangeleisky* in the 1960s helped lead to ONGC's discovery of Bombay High, which was successfully drilled with the Sagar Samrat, a Japanese-built platform. But after Bombay High, there were few occasions to celebrate. ONGC developed a poor record of domestic exploration and production. By the mid-1980s, its isolation from the advanced technology and techniques of international oil companies began to show. Recovery ratios of oil extracted to oil discovered in domestic fields were well below international averages.[5] By the end of the decade, India's oil consumption was increasing at a higher rate than production.[6] Unlike China, India ultimately failed to become self-sufficient in oil.

After two decades of strong overall economic growth, India is set to overtake Russia and Japan as the world's third largest consumer of energy in 2030, behind only the US and China.[7] In 2011, India's Ministry of Petroleum and Natural Gas (MPNG) estimated domestic oil reserves at

5.55 billion barrels,[8] compared with 30.9 billion barrels in the US and 14.7 billion barrels in China. India has 0.3 per cent of the world's total oil reserves, but needs to meet the energy needs of a fifth of the world's population. In addition, oil consumption continues to increasingly outpace production. India produced 858,000 bpd in 2011, up 8 per cent over the past decade, but daily consumption was 3.5 million bpd, up 52 per cent since 2001.[9] The widening gap must be filled with foreign oil imports.

While China did not become an oil importer until 1993, India has been importing well over half of its crude oil needs since 1965.[10] India's dependency on foreign oil, set at 75 per cent in 2011, is estimated to reach 90 per cent by 2025.[11] In 2012, 64 per cent of India's oil imports came from the Middle East, mainly Saudi Arabia and Iran.[12] Africa has also become a key source of oil for India—Nigeria has traditionally been India's major non-Middle Eastern oil supplier.[13] This longstanding oil deficiency at home and its dependency on Middle Eastern oil have troubled India's economy for decades.

The Indian economy was on its knees ready for the killing blow when Iraqi bombers streamed over Kuwait City on 2 August 1990. Saddam Hussein's occupation of his oil-rich neighbour was a short affair, thanks to the intervention of a US-led international military coalition, but the short spike in oil prices resulting from the Gulf War sparked a major financial crisis in India. To add to the loss of millions of dollars in remittances from Indian workers fleeing the Gulf, India's oil import bill rose by 60 per cent in 1990 following the spike in international prices.[14] After years of weak economic growth, India's meagre foreign exchange reserves could no longer carry the burden. In desperation, New Delhi even sold $200 million worth of gold—a symbol of honour in India—to the Union Bank of Switzerland.[15] But alarming as the 1991 financial crisis was, this was not the first time there had been economic fallout and severe political consequences in India stemming from trouble in the Middle East.

In the aftermath of the Yom Kippur war between Israel and several Arab states in 1973, the Arab oil embargo on the US and other Western countries sent international oil prices soaring. Even though India's oil consumption was but a fraction of current levels, the cost of oil imports increased drastically by 370 per cent from 1972 to 1974, driving up inflation and setting off massive popular protests.[16] There was high dependency on oil imports because, while ONGC discovered Bombay High during this period, it would take time to bring production up to high levels. The situation threw economic fuel onto political fires around Prime Minister Indira Gandhi's government, which suspended the constitution and declared a state of emergency in 1975.[17] It was during this short but tumultuous period that the Indian government established the Administered Pricing Mechanism (APM) to subsidise fuel prices.[18] The purpose of the APM was to use government borrowing to protect the Indian consumer from international oil price volatility. But the Indian government struggled to sustain the high levels of debt accumulated under the fuel subsidisation scheme.

When mass demonstrations broke out on the streets of Tehran in the 1979 Iranian revolution and oil prices once again went skyward, New Delhi was forced to take out a $5.65 billion loan from the International Monetary Fund.[19] In the early 1980s, oil import costs were so high that they represented half the value of India's total exports.[20] In theory, this means that half the value of Indian goods sold on international markets went to cover the oil bill. Bombay High helped to weather the economic storm of high international oil prices during the Iraq-Iran war in the 1980s, easing India's dependency on foreign oil to as low as 30 per cent by 1986.[21] But oil production stagnated by the end of the decade. India's entire economy was just waiting to buckle under the pressure, and it did when Iraq invaded Kuwait in the Gulf War of 1990.

The Indian government resembled a sorry game of musical chairs during the economic crisis sparked by the Gulf War. Lacking the political support to govern, Prime Minister V.P. Singh's coalition government fell in November 1990. The political situation only worsened when, seven years after the assassination of Prime Minister Indira Gandhi, a Sri Lankan suicide bomber killed her son, Rajiv Gandhi, who was campaigning for the Indian National Congress in the 1991 national elections. When Narasimha Rao of the Congress party became prime minister later that year, he faced the daunting task of taming double-digit inflation and turning around both a budget deficit and a trade deficit. Under Rao, Finance Minister Manmohan Singh sped up the liberalisation of India's state-run economy throughout much of the 1990s.[22] The crisis set off by rising international oil prices actually put Manmohan Singh, who later became India's Prime Minister, in the political position to build on previous government reforms by dismantling heavy state controls, commonly known as the 'License Raj', over the economy.

Reassembling the machine

The oil industry would not be spared from reform after the 1991 financial crisis. In 1995, the MPNG formed the Oil Industry Restructuring Group to develop and suggest deregulation methods. The Commission recommended a rationalisation of crude oil and fuel prices to international levels by the early 2000s.[23] However, while the APM was dismantled and crude oil prices were rationalised to international levels by 2002, the Indian government decided to prolong the subsidisation of most fuels. Kerosene and liquid petroleum gas (LPG) remained heavily subsidised because kerosene is largely used for cooking purposes by the poor and LPG as a motor fuel and for cooking and heating by the middle class in urban areas.[24] The political repercussions of rolling back fuel subsidies completely were too great for any Indian government to overcome at the time, and remained daunting in the coming decade.

The Indian government continued to be dissatisfied with ONGC into the 1990s. But even Indian socialists were now turning their backs on the once-cherished national company. The *Economic and Political Weekly*, the popular left-leaning magazine, strongly denounced the Indian government's slight opening of the oil industry to foreign companies in the late 1980s.[25] It called for New Delhi to support ONGC more directly, rather than become reliant on foreign oil companies. The Indian managers of ONGC were seen as 'true oil men, nurtured in the Malaviya tradition'; the magazine suggested that the iconic oil minister would not 'possibly feel elated by the return of oil multinationals'.[26] But by the late 1990s, the tables had turned. In the same publication, accusations were thrown at ONGC's 'true oil men' for neglecting their duties and damaging India's chances of maximising the ultimate potential of its oil fields.[27] The Indian government continued to try to attract private and foreign investment and technology to the oil industry.

The introduction of the New Exploration and Licensing Policy (NELP) in January 1999 redoubled India's efforts to find new oil reserves within its borders and presented a subtle but direct challenge to ONGC's dominance.[28] The response from private and international oil companies was quite mild.[29] But after some time, they warmed to NELP and started to command a larger share of domestic oil and natural gas production from ONGC.[30] By 2010, the new policies helped garner over 4.7 billion barrels of reserves of oil and oil-gas equivalent in the first eight bidding rounds for available concessions.[31] The incursion of private and foreign oil companies onto ONGC's once-hallowed turf pushed up India's total crude oil production by 17 per cent from 2000 to 2010, and important discoveries of natural gas were also made.[32]

Yet in contrast to the work of private and foreign oil companies, ONGC was still showing signs of decline. Industry experts continued to lambast ONGC's inability to make new discoveries and properly manage the oil fields it did find. Striving to ramp up domestic production levels, the company tried to improve its technological capabilities and managerial practices.[33] The advances and reorganisation helped, but were still inadequate. ONGC went from selling 459,000 bpd in the 2001 fiscal year to 463,000 bpd in 2011, a small increase.[34] Prospects for increasing production levels at home were so dire that the company signed an agreement with the MPNG in March 2008 to simply maintain the same production volume levels of the previous year.[35] The lack of oil remained a major drain on the Indian economy.

When US forces invaded Iraq in 2003, there were fears in India that history was repeating itself. More trouble in the Middle East, in tandem with rising demands for oil in China and India, pushed international oil prices past the $100 per barrel mark and beyond. As a consequence, India's oil import bill increased over tenfold since 2001, measuring $134 billion in 2011.[36] But the invasion of Iraq was not followed by a financial crisis; India's roaring economy had shored up enough foreign exchange reserves to cover its mounting oil import bills.[37] In 2004, Manmohan Singh, the Sikh technocrat turned politician, became prime minister and was met with the seemingly intractable problem that India's oil needs continued to drag down the economy. Over the past decade, oil had generally accounted for around a quarter of the total value of Indian imports, and it remains a major reason why India's trade balance continues to be in the red.[38] Persistently high international oil prices continued to exacerbate tensions between ONGC and its government handlers.

In the autumn of 2005 Mani Shankar Aiyar, Manmohan Singh's oil minister, took ONGC to task. He accused the company of failing in its duty to protect India's energy interests, noting that 20 per cent of the country's estimated oil reserves remained undiscovered.[39] Between 2000 and 2005, ONGC had a ratio of discoveries to exploration activities of 42 per cent, whereas the major private and foreign oil companies in India, Reliance Industries and Cairn, scored 71 and 80 per cent respectively.[40]

In early 2006, after a very public falling out with Aiyar, Chairman Subir Raha's contract was not extended. The company's poor performance in leveraging domestic oil production, the chairman's handling of a fire at a Mumbai High offshore oil platform that killed twenty-two employees, and his opposition to the appointment of government officials to the company's board of directors were all seen as reasons for the government to deny him the usual second term at the helm of ONGC.[41] Raha's dismissal was a clear indication of who was ultimately in charge.

ONGC is one of the few prestigious national-owned companies designated with the status of *Maharatnas*. The MPNG administers the state-owned oil and gas companies under the Directorate General of Hydrocarbons,[42] but in theory the *Maharatnas* status gives ample decision-making powers to corporate managers over capital expenditure, joint ventures and strategic alliances.[43] Exerting something similar to the powers of the Communist Party of China, the ruling coalition party in the Indian government controls the final decision on the appointment of ONGC chairmen and new members on its board of directors, with two government nominees from the oil and finance ministries typically holding membership. Changing political winds in New Delhi also influence board appointments.[44] For instance, when Manmohan Singh's Congress party took over the government from the Bharatiya Janata Party (BJP) in 2004, it sought to replace independent ONGC board members who had been appointed during its predecessor's time in office.[45]

But New Delhi has further reasons for maintaining leverage over the company through its main personnel. ONGC is a strategic piggy bank for the Indian government. US and European oil majors certainly provide billions in tax revenue as publicly traded companies, but ONGC's contributions are directly wired into government policies for providing affordable energy to the Indian population. New Delhi is not just interested in ONGC's corporate performance; it expects the company to contribute to India's energy security.

The company plays a vital role in New Delhi's subsidisation of fuel prices, which are historically a significant burden on government spending. In recent years, India has spent around $16 billion annually to subsidise fuel.[46] The formal cost of fuel subsidies alone amounted to 0.8 per cent of India's economy in 2011.[47] ONGC provides around one-third of the government's total subsidy payment each year to help cover losses of Indian national refiners, Indian Oil, Bharat Petroleum and Hindustan

Petroleum. From 2003 to 2008, ONGC provided \$12 billion to help subsidise fuel prices.[48] In 2011, the company gave \$8 billion, representing a staggering 57 per cent of its total sales.[49] In addition, ONGC transfers vast sums of its earnings annually to the Indian Exchequer in the form of levies, duties, royalties, dividends and taxes.[50] In effect, the subsidy payments and other contributions by ONGC ease the burden on the Indian government brought on by its fuel subsidy programme.

In May 2008, R.S. Sharma, the new ONGC Chairman, remarked that he was not 'unduly perturbed' by the company's subsidy burden. But he did express concern over the transparency of the subsidization program.[51] In 2011, Sharma's successor, Subhir Vasudeva, became more worried as subsidy levels from the government continued to rise. 'The single biggest reason for this decline or deficit in our profit as compared to the corresponding quarter last year is the burden of subsidy,' he said.[52] But at the same time, if the long view was taken, thanks to its national ownership ONGC was still in a privileged position. The combination of New Delhi's dismantling of price controls on domestic crude oil and the drastic rise in international oil prices enhanced ONGC's revenue levels immensely. Profits rose by over 300 per cent from 2001 to 2011, even though the company was producing very little more oil.[53] But it was clear that only one option remained for the company to find new oil: it had to leave India. By the turn of the century OVL, its international subsidiary, was suddenly crucial to the company's future.

A new man in charge

The story of the rise of OVL is best told through the feats of the Indian oilman Atul Chandra. Starting as Chairman of OVL in December 1995, Chandra had a hefty challenge in front of him. The company was running at a loss and its corporate parent ONGC was considering closing the subsidiary down. But Chandra was determined to draw from his vast knowledge of the domestic and international oil industry to move the company forward.

If anyone could turn around the fledgling overseas subsidiary, it was Chandra. In 1966, he graduated as a petroleum engineer from the Indian School of Mines in Dhanbad, India's 'Coal Capital'. Located northwest of Kolkata, the school was known for producing the elite of India's oil and mining business. Following graduation, he joined ONGC and became a rising star in the Indian oil industry. 'He is a hardcore explo-ration and production man, a good marketing man and an excellent dip-lomat,' said the former Indian Petroleum Secretary B.K. Chaturvedi.[54] At ONGC, Chandra worked in a wide variety of areas, gaining experi-ence in field operations, project management, research and development, and corporate affairs.[55] But reassembling OVL involved more than man-aging the discrete tasks of a multi-faceted enterprise: the entire company needed to be remade to escape from a long and tortuous past of failure.

Unlike China's CNPC, ONGC and OVL had over fifty years of inter-national experience, but this was largely a half-century of failure. OVL had been active overseas since its inauguration as Hydrocarbons India Limited in 1965. The company had made several forays in Malaysia, Thai-land, and the Sango Sango prospect in Tanzania, but these exploration efforts were largely unsuccessful owing to OVL's poor capabilities. In the 1960s, OVL made a minor oil discovery in the Raksh Rostum field of Iran, but the asset was later nationalised during the political turmoil of the Islamic revolution.

The state of affairs was so dreary during this period that OVL's cor-porate parent ONGC often scooped up the more prospective interna-tional opportunities for itself.[56] In the years to follow, some in the Indian oil industry began to regard OVL as a *gulag* for disgruntled managers from other state-owned oil and gas companies, who for political reasons could not be fired outright by the government.[57] After narrowly avoid-ing the chopping block, the company was restructured into ONGC Videsh Limited on 15 June 1989. But the results remained the same.

In the early 1990s, OVL drilled a series of dry wells in Egypt, Yemen and Tunisia that not only cost the company dearly, but also tarnished its reputation.[58] At the time, the company was simply not up to the task of navigating the tumultuous waters of major international oil bids. 'OVL was over tentative and unsure of the rules of the game in foreign envi-ronments,' recalls one Indian diplomat.[59] Its familiarity with the valua-tion and negotiation of international bids was at a novice level; it had few success stories of oil strikes to bring to the table.

Atul Chandra took part in the company's early overseas operations. From 1975 to 1977, he was head of production operations for the joint venture company Iminoco in Iran. The consortium included Philips Petro-leum, the Italian oil company AGIP, the National Iran Oil Company, and ONGC. 'I learned a lot during the two years with Iminoco. That was also my first experience of working with multinationals,' he said.[60] Iminoco provided Chandra with critical international experience, which he sought to exploit when he was put in charge of OVL in 1995.

Chandra's appointment as OVL's new boss did not immediately change the company's reputation. Shortly after he took over, ONGC decided to stop providing financial assistance to OVL, devised ways to shut down the subsidiary, and even refused to fund a temporary office after a fire destroyed the OVL headquarters. Business acumen within the company was in such dire straits that Chandra was forced to persuade his son, who worked at the international accountancy firm of Arthur Andersen, to teach the OVL staff how to construct a business plan.[61]

The Indian government was not much help; it placed stringent controls on OVL's international investment decisions until the turn of the century. The contrast with the politically powerful CNPC in China could not have been more stark. Chinese oilmen were able to exploit their Communist Party connections to garner support for overseas investments in the 1990s; OVL was utterly desperate for the government to release restrictions limiting its international activities. OVL lacked the quick reaction time to be competitive in the international bidding process for oil and gas deals. It needed permission from a number of ministries for any major international investment to go forward, and continually experienced political sparring between politicians and bureaucrats who wanted to stall the company's requests. 'When you are bidding for an asset, you need to respond in 2–6 weeks. Our procedures would take months and years,' said the ONGC Chairman Subir Raha. 'By the time the approvals came, six to eight months went by and nobody would wait ten months for India to decide whether to make a bid or not. This was a major reason why we couldn't do anything.'[62]

But Chandra had a plan to turn the ship around. He insisted that the company focus on expanding overseas as a participating partner in joint ventures rather than acting as operator where it contracted out management of activities from exploration to production.[63] 'At the time, OVL decided that rather than pursue organic growth through exploration and production, that it aim to access existing fields,' said a company executive.[64] Chandra apparently saw little use in taking on the majority of the risk, particularly since to date, the company did not have the experience and knowhow to succeed abroad. 'I realised I had no alternative but to think out of the box; at the same time I carried the people who thought differently along with me, and it worked,' said Chandra.[65] He also wanted OVL to 'farm-in', an industry term for an outside company purchasing an interest in an existing oil venture. Chandra's application of various industry and management mechanisms to the way OVL conducted its business gave the company the opportunity to learn the skills and techniques needed to manage large-scale overseas projects without undue risk. After all, Chandra himself had cut his international teeth working alongside international oil companies in Iran. He sought to bring the same learning experience to the entire company.

He was also confident that OVL could fill a gap in India's oil industry. 'India has no option but to go for equity oil overseas, and I just happened to be there to lead the mission,' he said.[66] 'Any oil company that wants to grow must find new reserves at least equal to its production. First, it tries to strike oil at home, but the balance must come from outside. That is why OVL exists,' said ONGC Chairman Subir Raha.[67]

In April 1998 B.C. Bora, Raha's predecessor, had established a four-pronged ONGC strategy to develop major domestic basins, improve oil recovery methods to increase productivity, explore frontier areas at home, and finally, acquire overseas concessions for exploration.[68] In May 2001, ONGC released its strategic vision, which included the securing of 20 million metric tons of oil and oil-equivalent gas per year from overseas by 2020.[69] This amounted to a goal of securing over 400,000 bpd. Suddenly, OVL was at the centre of its parent company's attention.

But the truth was that OVL was still up against stiff competition to win overseas bids. It simply did not have the capital and technology possessed by US and European oil majors. Atul Chandra could do all the strategic tinkering he wanted, OVL needed the Indian government to get behind its cause if it wanted to have a fighting chance overseas.

All hands on deck

While Atul Chandra was trying to reinvent OVL, the Indian government began efforts to shore up its energy security, which included reconsidering its support, or rather lack of it, to national oil companies operating abroad. In 1997 a parliamentary committee found that India lacked a long-term strategic plan on energy security. This was partly because there was a wide range of interpretation of energy security among politicians, the business community, academics and the media in India.[70] Some viewed it as attaining complete independence from oil imports, others focused on the energy needs of individuals, rather than the country as a whole. Rehabilitating India's poor energy infrastructure, the creation of a national gas grid, and enhancing India's nuclear power capacity were just some of the ideas on the table.

Any solutions for India's energy security problem would have to run through the reality of its democratic system, the often-constraining apparatus of its coalition government.[71] The political hurdles of existing incentive structures often delayed energy initiatives, such as fuel subsidy reform. With government decision makers faced with a long list of options, the more straightforward and recognisable projects in the oil industry often stand out.[72] Free of the constraints of domestic politics on energy projects in India, offering political support to the overseas investments of Indian national oil companies was an initiative that most Indian politicians could support.

In February 2000, the Indian government under the Hindu nationalist BJP and Prime Minister Atal Bihari Vajpayee released the 'India Hydrocarbon Vision 2025'.[73] The Vision aspired to build a cleaner and greener India through renewable sources of energy, and highlighted oil as central to energy security in India. Its main tenet called for India 'to assure energy security by achieving self-reliance through increased indigenous production and investment in equity oil abroad'.[74] When Manmohan Singh became prime minister in 2004, he continued to underline the importance of energy security. 'It is second only in our scheme of things to food security,' he said.[75] At the first meeting of the Indian Energy Coordination Committee in 2005, Singh stressed that India had 'to insulate the economy from any future shock' by diversifying energy sources.[76]

The following year, Manmohan Singh's government took a more comprehensive approach to energy than it had in the past by releasing the Integrated Energy Policy.[77] It stressed the importance of providing 'lifeline energy' to Indian citizens and underlined that the diversification of supply sources was important in minimising the risk of war, strikes and political upheaval in oil-producing countries upsetting the availability of oil to India.[78] More than ever before, energy security was now at the forefront of the Indian government's priorities.

The rising importance of energy security to New Delhi coincided with its growing support OVL seeking equity oil deals abroad. As a start, the

Indian Cabinet granted OVL special empowerment status in January 2000.[79] The company no longer had to seek acceptance from a line of government ministries on major investment projects. Rather, requests for approval were now fast-tracked through an empowered committee of secretaries and the Indian Cabinet.[80] Approval was still needed for investments over $50 million, which essentially meant that every investment would require government consent. OVL still regarded its investment limit as a major weakness, and sought a $500 million to $1 billion threshold.[81] But OVL's corporate parent, ONGC, was now flush with cash.

As with its counterpart CNPC in China, ONGC's control of the majority of India's oil production and the deregulation of domestic crude oil prices caused the company's profits to soar, despite its failure to ramp up production and reserves at home. 'Our thrust to procure more oil and gas equity at a global level was made possible by the deregulation of the oil sector in India last year,' said the Chairman Subir Raha in 2003. 'Now we have reached a stage where we cannot afford to stagnate; we either have to grow or fall by the wayside.'[82]

ONGC now looked for its future growth overseas. As a result, OVL was able to grab international opportunities by 'leveraging the farm' back home.[83] The majority of OVL's foreign investments would be funded by equity- and interest-free loans from its parent company. From 2002 to 2006, OVL borrowed a total of 157,618 million Rs ($3.15 billion) in largely interest-free loans from ONGC.[84] At OVL, Atul Chandra now had both strong backing from his corporate parent and the political winds of New Delhi behind him when he went out hunting for oil overseas.

For one of the first major deals, Chandra set his sights on Russia's vast oil and gas reverses. In 2001, OVL made a bid for a 20 per cent stake in the promising Sakhalin I project. Located offshore in the inhospitable Sea of Okhotsk, Sakhalin I was part of a series of major oil and gas finds in which Moscow and its national oil company Rosneft sought further foreign participation. The US giant Exxon, the largest oil company in the world, was already acting as the joint venture's operator, in charge of exploration and production activities. OVL initially made a bold $100 million bonus offer to the Russian government, but after an announcement was released during the bidding process that the field contained an estimated 1 billion barrels, BP entered the fray and outbid OVL with a $200 million offer.

In response to the emergence of BP as a rival for the Russian oil and gas assets, Chandra quickly called in the Indian oil minister Ram Naik for help. He pleaded with the minister to exploit India's close relations with Russia to win the bid. In response, Naik contacted the Finance Minister, Yashwant Sinha, to find a solution. Sinha then flew to Moscow to meet Russian officials and finally, in the eleventh hour, Prime Minister Vajpayee was called in to lend his political clout. In a telephone conversation with his counterpart, Vladimir Putin, Vajpayee promised that the Indian military would purchase Russian arms if OVL won the bid. When it heard this news, BP scrambled to bring in the British Prime Minister, Tony Blair, but it was too late. Putin insisted that Rosneft take on the Indian company as a partner. 'In the highest level of government there was involvement in the entire procedural negotiations,' said Subir Raha.[85] 'It is not usual for a company from a developing national to be associated with such a project,' boasted the Petroleum Minister at the time, Mani Shankar Aiyar, when production began in October 2005.[86] Together, the Indian government and OVL had taken down an oil major in a saga that the Indian media termed a 'corporate thriller'.

The Sakhalin bid was the first time that the Indian government had engaged in diplomacy to support an Indian national oil company. At $2.7 billion, it was also the largest foreign investment of any Indian company at the time. But the deal was worth the effort. Estimates of proven Sakhalin oil reserves rose to 2.3 billion by 2007.[87] The deal demonstrated that Vajpayee was committed to backing Indian oil companies abroad. After finalising the deal in 2001, OVL quickly began to look for other overseas opportunities. And when Talisman began to buckle under pressure from the US government and US activists and decided to leave Sudan the following year, OVL found its next target.

Early in Atul Chandra's tenure as OVL's leader, the company's poor competitive position was on full display in Sudan when OVL was present at the bidding for the oil concessions made available by Arakis in 1996. Former Sudanese oil officials in Khartoum only had disparaging comments about the company and its inability to make quick decisions and keep pace with the fast-changing bids during negotiations. They recall that Indian oil executives seemed more interested in taking tours down the Nile and enjoying parties in the capital than in the actual oil deal.[88] It did not take long for OVL to be sidelined as a serious contender and its Chinese and Malaysian rivals at CNPC and Petronas to win out.

Six years after it failed to enter Sudan, the doors were open to OVL once again. This time around, OVL had high-placed political friends in

New Delhi to help push the deal through. The rewards at stake were significant. The Greater Nile Petroleum Operating Company, a joint venture with CNPC, Petronas and Talisman, was producing over 200,000 bpd of crude oil in 2002. Talisman's decision to jettison the lucrative asset came just as the prospect of peace between the NCP government of President Bashir and the SPLA was on the rise. The Machakos Protocol, a cease-fire agreement named after the Kenyan town where it was signed in late July 2002, provided a framework for the eventual Comprehensive Peace Agreement of January 2005. Despite peace on the horizon, oil was still strongly associated with the killing and displacement of thousands of civilians by the Sudanese army and pro-government militias; but OVL and the Indian government paid little heed to the civil war's human rights abuses.

On 24 June 2002 two opinion pieces in *The Hindu*, one of the India's leading newspapers, summed up the Indian debate about OVL entering Sudan.[89] The first, written by Ninan Koshy, a political commentator and social activist, chronicled the horrors of Sudan's civil war and claimed the Indian government had committed a 'grave error' by seeking to invest in 'ethnically-cleansed areas' for the sake of oil. The second opinion piece, from C. Raja Mohan, one of India's leading foreign policy experts, argued that the investment was a necessary evil India had to accept. He applauded the move, writing that oil diplomacy needed to be added to the arsenal of India's foreign policy tactics in order for it to improve its energy security at home. Mohan felt that India had 'no option' but to take risks overseas, even by investing in war-torn Sudan in search of oil. After all, he wrote, the oil business was not for 'the faint-hearted'. In the end, there was little response from the Indian government to Koshy's warning. When questioned about the human rights situation in Sudan, the Petroleum Minister Ram Naik said that 'every country has different concerns and our concern is to have oil equity'.[90] For the Indian government, energy security trumped any ethical dilemmas.

It was no surprise that the discussion over the ethics of entering Sudan was short-lived in India. For the most part, the country's vibrant media and civil society focus on domestic and regional issues. Even if Indian activists had wanted, it would have been hard to shine the spotlight on an Indian national oil company financing an oppressive African regime. Child labour, poverty, AIDS, caste killings and women's rights are the critical issues constraining social and economic development in India.[91] Distant civil wars in Africa are exactly that, distant.

But despite increased government support for OVL's overseas ventures, the company nonetheless faced resistance from factions in the Indian government. Some members of Parliament and Cabinet led by the BJP under the ruling National Democratic Alliance regarded committing hundreds of millions of dollars to a war-torn country as a 'risky venture'. After all, India was still a developing country, and had to use its resources cautiously. If peace was to fail in Sudan, and it often did, OVL risked losing everything.

Furthermore, Sudan had also been the home of the international terrorist Osama bin Laden in the late 1990s, and India had its own problems with terrorism. Apart from security concerns, contractors in the Indian oil sector lobbied against the overseas investment for another reason altogether. They were worried that OVL's venture in Sudan would threaten the scope of ONGC's activities and investment at home. 'We are a poor country,' said the Communications Minister, Pramod Mahajan. 'Why do we need to invest so much money in faraway Sudan?'[92]

Political rivalries within the Indian government threatened to derail the Sudan deal for OVL. One of its opponents was Mahajan, a rising star in the ruling BJP in the early 2000s. He was joined in his discontent with the Sudan deal by the Disinvestment Minister, Arun Shourie. Both men had political reasons to question the deal. Mahajan saw his promising future as BJP leader threatened by Ram Naik, whose stature had been improved by the country's new energy security focus; the Sudan deal could only help build his portfolio in the BJP, and for Mahajan, sinking Sudan would weaken Naik's position. As for the Disinvestment Minister Shourie, he was pushing for India's national oil companies to be privatised, in opposition to Naik, who wanted to maintain state ownership for energy security purposes. If OVL was successful in making large investments overseas, it would help prove state-owned companies could be competitive, and the argument for keeping them out of public financial markets might be bolstered.[93] Seeing that political infighting was threatening the deal, OVL's parent company, ONGC, moved to counter the opposition.

Convinced that the presence of CNPC and Petronas in Sudan was evidence that OVL could also operate there successfully, ONGC Chairman Subir Raha stepped in to argue the case for the Sudan deal. Committed as he was to building ONGC's international presence through OVL, he saw Sudan as a golden opportunity. 'Why should we play politics with everything? Please understand that India has no alternative but to go overseas for equity oil,' said Raha.[94] 'We should learn from China.'

To counter concerns over the safety of the investment, Raha reminded Indian politicians that ONGC knew how to mitigate sabotage and conflict from its experience with insecurity right at home.[95] In the summer of 2002, separatist militants in India's rebellious Assam province had killed six ONGC workers; yet ONGC had soldiered on with its activities. OVL's Atul Chandra actually had experience in managing operations in Assam.[96] Raha was also keen on capitalising on opportunities in politically unstable countries where international oil companies from the US and Europe were wary of investing.[97] As the debate reached a feverish level, the Indian Ministry of External Affairs (MEA) weighed in. It was at first worried about OVL's bid to enter Sudan. 'We did not want it to be a political embarrassment to India,' said one former ministry official.[98] The ministry was afraid that the same events that led to Talisman's early exit might befall OVL. But after some analysis, it considered the Canadian company's departure as the result of civil society pressure in Canada and the US, rather than insecurity caused by the civil war.

The fact that CNPC and Petronas did not budge as Canadian and European oil companies pulled out was a further encouraging sign for the MEA. Since OVL was wholly-owned by ONGC, which was a majority-owned government company, it could easily avoid the same divestment pressures from activists that had plagued Talisman. In fact, the ministry felt that the activists strengthened the competitive position of OVL and the other Asian national oil companies by driving out their Western counterparts.[99]

Political leaders in the Indian government stepped in to settle the issue. L.K. Advani, the deputy prime minister, suggested that OVL take out political risk insurance before moving forward. In response, ONGC said that by purchasing the Talisman stake, it would be covered by a $1.2 billion insurance policy through the GNPOC joint consortium with the international bank HSBC in London.[100] Later, directed by the Finance Minister Jaswant Singh, the Indian cabinet instructed OVL to put a $1 billion cap on its investments as a 'de-risk' strategy, with any further investments to be made alongside other Indian national oil companies.[101] This was in stark contrast to the freewheeling investments of CNPC and Petronas in Sudan, but these measures helped to satisfy political opponents of OVL's Sudan investments. Prime Minister Vajpayee and the Indian Cabinet gave OVL the nod to proceed.

In the end, both OVL and the Indian government pushed aside any human rights qualms about entering Sudan and decided they were willing to take the risk of possible insecurity. As OVL managers later remarked, 'India has to decide whether it wants to make money or be worried about Sudan's lack of democratic credentials'.[102] A smiling picture of President Omar Bashir in military fatigues shaking hands with the newly-arrived Indian oilmen was hung in the company's Sudan headquarters in central Khartoum.

The drive to support Indian national oil companies overseas had accelerated in New Delhi. OVL now found politics on its side after decades of neglect by the Indian government. But the company was not exactly in the clear yet. As Indian politicians and bureaucrats bickered over the risks involved in entering Sudan, a familiar opponent was seeking to claim Talisman's oil stakes for its own. CNPC already dominated Sudan's oil industry, and it was hungry for more.

7

AN OIL TITAN REINCARNATED

May 2003: It was all smiles at Mangalore harbour in southwestern India. A group of men representing India's political and corporate elite waited at the docks for the arrival of a tanker carrying 600,000 barrels of Nile blend crude oil from Sudan. Deputy Prime Minister L.K. Advani, dressed in a signature Nehru vest, stood among them. The approaching tanker, the *Sea Falcon*, marked a victory for Advani; it represented the first time that Indian-owned oil had been brought home from a foreign source.[1] Arriving when it did during the run-up to the 2004 national elections, the oil was presented by Advani as proof that his ruling BJP was actively taking steps to secure India's energy future.[2] 'This is not imported oil, this is India's oil,' he said.

Flying down from New Delhi with the deputy prime minister was Ram Naik, India's oil minister. Advani praised Naik as 'far-sighted, enterprising and upright' in his efforts to bring Sudanese oil to Indian shores. Naik, in turn, said it was a 'golden day' and congratulated the MEA on its diplomatic success in sealing the Sudan deal for India's national oil company, OVL.[3] It was not long ago that the opportunity to produce oil in Sudan had almost slipped through OVL's hands in the face of Chinese opposition. Often portrayed as China's underdog in the race to capture oil assets in Africa, India had put up a united front to acquire oil stakes in Sudan and had won the day.

After struggling for decades to make a mark in the international oil industry, in a matter of years OVL had begun to win oil assets abroad, thanks to support from the Indian government. In March 2003, OVL invested $720 million to replace Talisman and join its Asian counterparts, CNPC and Petronas, in the Greater Nile Petroleum Operating Company (GNPOC) in Sudan. But the Chinese and Malaysians did not welcome the Indian company to Sudan with open arms; rather, they were eager to purchase Talisman's stake themselves. As China was Sudan's closest political and economic foreign partner, its opposition was particularly intimidating. It took New Delhi's full diplomatic support and, more important, the intervention of the Sudanese government to overcome China's opposition.

Subir Raha, the Chairman of ONGC, OVL's corporate parent, also attended the welcome ceremony at Mangalore. The rewards of acquiring oil stakes in Sudan went beyond the hundreds of millions in revenue that the Indian company would start to generate. Sudan was a demonstration for OVL that it could compete and operate successfully overseas, even against its Chinese competition. Standing with the politicians, Raha had cause to smile the broadest. This was a turning point for the company's international ambitions. In Sudan, OVL was born again.

The China threat

By the end of the summer of 2002, OVL had won the approval of the Indian government's Cabinet Committee on Economic Affairs to finalise an agreement with Talisman to purchase its stake in Sudan. But there was still one more hurdle standing in the way: CNPC and Petronas wanted the oil stake too. At first, the presence of the Chinese and Malaysians in Sudan encouraged India to invest there; OVL pictured its involvement as building an international relationship with its Asian counterparts.[4] CNPC and Petronas, however, knew the stakes at hand and were keen to compete rather than cooperate. Partnerships through joint ventures were a useful method to diversify risk, but if the terms were right and the oil was flowing, which was the case in Sudan, new partners were better avoided. Holding contractual rights of first refusal, both companies technically had initial access to Talisman's abandoned stake. If OVL did not do something to change matters quickly, it risked losing out on Sudan's oil before it had even landed there.

Both CNPC and Petronas had until the end of December 2002 to initiate their contractual rights. OVL Chairman Atul Chandra had been up against heavy competition before. As he had done during OVL's Sakhalin bid in Russia, Chandra asked the Indian government to lend a hand. He hailed the Sudan investment as a possible 'great leap forward in terms of national oil security'.[5] Raha, the ONGC Chairman, followed suit, saying that there was 'no alternative but to go overseas for equity oil' and that the rapid expansion of Chinese companies offered a lesson for India.[6] Raha implored the Indian Commerce Minister, Arun Jaitley, and the oil minister, Ram Naik, to promote OVL's position with the Sudanese government, which had the power to block CNPC and Petronas from buying Talisman's stake. It was no surprise then that in Sudan, OVL's bid to purchase the Talisman oil stake brought fears of the 'China threat' back to life in India.

It is an understatement to say that India and China have a complicated past in Africa. Mahatma Gandhi and Jawaharlal Nehru were prominent in helping South Africa's struggle against apartheid and the continent's struggle to sever its colonial bonds. But Indo-Afro solidarity was put to the test during the 1962 border war between India and China; many African countries did not provide the political support New Delhi had hoped for. While the peaceful ideals of non-violent resistance and cultural co-existence expressed by Gandhi and Nehru fell easily on the ears of African leaders, they could not match China's more tangible military, political and financial support.

The border war between the two Asian giants left a deep scar on India's political ambitions.[7] Indian leaders became particularly rattled during the Chinese Prime Minister Zhou Enlai's African tour in 1963–64, seeing it as an attempt to further dislodge India as the leader of the developing world.[8] India moved to correct its weakened position by trying to ramp up trade and investment on the continent during the 1970s. The External Affairs Minister Sardar Swaran Singh instructed Indian Foreign Service officers in Africa to be not only diplomatic agents but also 'trade agents' who 'should act like the commercial sales man on behalf of a private firm' and 'not consider this work as inferior or below their dignity'.[9] Over the following decades, the old political wound of the Sino-Indian border war slowly began to heal, but by the turn of the century, when China and India began to increase their trade and investment in Africa in search of natural resources, new economic sores would open up.

Over the past decade, both China and India have become increasingly significant economic and political players in Africa. However, India has not matched China's engagement. China's trade on the continent measured $160 billion in 2011, compared with India's $62 billion.[10] It is hard for an Indian diplomat or corporate executive to speak about India's role in Africa without having to answer questions about its competition with China. As India's Minister of State for Commerce, Jairam Ramesh, said on the eve of the 2008 India-Africa Summit, 'We can't race with them at all. There's no point. They have left us behind'.[11]

The same was true when it came to oil. In Africa and beyond, Chinese national oil companies were beating their Indian counterparts left and right. Just before the Sudan confrontation, Chinese national oil companies won exploration rights in Algeria and Tunisia and five Indonesian oil fields, all of which Indian companies were also vying for. 'The Chinese work with the single objective that they need more oil. They are very aggressive bidders,' said OVL's Chandra.[12] The Indian media were full of headlines reporting the sorry bidding results, often placing the blame on New Delhi for not allowing OVL to bid more aggressively.[13]

Officials at India's MEA attest that Beijing has a no-holds-barred approach in offering diplomatic support to the international bids of its national oil companies, whereas India is price sensitive and limited in what it can provide.[14] The Indian oil ministry sought to develop a special relationship with China to cooperate on energy security and energy conservation and promote joint ventures abroad between Indian and Chinese national oil companies.[15] But some in New Delhi worried that the Chinese were merely appeasing the Indians. China was expanding its oil interests abroad at a much more rapid pace than India and had little to lose in signing a cooperation agreement.[16] The joint deals to come between Indian and Chinese national oil companies, as in Syria and Colombia, were relatively small in scale,[17] whereas when the stakes were high, as in Nigeria and Angola, the gloves came off and China, more often than not, prevailed.[18]

India's presence in Sudan easily fell in the shadow of China's powerful and seemingly ubiquitous political and economic position. China is Sudan's largest trading partner, with over $9.5 billion in oil-powered trade in 2011, dwarfing India's otherwise impressive $1.2 billion.[19] India has longstanding ties with Sudan—at the 1955 Afro-Asian Relations Conference in Bandung in Indonesia, Nehru wrote 'Sudan' on his handkerchief to create an improvised flag for the soon-to-be independent country[20]—but despite this good-natured ingenuity with handkerchiefs, China's ample trade and investment, as well as its veto-wielding power at the UN Security Council (from 1971), offered Sudan tangible economic and political benefits. After China's CNPC made a move to capture Talisman's stake in Sudan in late 2002, the feeling in New Delhi was that the Chinese dragon had once again caught the Indian elephant tying its shoelaces.

In light of this longstanding rivalry, Sudan quickly became a decisive issue for the Indian government. No longer was Sudan seen as a risky investment. Rather, the eagerness of the Chinese and Malaysians to take on even more interests demonstrated to the Indians that Sudan was worth pursuing. To counter the opposition, New Delhi initiated a lobbying mission to persuade the Sudanese government to support OVL's entry.[21] Indian officials leapt at any opportunity to win over the Sudanese.

As it demonstrated during the effort to secure the Sakhalin deal in Russia, the Indians again chose to play diplomatic hardball. On his way to visit Indonesia in July 2002, Ali Osman Taha, Sudan's Vice-President, was transiting through Indira Gandhi International Airport in New Delhi.[22] Indian officials ushered the senior Sudanese leader quickly into the capital. During his six-hour stopover, Taha met Ram Naik and also had a *tête-à-tête* with Prime Minister Vajpayee.[23] Later that year, against Chinese and Malaysian wishes, the Sudanese sided with the Indians. Khartoum dispatched Foreign Minister Mustafa Osman Ismail to both Beijing and Kuala Lumpur to employ his charm and flair to persuade corporate executives and oil officials in those two Asian capitals to back down and yield to Sudan's political will. CNPC backed down outright; Petronas was offered the opportunity to acquire fuel retail assets from Mobil Oil Sudan if it also stood aside.[24] In March 2003, after months of delay, OVL's bid for the Talisman stake was finalised.

The real power behind giants

On the surface, OVL's arrival in Sudan was a rare example of India beating China at its own shrewd game of oil diplomacy in Africa. But India's entry into Sudan's oil industry was not simply determined by the Indian government's diplomatic push for OVL in an oil duel with the Chinese; the timely intervention of Indian diplomats to support OVL's investment in Sudan was only part of the picture. In the struggle between China and India over oil resources, the importance of Sudanese politics may become blurred. But African governments are far from bystanders in the competition between foreign governments and companies to capture oil on the continent. The ruling NCP was thinking pragmatically and was determined to diversify its external partners in order to avoid over-reliance on one country or company. In this case, the Sudanese government chose to balance its foreign partners in order to diversify its Asian political and economic friends and avoid placing all its eggs in one Chinese basket.

Khartoum favoured bringing in the Indians. It wanted to avoid another Talisman scenario and ruled out taking on another Western oil company. 'We preferred the Indian company because it is government-owned and pressures of non-government organisations on it are less than they are on private companies,' said Foreign Minister Ismail.[25] There was also growing concern about CNPC's dominance of the oil industry. The NCP still considered China its closest international ally, but was hesitant to provide CNPC with total control. If the Chinese oil company had split Talisman's share in the GNPOC with Petronas, it would have established majority control of Sudan's most important oil project. The Sudanese rejected the idea of any company owning more than 40 per cent in what was essentially the country's largest revenue producing asset.[26]

But there were limits to the importance of the Indian alternative to Sudan. In early 2004, stakes in the highly prospective Blocks 3 and 7 in southern Sudan were put up for sale. OVL, among other companies, was interested in adding these assets to its portfolio. The concessions were located in the Melut Basin covering over 72,000 square kilometres east of the White Nile in Upper Nile state. The Petrodar consortium that operated the concessions was led by CNPC. Petronas of Malaysia also held a large stake and Sudapet and two Middle Eastern firms, Al Thani and the Gulf Petroleum Corporation, held minor interests.

At the time, oil finds in the concessions were estimated to reach production levels of 200,000 bpd by 2005, with 1 billion barrels in reserves at Adar Yale, Agordeed and the giant Palogue oil field.[27] OVL entered talks with the Arab oil companies to purchase their combined stakes and secured acceptance from the Cabinet Committee on Economic Affairs in New Delhi to invest $125.4 million.[28] A 5 per cent share of the project alone was set to ensure 10,000 bpd for OVL.[29] However, in the week that it took the Indian Cabinet to ratify the cabinet committee's approval, the Chinese national oil company Sinopec made a higher bid and purchased Gulf Petroleum's stake.[30] The lucrative deal fell through completely for OVL.

The Indian media had a field day scolding the company and the government for their slow action. The Upper Nile oil concessions went on to produce roughly half of Sudan's 490,000 bpd in 2009. In contrast to the Talisman deal, the Sudanese government did not choose to impose its sovereign will over Chinese oil companies. Rather, Khartoum, with the Indians already in the fold, was continuing its diversification strategy by bringing in Sinopec. In the summer of 2004, Sudan continued to block CNPC from taking a major share in the Melut Basin project to develop infrastructure for Blocks 3 and 7. CNPC and Sinopec were in opposing bids for pipeline projects. The Chinese Ministry of Foreign Affairs urged the two oil giants to avoid directly competing in Sudan, and Sinopec proposed pulling out. But the Sudanese government, playing its sovereign card again, retorted that regardless of Sinopec's withdrawal CNPC would not win the bid.[31] Sinopec was part of the winning bid from a Malaysian-led international consortium.[32] After heavy lobbying by Petronas, Malaysian construction and engineering companies, including Peremba Construction, MMC, and Ranhill, were well represented in projects valued at $900 million.[33] Khartoum was balancing not only between countries, but also between companies. While OVL was not successful in obtaining all the investment it sought in Sudan, the company could now boast that it had beat its larger Chinese competition. In dramatic fashion, India was suddenly engaging in Sudan as never before.

In October 2003 India's President, A.P.J. Abdul Kalam, paid an official visit to Sudan; he was the first Indian president to step foot in the country in twenty-eight years. He met Sudan's President Omar al-Bashir and the Minister of Energy and Mining (MEM), Dr. Awad Al-Jaz, in Khartoum and signed a number of trade and investment agreements.[34] Kalam ostentatiously praised the two countries' 'centuries-old and time-tested relations'.[35] In a joint statement, the two sides asserted that India and Sudan were both 'multi-religious and multi-ethnic societies, committed to pluralism, harmonious co-existence, and the concept of unity in diversity'.[36]

But the sentiment rang hollow. Kalam was the embodiment of India's diverse society, a Muslim president in a country led by a sikh prime minister despite its Hindu majority. Despite its religious and cultural diversity, Sudan under the NIF, later known as the National Congress party (NCP), was living under *shari'ah* law, the media were heavily censored, and political oppression was rife. When the NIF seized power in 1989, a statue of Gandhi in Khartoum's twin town of Omdurman was beheaded—a sign of things to come for religious and political freedom under the new Islamist regime.[37]

Along with much of the rest of the world at the time, Kalam was either unaware, or chose not to mention, that the Sudanese government was laying waste to Sudan's western region of Darfur in a brutal counterinsurgency that would leave hundreds of thousands of largely Muslim civilians dead. The Indian president was preoccupied with other matters. Kalam was in Khartoum to help steer forward the booming economic relationship between India and Sudan developed by OVL's investments. In a joint statement, he underlined that Sudan's 'unity and territorial integrity' should be protected, echoing a similar Chinese foreign policy approach in Sudan.

India had long maintained cordial relations with Sudan. The two countries shared a common history as colonies of the British Empire. During the late colonial period, Indian political leaders would stop in Sudan on their way to Britain during the lead-up to its independence. Mahatma Gandhi visited Port Sudan in 1935, followed three years later by Nehru, accompanied by his daughter Indira, the future Indian prime minister. India's founding fathers influenced Sudan's own pursuit of independence: the Sudan Graduates' Congress, which led the Sudanese struggle for independence, modelled on the Indian National Congress.[38] Later, India provided Sukumar Sen as the chief election commissioner for Sudan's first multi-party election in 1953. In April 1955, India opened a Liaison Office in Khartoum before Sudan's official independence was declared in January 1956. By the late 1960s, the two countries had become close trading partners, particularly through Indian purchases of Sudanese raw cotton.[39] In the coming decades, both countries saw their relations as a model of South-South cooperation and supported the restructuring of the UN.

But OVL's investments in Sudan's oil industry in the early 2000s took Indian-Sudanese relations to a whole new level. Sudan's crude oil exports constituted the bulk of its commerce with India. From 2001 to 2011, trade between the two countries increased more than sevenfold to over $1.15 billion.[40] Sudan became one of the largest destinations for Indian foreign investment between 1995 and 2005, representing 11 per cent of total Indian foreign investment, behind only the US and Russia.[41] 'Sudan is our hope in Africa,' said Deepak Vohra, the Indian Ambassador in Khartoum.[42]

Indian diplomats undoubtedly made promises to the Sudanese during their push to help ensure that OVL would be able to purchase Talisman's stake in the GNPOC oil venture. In the coming years, the India EXIM Bank granted a total of $567 million in lines of credit to Sudan, almost exclusively involving Indian national-owned companies.[43] The largest, at $350 million, aided the Indian national power and energy company Bharat Heavy Electricals Ltd. (BHEL) to set up a power plant at Kosti in White Nile state in central Sudan. India also supported peace-building efforts in Sudan. In 2005, after the signing of the Comprehensive Peace Agreement between the Sudanese government and the SPLA, India committed almost 3,000 troops to the UN Mission in Sudan in Sudan.[44] It was not easy to enter Sudan. But thanks to the support of New Delhi, and with Sudanese political winds blowing in their favour, the Indian oilmen could now claim their prize.

The rewards of oil

It was an odd place for a celebration. North of the Bahr el Ghazal river in Sudan, in a region widely known for violent conflict, severe poverty and human suffering, a group of Indian oilmen were cutting a cake to the tunes of the Sudanese musical troupe Balimbo.[45] Employees of OVL were hoisting the Indian tricolour at GNPOC's base camp at Heglig to mark their arrival in Sudan's oil industry. OVL moved quickly to add other investments to its Sudan portfolio after winning the Talisman stake. In August 2003, the company won government approval from the Cabinet Committee on Economic Affairs to buy the stakes of the departing Austrian company OMV in Blocks 5A and 5B of southern Sudan for $115 million.[46] It went on to purchase OMV's concessional rights in each block. Within Sudan's massive swampland of the Sudd, where Chevron's oilmen once worked, Block 5A held oil reserves of almost 150 million barrels in early 2001. Block 5B, located further south, was largely unexplored; the hostilities of the civil war had made the concession a no-go area. But by 2003, the Sudanese government and the SPLA were making progress in peace talks; a ceasefire gave hope that exploration activities could begin in the near future.

OVL also made plans to build an oil pipeline in Sudan. In June 2004, the company agreed to construct a 741-kilometre oil pipeline from Sudan's Khartoum refinery to the export terminals of Port Sudan at a cost of almost $194 million. The pipeline was estimated to take sixteen months to complete, with the Sudanese government reimbursing the Indian company biannually for nine years.[47] OVL put forward $110 million for the project, leading a team of Indian national oil companies in order to comply with New Delhi's directive that it should not overburden itself in Sudan. Oil India was a minor investor and the Indian Oil Corporation was brought in to train Sudanese engineers to operate and maintain the pipeline.[48] This project was OVL's first major infrastructure venture abroad, but before the project got underway, the company received a fright when the required approval from the Cabinet Committee on Economic Affairs was delayed. A 2004 change of government from the BJP-led National Democratic Alliance to the Congress-led United Progressive Alliance put the approval on hold until the new Cabinet under Prime Minister Manmohan Singh could review the terms.[49] But it did not take long for the project to be accepted.

Regardless of which party was in power, thanks to the rising importance of energy security in India OVL was benefiting from its elevated status with political leaders in New Delhi. The previous government's demand that the company purchase political risk insurance for Sudan was shelved, as it was regarded as too costly.[50] But not all OVL's ambitions in Sudan found support back home. Shortly after the pipeline project was launched, the Sudanese government offered to award a contract to upgrade and revamp the Port Sudan refinery. Quick to announce the news, the Indian media reported that the deal was in place and OVL had beaten its Malaysian rival Petronas.[51] But the project never saw the light of day.[52] In early 2005 Indian and international banks, such as State Bank of India and BNP Paribas, were exploring the formation of a consortium to offer a commercial loan to OVL for the refinery. But the banks were unwilling to accept the $600 million non-recourse terms the company was seeking, feeling the investment was far from sound owing to Sudan's political instability.[53] Without the bank loan, and already stretching the limit of its investment in Sudan dictated by the Indian government, OVL could not move forward with the refinery project. Shortly afterwards Petronas sought to take up the project, but finally shelved it in 2008, after soaring world steel prices upped the necessary investment from $1 billion to $5 billion.[54]

In 2003, Sudan became OVL's largest revenue earner. This was not a difficult feat. The company had no other oil producing assets at the time;

Sudan was where it earned its first oil revenue. Thanks to rising production levels, the hundreds of millions of dollars that Indian politicians worried about losing by investing in a war-torn country were rapidly recovered. 'Our investment will pay off in under three years,' said Naik in January 2004.[55] But with rising international oil prices the investment was recovered nearly a year ahead of schedule.[56]

OVL became India's second largest oil producer behind its corporate parent ONGC. From 2003 to 2010, Sudanese crude made up an average of over 46 per cent of the company's annual production.[57] Even after production in its Russian oil and gas field at Sakhalin I came onstream in 2006, Sudan was still OVL's highest oil producing venture. The company went from reporting Rs 4,284 million total profit in 2003 to Rs 26,905 million by 2010 (roughly from $79 million to $496 million), a more than sixfold increase.[58] 'We are looking very keenly at many countries in Africa and hope to repeat the Sudan experience in other parts of the region,' said V. Ravindranath, an OVL executive director at the 2005 India-Africa Project Partnership conclave.[59]

Sudan was not only a crucial investment for OVL, but also the entire ONGC Group. In 2002, under Chairman Raha, ONGC expanded the scope of its activities by becoming the first company in the Indian oil industry to operate both upstream and downstream activities by purchasing majority ownership in Mangalore Refinery and Petrochemicals Ltd.[60] The MPNG was not entirely on the same page with the company's expansion into refining, reminding ONGC to stick to its core competencies and not 'fritter away national resources in chasing chimera'.[61] But ONGC wanted to invest further in its downstream activities to offset financial losses brought on by the stagnation of domestic oil fields.[62] Supporting the ambitions of its international arm OVL served the same purpose. From the African to the Indian coast, OVL's investment in Sudan allowed ONGC to internationalise its integrated operations.[63] 'ONGC Videsh is the growth vehicle of the group,' said the ONGC Chairman R.S. Sharma in 2006.[64] The subsidiary had borrowed over Rs 47,679 million ($900 million) from ONGC in 2002, primarily to purchase Talisman's stake. But after four years of profiting in Sudan, it paid off the loans.

OVL's confidence appeared to be growing by the day; it now looked to make a big splash. In 2009, it purchased the British oil company Imperial Energy for $1.9 billion. This move to capture Russian and Kazakh oil and gas assets owned by Imperial demonstrated the durability of OVL's rise as a player in the international oil industry. Its success in Sudan opened the door for Indian government approval for larger investments overseas.[65] OVL delisted Imperial from the FTSE 250 London stock exchange and brought it under its own national ownership model.[66] The ONGC Chairman Sharma was quick to praise New Delhi for the Imperial deal, saying that the company owed the acquisition, along with its massive international expansion, to government support.[67]

Since OVL was still relying on its corporate parent for financing its overseas deals, ONGC provided the subsidiary with the equivalent of $1 billion for the Imperial deal. But ONGC was now demanding 6 per cent interest in contrast to the interest-free and other easy financing it had provided to enter Sudan. OVL no longer needed the padded crutch of interest-free loans from ONGC, it had finally stepped out of its corporate parent's shadow.

By 2010, OVL was producing oil and gas in Sudan, Russia, Syria, Brazil, Colombia, Venezuela and Vietnam, along with a long string of other exploration and development activities stretching around the world. With a production total of 189,575 barrels of oil and oil-gas equivalent per day, OVL was approaching the halfway mark towards its target of producing 400,000 bpd by 2020.[68] Along with Raha at ONGC, OVL's Chandra had taken advantage of the rising political significance of energy security to empower OVL to become a global player.

Company before country

In 2004, Atul Chandra left OVL. Unlike Zhou Yongkang at CNPC, he chose not to enter political life and joined the private sector company Reliance Industries. But Chandra certainly left his mark on OVL. From the beginning to the end of the decade, the company went from one gas project in Vietnam to thirty-three projects in fourteen countries. 'It feels good to see where OVL stands today in terms of size, profile, and image,' Chandra said.[69] The distinction between oilmen and politicians was clear in India compared to China, but OVL still had an influence on Indian foreign policy by pulling the country deeper into relations with Sudan than it would otherwise have gone. As was the case with CNPC, OVL's overseas oil assets also did little to help India's energy security.

When OVL first entered Sudan in March 2003, the Indian oil ministry advised the company not to enter into any long-term supply contracts in order to ensure that supplies to India would have priority.[70] New

Delhi saw trouble brewing in the Middle East again (the US invasion of Iraq was gathering steam at the time) and wanted to ensure that it was ready for another oil shock.[71] But Sudanese oil fields do not offer copious amounts of crude to India. In a crisis, if the Indian government did force the company to ship all its Sudanese crude home, it would not make much difference. At best, the oil available to OVL from its stakes could only marginally cover India's staggering oil import needs, offering around 3 per cent of the total.[72] In fact, if it was sent to India, the company's entire overseas production would amount to only 7.5 per cent of total Indian oil imports.[73]

But OVL was not bringing home the majority of its Sudanese crude. While it had shipped its first batch of Nile crude from Sudan to its refinery in Mangalore in early 2003, in a matter of months the company opted to sell most of the oil on international markets instead.[74] The following year, only 6,627 bpd of its roughly 74,000 bpd allowance went back to India.[75] Despite OVL's sizeable investment, Sudan was far down the list of oil importers to India, providing only 0.34 per cent of India's total imports in 2004.[76] In the years to come, the high price of oil continued to push OVL to sell Sudanese oil on the international market, rather than ship it home.[77]

It is difficult to assess how OVL's oil production in Sudan and other overseas ventures could measurably improve India's energy security. Even if OVL brought its overseas oil home, the price of that oil, as a global commodity, would be governed by international market prices. OVL would still sell its oil to other Indian refiners at international prices, saving India next to nothing, but allowing the ONGC group to bypass trader's premiums charged on the open market if OVL sold the oil to ONGC's Mangalore refinery. At best, the profits generated from Sudan helped to maintain the financial health of OVL and ONGC, and thus helped the Indian government to use the parent company as a funding source for its subsidy programme to provide cheap fuel for the population. But if there was a clear beneficiary from OVL's operations in Sudan, it was the company itself, not India.

The 2006 Integrated Energy Policy devised by India's Planning Commission actually cautioned against making a link between the overseas investments of Indian national oil companies and energy security. 'Obtaining equity oil abroad does not particularly increase oil security beyond diversification, if any, of supply sources,' the report argued. 'Thus, we should explore and seize economically attractive opportunities for equity energy abroad. However, such investments must factor in all country, political and logistic risks.'[78] Sudan was certainly a viable investment for OVL. But even though the Planning Commission regarded overseas investments as providing only marginal benefits for energy security, many of India's political leaders portrayed overseas deals by Indian national oil companies as a boon for energy security.

In 2004, Ram Naik, the BJP oil minister, said that 'for a country 70 per cent import dependent to meet its oil needs, acquiring oil assets abroad was the answer for attaining energy security'.[79] Six years later, the Congress oil minister, Murli Deora, stayed on message, declaring that the 'acquisition of exploration and oil producing properties overseas is a key strategy to enhance oil reserves in the country and reduce our dependence on the world's oil reserves'.[80] Even investments as far away as Venezuela were described by Deora as strategic moves for India's energy security.[81] The MEA established an Energy Security Unit in September 2007, upgraded to a division in 2009, which sees as one of its core objectives 'to support efforts of our corporate entities, in acquiring energy assets overseas, and in building strategic partnerships with foreign companies'.[82] Bureaucrats in the Energy Security Division were prepared to intervene and support Indian national oil companies abroad by organising 'sweeteners' of aid and loan packages to oil producers to win deals. The posting of an ONGC representative in the Division for help on technical issues established a direct link between the government and the national oil corporation.[83] The MPNG also created an International Cooperation Division for similar purposes and sought to enhance India's energy security by supporting Indian national oil companies overseas.[84]

While there has been bureaucratic infighting between the two ministries,[85] over the past decade, regardless of the political stripe of the ruling government, overseas oil investments by OVL and other Indian national oil companies were promoted as contributing to energy security. In a similar vein, the Indian media often portray OVL's international investments and successful competition with Chinese companies as enhancing India's energy security.[86] The political importance of meeting India's energy security challenge was a symbolic boon for OVL. Certainly, it was in the interest of the company to be seen as a major contributor to India's energy security.

Corporate executives at ONGC and OVL are quick to promote the idea that overseas investments are a path to energy security for India. In

2004, ONGC Chairman Raha said the Indian government was becoming aware of the energy problem at 'every level', particularly in the MEA, where 'the sense of urgency of the strategic priority of energy security had grown significantly'.[87] At times, ONGC used the drive to acquire oil abroad as a shield to deflect its failings at home.

In 2006, when facing down pressure from the oil ministry over poor domestic production and reserve levels, Raha guardedly placed the onus on India's lack of energy potential. He said the belief that the country had the resources to be energy independent or even significantly reduce its imports was a 'bogey', and argued that India's energy security lay in acquiring equity oil opportunities abroad.[88] OVL argued in its annual report that year that the geopolitical environment of the international oil industry demanded that it coordinate efforts with New Delhi.[89] 'Entrusted with the responsibility to ensure energy security for India, ONGC Videsh Limited (OVL) continues its journey across seas exploring, developing and acquiring new oil and natural gas for the country,' read the first page of its 2011 Annual Report.[90] Yet in reality, OVL was primarily fulfilling its own corporate objectives abroad with only marginal benefits for India's energy security.

OVL's presence, and its success in Sudan, demonstrated the lengths to which the Indian government was willing to go to support its overseas investments under the mantra of energy security. OVL and CNPC competed for Talisman's abandoned oil stake, but after the Sudanese government's intervention in favour of the Indians, they were now partners in Sudan's largest joint venture oil company. Chinese and Indian oilmen were now in the same boat in Sudan, and would sink or swim together.

PART IV

DARFUR

8

THE RISE AND FALL OF AN
ACTIVIST CAMPAIGN

February 2007: The afternoon sun was out in full force in Khartoum. Apart from the occasional battered yellow taxi kicking up dust and dirt, there was little traffic on the baked streets of the city centre. Sudanese men sat on rickety plastic chairs in the shade of aged shopping arcades waiting for the sun to begin its descent. All in all, it appeared to be a typical day in Sudan's capital.

It was only the sight of a black military helicopter sweeping by overhead that was out of the ordinary. Helicopter gunships were a particularly menacing part of the attacks by the Sudan Armed Forces and pro-government militias against southern Sudanese communities during the second civil war. Years later, the military helicopter over Khartoum was a sad demonstration that President Bashir and his ruling National Congress party were willing to protect their foreign visitors, but employed the same means to terrorise their own people. Its presence in the clear blue sky marked a special occasion: Hu Jintao was in town.

The Chinese president was in Khartoum for good reason. China's trade with and investment in Africa were booming. CNPC was Sudan's largest investor and Chinese refineries bought the majority of Sudanese crude. Sudan, the recipient of multi-billion dollar investments from China, was the centrepiece in the Asian oil giant's African engagement. Hu's arrival in Khartoum marked the culmination of a long line of Chinese political leaders visiting Sudan to forge closer ties with the Sudanese and commemorate the accomplishments of Chinese oilmen. But there were also more complicated reasons for his visit. President Hu may have been in Khartoum to praise the accomplishments of Chinese oil-men, but he was also there to try to clean up the political mess CNPC had created for China.

In 2003, longstanding resentment in the western region of Darfur against neglect and exploitation by the central government in Khartoum led to a new civil war in Sudan.[1] Over the coming years, a shifting *mélange* of Darfuri rebel groups, including the Sudan Liberation Army and the Justice and Equality Movement (JEM), fought against the Sudanese army and pro-government militias. The Sudanese government in Khartoum exercised the same counterinsurgency tactics as it had used in southern Sudan during the second north-south civil war, driving civilian popula-tions from their land to drain the sea of rebel support. Consequently, an estimated 300,000 had died since the start of the Darfur conflict, mostly from hunger and disease brought on by the fighting, and millions more were displaced in refugee camps along the border with Chad.[2] Again, oil acted as a means for the Sudanese government to wage war.

The outbreak of the Darfur civil war sparked an unprecedented surge of activism in the US to put an end to the violence. The American gov-ernment and activist groups accused the Sudanese government of wag-ing genocide against the Fur, Zaghawa and Masalit civilian populations of Darfur. In the summer of 2004, the Save Darfur Coalition brought much of this activism under a common banner. Acting as a financial weapon of coercion for Save Darfur was the university student-led Sudan Divestment Task Force. It called on investors to sell their shares in CNPC, Petronas, OVL and other foreign companies operating in Sudan. The goal was to use divestment as an economic lever to change the polit-ical behaviour of Khartoum and help resolve the civil war in Darfur.[3] While the divestment campaign produced popular support in the US, it failed to have any noteworthy impact in Sudan. Even after Save Darfur targeted the 2008 Beijing Summer Olympics, challenging the Chinese government's longstanding foreign policy of non-interference in the domestic affairs of other countries, CNPC's activities continued unabated. Although US activists were able, through the Beijing Games, to move China's behaviour away from its position of non-interference,[4] this epi-sode also showed that the countervailing power of Chinese national oil companies would give the oilmen higher priority in Beijing's foreign policy. However, in the end, the efforts of divestment activists inflicted collateral damage on CNPC by helping to build political opposition to Chinese national oil companies investing in the US. This frustrated the efforts of Chinese national oil companies in moving forward with their international expansion.

Sudan seen from California

The Sudan Divestment Task Force was born in late 2005 with the aim of coordinating divestment activities in the US and abroad. The following year, it joined another student-led advocacy organisation, the Genocide Intervention Network, as part of the wider Save Darfur Coalition. While Amnesty International, Human Rights Watch, and other human rights groups spearheaded initial advocacy efforts, Save Darfur was instrumental in widely broadcasting the issue throughout the US. In contrast to past US-based human rights movements targeting Sudan, Save Darfur's speed of formation and its size were impressive.

Save Darfur would amass over one million activists from 180 faith-based, advocacy and humanitarian organisations, with conservative and evangelical Christian and Jewish grassroots groups representing the cornerstone of the coalition.[5] Its immense size and its ability to develop existing channels in the US Congress from its inception produced significant support in Congress in a relatively short period of time. The campaign also conjured up the ghosts of the failure of the US to respond to the Rwanda genocide in 1994, as a powerful rallying point. Propelled by the growth of Save Darfur, the emergence of the divestment campaign provided new weapons of coercion against the Sudanese government.[6] The Task Force acted as the main organisational thrust for divestment.

What was at first a collection of unconnected divestment campaigns on university campuses in the US started to take steps to become a nationwide movement in Venice Beach, California. Adam Sterling, a student of the University of California, Los Angeles, first became interested in Darfur in 2005 and began handing out flyers to build awareness along the city's ocean-side promenade. 'We felt like we really wanted to make an impact on the ground, beyond just kind of telling others that they should do things,' he said. 'We wanted to do something ourselves.'[7]

The following year, Sterling co-founded the UC Sudan Divestment Task Force with Jason Miller, a fellow student; the two led an initiative calling on the endowment fund of the university to divest its tens of millions of dollar investment in energy, telecommunications and oil companies operating in Sudan.[8] 'We are witnessing a genocide that's ongoing and we have the power to stop it and economic pressure has been the most effective tool …' said Sterling to university regents in March 2006.[9]

Sterling and Miller did not start the Sudan divestment movement. During the autumn of 2004, students at Harvard University forced their university endowment to sell Sudan-related investments.[10] But after Harvard and a few other universities dropped their Sudan-related stock, there was little immediate growth in divestment. It was not until Sterling and Miller gave the movement a common voice in California that divestment really took off.

By April 2006 the divestment campaign was gaining traction, with a growing number of universities, cities and state pension funds beginning to apply a targeted approach in their investment funds. 'It can't just be the sort of piecemeal one-or-two companies symbolic approach,' said 19-year-old Daniel Millensen, a Task Force executive director and freshman at Brandeis University in Massachusetts. He admitted there was still little impact from the divestment campaign to date, but said he hoped to see the movement induce a drop in the share prices of targeted companies, which in turn would propel them to question their relationship with the Sudanese government.[11]

Others were more optimistic. 'This is an explosive campaign, and I think we'll see some major announcements in the coming months,' said Eric Reeves, a long-time Sudan activist.[12] Reeves was participating in his second divestment stint, after playing a leading role in forcing Talisman out of Sudan in 2003, a result that changed very little in Sudan when OVL replaced the Canadian company.

The Task Force received a jump start in the autumn of 2006 when the Governor of California, Arnold Schwarzenegger, flanked by the celebrity activists George Clooney and Don Cheadle, adopted a targeted divestment model for investment portfolios run by the state's public employee and teacher retirement pension systems. Standing front and centre at the ceremony announcing the initiative in Sacramento, Adam Sterling issued a warning to the Sudanese government with the Hollywood stars looking on: 'To the government of Sudan. We're coming! Your genocide will not occur on our watch, and it will not occur on our dime!'[13] He was confident about where the divestment campaign was headed: 'At this point, we are approaching that critical mass where it is past symbolism.'[14] The following year, the Task Force received critical and timely support from Calvert Investments and the divestment campaign was poised to spread rapidly across the US.

Outside Washington, in the small but affluent town of Bethesda, Bennett Freeman has a rather interesting job at Calvert Investments. As a Senior Vice-President for Sustainability Research and Policy, one of Freeman's many responsibilities is to advocate divestment, the selling of publicly traded shares in companies that fail to meet international standards on environmental, social, and governance issues. Calvert specialises in providing socially responsible investments for its clients; it was the first US-based mutual fund to rule out investing in companies active in apartheid South Africa in 1982. Freeman had participated in the South Africa movement as a student at the University of California, Berkeley in the late 1970s.[15] Two decades later, he was known as 'the lion of the field' of socially responsible investment and led Calvert's efforts to support a new generation of university student activists calling for divestment from Sudan.[16] In the years following the outbreak of the Darfur civil war, Freeman identified CNPC, Petronas, and OVL operations in Sudan as his main targets for divestment.

Beginning in 2007, Calvert began to provide analytical and advocacy support to the Task Force, which was calling for the Asian national oil companies and other foreign companies to put pressure on the Sudanese government to end its abuses against civilians in Darfur and help resolve the civil war. The divestment campaign had already built up plenty of steam in the US; Calvert's assistance promised only to strengthen the campaign's hand.

The battle on the Home Front

Divestment activists saw US government action on Sudan as only going so far. Most US companies were already restricted from operating in Sudan on account of longstanding unilateral sanctions. But the activists saw a further opportunity to make an impact on Sudan through private sanctioning. The Task Force focused on foreign companies raising capital from US and international financial markets whose activities were closely linked to the Sudanese government. 'The goal is to put economic pressure on Khartoum to stop the killings in Darfur,' said Sterling.[17] The

Task Force aimed to promote its targeted model among diverse divestment policies across the US. While universities often chose to divest from just a select few companies in Sudan's oil industry, individual states often divested from all non-humanitarian ties.

The divestment campaign activists recognised that a country-wide blanket divestment could potentially lead to more hardship for Sudan's civilian population by undercutting beneficial foreign investment in agriculture, consumer goods, and education. Responding to this concern, the Task Force called for targeted divestment based on a ranking of companies that provided substantial revenue to the Sudanese government, produced little benefit to disadvantaged populations, and failed to lobby Khartoum to alter its destructive practices in Darfur.[18] As a result, the list included in large part companies from the oil, mining, power and, for more direct reasons, military sectors.

As in the US television show *America's Most Wanted*, the Asian national oil companies occupied the position of 'highest offenders'. CNPC was at the top of the list and Petronas and OVL filled the top three positions, followed by other Asian, Middle Eastern, and European companies. The Asian national oil companies were the right targets; they held stakes in Sudan's various oil consortiums amounting to 90 per cent of total oil production, with CNPC at 46 per cent, Petronas at 34 per cent, and OVL at 10 per cent in 2009.[19] The campaign honed in on CNPC, which it saw in particular as the linchpin holding together the Chinese government's economic and diplomatic support that made it possible to continue Khartoum's genocide in Darfur.[20] The aim was to push the Asian and other foreign companies to exit Sudan or significantly alter their behaviour by implementing social projects and placing pressure on Khartoum to change its political stance on Darfur.[21] More than a decade of US sanctions against Sudan helped to ensure there would be little opposition at home, as there were no US companies on the radar.

But activists shrewdly tried to dampen the wider financial concerns attached to divestment. 'They wanted to work with us. They were patient,' said Craig Carnaroli, Executive Vice-President of the University of Pennsylvania. 'I remember in my day, students threw their buttons at the trustees. ... This group, they came to meet with me in ties.'[22] Sterling noted that the Task Force had learned to craft its message over time, appealing to financial sense rather than just moral concerns.[23] The meticulous attention that it paid to designing and promoting its targeted divestment model would be tremendously successful in garnering support in the US.

Five years after the beginning of the divestment movement at Harvard, twenty-seven states, sixty-one universities and twenty-three cities in the US imposed restrictions on their investments linked to Sudan.[24] 'The burgeoning Sudan divestment movement has already facilitated a response from companies operating in Sudan, institutional investors and mutual fund managers,' said Sterling in the summer of 2007.[25]

But not everyone was eager to rally around the divestment flag. Despite the efforts of divestment activists to sway large US and international private investors and financial institutions, they continued to insist that investment decisions be made on financial and legal merits alone. Activists did succeed in putting the issue on the agenda at annual shareholder and board meetings; some decided to remove the targeted companies from their portfolios. But the majority of financial institutions rejected the idea of divestment.[26]

In late 2007, the Swiss firm UBS was pushed by activists with the symbolic support of Romeo Dallaire, the Canadian general who had been UN commander in Rwanda, to refuse to 'underwrite genocide' by aiding the bid of PetroChina on the Shanghai Stock Exchange.[27] But UBS went ahead with the deal; with a market capitalisation to the tune of almost $1 trillion, PetroChina was worth more than Exxon Mobil and General Electric put together at the time.[28] Activists could not put a dent in the value of PetroChina shares on the NYSE as their predecessors had done with Talisman years earlier.

Another confrontation between divestment activists and US investors involved Warren Buffett, the legendary American finance guru. His holding company Berkshire Hathaway invested heavily in PetroChina in 2002 and 2003. Later, when the divestment movement gained steam, Buffett openly disagreed with the campaigners on the use of divestment as a political instrument.[29] Nonetheless, Berkshire gradually began to unload all its PetroChina stock by October 2007.[30]

While the divestment campaign expected that PetroChina's share price would suffer greatly if Berkshire and other major investors sold out,[31] this did not occur. The value of PetroChina stock had increased sevenfold since Berkshire's original purchase, resulting in a hefty $3.52 billion profit.[32] Buffett said that he sold the shares when he concluded that PetroChina was at a market value comparable to oil majors; he saw the sale as a contribution to the US government rather than to the Sudan divestment campaign. 'We paid the IRS tax of $1.2 billion on our PetroChina gain. This sum paid all the costs of the US government—defense, social security, you name it—for about four hours,' he said.[33] American financial investors were not the only ones wary of the results of divestment from Sudan.

The divestment campaign was able to win US federal action less than three years after the first universities started to delink their investments from Chinese and other foreign companies in Sudan. On 31 December 2007 President George W. Bush signed the Sudan Accountability and Divestment Act into law. The act allowed US state and local governments, as well as asset managers, to divest under the legal protection of the federal government.[34] It also prohibited federal and state contracts with those foreign companies active in Sudan's oil, mining, power and military sectors.

But President Bush did not immediately support passing the divestment law. There was a long list of countries around the world with poor human rights records, including US allies, and the Bush administration worried that the act might become a precedent for similar measures in the future and upset wider US diplomatic and trade relations. In the run-up to the signing of the Divestment Act, some were concerned that Bush might veto it; after all, because of broader US interests, the 2002 Sudan Peace Act did not include capital market restrictions on foreign companies in Sudan's oil sector. When Bush signed the divestment legislation, he included a caveat: he would choose to intervene if he felt divestment activity was not congruent with US foreign policy.[35] The outcome was no small victory for the activists: they had brought about change at the very top of the US political establishment. But the new divestment law was very limited: it merely facilitated divestment; it did not impose it on local, state or private fund managers.

While activists did not believe that divestment alone would end the conflict in Darfur, they certainly saw it as an important part of the wider advocacy and diplomatic effort. 'Targeted divestment is a well-crafted, well-timed tool that combines economic and political pressure,' said Freeman.[36] When the Sudanese government published a six-page promotional ad in the *New York Times* to promote investment in Sudan, the activists saw this as proof of the impact of divestment. 'These and similar activities indicate the Sudanese government is taking the growing pressure for divestment seriously,' Freeman testified at a US Senate committee hearing in October 2007. But as the activists enjoyed the heady feeling of the success of their efforts in the US, it became clear that they had neglected to consider how the model would affect Sudan. Over the years of the divestment campaign's remarkable growth in the US, Sudan's oil boom was in full swing.

Missing the target

Longstanding US sanctions and the divestment campaign did deflate foreign investment in Sudan, but not to their desired effects. Financial transaction restrictions using US dollars made business harder to conduct and the reputational risk of involvement in Sudan was a particular concern for Western companies.[37] A larger influx of Western technology would have also helped Sudan avoid some of the technical difficulties that were threatening long-term oil production and exploration.[38] But there were still plenty of investors willing to come to Sudan. And thanks to diminished competition from the US and Europe, the risks of entering Sudan also produced higher rewards for those companies willing to take the plunge. The oil boom could have been larger and longer lasting if not for US sanctions and divestment, but the political power of the Khartoum government was nonetheless solidified by the strong economic growth from oil production. Sudan did not bend to the demands of American activists.

The pledge of the Task Force to leverage foreign companies to alter the Sudanese government's behaviour in Darfur went unfulfilled. As the divestment campaign grew, Sudan's economy and its oil industry moved forward.[39] Oil development spurred an average economic growth rate of close to 8 per cent in Sudan between 2004 and 2008, leading to a noticeable expansion of the construction and service sectors in Khartoum and the surrounding Nile valley region.[40] During this period, the Sudanese government earned a record level of revenue; annual oil windfalls from exports and sales to local refineries were on average over $4 billion.[41] Crude oil made up around 90 per cent of Sudan's total exports by value. China was Sudan's top trade partner, purchasing over 80 per cent of Sudanese crude, with Japan the second largest buyer.[42]

The divestment campaign had no discernible influence on Asian national oil companies. In May 2008, a study conducted by the Task Force demonstrated that companies investing in Sudan were underperforming their peer group average in share price on international financial markets.[43] But this disregarded the fact that the main targets, CNPC and the other Asian national oil companies, were generally not susceptible to divestment pressures because they were state-owned and had only small capital positions on international financial markets.[44] They simply could not be influenced in the same manner as Western companies, which are typically prone to divestment pressures through their capital positions and consumer reputations in home markets. The fact that Asian oil companies are relatively immune to divestment pressures is reminiscent of a Sudanese proverb invoked by the Sudanese academic Ali Abdalla Ali to describe the response of China to US pressure on Darfur: 'the dog barks, but the camel goes on its way'.[45]

From its conception, the Task Force had gradually put more focus on promoting corporate responsibility in Sudan and began to view divestment as a tool of last resort to help open doors to companies and engage with them. The original approach of the divestment campaign was now seen as 'too adversarial', said one divestment analyst, after greater potential for responses from companies and long term success was seen through constructive engagement. The activists' approach morphed from idealistic to pragmatic.[46] But even as advocates of corporate responsibility, the activists only achieved ambiguous results in Sudan.

During the Task Force campaign, activists offered targeted corporations the opportunity to avoid divestment calls in return for 'engagement' with the Khartoum government and 'substantial' humanitarian action in Sudan.[47] By the end of 2008, the campaign announced that thirteen foreign companies had ended their operations altogether or significantly altered their behaviour, claiming these results had had an impact on the ground by promoting ethical investment in Sudan.[48] Out of the dozens of foreign companies targeted by the divestment campaign, those that left Sudan or changed their behaviour according to the wishes of activists were mostly European.

Growing divestment pressure was certainly part of the reason why Rolls Royce, responsible for power generation along much of Sudan's oil pipelines, withdrew progressively from Sudan, citing political and humanitarian concerns.[49] However, despite Rolls Royce's decision to withdraw, its main client, the oil operating company GNPOC, continued to have access to the supplies needed to maintain the engines, and it could simply engage another supplier from a variety of Asian and Western possibilities.[50]

Even companies that engaged with the activists directly produced few results that would satisfy the most urgent human rights concerns in Sudan. In 2007 Schlumberger, the French-American oil service provider, established an agreement with the divestment campaign to be taken off its list of companies warranting divestment if it expanded its community development projects in southern Sudan.[51] However, despite the benefits of Schlumberger's education and water programmes to local communities, the agreement with the divestment campaign also allowed the company to continue to offer its experience and expertise to Sudan's oil industry. In the end, the Sudanese government maintained its relationship with the world's leading oil service company, and Schlumberger continued to operate and make a profit.

There were no easy answers for the divestment activists. Development benefits for local communities from enhanced corporate responsibility in the oil industry are anything but clear-cut; the advantages of corporate responsibility programmes are far more evident in improving the company's reputation back in home markets.[52] The divestment campaign's evolution into a socially responsible investment service was not necessarily a move in the right direction, but was a step towards adopting a 'better-than-nothing' approach after the campaign had failed to find leverage with its Asian targets. In fact, the Asian national oil companies were also adjusting to corporate responsibility standards in the international oil industry, but not in the way the divestment campaign had originally sought. Asian national oil companies still lag behind their Western counterparts on the learning curve of corporate responsibility, but CNPC, Petronas, and OVL had begun to make social investments in Sudan before the divestment campaign was underway.

Qin Anjiang, CNPC's chief representative in Sudan, exulted in the company's job creation, training, and community development at a 2006 trade and investment conference in Khartoum.[53] A few years later, CNPC Vice-President Wang Dongjin said that the company had provided a total of $50 million in social and economic development since its arrival in Sudan in 1995. This consisted mainly of construction of roads and bridges, and drilling of water wells, along with ten hospitals and twenty-five schools, training of Sudanese oil professionals, and the provision of scholarships in Chinese universities and educational materials for Sudanese students.[54] One CNPC manager in Beijing argued that the company was adjusting its initial 'Chinese way of doing business' to international standards in corporate responsibility as it expanded abroad.[55]

Malaysia's Petronas also adapted corporate responsibility to its overseas investments. Focusing on education and capacity building, the company has been engaged in community development programmes supporting permanent and mobile libraries to enhance primary and vocational education in Sudan since 1998.[56] Petronas was also a supplier of diesel and aviation fuel to the UN-African Union Mission in Darfur.[57] The contrast in Petronas' business in Sudan is ironic: through its financial relationship with the Khartoum government, Petronas was generating oil revenues for Sudan that went towards the purchase of Antonov bombers and helicopter gunships that brought violence to Darfur on the one hand, but was fuelling the planes and vehicles of the Darfur peace mission on the other.

OVL also engaged in corporate responsibility in Sudan. Around its concession areas in the south, the Indian oil company provided medical and ambulance services as well as school bags and educational kits. In the Khartoum area, it supplied 1,500 artificial limbs to amputees, donated cancer treatment equipment, set up a clinic for the hearing impaired, provided assistance to farmers, and built football facilities.[58] 'Wherever we operate, ONGC Videsh (OVL) strives to make a positive and meaningful contribution to community activities, and learn from the cultures in which we work,' said R.S. Sharma, ONGC Chairman.[59]

On the whole, the corporate responsibility efforts of the Asian national oil companies were limited in scale and almost irrelevant when compared to the negative consequences oil development had on the lives of the people in southern Sudan. There was certainly room for improvement and the divestment activists' goal of promoting better corporate responsibility practices in Sudan was a credible one. But despite their efforts to use the Asian national oil companies as levers to pressure the Sudanese government to resolve the Darfur civil war, their campaign missed its target.

The development of the Sudan Divestment Task Force into the Conflict Risk Network (CRN) in early 2009 signalled the campaign's inability to use divestment as a tool of coercion against Asian national oil companies and the Sudanese government. Adam Sterling left to attend law school in the autumn of 2009, with plans to pursue a political career.[60] Much of the campaign's funding had dried up; the new organisation operated with a skeleton staff. Although constituting only a small part of its operations, CRN began working beyond Sudan on other conflict-affected countries, such as Myanmar and Iraq.

Long-time human rights activists working on Sudan were critical of the lack of connection between external campaigns—the divestment campaign and Save Darfur—and local civil society in Sudan.[61] They implored activists to work 'with' the Sudanese people, not 'for' them.[62] Divestment activists failed to engage and lend their expertise and resources to those few local groups in Sudan seeking to change the social and environment conditions in which the oil industry operated. As a result, some in Sudan saw the campaign as a 'Western conscience-clearing exercise', rather than part of the solution to long-standing conflict and poverty.

Some divestment activists were also disappointed. One leading student activist in London, who originally joined the campaign after visiting Rwanda and seeing first hand the result of genocide, was disillusioned by the Sudan divestment experience: 'We didn't plan for such long-term engagement. We thought it would all be over in a couple years.'[63] He felt the Rwanda narrative was a tremendous rallying point in drawing support, but it also led activists to build a limited understanding of Sudan and to paint the Darfur conflict in the most simplistic of terms.

Back at Harvard, where the first divestment campaign was launched, there was a similar feeling of disenchantment. After being inspired by leading Darfur activists—Samantha Power, John Prendergast and Eric Reeves—to do something to stop the killings in Darfur, student activists soon realised that divestment was largely a symbolic act; while it built some awareness of Darfur, it had limited on-the-ground impact. 'We needed to generate front page news,' said one former Harvard activist. But getting Americans to pay attention to Darfur meant getting the American media to pay attention, and for that to happen the activists needed to have events in the US for the media to cover.[64] Publicity was certainly needed to build awareness and support, but this involved striving to get 'A1 stories' on the cover of national newspapers.

Other activists saw a silver lining in the Sudan issue. Bennett Freeman spoke more candidly than most activists about the successes and failures of the divestment campaign. By mid-2008, he admitted there were few hard economic results from divestment to show in Sudan. But Freeman was certain that the impact of the Sudan divestment campaign had not yet shown its true force. He felt that the campaign offered a unique opportunity to engage Chinese companies and the Chinese government on international human rights standards.[65] In his opinion, the most serious achievement of the Sudan activists was putting the human rights spotlight on Chinese national oil companies and their actions abroad.[66] Having had little luck in engaging the Asian national oil companies in the past, divestment activists under the newly-formed CRN, with its corporate responsibility-orientated approach, began to make inroads in establishing contact with CNPC and OVL in 2011.[67] The subsequent response of Asian national oil companies to the invoking of corporate responsibility demonstrated that Freeman may have been right, but it mattered little to Sudan and the ongoing Darfur civil war. Instead, the tendency for divestment activists to fail to connect their efforts with actual results in Sudan would be repeated, when the Save Darfur campaign sought to shame the Chinese government in the run-up to the 2008 Beijing Summer Olympic Games.

Challenging China

The Sudan divestment campaign and the wider Save Darfur movement were not short on star power. George Clooney and Don Cheadle were long-time supporters. In the spring of 2007, Mia Farrow, another celebrity activist, began to focus intensely on the role of China in Sudan. Farrow and other activists branded the upcoming 2008 Beijing Olympic Games as the 'Genocide Olympics', as part of their growing campaign to shame the Chinese government into pressuring Khartoum to end its abuses against civilians in Darfur.[68] Activists saw CNPC's oil investments, Chinese arms sales to Sudan, and China's powerful position on the UN Security Council as serving to delay and dilute potentially strong multilateral sanctions against Khartoum's ability to wage war in Darfur.

For years, China had stood behind its longstanding foreign policy of non-interference in the domestic affairs of other countries. 'Business is business,' said Deputy Foreign Minister Zhou Wenzhong. 'We try to separate business from politics.'[69] The Sudanese did not shy away from praising China's support. 'The Chinese are very nice,' said the oil minister Awad Al-Jaz. 'They don't have anything to do with any politics or problems. Things move smoothly, successfully. They are very hard workers looking for business, not politics.'[70] But the Beijing Olympics offered a unique moment for US activists to exert power over China and its close ties to Sudan.

The Beijing Olympic Games appeared to be the Communist Party's time to shine under the international spotlight and demonstrate to the world and its own people China's achievements of economic growth and modernisation.[71] As a 'core interest' of the Communist Party, the Chinese government was keen to eliminate all obstacles standing in the way of the success of the Games.[72]

After Save Darfur's China campaign began, there appeared to be a response from the Chinese government. Beijing dispatched Assistant Foreign Minister Zhai Jun to Sudan to visit three Darfuri refugee camps in April 2007.[73] A month later, the Chinese government appointed Liu Guijin, former Ambassador to Zimbabwe and South Africa, as its first Special Envoy for African Affairs, with a particular focus on Sudan.[74] In July, China helped pressure the Sudanese government to allow the deployment of a hybrid United Nations-African Union peacekeeping force to Darfur. According to a leading Chinese foreign policy scholar, this was accomplished through 'gentle' diplomacy: respect for Sudan's sovereignty, private persuasion, and close consultations.[75] In the face of activist pressure, the Chinese government wanted to make a clear, public demonstration of its commitment to helping the international community resolve the Darfur civil war. But these actions were only accelerating policy changes that were already underway before activists began the campaign to shame the Beijing Olympic Games.

In November 2006 China's UN Ambassador, Wang Guangya, played a large role in reaching a compromise between Sudan and the international community by pushing through plans for the UN peacekeeping force to play an expanded role in Darfur.[76] China saw that the conflict was dragging on and reacted to diplomatic pressure from the UN, the African Union, the US government and other Western countries to become more engaged in helping bring about peace.[77] 'Darfur is a part of Sudan, and you have to resolve this problem,' Chinese President Hu Jintao told President Bashir during his February 2007 visit to Sudan.[78] (Originally, Sudan was not supposed to be on Hu Jintao's eight-nation Africa tour, but in order to decrease international pressure on Beijing, China's Foreign Minister Li Zhaoxing suggested that Hu go and try to persuade Bashir to soften his opposition to UN peacekeepers.)[79]

Activists wrote off the private intervention of President Hu in Sudanese affairs. They saw China's provision of financial assistance to Bashir for a new presidential palace as evidence that his efforts to pressure the Sudanese president were not sincere. But Hu's stance that 'it is imperative to improve the situation in Darfur and living conditions of local people' was perhaps the closest any Chinese leader had come to offering recognition and support to the ideal of a 'responsibility to protect' civilians from violent conflict.[80] Certainly Hu's statement blurred Beijing's longstanding foreign policy of non-interference in the domestic relations of other countries.[81]

The Chinese government chose to intervene with the Sudanese government on the issue of Darfur because it had determined that its national interests were in jeopardy from the international pressure the Darfur civil war created on the Beijing Olympic Games.[82] China's non-interference stance has proven to have pragmatic elasticity, but it still fundamentally shaped the manner in which the Chinese government sought to pressure Sudan. China's apparent retreat from non-interference in Sudan did not necessarily mean it was falling completely in line with the demands of the US government or the activists.

China wanted a peaceful resolution to Darfur, but one that kept the Sudanese government in the driver's seat. Despite President Hu's overtures, he still called for the international community to 'respect Sudan's sovereignty and territorial integrity'.[83] China also demanded that Western governments do more to get rebel groups to join peace talks, rather than putting most of the onus on the government in Khartoum.[84] 'China is a mediator between Sudan and the West,' said one former Chinese diplomat.[85] It was also clear that Beijing was unwilling to apply pressure on Sudan through oil.

In fact, China's support for Sudan on the UN Security Council was not simply a pact sealed in oil, as many American activists believed. Rather, even before CNPC invested in Sudan, Western observers worried that because of its policy of non-interference, China might use its veto power on the UN Security Council to block US efforts under President Clinton to pressure Sudan over its human rights record and links to international terrorism.[86] But once CNPC had made its first investment in Sudan in 1995, there was even greater reason for the Chinese government to protect Sudan's sovereignty from international intervention.

In 2004, the US and other Western countries were pushing for multilateral oil sanctions to be included in a UN resolution on the situation in Darfur. China had never used its veto against sanctions directly, but it made sure that the possibility was dead in the water before any vote came about. 'I hope the US will come up with a good draft because if it is not a good draft then I do not know the fate of this resolution. As the draft stands now, it would be very difficult for China to support it. They know my instructions,' said Wang Guangya, China's UN Ambassador.[87] This position was in line with China's traditional non-interference policy. But there was another longstanding norm in Chinese foreign policy that also stood in the way of Western efforts to impose multilateral sanctions against Sudan: 'For China, foreign policy serves economic trade and investment,' said a leading Chinese scholar.[88] Thus, even in the face of activist pressure leading up to the 2008 Summer Olympic Games in Beijing, CNPC's investments in Sudan were safe from intervention by the Chinese government and Party leadership.

The Olympic torch relay in the lead-up to the Beijing Games encountered protests and demonstrations in London, Paris, and San Francisco from pro-Tibetan groups and activists condemning the Chinese government's human rights record and China's role in the Darfur civil war. When the relay finally arrived at Beijing International Airport in April 2008, the first man to meet the Olympic torch was none other than Zhou Yongkang.[89] Zhou's role that day was practical: he was China's security chief, as head of the Party Central Committee's Politics and Law Commission, and charged with overseeing the torch's tightly-controlled transit to Tiananmen Square. But he also played a symbolic role where Sudan and Darfur were concerned: as former head of CNPC, he was instrumental in bringing China closer to Sudan in the first place.

If the Party leadership was excessively concerned about activist pressure over the connection between the Olympics and Darfur, Zhou's presence was hardly a conciliatory move. But the connection was lost on Save Darfur activists. They failed to understand CNPC's key role in fostering ties with the Sudanese government. Government officials or even Party leaders did not hold straightforward control over the company.[90] In fact, Chinese business interests have become increasingly politicised inside and outside China over the past two decades. Foreign policy decision-making is becoming more complex, with actors ranging from local governments to the media and large energy companies interacting and at times supplanting government interests.[91] In fact, there was considerable debate inside the Chinese government on how to manage international pressure arising from CNPC's oil investments in Sudan.

Conservatives among China's policymaking elite saw US pressure on Darfur as hypocritical, because of the close ties that exist between the US and other autocratic and corrupt African regimes, such as that in Equatorial Guinea. But progressives felt that in the long run Sudan's oil resources would not be worth the loss of China's image and international reputation in the US and other Western countries over Darfur. Although CNPC had invested in Sudan long before the Darfur conflict began, some Chinese foreign policy experts spoke out against the company and the oil industry as a powerful interest group 'hijacking' Chinese foreign affairs for the sake of profits.[92] However, the Chinese Ministry of Foreign Affairs and other government ministries had little power over CNPC's decision-making. CNPC was heavily shaping China's foreign policy on Sudan.

Within the Party, Zhou Yongkang and others inclined to support the oil industry were well positioned to influence foreign policy. The Party's International Department offered a vehicle for Zhou to visit Sudanese leaders through party-to-party ties after 2007 when he no longer held a Chinese government post.[93] Zhou's position on the Politburo Standing Committee was even more influential: it put him well above Foreign Minister Li Zhaoxing and his successor, Yang Jiechi, in Party ranking. If President Hu Jintao, Premier Wen Jiabao or other Party leaders were interested in using CNPC as a tool of foreign policy to lever the Sudanese government's behaviour in Sudan, Zhou was in the right place to counter such positions.

The end of the Beijing Olympic Games marked the passing of the high point of activist pressure on China; CNPC's oil interests with Sudan remained steadfast. CNPC, Petronas and OVL may have been developing an increased awareness of corporate responsibility in Sudan and beyond, but as the investment demonstrated, this was not in the way American activists hoped, by the Asian national oil companies putting pressure on the Sudanese government to change its behaviour in Darfur. The largest potential corporate levers on Sudanese government behaviour in Darfur were the most difficult for activists to access and influence. Asian national oil companies were largely unresponsive to both the divestment campaign and Save Darfur's tarnishing of the Beijing Olympic Games. But they were becoming increasingly aware of how Sudan might affect their expanding international operations.

Collateral damage

'We don't want you to write about us.' This was the response of Zhang Yuzhen, the head of the CNPC public relations department, to a reporter who asked for basic information on the company's international expansion in 1998.[94] A decade later, when divestment activists accused CNPC of 'perpetrating genocide' in Darfur, the company had hardly changed its position towards engaging the media and civil society. Company managers were certainly aware that the divestment campaign was underway; they just did not think that it was a serious threat to their Sudan operations.[95] Rather, they saw the campaign as another sign that the US and Europe did not want Chinese national oil companies to establish a footing in the international oil industry.

In 2003, CNPC's national counterparts, CNOOC and Sinopec, each failed to buy a stake in the highly-touted Kashagan oil field in Kazakhstan when an existing group of six Western oil companies exercised its right of first refusal to block the Chinese buyers.[96] The same year, the US invasion of Iraq and the ousting of Saddam Hussein put CNPC's investments in several major oil fields there in jeopardy.[97] Chinese resentment grew when in 2005 the US Congress derailed CNOOC's $18.5 billion bid to purchase the US oil company Unocal. CNOOC's bid for Unocal was over $2 billion more than the next highest offer from the American oil major Chevron, but the political pressure in Washington to reject the blockbuster deal on national security terms drove the Chinese national oil company away.[98] In Hong Kong, Yang Hua, CNOOC's Chief Financial Officer, said the political opposition to the bid was a human rights violation. 'What are human rights? I'll tell you what it means. It means having guaranteed access to energy. It means have petroleum to run your car,' he said.[99] In the immediate aftermath of CNOOC's failed 2005 bid for Unocal, Chinese national oil companies began to regard investing in the US as more politically risky than investing in Sudan.[100] As a result, when American divestment activists called for investors to sell their stock in PetroChina because of CNPC's operations in Sudan, Chinese oilmen saw another example of the US trying to block their international expansion. Other Asian oil executives were similarly dismissive about the motives of the US.

Sanjeev Kakran, a Vice-President at OVL, summed up his company's opinion when he remarked in early 2005 that 'the shadows of Darfur don't affect us'.[101] Foreign institutional investors in OVL's parent ONGC held just over 5 per cent of the company through the Bombay Stock Exchange in 2009.[102] Even so, ONGC felt that such low percentages of publicly available stock could easily be replaced should institutional holders decide to divest in response to pressure from international activists.[103]

OVL Chairman Chandra saw a smattering of double standards in the agenda of US pressure: 'Coca Cola requires gum arabic, which comes out of Sudan, but it is not banned by the US. Why should oil production be banned?'[104] (Indeed, US companies had lobbied President Clinton's administration to win an exemption from sanctions for gum arabic in 1997.)[105] There was ample resentment at pressure from US activists on OVL. 'India is the home of non-violent resistance, human rights, and a strong supporter of UN peacekeeping,' said one official at the Indian Ministry of External Affairs. 'Any lecturing from the West on human rights will fall off India like water off a duck's back.'[106]

During the US divestment campaign, India's vibrant media and civil society expressed interest in OVL's operations in Sudan in relation to human rights issues. 'We are shocked to learn how ONGC (OVL's corporate parent) is indirectly linked to the gross human rights violations going on in Sudan,' said Colin Gonsalves, founder of the Human Rights Law Network, a lawyers' and social activists' organisation defending human rights in India.[107] Gonsalves was approached by the Sudan Divestment Task Force in 2008 to form a partnership with US activists to engage OVL on pressuring the Sudanese government over Darfur and improving its corporate responsibility practices in Sudan. But Gonsalves said there were too many human rights issues in India that he needed to prioritise over Sudan and felt that engaging OVL would require high profile political support if a campaign on Darfur was to get off the ground in India.[108]

There was little traction available to the activists to change the behaviour of Asian national oil companies in Sudan. But divestment activists did have an influence on their global operations by raising the possibility of a threat to Asian national oil companies' investment in US and other Western markets because of their Sudan connection.[109] Sudan was where the Asian companies launched their major international operations and gained crucial experience for further overseas ventures after US foreign policy, through unilateral sanctions, opened the door in 1990s. But as their international activities grew over the following decade, the Asian companies found that Sudan's foreign relations with the US had negative side effects as well.

The unprecedented surge of US activism towards ending the civil war in Darfur cemented the imposition of US economic sanctions against Sudan. As the Darfur civil war dragged on, both the George W. Bush and Obama administrations pushed increasingly to find a diplomatic solution with Khartoum, suggesting a normalisation of ties and the eventual removal of sanctions, in return for concessions on Darfur.[110] But at the same time, American special envoys to Sudan appointed by the two administrations would face a tidal wave of criticism from the Save Darfur movement for negotiating with the Sudanese government. The idea of a complete removal of US sanctions on Sudan without the consent of the large civil society movement seemed doubtful. Consequently, the opposition to Chinese national oil companies in Washington only grew because of CNPC's operations in Sudan.

'Darfur affected CNPC's ability to invest elsewhere,' said one Chinese oil analyst in Beijing.[111] Five years after PetroChina's IPO on the New York Stock Exchange faced harsh criticism in the US, CNPC was still unable to fully launch the subsidiary as its international arm. In 2005, CNPC sold 50 per cent of its foreign assets to PetroChina, but it deliberately left out of the sale its assets in Sudan and other countries facing US sanctions, such as Iran, Syria and Myanmar. This limited the potential of PetroChina's global ambitions.[112] Sudan hindered CNPC's ability to become a global corporation with integrated exploration and production, refineries and filling stations around the world. In fact, Sudan also constrained CNPC's ability to operate within its own borders.

In July 2010, PetroChina was warned by the US government not to process Sudanese crude oil bought from its corporate parent CNPC at its new $2.2 billion refinery at Qinzhou in the southern Guangxi region. The refinery was constructed specifically to handle highly-acidic crudes such as Sudan's Dar-blend, but PetroChina took the warning seriously and indicated that it would retool the refinery's facilities with new units to handle West African crude blends instead.[113] Longstanding sanctions on Sudan were effective in halting efforts in the CNPC group to efficiently run a global corporation by bringing its Sudanese crude to the specially designed PetroChina refinery.

The international expansion of Chinese national oil companies into Sudan, Iran and Venezuela, considered rogue states by the US government, had irked many in Washington. 'At some point in time you are judged by the company you keep, and that is not always the best company to keep,' said Deputy Secretary of State Richard Armitage on China's expanding energy ties in 2006.[114] China was already the holder of close to $2 trillion in foreign currency reserves at its disposal, much of it in US government debt, and its booming economy and modernising armed forces made many in Washington worry that it was challenging US power in the world.[115] The focus in the US on Chinese oil interests around the world was perhaps one of the only occasions when the Indian national oil companies were thankful that they were behind their Chinese counterparts in the race for foreign oil and gas assets. In particular, Sudan had stained the reputation of Chinese national oil companies in Washington to the degree that US Congressmen could hardly tell the three Chinese oil giants apart.

In 2009, US Representative Frank Wolf, one of the leading advocates on Sudan in Washington, challenged the nomination of Charles Freeman, former US Ambassador to Saudi Arabia, as chairman of the National Intelligence Council, in part because of his apparent connection to Sudan. Wolf cited Freeman's previous position on the advisory board of the China National Offshore Oil Corporation (CNOOC) as compromising his candidacy for the intelligence post.[116] 'Freeman's appointment to this high-level post would have undermined the policy of US divestment from the genocidal regime of Sudan,' Wolf wrote in the *Washington Post* after Freeman had withdrawn his candidacy for the position. But as Freeman noted in his rebuttal to Wolf, CNOOC had never been in Sudan:[117] CNPC and Sinopec were the Chinese national oil companies there.

As Chinese national oil companies continued to expand overseas in the 2000s, Chinese oil executives were increasingly worried that their poor reputations in the US would limit access to technology in deep-sea and unconventional shale oil and gas drilling that many American and Western oil companies possessed, and that Chinese companies wanted. If mergers and acquisitions continued to be obstructed by the US government, then it would be more difficult to acquire such technology and expertise, which would ultimately limit the growth potential of Chinese national oil companies. This combination of demand for technology and political opposition in the US began to force Chinese national oil companies to better understand the political environments in the US and other Western countries, understanding among other things the influence of American civil society organisations, such as Save Darfur and the Sudan Divestment Task Force, on the US government.

The divestment campaign largely failed as a force for real change in Sudan, but it did manage to have a discernible impact on the international activities of Asian oil companies. As with all international oil companies, the convictions of Asian national oil companies are tied more closely to an economic mindset than to human rights. As Chinese national oil companies became increasingly concerned about future investment possibilities in the US, the ongoing violent politics of oil in Sudan gave the Asian oilmen another reason to rethink their problematic relationship with the Sudanese government. For if US activists were unable to succeed in their efforts to pressure Asian national oil companies on Sudan, perhaps the Sudanese could.

9

WAR IN PEACE

October 2008: Cui Leilei was running for his life. His nine-day ordeal as a hostage had just come to an abrupt and violent end. The young oil worker from China's Shandong province had been kidnapped with eight of his colleagues near the village of Al Agad in Southern Kordofan, a vast and desolate state of endless plains and woodland marked only by the Nuba Mountains to the east.[1] The Chinese oilmen were conducting maintenance on a pipeline when armed men from the Arab Misseriya ethnic group that called the area home came upon them. Leilei and his colleagues were led on what Sudanese authorities later called a 'death march', which brought on exhaustion and sickness.[2] Surviving only by drinking pools of stagnant water, some men become violently ill. Several days after the Chinese oilmen were taken, Misseriya tribal leaders started negotiations for their release.[3] The kidnappers demanded that Chinese oil companies leave the region because oil had brought no jobs or development. It was not long after negotiations broke down that shots were fired. Leilei was lucky to escape the fighting, but was wounded in the crossfire and later became lost in the Sudanese bush. When he was found two days later, he had already succumbed to his wounds.[4] In what became known at CNPC as the 10.18 Incident, marking the exact date of the kidnapping, Leilei was one of five Chinese oilmen who died.

This is what peace looked like for Asian national oil companies in Sudan after the country's second civil war ended. In January 2005, the NCP and southern rebel group, the SPLA/M, inked the Comprehensive Peace Agreement (CPA) ending a twenty-two year civil war that had killed two million and displaced four million Sudanese. But Sudan was not destined to enjoy the fruits of peace. After a decade of operating in the midst of a civil war, the oilmen were now more vulnerable than ever during what was suppose to be peacetime.

Khartoum had not changed its style of governance. Marginalisation and exploitation by the ruling National Congress party (NCP) stretched far and wide and resentment towards the government often burst into violence. The oil boom was one of the most significant developments in Sudan's economic history, but rather than harness the flood of incoming petrodollars for social and economic development, the NCP exploited oil as a means to build political power and pursue personal enrichment. Over a decade of acting as the 'right-hand man' of the Sudanese government did little to help China's image among most Sudanese. CNPC had made few friends outside the presidential palace and government ministries in Khartoum. Moving Sudan's oil industry forward, the Chinese company and its Asian partners were prime targets for those seeking to harm the Sudanese government. The closer one got to the oil, an unprecedented source of power and wealth in Sudan, the bigger the grievances. The corporate responsibility of the Asian national oil companies was misplaced and manipulated by the Sudanese government and the destructive environmental impact of the oil industry threatened the livelihoods of local populations.

A growing number of security incidents made peacetime very insecure for CNPC and its Asian partners. Misseriya armed groups, which had fought on the side of the Sudanese government as part of the Popular Defence Forces, alongside the Sudanese armed forces during the second civil war, now saw little peace dividend after 2005. They were turning their anger towards the Chinese oilmen who fuelled Sudan's rapid yet inequitable economic growth. Darfur rebels fostered ties with the Misseriya to strike at the government's economic heart. Several years after it began in 2003, the new civil war in Darfur reached east to meet the ghosts of Sudan's old civil war at Chinese oil fields. CNPC discovered that the Sudanese government was hardly a reliable partner in mitigating security risks and their rising consequences for the company in Sudan.

The oil curse

The oil boom arrived in Sudan after the signing of the CPA in 2005. Production went from 305,000 bpd in 2005 to 480,000 bpd by 2008; the average price of Sudanese crude rose 42 per cent on international markets.[5] Sudan became sub-Saharan Africa's third largest oil producer behind Nigeria and Angola. As a result, the Sudanese government experienced a massive influx of revenue from oil export sales. On average, between 2005 and 2010 oil revenues were over $5.7 billion, representing nearly 60 per cent of total government revenue.[6] The World Bank reported that the Sudanese economy grew fivefold from 1999 to 2008, with oil enabling a massive expansion of physical and social infrastructure, including a doubling of road networks, increased electricity generation, and a sharp rise in primary-school enrolment.[7]

But as happened with West African oil-rich countries, the threat of the oil resource curse loomed. This is a phenomenon in which countries with an abundance of oil and minerals paradoxically suffer from economic underdevelopment, government corruption, and civil war despite the influx of oil revenue.[8] Apart from the revenue transfers to the new, semi-autonomous Government of Southern Sudan, investment in services and infrastructure from incoming petrodollars focused in large part on Khartoum and the Nile Valley heartland. In 2009, the United Nations Development Programme found that 60–75 per cent of the population in the north and 90 per cent in the south lived below the poverty line, most acutely in rural areas.[9]

Oil revenue did not change the way political business was conducted in Sudan. Oil as a new source of wealth simply fed longstanding practices of economic mismanagement, political patronage, militarisation and corruption displayed by Sudan's ruling elite in Khartoum since the country's independence. In fact, to call oil a resource curse is wrong: the NCP's methods of governance before oil were already a cancer on the body politic, affecting both social stability and equitable development. The coming of oil did not change this entrenched political system.

The NCP showed little interest in harnessing oil for the good of Sudan's fledgling economy. During a period of record economic growth, it presided over one budget deficit after another from 2005 to 2011, with its total debt amounting to $41.4 billion.[10] Instead, NCP officials used the oil windfall to cement their own political power and personal wealth. Oil wealth was not used to develop other sectors of the economy. Rather, the process known as 'Dutch Disease' was allowed to take effect, by which significant inflows of foreign currency from oil exports appreciate the value of a country's currency. As a result, the competitiveness of Sudan's agriculture industry, which employs two-thirds of its population, suffered immensely. Sudan's non-oil exports, composed largely of sesame and live-stock, fell from $677,000 million in 2004 to $545,000 million in 2008.[11]

An average of 71 per cent of the Sudanese government's annual expen-diture between 2005 and 2007 went to the defence, security and police sectors, mainly to cover salaries, providing little room for pro-poor spend-ing.[12] There also remained largely invisible avenues of personal enrich-ment within the security, commercial and political cabals of the government, upon which NCP-affiliated oil service companies were quick to capitalise.[13] High-level NCP officials were reported to have funnelled government funds through private oil service companies and abroad to Islamic banks in Bahrain, Malaysia and Singapore.[14] President Bashir's brother helped run a construction company under the High Tech Group that charged inflated sums for setting up camps for oil companies.[15] 'Peo-ple can make millions just off of the issuing of contracts,' said one Suda-nese service company manager.[16] But the majority of Sudanese saw little benefit from oil.

The role of China in empowering the NCP and fuelling Sudan's uneven distribution of the benefits of oil was not overlooked by the people of Sudan. China was investing billions in Sudan's oil and infrastructure sec-tors, but many Sudanese were wondering what Sudan was actually get-ting out of it. Sudanese academics and intellectuals were most critical of Sudan's relations with China. 'They send (Sudanese) government offi-cials to China in business class, show them the Great Wall, and give them expensive gifts. And no one wants to talk about it because their mouths are full of money,' said one Sudanese academic.[17] There were also increas-ing complaints from the Sudanese private sector about Chinese imports flooding the market, as well as general popular grievances against the thousands of Chinese workers and small businesses coming into the country.[18] The billions of dollars of investment made by CNPC in Sudan's oil industry stood out in particular. The hospitality to Chinese oilmen in Sudan did not extend far from the centre of power in Khartoum.

Chinese oil executives like to engage in a counting exercise of hospi-tals, schools and water wells when asked about their corporate respon-sibility in Sudan. But it is not simply the number of schools or hospitals that is at the heart of the grievances. Rather, it is the negative impact of the oil industry on an environment that sustains the livelihoods of local communities, and the lack of job opportunities in oil regions.[19] The death and displacement suffered by the Dinka and Nuer communities living in and around Sudan's oil fields largely subsided following the civil war, and there have been pockets of development. In Unity state there has been some investment in education and agriculture, and the expansion of oil infrastructure has brought more roads and public transport, access to markets, and wider mobile phone network coverage.[20] But these are shallow benefits in light of the detrimental environmental impact of the oil industry.

In oil regions of southern Sudan, seismic surveying has carved up hundreds of kilometres of 12-metre-wide bulldozed tracks, destroying farmland and leading to deforestation and devegetation. Road construction has dammed water flows, upset irrigation for agriculture, and led to the evacuation of several communities.[21] But the most damaging environmental impact of the industry has been the discharge of contaminated 'produced water' generated from oil reservoirs and the improper disposal of drilling mud and other waste, killing livestock and causing serious illness among locals in oil regions.[22] The corporate responsibility investments of CNPC and other Asian national oil companies have not made up for such losses.

It was no surprise that CNPC, through its joint venture companies in Sudan, was caught up in practices of environmental degradation; the company has a deplorable track record in environmental management at home. But the Sudanese government in general and Sudan's Ministry of Energy and Mining (MEM) in particular were responsible for upholding environment laws and regulations over the oil industry, not the Chinese company. The Petroleum Wealth Act and the Sudan Environmental Protection Act provide a set of rules for environmental preservation. For example, the MEM could revoke certain contractual rights, including those for Blocks 1, 2, and 4 of the GNPOC concession, if environmental measures are not undertaken.[23]

However, there has been an extreme absence of political will to enforce these regulations. Sudanese government officials have historically given precedence to the advancement of the oil industry over environmental laws. As a result, in the absence of governmental oversight, the self-regulation of the industry by oil companies has encouraged poor environmental practices.[24] Not surprisingly, environmental impact assessments by oil companies in Sudan have often been substandard, conducted after operations had already begun, and shelved upon completion with little follow-up.[25] In other areas, the NCP has closed off possibilities to build goodwill between oil companies and local communities.

CNPC and the other Asian national oil companies did make social investments in Sudan. But the Sudanese government directed corporate investments in social development to reward political allies or pacify local resistance. It is common practice for corporations to require clearance from the MEM before engaging in community development pro- grammes. Khartoum also controlled many employment decisions, even for temporary, low-level positions, with the result that mainly northern Sudanese and foreigners were hired, not local workers.[26] Neither was there much compensation for southern Sudanese communities harmed by the oil industry's environmental impact. Standards and modes of com- pensation were not specified in the CPA and enforcement mechanisms are non-existent.[27] There were few opportunities for local communities to address their grievances. Instead, some people took to stealing the cop- per wire used in oil well logging and selling it on local markets.[28]

But it was not just the Dinka, Nuer and other communities in south- ern Sudan that were suffering under the oil industry's expansion after the CPA. New grievances against the Sudanese government were to arise among the Misseriya on the northern side of the border with southern Sudan. Chinese oilmen found themselves the main targets of this vio- lent recoil against oil development.

Old greed, new grievances

On the roof of CNPC headquarters in Khartoum near the Nile, Chinese oilmen were still doing their early morning exercises before temperatures soared by mid-day. But it was far from a good vantage point to see the trouble brewing in their prized oil fields to the south. Sudan was the beginning of major international operations for CNPC, but it was also the beginning of serious security and political risks. The close affiliation of the Chinese company with the NCP increasingly threatened its invest- ments, as one civil war ended in southern Sudan and another began in Darfur.

Insecurity was an inherent part of the international oil industry; no company chooses where oil is located. US and European oil compa- nies are no strangers to operating in physically insecure and politically risky countries. Decades of kidnappings and killings of Western oilmen in Nigeria illustrate the constant insecurity faced by international oil companies.

Declining oil reserves and production in China forced the big three Chinese national oil companies CNPC, Sinopec and CNOOC to go overseas wherever oil may be. But the Chinese newcomers faced ferocious competition in a global industry dominated by Middle Eastern and Russian national oil companies and Western oil majors. Like mid-sized Western oil companies, such as Talisman and Lundin, Asian national oil companies have followed a strategy of going after more risky ventures to access overseas oil without facing too much competition. 'The potential reward outweighed the potential risk,' said one former Chinese oil executive in Beijing.[29] But over time, the risks involved in investing dangerously would catch up with the Chinese national oil companies as they tried to close the gap between themselves and the leaders of the industry, such as ExxonMobil and Royal Dutch Shell. The 10.18 Incident in Sudan was one of a growing number of attacks the companies faced as they expanded into the frontiers of the international oil industry.

The deadliest attack against Chinese national oil companies to date actually occurred over a year before the 10.18 Incident. At an oil field near the small town of Abole in the Ogaden region of eastern Ethiopia, dozens of armed rebels from the Ogaden National Liberation Front (ONLF) launched a dawn attack on a heavily-guarded compound of China's Zhongyuan Petroleum Engineering Co. Ltd. (ZPEB). In an hour-long battle, over sixty government soldiers and nine Chinese oil workers were killed.[30] In Ethiopia, Malaysia's national oil company Petronas had contracted the ZPEB, a Sinopec subsidiary, to carry out exploration work in 2006.[31] The rebels of the ONLF were seeking independence for the ethnic Somalis of the Muslim Ogaden region. Chinese and other oil companies were regarded as collateral damage in a war against the Ethiopian government. Elmi Mohammed, an ONLF commander, said the rebel group had sent letters to the Chinese embassy in Addis Ababa warning its oil companies not to work in the region. The Chinese company 'came into a burning fire where people are fighting,' he said.[32] 'They never listened to us. They listened to (Ethiopian Prime Minister) Meles Zenawi.'

A harsh counterinsurgency operation by the Ethiopian army followed the attack in Ogaden, but persistent insecurity had a 'dampening effect' on investment.[33] ZPEB halted its operations after the Ogaden attack and by 2010 Petronas had sold all its oil concessions in Ethiopia in an effort to improve the quality of its overseas assets.[34] The private, Hong Kong-based Petrotrans later picked up the abandoned assets, and immediately received a warning from rebels not to proceed with its operations.[35]

On the other side of Africa, Chinese national oil companies were also under fire. In March 2006, a car bomb went off near an oil refinery in the city of Warri in the Niger Delta. Following the visit of Hu Jintao to Nigeria that year, during which CNPC was granted four exploration licenses, the Movement for the Emancipation of the Niger Delta, a large rebel movement against oil companies' exploitation, said the explosion was a special message to Chinese oil interests.[36] Two months earlier, nine CNPC oilmen were kidnapped in one of many incidents targeting Chinese oil and telecom companies in Nigeria.[37]

These attacks in Ethiopia, Nigeria, and elsewhere were demonstrating that Chinese national oil companies, like their American and European counterparts, had become entangled in the domestic politics of oil-rich countries. In Sudan, CNPC was now playing the role its American counterpart Chevron once held twenty years earlier. Rebel groups and local communities across the oil regions regarded the company as an economic arm of their oppressive government that was reaching out from Khartoum into the marginalised periphery that they called home.

The Misseriya who carried out the kidnappings of the nine Chinese oil workers in the 10.18 Incident in 2008 were an unexpected enemy for CNPC and the oil industry in Sudan. The Arabic-speaking Misseriya, a cattle-herding nomadic ethnic group, have two sub-groups, the Zuruq and the Humr. The Misseriya Humr in particular developed strong grievances against the Sudanese government after the CPA. Much of their discontent revolved around a longstanding dispute between the Sudanese government and the SPLM over the region of Abyei.

Between the states of Southern Kordofan in the north and Bahr el-Ghazal in the south, Abyei was home to the southern Sudanese Ngok Dinka, but was also where the Misseriya traditionally crossed to graze their cattle. During Sudan's civil wars, these two communities supported opposite sides. The Ngok Dinka were instrumental in forming the SPLA after 1983 and much of the Dinka population in Abyei was displaced by the war. Along with the Rizeigat of South Darfur, many Misseriya enlisted in the Sudanese government's *murahaleen* militias. Beginning in the mid-1980s, they fought the SPLA and terrorised southern villages on horseback as a key part of the Popular Defence Forces, and essentially acted as a buffer between the rebellious south and the oil fields.[38] But after the

CPA, the Misseriya felt abandoned and betrayed by Khartoum. They recognised that they had little to show for siding with the government in the civil war. Many Misseriya fighters received no compensation when they were disbanded after the war, and relations with the Ngok Dinka communities in Abyei were severely strained after years of fighting.[39] Some Misseriya leaders thought they had protected the oil companies from the war, making it possible for the oil industry to be opened up for the entire country; yet they saw little benefit from oil development.[40]

In 2006, Misseriya settlements were cleared to make way for oil activity in the Muglad area. In response a group of Misseriya blocked a main road used for oil work, which brought in Sudanese soldiers and led to the deaths of several civilians in the resulting fighting.[41] The Misseriya also saw little of the 2 per cent share of oil revenue, generated from the region's production, the government had promised them in the peace agreement, and virtually no jobs or development from the oil industry.[42] Much of the funds going to Southern Kordofan for its share of oil production went to pay the wages of state government officials supportive of the NCP in Khartoum.[43] 'Having oil in Abyei is like planting a palm tree in your own yard. As the tree grows so tall, it only gives shade to your neighbor,' a member of a prominent Misseriya ethnic group and head of a Sudanese oil service company told US officials in Sudan.[44]

The Misseriya asserted that they were experiencing only the negative consequences of the oil industry through environmental degradation. They called the few boreholes the GNPOC consortium drilled for water 'peanuts' in comparison with the damage the oil industry had done to their livelihoods by contaminating water supplies and pastures. The geological formation of Sudan's oil fields, numerous and small rather than few and large, gave Misseriya armed groups plenty of targets.

Protectors become predators

Once protectors of CNPC's interests in Southern Kordofan, armed groups of Misseriya, together with Darfur rebels, were now turning their anger towards the Chinese company. In late March 2004, two Chinese oil workers from the Liaohe Oilfield Road Construction Company, a subsidiary of CNPC, were killed while driving near the Heglig oil field. Their deaths were not attributed to a road accident, as most Chinese deaths had been during the civil war, but to a violent encounter with a local armed group.

Chinese state media claimed there was no political motive behind the attack: the men were killed for their truck and equipment. Weeks earlier, two Chinese workers were kidnapped in the neighbouring state of Southern Darfur. The men were treated well by their captors, and served hot tea. One managed to escape and the second was released with assistance from the International Federation of the Red Cross and Red Crescent Societies. The Chinese embassy in Khartoum described the incident as a local affair in which the kidnappers took the Chinese men in hopes of gaining protection after robbing a local police station.[45]

Chinese diplomats may have been strictly correct when they suggested that CNPC was simply becoming caught up in local affairs out of their control. But the attacks and kidnappings of Chinese and other foreign oilmen were also part of national politics and civil war. In November 2006, an alliance of Darfur rebel groups under the banner of the National Redemption Front attacked CNPC's Abu Jabra oil installation on the border between Southern Kordofan and Southern Darfur. Abu Jabra was where Chevron had made its first oil discovery in the late 1970s. The area had been relatively safe back then; the Misseriya communities remember fondly the training programmes carried out by Chevron and the subsequent community development work conducted later by Talisman.[46] Nearly three decades later, Abu Jabra was a target of Darfur rebels and Misseriya armed groups looking to strike at the ruling NCP. It appeared by now that CNPC had become a pawn in the Sudanese government's strategy of divide and rule.

Rumours persisted that Khartoum knew the attack on Abu Jabra was coming, but hoped it might be able to turn the Misseriya living in the area against the Darfur rebels. However, while some Misseriya were unhappy with the incursion of outsiders on their territory, it was clearly understood that the Darfuris were after the Chinese oil company and through it, the Sudanese government. This was a cause of growing sympathy among many in the Misseriya community.[47] In fact, local Misseriya who knew the area well assisted the rebel group in the attack.[48] Afterwards, an official at the Sudanese oil ministry admitted that facilities were damaged in the fighting. But the attack would have little impact on Sudan's overall production, as Abu Jabra produced only 10,000 bpd of Sudan's 330,000 daily output that year.[49] The attack, however, was a sign of things to come.

There was another strike against Chinese oil installations by a Darfur rebel group less than a year after Abu Jabra. The Justice and Equality

Movement (JEM) captured an Egyptian and an Iraqi oil contractor and several Sudanese workers after its attack on the Chinese-run Defra oil field in October 2007. The kidnapping of the two foreign nationals was another local affair with national underpinnings. A Sudanese field production manager had warned his superiors that the road between Muglad and Heglig was unsafe, 'mainly due to local people demanding for compensation,' he wrote in an email. Chen Shudong, the CNPC manger, replied that the company was coordinating with national security authorities to resolve the situation.[50] A JEM political affairs officer told US officials that all the men who had participated in the operation were from the Kordofan region and had chosen to 'join the revolution'[51] under the command of Mohammed Bahr Ali Hamadain, leader of the local Shahama movement and JEM's Kordofan division. He saw the Defra attack as 'a message to the Chinese companies in particular'. Shahama, which means 'valiant' in Arabic, was formed in 2004 and had ties to JEM rebel leader Khalil Ibrahim and the Popular Congress, the political party Hassan al-Turabi formed after his falling out with President Bashir.[52] They shared many of the concerns of other political groups in the Kordofan region, which were seeking jobs and development from the oil industry but were looked down on by many for their violent approach.[53]

A month after the Defra attack, the JEM leader Khalil Ibrahim issued a veiled threat to 135 Chinese engineers joining UN peacekeeping forces in Darfur. 'China has so far only offered $1 million for displaced Darfur people. Meanwhile, they are sucking a million barrels of oil out of Sudan every day. We do not welcome them,' he said of the Chinese peacekeepers.[54] A JEM representative later backed away from his leader's comments, saying that the Chinese contingent was part of the international community and was not a target.[55]

These violent attacks against Chinese oil operations did not constitute an all-out war against China; rather, they were directed against those Chinese interests supporting the Sudanese government, particularly CNPC's investments. In December 2007, JEM kept the pressure on with an attack on the Rahaw facility run by CNPC's Great Wall Drilling Company.[56] 'We are implementing our threat of attacks against foreign companies, particularly Chinese ones, and we will continue to attack,' said the JEM commander Ashr.[57] As with the attacks against oil targets before, there was minimal impact on actual oil production, but concern was growing in Beijing. In response to the attacks, the Chinese foreign ministry said in a statement that 'the safety of Chinese personnel in Sudan must be effectively guaranteed'.[58]

The growing strength of JEM culminated in a daring attack on Khartoum in May 2008. Pickup trucks carrying thousands of rebels crossed the desert from Darfur and clashed with government security forces in Omdurman, one of the three towns that constitute Sudan's capital.[59] The rebels were eventually pushed out of the city; among the hundreds of Darfur rebels captured was Mohammed Bahr Ali Hamadain, JEM's Kordofan chief and head of the Shahama movement, who had led the earlier attack on CNPC's Defra oil field.[60] In a major escalation of the Darfur civil war, fighting had come to the capital for the first time. If the links between Shahama and other Misseriya armed groups with Darfur rebels had not yet disturbed the ruling NCP, assault on the Sudanese capital certainly heightened their concern.

Chinese oilmen were not the only ones under attack. In the same month that JEM attacked Khartoum, four Indian oil contractors were taken at gunpoint outside the town of Heglig. Again, a Misseriya armed group was behind the kidnapping. Deepak Vohra, the Indian Ambassador in Khartoum, quickly set negotiations in motion to free the hostages. He assured the Sudanese, Indian and international press that the men were 'in fine fettle,' and added, 'We believe the abductors didn't know they were Indian,'[61] as if suggesting that the kidnapping was a case of mistaken identity for another nationality and that Indians were free from the divisive politics of oil in Sudan. 'I can confirm that four Indians have been abducted and every effort is being made to secure their release,' Vohra assured. 'I am hopeful that they will be released in the near future.'[62] But the men were not freed until two months later.

As the kidnapping dragged on, Abdel Rahman Mohammad Bekheit, the Sudanese Ambassador to India, was summoned to the Ministry of External Affairs by N. Ravi, the Secretary for the East. Ravi pressed the ambassador to ensure that Sudanese authorities were doing everything in their power to resolve the issue.[63] Back in 2003, Bekheit's predecessor, the fast-talking Abdalmahmood Abalhaleem Mohamad, had assured the Indians that Sudan was safe. The wisdom of supporting OVL's venture in the conflict-prone country had been weighed heavily by Indian politicians for some time; now the kidnapping incident threatened to reopen the debate.

Three weeks after the kidnapping, one of the Indian workers, Mohammed Aseeb Shaikh, managed to escape. 'I felt I would never reach home.

As I escaped, the only thought racing through my head was to not give up hope,' Shaikh said upon his return to his home in an eastern Mumbai suburb, where locals triumphantly raised him up on their shoulders. 'I kept walking to reach a remote road ... at times I drank my own urine when there was no water.'[64] But Shaikh's return was bittersweet. A colleague who had escaped with him went missing when he went searching for water and was presumed dead.[65] Some weeks later another technician eluded the kidnappers and found his way to the nearby Heglig oil base camp.

Seventy-four days after the beginning of the ordeal, a ransom agreement was made for the release of the remaining Indian worker and the Sudanese driver.[66] Upon his return home to India, Shaikh stressed that he had no intention of going back to work in Sudan and other Indians did not want to be there. 'Workers who are not keen to work (in Sudan) should be allowed to leave,' he said.[67] A little over five years after Indian oilmen had celebrated over cake their arrival in Sudan, they found themselves caught in the often violent and rapidly developing politics of oil.

Malaysia's Petronas also faced similar security threats. Its workers considered that their enduring the weather, isolation, long hours, and insecurity in Sudan was a national service.[68] But the Sudanese backlash against CNPC was strongest. CNPC was the Sudanese government's largest investor and the relatively large number of Chinese personnel in southern Sudan, by comparison with their Asian counterparts, provided armed groups with an abundance of targets, and the Sudanese government's protection of CNPC was wearing thin.

10.18

It was in the early morning on 18 October 2008 when Cui Leilei and his eight colleagues were taken at gunpoint by a group of Misseriya between the Diffra oil field and the village of Al Agad near the disputed Abyei region. The three engineers and six workers were from the Huabei division of the China Petroleum Engineering and Construction Corporation, CNPC's main construction subsidiary. The following day, when news of the abduction arrived in China, CNPC Chairman Jiang Jiemin called an emergency meeting at company headquarters in Beijing. He dispatched the newly-appointed Vice-President Wang Dongjin to head a company team to oversee the rescue work. Wang was one of several

CNPC executives with experience of Sudan, having previously served as General Manager of CNPC's Sudan operations.

When they arrived in Khartoum, Wang's team and the Chinese Ambassador Li Chengwen met President Bashir and several high-level Sudanese government officials. The Chinese implored Bashir to send more troops to the region to strengthen the rescue efforts.[69] On 22 October the Sudanese army commander in charge of the rescue mission informed the Chinese team that the troops had located the kidnapped workers.

'We don't have any material demands. We want Chinese companies to leave the region immediately because they work with the government,' said Abu Humaid Ahmed Dannay, the leader of the kidnappers.[70] Dannay said he was a former Popular Defence Forces government fighter now acting as the Kordofan commander for JEM, the Darfur rebel group.[71] 'China supports the Khartoum government militarily and helps it marginalize our region. But our case is with the government in Khartoum and it bears the consequences of what is happening in the region and in Sudan in general,' he said. On 24 October Dannay reported that his men pushed back government security forces in a firefight, but that ground troops and helicopters now surrounded them. He warned of a 'bloodbath' should the government security forces attempt to free the Chinese oilmen by force.[72]

Three days later, Misseriya tribal leaders from Khartoum joined their local counterparts to meet the kidnappers to try to negotiate a release of the Chinese hostages.[73] Mukhtar Babu El-Nimer, the Amir, or chief, of the Misseriya in Muglad, a town near where the incident took place, confirmed that the kidnappers were from his ethnic group. 'They are Misseriya, but they are associated with the Justice and Equality Movement of Khalil Ibrahim,' he said. Nimer also spoke out against oil development: 'This area has no development and the oil is pouring out of it. The government has done nothing for them. The oil is being pumped, but they haven't seen any benefits.'[74]

Shortly after the talks between the tribal leaders and kidnappers broke down, shots were fired. CNPC reported that three workers were killed in the ensuing gunfire, three were rescued, and another two went missing. Hundreds of Sudanese soldiers and police spanned out across the area in search of the missing workers, but only one man would be found alive.[75] Wounded in the fighting, Cui Leilei was found too late.[76]

Both the head of Sudan's Criminal Investigation Directorate and a Chinese embassy official in Khartoum told US diplomats that the killings took place when one of the kidnappers panicked after seeing a Sudanese security helicopter. The hostages were lined up to leave the area after the helicopter was spotted, but the 'deranged' kidnapper opened fire on the Chinese workers and the 'bloodbath' that Dannay warned about took place.[77] A CNPC official in Beijing confirmed this version of the killings.[78] But other Sudanese and Chinese officials, including the Sudanese foreign minister and a Chinese foreign ministry spokeswoman, said that Sudanese security forces had launched a rescue attempt that went horribly wrong and the Chinese oilmen were caught in the crossfire.[79]

Ibrahim Mahmoud Hamad, the Sudanese Minister of the Interior, said that the Shahama or another armed Misseriya group affiliated with the Darfur rebel group JEM were probably responsible.[80] For its part, JEM immediately distanced itself from the killings. 'We have forces in the region, we have the support of the people there. Some of the (Misseriya) people are affiliated to us. Some of them may take actions, but not in the name of JEM,' said Tahir el-Faki, a London-based JEM representative.[81] Since late 2006, because of JEM's rapid growth, its leaders had been unsure of the precise number of fighters under their command. 'There are no hard numbers. It is a revolution: fighters join us, then leave....' said one JEM cadre.[82]

Shahama's ties with JEM had waned after the battle of Omdurman in Sudan's capital that May. In addition to the loss of its leader, many in the movement were disappointed by JEM's lack of attention to Misseriya concerns. Yet this did not mean that CNPC was out of harm's way. JEM and Shahama were not the only groups looking to harm the Sudanese government by targeting Chinese oil interests. Before the nine Chinese oil workers were kidnapped, a group of well-trained Misseriya veterans of the Popular Defence Forces sent an ultimatum to the government demanding that their military service be acknowledged and proper compensation and jobs be provided by 15 October 2008, or else they would continue to attack oil companies.[83] Regardless of the group the kidnappers were affiliated with, if any, it was clear that CNPC had a long list of enemies in Sudan thanks to its affiliation with the Sudanese government.

The 10.18 Incident revealed the growing friction between the Chinese company and government officials and their Sudanese hosts around security issues. Public statements from the Chinese government about the killing of the CNPC oilmen were diplomatically balanced, but contained a rare dose of criticism. 'In the future we will continue to value and implement a friendly policy towards Sudan; meanwhile, we hope that Sudan will provide good conditions for the people-to-people relations between the two countries,' said Jiang Yu, a Chinese foreign ministry spokeswoman in Beijing.[84] The CNPC Chairman Jiang Jiemin echoed his government's sentiments following the 10.18 Incident: 'CNPC can promise that as long as Sudan can provide a secure environment, CNPC will never give up our cooperation in oil exploration.'[85] Chinese diplomats and oilmen, who had been trying to put an end to the kidnappings peacefully, were stunned by the violent outcome.[86]

The Chinese foreign ministry was involved in the ongoing negotiations with the kidnappers when the killings took place. A Chinese embassy official told his US counterparts in Khartoum that he had travelled to an oil camp near where the oilmen were taken and was overseeing the negotiations with Misseriya tribal leaders. There was daily contact with the kidnappers; at one point, the Chinese official even spoke by satellite phone to the hostages through their kidnappers. 'We knew we would have to pay something, and we were prepared to do so,' he said. 'We put our people's lives first,' he added, while certainly aware that a ransom payment would only encourage further incidents in the future.[87] However, the official was miffed about the demands of the kidnappers for jobs and development, claiming that China had built over 100 schools in the region. 'But some people are never satisfied,' he explained. 'Rome wasn't built in a day.'

After the 10.18 Incident, the Chinese embassy requested that the Sudanese improve security by deploying Joint Integrated Units, or JIUs, of the Sudan Armed Forces and SPLA troops to the disputed area.[88] Mandated by the CPA, JIUs were to form the nucleus of a future national army if unity was maintained after 2011. They were stationed around southern Sudan and in Southern Kordofan, Blue Nile and Khartoum. In border areas, they were supposed to fill the security vacuum after the civil war, particularly in oil-rich regions of Southern Kordofan, Unity state, and Upper Nile state, after the SAF withdrew forces from the south and the SPLA from the north. But the JIUs provided little security. Rather, the Sudan Armed Forces and SPLA forces in JIUs operated for the most part under parallel command structures.[89] In fact, JIUs were often sources of insecurity in and around oil areas. The most severe incident took place in the contested region of Abyei in May 2008, when fighting between SAF and SPLA forces led the JIU brigade to quickly disintegrate.[90]

Ninety people were killed and 50,000 civilians displaced after the town was overrun during the battle.[91]

Sudanese authorities were adamant that those responsible for the 10.18 Incident would be brought to justice. The interior minister said that new security measures would also be taken in and around Sudan's oil fields. Oil companies would now be required to inform government security forces of travel outside their main camps so that an armed escort could be provided.[92] The SPLM feared that the government was using the incident as a 'power grab' to improve its military position against southern forces along the already heavily militarised border between northern and southern Sudan.[93] A month after the 10.18 Incident, the Sudanese government began to reorganise and rearm its Popular Defence Forces in Southern Kordofan.[94] By 2010, the Shamama movement and other organised paramilitary forces in Southern Kordofan were defunct.[95] But there was a noticeable shift in the allegiance of the Misseriya. Some would remain under the government's fold, but others were integrated into the JEM and even the SPLM/A.[96] The Misseriya groups of Southern Kordofan had their differences with the southern Sudanese and Darfuris, but they united under their common grievances against the ruling NCP in Khartoum.

After the 10.18 Incident, the sight of coffins draped in the five-star red of the Chinese flag at Khartoum International Airport sent back to China an entirely different image of CNPC's involvement in Sudan from those that the country had witnessed over the past decade. Sombre Chinese and Sudanese officials carried the remains of the killed oil workers across the tarmac, while blue-bereted Chinese peacekeepers saluted their fallen countrymen.

Losing trust

Zhou Yongkang, the former CNPC boss, arrived in Sudan in November 2009 to commemorate fifty years since the establishment of diplomatic ties between China and Sudan. Ten years had passed since Zhou was last in Sudan. As a member of the Politburo Standing Committee of the Communist Party, he was now one of China's most powerful men. During his visit to Sudan, he toured Khartoum with President Omar al-Bashir. They signed an agreement on agriculture, attended the launch of direct flights between China and Sudan, and opened a Confucius Institute at the University of Khartoum.[97]

But Zhou and Bashir did not forget what had brought their two countries closer together over the past decade. 'As an old friend of the Sudanese president, I got a full sense of the profound changes that have taken place in Sudan under your leadership as soon as I stepped on Sudanese soil,' said Zhou. 'This morning I visited the Khartoum Oil Refinery. Ten years ago, it was a mere construction site. Today it is covered with one modern plant after another.' In turn, Bashir praised Zhou. 'You have been an important promoter of oil cooperation between Sudan and China and the people of Sudan have special feelings for you,' the Sudanese president said. 'China is a true friend and partner of Sudan. Oil cooperation between Sudan and China has brought not only oil to the people of Sudan, but also peace.'[98]

Despite the public celebration between Zhou and Bashir in Khartoum, the relationship between China and Sudan was under considerable strain in 2009. Distrust was brewing on both sides. President Bashir and his ruling NCP were critical of China's lack of response to international pressure on Sudan. The International Criminal Court (ICC) prosecutor had requested an arrest warrant for Bashir for war crimes and crimes against humanity in Darfur which was issued in March 2009; he was the first sitting head of state to be charged by the ICC.[99] China, along with the US, India, and several other countries, was not a signatory to the Rome Statute which established the ICC in 2002; but when the UN Security Council passed a resolution to refer Darfur to the ICC in 2005, China did not use its veto to block it, but instead abstained from the vote.

Neither the Sudanese nor the Chinese foreign ministry prioritised this issue in 2005, believing that the US would block the resolution because of its own disdain for the international court.[100] But now that Bashir was a wanted man, the NCP was upset that China, as Sudan's closest foreign partner, did not intervene on its behalf at the time. The Chinese government did not support the international warrant against Bashir, but also did not expect that the ICC would go after the Sudanese president when it began its investigations on Darfur.[101] Years later, this issue festered as a major point of contention between the two countries, reflecting deteriorating relations between Zhou's former company, CNPC, and the Sudanese government.

While the company's former leader was glad-handing with Omar al-Bashir in Khartoum, current CNPC executives and managers were questioning their longstanding relationship with the Sudanese government.

During his 2009 trip, Zhou did not travel to Darfur where the civil war was still simmering, nor did he venture to CNPC oil fields, which were under fire from local Misseriya and Darfuri rebel groups.

For CNPC and its Asian oil partners, the glory days of operating in Sudan had clearly come to an end. The Chinese oil giant was increasingly regarded as an arrogant empire builder by the Sudanese government, whereas the company saw the government as an increasingly problematic partner to deal with.[102] The 10.18 Incident had driven a wedge between the two. When the company had first arrived in Sudan during the second civil war, CNPC security officers had assessed the security conditions faced by the company, but felt generally well protected. 'Ten years ago security was not a big issue,' said one CNPC manager in Beijing. 'It was dealt with on a case-by-case basis.'[103] CNPC gave little attention to prevention or early warning security systems at that time; it simply placed its safety in the hands of the Sudanese government and the Sudan Armed Forces.

Talisman, CNPC's former GNPOC partner until its departure in 2003, was seen as the member of the consortium most concerned with security. Talisman kept a minimal number of personnel on oil rigs outside its base camp, engaged a network of contacts in the Sudanese military and security apparatus, and was the only member of the consortium to regularly make security demands of Sudanese authorities. Talisman's caution certainly did not spare it from attacks and it admitted to a number of security incidents, including one in which six local members of a road construction crew subcontracted by GNPOC were killed by SPLA forces.[104] In contrast, CNPC and Petronas were not perturbed about associating with Sudanese military, and frequently travelled with government security vehicles.[105] The strategy largely worked during the second civil war, but in peacetime, conditions in the oil fields changed.

After the signing of the CPA in 2005, everything from theft to the commandeering of oil company equipment and vehicles to armed kidnappings and killings was undermining CNPC's work. From 2007 to 2009, CNPC reported 500 security emergencies in its oil fields.[106] CNPC officials gave a number of reasons for the waning of security since the end of the second civil war. After the outbreak of the Darfur conflict in 2003, CNPC witnessed tens of thousands of soldiers from the Sudan Armed Forces leaving the oil fields to wage war in Sudan's western region. Along with southern pro-government militias, these forces had been critical to the protection of oil companies during the civil war. CNPC officials found the JIUs of northern and southern forces to be almost useless security providers.[107] This relative security vacuum provided opportunities for local armed groups to target oil companies, particularly within the 'no man's land' on the border, where neither side held control.[108] There were still government security forces in oil regions, but CNPC experienced a significant decrease in security after 2005. The 10.18 Incident escalated the company's rising concern with the level of security the Sudanese government was providing.

CNPC closely followed rescue work by the Sudanese authorities during the 10.18 Incident. After negotiations between the kidnappers and local tribal leaders broke down, Sudanese authorities were determined to pursue the kidnappers. CNPC officials were against the idea; they did not want to provoke them in any way.[109] But the Sudanese government asserted its political authority and went forward with the rescue operation. The violent result left CNPC executives furious. 'The attack freaked them out,' said one Chinese oil industry insider. 'They started looking for answers to developments in Sudan outside of the Khartoum government.'[110]

Because the 10.18 Incident kidnapping and killings took place in Sudan, the heart and soul of CNPC's 'go global' campaign, it had a markedly different impact compared to other attacks on Chinese national oil companies abroad: it galvanised strategic thinking at CNPC on overseas security. Established in December 2004 within the CNPC International Department, it is the Overseas Security and Health, Safety and Environment Office, which translates directly into 'anti-terrorism' in Chinese, that largely shapes company policy on security.

After the 10.18 Incident in Sudan, the priority attached to security by CNPC rose significantly. The Overseas Security office was expanded and security training was subsequently provided to all of the 56,000 CNPC employees in the international staffing rotation.[111] A command centre for emergencies was established in Beijing and each subsidiary around the world was required to have a security division. 'Safety comes first. In no way do we want profits stained with blood,' wrote the International Department head Wang Hongtao and other CNPC officials in 2009.[112]

One new security method to decrease the danger facing Chinese workers employed by CNPC was to use more local labour overseas. CNPC estimates that 60 per cent of its workforce sensitive countries is made up by Chinese nationals because of the large number of Chinese oil service subsidiaries that have accompanied CNPC abroad.[113] CNPC, Sinopec and other large Chinese companies were also increasingly providing personal security training for employees, who learned about religious taboos in foreign countries, how to give first aid, and self-defence.[114] When the body of Cui Leilei was found by rescuers in Southern Kordofan in late October 2008, it was determined that he had only recently died from wounds sustained in the confrontation with the kidnappers and Sudanese security forces; if he had known simple navigation techniques, he would more than likely have been able to be spotted by the search teams.[115]

The security-training certificate that each CNPC employee was required to earn provided the basics on how to spot a possible kidnapping attempt before it happened, and if taken hostage, how to cope with long periods of captivity and capitalise on possibilities to escape. Some techniques were more useful than others. For example, company training programmes initially taught employees physical gestures to use to alert local police that were more suitable for urban settings than for the empty savannas of southern Sudan. CNPC quickly learned that new training methods to take account of the various work settings abroad were needed.[116]

In the aftermath of 10.18, it became clear that CNPC had learned an important lesson. Albeit not without incident, the Sudanese government was a capable enough partner in providing security during wartime, when it could unleash brutal counterinsurgency measures and manipulate southern rebel divisions to ensure that oil production moved forward. But Khartoum was hardly a reliable partner in protecting the company's interests during peacetime, when governing, not violence, was necessary. If CNPC was to ensure its long-term well-being in Sudan, it needed to step out of its normal pattern of dealing exclusively with the government and engage with a number of groups and organisations to protect its interests. With southern independence approaching after an affirmative vote in a referendum held in January 2011, Sudan's political landscape was moving beneath the feet of the Chinese oilmen, presenting an entirely different set of risks.

PART V

TWO SUDANS

10

NEW COUNTRY, OLD PROBLEMS

November 2010: 'It's a catastrophe!' Less than two months before southern Sudan was to hold a referendum to determine whether it would separate from Sudan and become an independent country, a senior Sudanese oil official was fuming about the work of CNPC. Dressed in the traditional long white robes of the *jellabiya* and sitting under the dim lighting of a hotel terrace in central Khartoum, he startled a pink lizard scaling the nearby wall with his angry shouts. 'They are producing more water than oil and drilling only dry holes,' he claimed.

Sudan's total oil production began to decline steadily from 2007, and the official thought that CNPC was to blame. Its subsidiaries could recover their expenses for drilling and other exploration and development work even if Sudan's main oil consortium, GNPOC, was producing less and less oil with each passing month. 'We want to bring in local companies instead,' he said.[1] In the wake of the 10.18 Incident, CNPC may have been wondering if it was too close to the Sudanese government for its own good, but in the years preceding southern Sudan's historic referendum vote, Sudanese oil officials were also questioning their over-reliance on the Chinese oil company. Sudan's oil industry was cracking under the pressure of years of pent-up political tension, and the Asian national oil companies and their home governments in Beijing and New Delhi could do little to keep things from falling apart.

At the halfway point of the six-year Comprehensive Peace Agreement (CPA), it was clear that production in Sudan's coveted Unity and Heglig oil fields was falling. The instability and insecurity brought on by the possibility that southern Sudan would separate after the January 2011 referendum, taking three-quarters of Sudan's oil wealth with it, dissuaded much-needed investment in the ageing oil fields by CNPC and its Asian partners.

After South Sudan won its independence in July 2011, the Asian national oil companies were to discover that the new country offered its own set of challenges. The oil companies and their home governments made positive steps to build relations with South Sudan, but after more than a decade of close ties with the south's long-time enemy in Khartoum, the companies faced the prospect of having their oil rights stripped away from them. After the January 2011 referendum, the two Sudans continued to skirmish over disputed borders while negotiating on a possible agreement to continue to pipe South Sudanese oil north. As political tensions between the two Sudans rose, CNPC and OVL discovered that although their respective home governments in Beijing and New Delhi were helpful in entering Sudan in the first place, neither was able to ensure the sustainability of their investments in the face of severe political turmoil in Sudan.

Oil games

From the signing of the CPA in 2005 until the 2011 referendum on South Sudan's independence, intense jockeying for power occurred between the NCP and SPLM, particularly over oil. Under the peace agreement, the NCP and the SPLM, the political wing of the former rebel group SPLA in southern Sudan, agreed to share political power in a Government of National Unity. National elections were planned for 2009 and the referendum for southern independence in January 2011. During the six-year interim period, the former rebels of the SPLM won regional autonomy for the south and formed the Government of Southern Sudan (GOSS). They were allocated half of the oil revenue generated by southern production, where the large majority of reserves was located.[2]

The peace agreement brought plenty of hope to Sudan's oil industry. Security in war-torn regions of southern Sudan gradually improved, which allowed for new investment to increase oil production. But it did not take long for the divisive politics between the NCP and SPLM to deflate expectations that after decades of war political stability had arrived. On the face of it, oil revenue transfers from Khartoum to GOSS in the southern capital of Juba were an enormous change from the long-standing economic and political marginalisation and exploitation of the southern region by the national government. Under the surface, however, the opaque manner in which the NCP continued to manage Sudan's oil industry soon stirred questions within the SPLM about whether it was receiving its fair share of oil revenue.

A Joint Technical Committee for Oil Revenue Sharing composed of northern and southern officials regularly assessed production and revenue allocation, but in addition to delays in revenue transfers to the south, southern officials were kept in the dark about the parameters behind the numbers.[3] In October 2007, the SPLM suspended its participation in the Government of National Unity, in part because it was not allowed to participate in management of the oil industry in the southern region. While it rejoined the government two months later, after striking an agreement that promised an increased oil management role,[4] southern officials continued to question whether secret, off-the-book deals were being conducted by the NCP with international oil traders in order to avoid north-south revenue sharing.[5]

These suspicions grew when Global Witness, an international advocacy group, published a report in 2009 claiming that there were multiple discrepancies between CNPC's oil production figures and those of the Sudanese government.[6] The SPLM leadership was adamant that Khartoum was manipulating the figures. 'After four years of our sole, lonely voice, it has been confirmed that there (have) been serious discrepancies that might mean that the government of South Sudan has been cheated for hundreds of millions of dollars,' said the SPLM Secretary-General, Pagan Amum.[7] 'We need transparency, and we are calling for transparency now.'

The Sudanese government immediately rejected these allegations. 'The report of (the) Global Witness group depended on inaccurate information and had not asked the Sudanese government about the real situation,' said the oil minister Al-Zubair Ahmed Hassan.[8] In a rare public response to an advocacy group, CNPC rebutted the findings. It claimed that production figures were different between the government and the company because they were measured at different points of the production process; while the company was reporting output from wellheads at its oil fields, the government measured at the point of export. According to CNPC, losses in total volume of oil occurred along the way through the pipeline and infrastructure, as the oily-watery mix of crude oil was transported and processed.[9] Global Witness argued that the discrepancies in production figures between the Sudan government and CNPC were still too large (when measured by industry standards) to be accounted for solely by losses in processing and transport.[10] In turn, the Asian national oil companies concluded that Global Witness was driving an unnecessary wedge between the north and south.[11] This dispute did not die down, and did little to help ongoing negotiations between northern and southern officials on how to manage the oil industry in the event of southern Sudan's separation.

But this was not the only oil-related conflict between the NCP and SPLM. As part of the CPA, the contested region of Abyei along the north-south border was designated as one of the 'Three Areas', along with the Nuba Mountains and Blue Nile.[12] Abyei was granted special administrative status, a small share of oil revenue, and the right to hold its own referendum to decide whether it would join the south or the north.[13] To start the process, the Abyei Boundaries Commission (ABC) was appointed to demarcate the borders of the region. But the NCP rejected the ABC's findings, which placed a number of oil fields, including Heglig, inside the Abyei region. The parties then agreed to take the dispute to the Permanent Court of Arbitration (PCA) in The Hague for a final ruling. In July 2009, the PCA found that the ABC had exceeded its mandate on certain points of border demarcation.[14] The PCA changed the eastern boundary of the area demarcated by the ABC's findings, placing Heglig outside the Abyei area.[15] Khartoum was quick to declare that future oil revenue transfers to the south would not include earnings from oil fields ruled to lie outside Abyei. But the ruling only determined the borders of Abyei, not whether Heglig and other oil fields were in the north or the south.

SPLM officials insisted that the decision about the location of the oil fields would have to be determined by the Technical Ad hoc Border Committee set up in the CPA.[16] After much delay, the committee announced in May 2010 that 80 per cent of the demarcation process was complete, but critical areas, such as Heglig, remained in dispute.[17] The southern Sudanese knew Heglig as Panthou or Aliiny, and as part of their territory. The location of the oil field remained a point of friction as the referendum vote drew near. The undecided border between the north and south and the political bickering over oil revenue transfers did little to help either the NCP or the SPLM focus on the deteriorating health of the oil industry.

Stagnation

In the middle of the hustle and bustle of Beijing's Wudaokou student district, Su Yongdi was hard at work. After leaving Sudan in 2005, Su became a chief geologist in the Africa department of the Research Institute of Petroleum Exploration Development, CNPC's research and development centre. In this centre located on the former campus of Beijing Petroleum University, where a large white statue of Mao Zedong greets visitors at the main entrance, Su presided over two large computer screens in an otherwise simple office overlooking the institute's well-kept grounds. On a large map on the wall the locations of CNPC's exploration and production activities around the world were marked with tiny red flags. Although the company's international activities had grown significantly since Su first went to Khartoum in 1997, a number of geological maps of the Bentiu area of southern Sudan on a table demonstrated that he was still very much preoccupied with the company's most cherished investments.

Ten years after the GNPOC began operations and thousands of Chinese workers helped construct Sudan's first oil pipeline, flattening production levels and a lack of new discoveries were clear signs that the strength of the industry was diminishing. The Unity, Heglig, and other oil fields of Blocks 1, 2 and 4 in Unity state operated by GNPOC, and those of the Petrodar Operating Company, or PDOC, in Blocks 3 and 7 of Upper Nile state made up nearly 90 per cent of oil production.[18] The remainder was brought to export by the White Nile Petroleum Operating Company (WNPOC) in Block 5A of southern Unity state and the CNPC-run Petro Energy in Block 6 of Southern Kordofan. According to Sudapet, the Sudan National Petroleum Corporation, production hit a peak of a little over 483,000 bpd in 2007.[19]

There were differing estimates of how much oil was left in Sudan. In 2010, the influential *Oil and Gas Journal* estimated that Sudan had around 5 billion barrels, which would last at current production levels for three decades. But Sudan's own Ministry of Energy and Mining thought there were only 2.35 billion barrels left, leaving a little over a decade of supply at current production levels.[20] Output levels of the high quality Nile-blend oil drilled by GNPOC fell from a peak of nearly 287,988 bpd on average in 2004 to 124,766 bpd by June 2011.[21] Since going onstream in April 2006, production from Blocks 3 and 7 in Upper Nile of the lower quality Dar-blend crude compensated for the loss, but a Chinese geologist said that Petrodar passed its own output peak in 2010 and was expected to drop sharply in the coming years.[22] A lack of new discoveries was shortening the oil industry's lifespan.

Sudanese oil officials felt that CNPC was not interested in the long-term maximisation of oil production during its initial years of operation. They argued that continuous studies of the oil fields were not undertaken to learn how to improve recovery rates as production moved forward. 'These are all national oil companies,' said one Sudanese oil company manager. 'They don't invest in research and development like the Western firms do.'[23] A decade later, the proof of poor reservoir management was evident in a shortened plateau period of high levels of oil output and a sharper drop in production than had been forecast earlier.[24] Indications of premature high water content in production also increased concerns that the Chinese-led GNPOC did not manage its oil fields with the long term in mind.[25] 'CNPC was working to produce, not working on how to produce,' said a former Sudanese oil official.[26] The rapid decline of the Unity and Heglig fields caused some in the oil industry to suggest that GNPOC was pumping as fast as possible to recover its investment because it was afraid that the civil war would halt its activities.[27] Although a detailed examination of all the wells GNPOC drilled over the years would be needed to prove that intentional over-pumping took place, many Sudanese oil officials had already made up their minds that CNPC in particular was at fault for the early fall in production.

The Ministry of Energy and Mining signed a cooperation agreement with Norway in 2008, in part to receive technical assistance in improving oil recovery. A Norwegian study found that the average recovery rate in Sudan of 23 per cent could be pushed up to an international average of 30 per cent and generate billions in new revenue if the proper investment was made.[28] But Sudapet estimated that investment in technology to improve recovery would cost up to $300 million for a single field.[29]

CNPC got serious about improving oil recovery rates in Sudan from 2009 onward by conducting studies, convening technical seminars and starting pilot projects where new recovery techniques were put into practice.[30] But speculation continued that corners had been cut in the past in developing Sudan's oil fields, in a way that would depress future production. 'An oil reservoir is like an elephant,' said an oil service company manager in Sudan.[31] 'It has a long memory, and if you mistreat it, it could take decades until it produces more oil again.'

From 2005 the exploration work of all oil companies in Sudan, not just CNPC, was disappointing. Block 5B was considered a highly prospective concession made accessible by the end of the civil war. But in 2008, the WNPOC consortium, made up of Petronas, Lundin and OVL, drilled three unsuccessful exploration wells.[32] One company manager said that not only did they fail to discover oil, but in addition there was little evidence of any source rock, the type of rock where oil is typically generated over time. This spate of dry wells drove fears that the further one went south in search of oil in Sudan, the worse the chances were of finding it.[33]

There was also a lack of exploration work in Sudan's massive oil concessions. 'We have no idea what is going on there, because smaller companies do not have the money or the foreign ones from China or India are not willing to spend on exploration,' said a Sudanese oil company manager.[34] There were some possibilities of oil deposits in north-western Darfur, but the size of the prospects was not considered to be commercially attractive, especially considering the insecurity due to the ongoing civil war in Sudan's western region.[35] Much of the hope rested in the enormous oil concession Total had abandoned at the beginning of the second civil war. At 118,000 square kilometres, Block B in Jonglei and Lakes states of southern Sudan had the most potential to boost flattening Sudanese production levels. But Total did not advance with exploration activities during the six years of the CPA. Instead, Sudanese oil officials were increasingly turning their attention to the failure of the Asian national oil companies to improve productivity in their main oil fields.

CNPC and its Asian partners may have cut their international teeth in Sudan during the late 1990s, but according to Sudanese oil officials in Khartoum, the use of Sudan as a training ground came at a cost. The GNPOC consortium quickly constructed its oil pipeline after it was established in 1997, but there were long delays in getting oil from Blocks 3 and 7 run by PDOC in Upper Nile state to international markets. Segments of the pipeline were misaligned by some 50 metres by the various oil service companies involved in its construction. As a result, in late August 2006, government reductions to petrol and sugar subsidies to offset delayed oil revenue in the planned national budget sparked public protests on the streets of central Khartoum, which were met by police with violence.[36] The delays were blamed on a lack of managerial efficiency among the Asian national oil companies.[37] There was a growing sense that while CNPC and Petronas were happy to champion their own service companies in large projects, at times, they were not able to work together effectively for the good of Sudan's oil industry.

Overseeing large overseas projects was a challenge for all international oil companies. But the mismanagement problems of CNPC in Sudan revealed a major problem at the Chinese oil giant. CNPC may have been steering Chinese government policy on overseas investments, but managing a company of 1.6 million employees was a nightmare; the long line of subsidiaries working under CNPC, each with numerous departments and offices, would challenge the most gifted corporate executive.[38] The company was still in the process of testing the ability of an assortment of subsidiaries to operate overseas when it first entered Sudan; these were companies accustomed to working independently of one another across China.[39] As a result, they were not necessarily doing what was best in the long term for the parent company's interests, but were rather leveraging their own revenues and profits first. It was not until 2008 that CNPC began to reorganise its subsidiaries to provide integrated services that focused on project-wide efficiency.[40] But by then, Sudan's oil industry was already in steep decline.

The oil companies were not exclusively to blame for the poor state of Sudan's oil industry. Accusations of mismanagement thrown at CNPC neglected the government's own role. One Sudanese oil official felt that the NCP leadership suffered from a 'war legacy' where oil production was concerned.[41] During the civil war in the south, the NCP pushed CNPC and other oil companies to quickly develop infrastructure and ramp up production to generate revenue for fighting the SPLA. During the interim period of the peace agreement, the NCP's demand for steady increases in oil production was designed to gain as much revenue as possible before the very likely separation of southern Sudan. When it became evident that output was peaking early, the government changed its approach and demanded that the companies focus on enhancing their recovery rates. But the new-found attention to efficiency coincided with a sharp drop in oil prices in mid-2008 and rising insecurity in and around the GNPOC oil fields, which together dissuaded new investment by

Asian national oil companies.[42] In a way reminiscent of Chevron's reluctance to invest in Sudan in the face of insecurity in the 1980s, CNPC and its Asian partners were not willing to invest hundreds of millions of dollars in enhanced recovery techniques with the potential separation of southern Sudan approaching and the prospect of an unknown regulatory landscape that might accompany its independence.

The Asian national oil companies would suffer the consequences of neglecting the oil fields. Both OVL and Petronas experienced a drop in total overseas oil production levels in 2008 and 2009, which was largely the result of falling levels in Sudan.[43] As the largest stakeholder in the GNPOC consortium, CNPC was losing the most. But the company stayed quiet. True to its traditional secretive demeanour, it released very little information about its international oil field production. Together with its Asian partners, CNPC avoided much of the political instability and insecurity during the civil war. But as one Sudan became two in July 2011, the risk it had initially taken to invest and produce in a highly unstable country was coming full circle for the company.

The state to come

On 9 July 2011, tens of thousands gathered at Freedom Square in Juba to witness the birth of South Sudan. Close to 99 per cent of the southern Sudanese voters chose to break away from Sudan six months earlier. Wearing his trademark black cowboy hat, a gift from US President George W. Bush, Salva Kiir was sworn in as the new nation's first president. 'Our martyrs did not die in vain....We have waited for more than 56 years for this day,' said Kiir, remembering the terrible sacrifices that millions of people had made to attain independence.[44]

The man who originally led the SPLA into rebellion in 1983 was buried not far away from Freedom Square. The southern rebel leader John Garang was made First Vice-President of Sudan at the end of the civil war in 2005, but within months the charismatic SPLM leader was killed in a helicopter crash on his return from a trip to Uganda. The chances of the CPA fulfilling its goal of 'making unity attractive', of a new but united Sudan, were greatly diminished by his death.[45]

William Doh, who had transformed from a storeroom assistant in Chevron's operations to a rebel fighter with the SPLA, lost three of his brothers in the civil war. He went on to obtain a Master's degree in England after the civil war, but would not see South Sudan win its freedom; in March 2011, he died from tuberculosis and heart complications in a Nairobi hospital. SPLA comrades remembered Doh for his brave acts in battle during the civil war. But the South Sudan that he helped free from decades of political and economic marginalisation and manipulation was now facing many challenges of its own. The southern migration of Asian national oil companies to South Sudan was fraught with danger.

During the six-year interim period, southern Sudan demonstrated that it was in no way on the path to becoming a stable and secure state for Asian national oil companies to operate in after it attained independence. The ruling SPLM in southern Sudan did little to improve the standard of poor governance established by the NCP in Khartoum. After the petro-dollars started to flow following the signing of the CPA, glaring examples of fiscal mismanagement and graft rose to the surface. From the time the former rebels began to receive oil revenue transfers from Khartoum in 2005 until South Sudan's independence in 2011, they earned over $13 billion.[46] But the SPLM, acting like the Sudanese government, allocated the majority of oil revenue to the GOSS' and SPLA's salaries and security expenditure rather than to development. The SPLM also followed in the NCP's footsteps by centralising resources and expenditure: 90 per cent of salaries and 67 per cent of development expenditure were concentrated in the capital, Juba.[47] While the capital may have been undergoing fast-paced urbanisation, it and other major towns remained crippled by a lack of investment in health care, infrastructure and education.

In 2009, operating on a constrained budget owing to a sharp drop in international oil prices the year before, southern Sudanese officials' frivolous expenses, such as overseas training courses and huge sums spent on travel and hotel bills, were aired in public.[48] While these expenses were not necessarily illegal, they were certainly wasteful uses of southern Sudanese oil wealth and did not impress the wider impoverished population. More alarming were reports from the southern Sudanese Auditor General that billions were missing through fake contracts and inflated salaries paid by government ministries.[49] In May 2012, eleven months after South Sudan became independent, President Kiir sent a letter to seventy-five former and current government officials stating that $4 billion in government funds had been stolen over the years. 'We fought for freedom, justice and equality,' the letter read. 'The credibility of our government is on the line.'[50] But more than the new country's character and integrity was in jeopardy. The SPLM's shoddy management of oil revenue fuelled grievances that threatened to seriously destabilise the already politically fragile country.

Some of the worst periods of violence during the second civil war arose from southern infighting. The Sudanese government supported a number of southern militias to fight the SPLA. Consequently, during the interim period of the CPA, Salva Kiir and the SPLM sought to make amends and integrate southern militias into the SPLA. The largest of the militias was the South Sudan Defence Force (SSDF) led by Paulino Matip, who had been an Anyanya fighter during Sudan's first civil war and was implicated in the attack on Chevron's Rubkona facility in 1984. He subsequently became a close ally of Khartoum in the second civil war. After the 2006 Juba Declaration with Salva Kiir and the SPLM, however, Matip was made Deputy Commander-in-Chief of the SPLA and his SSDF was brought into the South Sudanese army. But the wider integration of the SSDF into the southern forces was far from complete.[51] In many respects, it was a financial pay-off with little actual political power passed to former SSDF leaders.[52] As the south headed towards independence, the SPLA remained far from a cohesive unit.

After delayed national elections were held across a still united Sudan in April 2010, over half a dozen southern Sudanese rebel groups, some led by high-ranking former SSDF commanders, others by SPLA officers, announced their opposition to Juba. In Unity, Jonglei and Upper Nile states, the southern rebel groups were driven by a mix of personal ambition, motivation and support from Khartoum to destabilise the south, but also by grievances against SPLM rule.[53] Together, they did not necessarily pose an outright threat to the SPLM's rule, but they kept large parts of southern Sudan insecure.[54] Some of the rebellions fed off wider grievances among the ethnically diverse southern Sudan population. In Jonglei state, some 2,500 people had been killed and almost 350,000 displaced in 2009 as a result of inter-tribal violence among the Lou Nuer, Murle, and Dinka ethnic groups. The SPLA's heavy-handed response to the fighting was directed for the most part at the Murle community and played a large part in bolstering subsequent recruitment drives of the main southern rebel group.[55]

China's hand was seen in the southern fighting. After CNPC led the way, Chinese state-owned arms manufacturers, also profit-seeking, commercially-motivated and nationally-owned companies, were opening up new markets of their own in Sudan.[56] Quite paradoxically, while Chinese oil executives were trying to befriend the SPLM in Juba, southern Sudanese rebels armed with new Chinese-made assault rifles were threatening to overthrow the southern Sudan government. While the insecurity of southern Sudan during the interim period of the CPA did little to encourage hopes on the part of CNPC and its Asian partners for stability in South Sudan, it was the SPLM's management of the oil industry that was the most worrying sign.

The CPA stated that all existing oil contracts in Sudan made before its signing would be protected from renegotiation. As the leading partner in an international consortium, Total had maintained rights to all of Block B during the civil war after declaring *force majeure*, and it renewed its contract with the Sudanese government shortly before the signing of the CPA. Fearing that Khartoum would sell off all the oil rights without their consent, some high-level SPLM officials moved ahead with plans to sign their own agreements with different oil companies.[57] In one of these deals, the rebel leader John Garang engaged a fledgling British corporation, White Nile Ltd.[58] SPLM officials decided to carve up the Block B oil concession into three segments and granted White Nile a section in Jonglei state, Block Ba. These conflicting contracts led the French oil major to take the British oil minnow White Nile to a London court. Total had conducted aeromagnetic and seismic surveys on the concession in the 1980s, and regarded Block B as a rare opportunity.[59] A study by independent geologists commissioned by White Nile found that Block Ba alone could contain up to 5 billion barrels from extensions of the Muglad and Melut basins and new basins.[60] Block B held the possibility of renewing a stagnating oil industry and was heavily contested.

White Nile appealed to many in southern Sudan. It granted the newly-established southern oil company Nilepet 50 per cent ownership and promised much in terms of community development projects. 'We started out by saying to the southern Sudanese: 'This is your land. We'd like to develop oil. What are your expectations?', said Philip Ward, Chief Operating Officer of While Nile.[61] Philip Thon Leek, the governor of Jonglei state where the disputed block was located, backed White Nile's claim. 'A court in the UK has no right to decide who I should give my land to carry (on) oil exploration in,' he said in May 2007.[62] White Nile also had friends in high places. It worked closely with Riek Machar and his wife Angelina Teny, who acted as State Minister of Energy and Mining in the Government of National Unity formed between the NCP and SPLM during the interim period of the CPA. But at the end of the day, it did not have the technical capacity or the finance to explore the concession properly.

At first, the GOSS President Salva Kiir was not concerned about the White Nile affair in 2005. It demonstrated southern authority at a time when the SPLM was trying to manage the oil industry. But after the fledgling company drilled its first well in Jonglei state in 2007, Total turned up the pressure on the southern Sudanese government. It stressed that, as an oil major, it was far more capable of developing the concession with state-of-the-art technology and ample financing. Kiir ordered an investigation into the White Nile dispute and later decided to expel the British company.[63]

The White Nile dispute revealed friction over oil among the southern leadership cadres. The main dividing lines were personal, professional and ethnic, highlighted by occasional power struggles between President Salva Kiir, a Dinka, and Riek Machar, his Nuer Vice-President and a former SPLM defector.[64] Kiir's decision to oust White Nile was regarded as a move to take better control of the oil industry.[65] 'White Nile became an embarrassment for Kiir,' said a former SPLM oil adviser.[66] While the company was regarded as a vehicle for some SPLM officials to enrich themselves through speculation in its London stock market listing, in the end it was not seen as capable enough to take part in the development of southern Sudan's oil industry.

Before the CPA, SPLM officials also signed a deal with the Moldovan company ASCOM for rights in Block 5B of the WNPOC, of which Petronas and OVL were members. But instead of dropping ASCOM, as the SPLM eventually did with White Nile through the National Petroleum Commission, it allowed ASCOM to remain. Unlike White Nile, ASCOM had the capacity to conduct serious oil development work. It drilled a number of oil wells and reported $150 million in investment.[67] Kuol Manyang, the southern Sudanese Governor of Jonglei state where the concession was located, told WNPOC representatives not to take their operations east of the White Nile river.[68] For the WNPOC partners, the political intervention of the southern regional government added to existing concerns the consortium had about security in the concession. But there was nothing WNPOC or Sudan's oil ministry could do. Block 5B was deep in southern territory and the SPLM was flexing its new-found political muscle. But in the end, the result was the same for both WNPOC and ASCOM.[69] Wells drilled on both sides of the river came up dry.

These various oil concession disputes in southern Sudan set the stage for the main event: the question of whether the SPLM would recognise the rights of Asian national oil companies as the operators in the main oil concessions once South Sudan won its independence. The oil consortia run by CNPC, OVL, and Petronas in Unity and Upper Nile states may have been in decline, but they were still producing hundreds of thousands of barrels each day and generating tremendous profits for the Asian national oil companies. But there were plenty of reasons why the companies should have been worried. It would be an uphill climb to keep their oil interests intact in South Sudan.

Getting acquainted

China had little official contact with the SPLM prior to the signing of the CPA. While it may have pursued a policy of non-interference in Sudan during the civil war, southern Sudanese rebels certainly thought China was supporting the enemy through its political and economic engagement with Khartoum.[70] This put CNPC's oil investments at risk in an independent South Sudan. 'The suffering of the people is on the hands of the Chinese,' said one SPLA commander at the end of the civil war. 'The agreements for the Chinese company may be terminated.'[71] The uncertain future facing CNPC's oil interests became clear when President Kiir made an official visit to Beijing in July 2007. As GOSS President at the time, he clearly spelt out to Chinese President Hu Jintao that the majority of Sudan's oil was in the south and that the southern Sudanese would exercise their right of self-determination in four years.

From that point on, Beijing saw the writing on the wall. The Chinese government moved to enhance its relations with Juba in an effort to ensure that CNPC's investments would remain unscathed after South Sudan's separation.[72] In August 2010, China's Deputy Foreign Minister Zhai Jun told Scott Gration, the US Special Envoy to Sudan, that 'China respects the will of the people, no matter the result of the referendum in Juba.'[73] Beijing would remain a close partner of the ruling NCP in Sudan, but would also attempt to balance this engagement with new relations with the ruling SPLM in the south.

Beijing went on a diplomatic offensive to win over the SPLM. In October 2011, the SPLM Secretary-General Pagan Amum travelled to Beijing to meet Li Changchun, a member of the Communist Party's Politburo Standing Committee. Amum hailed China as a 'strategic partner' and promised to protect its oil interests. This position was a far cry from the SPLM position during the Sudan's second civil war, when Chinese oil interests were military targets for the southern rebels. But the calculations of the SPLM were in flux and there was much an independent South Sudan could gain from China. 'During the struggle of the people of South Sudan, China took the side of the government in Khartoum,' Amum said. 'But that is history, a troubled history, and we will not allow ourselves to be hostages of the past.'[74] In return, Li committed China to building a 'win-win cooperation with South Sudan'.[75] This exchange was a clear sign that both the South Sudanese and the Chinese were more pragmatic than principled. It was not the first time Li had made such a promise; six years earlier, he had conveyed a similar statement to the Sudanese Vice-President Ali Osman Taha in Khartoum.[76] But now China found itself between the two opposing sides. 'They want to be close to us and close to Khartoum,' said South Sudan's oil minister, Stephen Dhieu Dau.[77] 'But Jesus said you cannot serve two masters.'

Chinese oilmen thought that working in Khartoum in the late 1990s was a challenge because of the lack of infrastructure and the dry, hot climate. In April 2010, after coming to Juba to establish an office, they found the southern capital refreshingly lush, but lacking roads and infrastructure altogether. Some initial arrivals from the company contracted malaria and were so disturbed by the insecurity that they looked into ordering bulletproof vests.[78] The company established a temporary office near the Beijing Juba Hotel, where other Chinese companies and the embassy were also established after South Sudan's independence.[79] Other joint venture companies would follow slowly, moving from their soaring glass headquarters in Khartoum to the prefabricated container houses of Juba.

In 2009, CNPC senior management put on a brave face concerning the upcoming separation of South Sudan. Vice-President Wang Dongjin said his company was taking a 'wait-and-see' attitude about the southern referendum, but hoped to continue to produce oil along the disputed border region regardless of the results.[80] But this public posture masked pressing internal concerns. When CNPC staff first arrived in Juba a year later, their first goal was to 'learn how to relate to the southern government'.[81] The company did not sit idly by as the political ground changed beneath its feet. It was well aware of its links with the violent history of the civil war. CNPC built a new computer lab at the University of Juba to show its goodwill, and together with its Asian partners funded new tarmac at Juba International Airport to receive international arrivals for the 9 July 2011 independence ceremony.[82]

CNPC maintained contact with the Chinese diplomatic presence in the Sudans, but also sought to manage its own affairs. In parallel to its government's efforts to establish smooth relations with South Sudan, CNPC carried out some diplomacy of its own when Amum was in Beijing in October 2011. During a banquet held at company headquarters, Amum was told by CNPC President Jiang Jiemin that, 'if anything bad happened, it was not from them but from the government of Sudan'.[83] The Chinese company, Jiang assured Amum, wanted to 'sort things out, to heal'.

India followed a similar line to China. India was the first Asian country to open a consulate in southern Sudan's capital Juba in October 2007.[84] In the run-up to southern Sudan's referendum, a senior Indian official in Khartoum called for a 'timely, credible, and transparent' vote in which the 'popular will' of southerners would be respected.[85] After a visit from a southern Sudanese special envoy to New Delhi in April 2011, the Indian Ministry of External Affairs was confident that OVL's interests would be protected. 'Our understanding is that the agreements pertaining to India will be honoured,' said one MEA spokesman.[86] But months later, fears were rising in New Delhi that the oil contracts between OVL and South Sudan would in fact be rewritten.[87] For its part, OVL was particularly disturbed by the possibility of losing its contractual rights and the operational risks of insecurity in concession areas.[88] In the end, OVL largely piggybacked on Chinese efforts to protect their joint investments. But, unfortunately for the Indian company, it appeared that CNPC was making little progress in effectively managing the oil industry under the new South Sudanese government.

The International Energy Agency estimated that in December 2011, before the oil shutdown, Sudan was producing 110,000 bpd and South Sudan 260,000 bpd. This was a noticeable decrease from the first half of that year, when a united Sudan churned out 450,000 bpd.[89] Part of the reason for this shortfall was that South Sudan lacked trained personnel to work in the oil industry.[90] CNPC was bringing Southern Sudanese to

Beijing for training and carrying out vocational workshops in Juba,[91] but in the meantime the South Sudanese oil ministry would not provide approval to bring in more Chinese manpower, equipment and materials to maintain the oil fields. Instead, the Chinese oilmen watched with suspicion as US advisers to the South Sudanese government visited their central and field processing facilities in Upper Nile state.[92]

South Sudan's close relationship with the US was viewed as a possible threat to the Chinese oilmen. The South Sudanese government was engaging Halliburton and other US and Western oil service companies with an eye to convincing these companies to invest and improve oil field recovery rates.[93] Although CNPC was already working in Sudan with Western oil services companies such as Schlumberger, CNPC saw Juba's engagement with US officials as a possible sign that US oil companies were coming to South Sudan. As things stood, it could not be much worse for the Chinese company. It had strained political relations with the Sudanese government and was struggling to foster new ties with Juba. But standing as it did between the feuding Sudans, CNPC was about to discover that the worst was still to come.

Shutdown

When South Sudan won its official independence, Khartoum and Juba still faced an oil conundrum. Three-quarters of oil production was located in South Sudan, but the only route to bring the oil to market was via pipelines heading through Sudan. Beginning in June 2010, an African Union High Level Implementation Panel, led by former South African President Thabo Mbeki, was charged with facilitating negotiations over outstanding issues between the Government of Sudan and, after July 2011, the Government of the Republic of South Sudan. These included disputes over security, citizenship, borders, and not least, oil. Sudan and South Sudan committed to becoming two mutually viable states at peace with one another. Offsetting the loss of oil was key to the economically viability of Sudan, while maintaining oil production was crucial for South Sudan's economic future.

Sudan and South Sudan agreed that their economies were interdependent through oil. But there was no consensus on how the south should provide payment to the north for usage of its pipeline infrastructure. As the official separation of South Sudan in July 2011 approached, progress was made as the talks were steered forward by a Norwegian petroleum envoy. In March, at the Ethiopian resort Kuriftu, the two sides agreed that a transit fee and a transitional financial arrangement would be established for Sudan to account for the use of its oil infrastructure and its loss of oil revenues. Later that year, Sudan and South Sudan decided that the south alone should not be expected to cover Sudan's entire financial gap. Rather AU mediators suggested that Sudan invoke austerity measures to cover around one-third of the losses while South Sudan and the international community split the rest.[94] Between 2011 and 2015, Sudan's revenue gap from the loss of oil was estimated to measure $7.7 billion by the IMF.[95] While negotiations continued in Addis Ababa at the end of the year, South Sudan's oil continued to flow through Sudan. Even though an agreement was not in place, South Sudan raised $3.2 billion in revenue from oil during its first six months of independence.[96] But at the end of the year, Sudanese and South Sudanese officials were still unable to come to an agreement. On the one side, Juba wanted the transit fee to be based on international examples, such as the 1,000 kilometre Chad-Cameroon pipeline, for which Chad paid Cameroon 41 cents per barrel. Since the GNPOC pipeline was roughly 1,600 km long and the PDOC pipeline 1,500 km, southern officials decided on 69 and 63 cents per barrel respectively as fees, and later raised their proposal to a $1 fee for each. But Sudan wanted a total of $36 dollars per barrel in pipeline fees, plus a transitional financial arrangement with South Sudan, to offset the loss of oil. Northern officials said that their calculations included costs associated with using the pipeline, central processing facilities, the marine terminal and other infrastructure that they had originally invested in.[97] Such a transit fee was unprecedented in the international oil industry; not surprisingly, negotiations moved nowhere. Instead, fighting continued along the now internationally disputed border between Sudan and South Sudan.

In May 2011, two months before South Sudan's independence, the Sudanese army, supported by Misseriya militias, took control of Abyei town by force. As in the fighting three years earlier in the disputed region, tens of thousands of civilians were forced to flee as Sudanese planes, artillery, tanks, and soldiers attacked.[98] A month after overrunning Abyei, the Sudanese army moved against forces of the SPLA-North in Southern Kordofan and later in Blue Nile. The SPLA-North was made up of an assortment of former SPLA fighters. Discontent with Khartoum's unwillingness to implement popular consultations in Southern Kordofan and Blue Nile, as stipulated in the CPA, the SPLA-North took up arms after the Sudanese army tried to forcefully disband the group. The fighting displaced hundreds of thousands of civilians with government bombing raids on civilian targets in both Sudanese and South Sudanese territory, and led to a humanitarian disaster.[99] While the fighting was generally a good distance from CNPC's oil fields, other Chinese companies would be affected. Ironically, while the oil giant had paved the way for China's wider economic involvement in Sudan, its Chinese counterparts were now under fire as well.

In an attack on a town in Southern Kordofan, twenty-nine Chinese employees of Sinohydro, a hydropower engineering and construction company, were captured by SPLA-North rebels.[100] Chinese officials were quick to hold direct meetings with the leaders of the SPLM-North, Malik Aggar and Yasir Arman, to help facilitate the release of the hostages.[101] The men were released shortly afterwards, with help from the International Committee of the Red Cross. The Chinese government appeared to be developing a better understanding of the lie of the land in the Sudans by comparison with its response to CNPC's 10.18 Incident, in which it had relied heavily on Khartoum. But the ability of both the Chinese and Indian governments to adapt to a changing political landscape in order to protect the investments of their national oil companies would be put to the test.

The oil impasse between the Sudans was increasingly putting Asian oil interests in jeopardy. South Sudan sold its first shipment of oil to the CNPC subsidiary Chinaoil just weeks after becoming independent. This gave CNPC hope that it was business as usual despite the separation.[102] But in the coming months Sudanese authorities delayed and confiscated shipments of South Sudanese oil in a unilateral move to claim its share of revenue for a yet-to-be established transit fee.[103] One of the shipments was destined for China and was the property of China's main refiner, the national oil company Sinopec. Khartoum was also blocking equipment and materials for the oil industry from entering landlocked South Sudan. A shipment of specialised pumps destined for southern oil fields was delayed at Port Sudan in October 2011.[104]

This series of obstacles roused the Chinese government. China showed a rare open display of displeasure in the growing feud between the two Sudans. Luo Xiaoguang, China's Ambassador to Sudan, called Khartoum's

detainment of oil tankers 'very serious and unjustified'.[105] A Chinese foreign ministry spokesman in Beijing called on the two sides 'to exercise
calm and restraint' and China's special envoy Liu Guijin was dispatched
to Juba and Khartoum in early December 2011.[106] Liu's trip marked
another step towards the Chinese government playing a more direct role
in mediation between the two Sudans, particularly on oil. The venerable
Chinese diplomat was first tapped as Beijing's top man to help bring
peace to civil war in Darfur back in 2007. But over time Liu's attention
had gravitated towards the pending separation of South Sudan and fes-
tering tensions over oil. 'My message to Juba and Khartoum is that…as
people who used to be one, and now with a long border, you have no
other option except peaceful negotiations,' he said in Khartoum.[107] If this
was China exerting its diplomatic force, it did not work: both the Sudanese
and the South Sudanese were non-responsive.

In Khartoum, despite the Chinese special envoy's calls for restraint,
the Sudanese parliament passed a law authorising the confiscation of oil
passing through its pipeline as payment for transit fees. Back in Juba,
South Sudan threatened to turn off the oil taps altogether.[108] CNPC
feared for the worst. If there was a forceful stoppage without the pipeline being properly flushed, the heavy oil would solidify and cause extensive and costly damage.[109]

China's efforts to balance its interests between Sudan and South Sudan
were under strain as conflict on the battlefield and at the negotiation
table grew. China did not hold sway over the two Sudans. On the con-
trary, each side was pushing Beijing to support its position in the negotiations. While Khartoum had fostered close relations with Beijing in
the past, the South Sudanese now had the upper hand. Fears that the
new South Sudanese government would kick out the Asian companies
because of their close connections with Sudan during the civil war did
not come to pass, but this was not simply the result of the goodwill gestures of the Asian companies. Pragmatists in the South Sudanese government saw that replacing the current operators in the oil industry would
create serious reputational and legal complications for their oil industry's
future. Instead, the South Sudanese government shrewdly threatened to
nullify CNPC's oil contracts in order to leverage China. It pushed CNPC
and its partners to support its position in negotiations with Sudan on
the pipeline transit fee.[110] It also demanded that the oil companies accept
changes to environmental, social and local employment provisions of the

existing contracts, and the inclusion of a new clause, Article 19, that freed the South Sudanese government from liability or any compensation obligation in the event of an oil shutdown.[111] CNPC was naturally uneasy about the new condition.

On 13 January 2012, when a high-level Chinese delegation including Li Yuanchao, a Politburo member and future Chinese Vice-President, was due to arrive in Juba, a series of alterations to the new contracts was handed to South Sudanese officials at the last moment by the Chinese side. The revisions basically omitted Article 19 and stipulated that oil would continue to pass through the northern pipeline. But the South Sudanese did not yield on their terms. They dismissed the last minute changes and the Chinese company and its partners backed down.[112] By this time, a company so accustomed to getting its way in shaping government policy at home in China must have been feeling out of sorts in South Sudan.

The inclusion of Article 19 in the new oil contracts left the Asian national oil companies vulnerable to rapidly deteriorating relations between Sudan and South Sudan. It took just a week following the high-level Chinese delegation's visit to Juba for the oil shutdown to become a reality for CNPC and its partners. In the planning for months as a possible idea for South Sudan to leverage Sudan in negotiations and protect its national wealth, the South Sudanese Council of Ministers moved forward and announced the shutdown on 20 January 2012.

Sudan had forced the South Sudanese President's hand by delaying and confiscating oil shipments at Port Sudan to pressure his country into paying an exorbitant fee to pipe its oil north. 'At this time, we have no guarantee that oil flowing through the Republic of Sudan will reach its intended destination,' Kiir told his parliament on 23 January 2012. 'We cannot allow assets which clearly belong to the Republic of South Sudan to be subject to further diversion.'[113] Three days before his address, Kiir and his cabinet had unanimously agreed to halt oil production and then quickly pushed the oil companies to implement the decision. US, Norwegian and British advisers, along with Chinese officials in Juba, were not informed beforehand.[114] It was a bold move on the part of Kiir; oil revenue made up roughly 98 per cent of the new government's total revenue.[115] But after decades of Sudan extracting oil from southern soil, the shutdown was a clear sign that South Sudan was now in charge of its oil production.

There was still a chance to stop the shutdown. It would take a number of weeks to close all the oil wells and flush the pipelines properly without causing irreparable damage to the infrastructure. At the end of January 2012, the AU was holding one of its planned bi-annual summits in Addis Ababa. Along with other African heads of state and government, South Sudanese President Salva Kiir and Sudanese President Omar Bashir, would be on hand. The late Prime Minister Mele Zenawi of Ethiopia, who was chair of the Intergovernmental Authority on Development (IGAD), an eight-country regional organisation in East Africa, decided to convene an extraordinary summit of IGAD on the sidelines to try to reach a settlement of the oil crisis. It was a ripe opportunity to bring the two sides back from the brink of the oil shutdown.

The AU mediators were now in a frantic race against time. In the week before the IGAD summit meeting they worked intensely to table an oil package for the two sides to consider. The Sudanese were warming to the possibility of the proposal, but South Sudan's chief negotiator and SPLM General Secretary, Pagan Amum, was adamant that the oil shutdown would go ahead. President Kiir, however, had a different opinion when he later arrived in Addis Ababa. Before the evening summit meeting on 27 January, Kiir informed Zenawi, Mbeki, President Bashir, and other East African leaders, that he was prepared to sign.

It seemed that the shutdown could be averted after all. 'We had informal discussions this morning to deal with the current crisis between the republic of Southern Sudan and the Republic of Sudan,' said Zenawi. 'I believe we will have an announcement to make on this matter at the end of our meeting.'[116] But in a dramatic twist of fortune, when Kiir returned for the official summit meeting that evening, he abruptly reversed his earlier position in front of the other regional heads of state.[117] Later that night, South Sudan's Pagan Amum gave a press conference. 'These talks could not go anywhere because Khartoum is insisting to continue stealing,' he told journalists.[118] He stated that South Sudan would explore developing alternative pipeline routes through Kenya, Djibouti, and Ethiopia and insisted that there was no division within the SPLM regarding the decision not to sign the AU's oil proposal.

The Chinese government supported the AU's mediation and along with CNPC began to play a more active role in the process as the shutdown loomed. In the hope of bringing the sides together, CNPC leadership called on Bashir to release the detained oil tankers. CNPC and its partners in Sudan also suggested that a $600 million crude oil package be offered to Khartoum to avoid a shutdown, with the consortium covering one quarter and South Sudan three quarters of the costs.[119] In a last ditch effort, Yang Jiechi, the Chinese Minister of Foreign Affairs, urged President Kiir at the February 2012 AU Summit to reconsider the oil agreement tabled by the mediators. Jia Qinglin, a member of the Party's Politburo Standing Committee, also met President Bashir on the sidelines of the summit. Kiir stood his ground and the oil taps were turned off in South Sudan.

CNPC and its partners were shocked at the recklessness of the South Sudanese in shutting down their oil production. The decision had been taken without any preparatory studies regarding the possible damage to oil wells and infrastructure. There was also a potential for loss in future production as it would not be economically viable to reopen many of the wells after the shutdown. At the same time, no feasibility studies had been carried out on possible alternative pipelines for South Sudanese crude to flow through Kenya or other third countries.

Pagan Amum and others in the SPLM leadership were not ready to accept an oil deal with Sudan in early 2012.[120] Some were pragmatic and open to working with Sudan. Others were dogmatic in their approach. They were keen to pursue a military plan to overthrow President Bashir and the National Congress party in Khartoum. A similar sentiment was present in the Sudanese military. It hoped the economic consequences of the oil shutdown—petro-dollars accounting for 98 per cent of the southern government's revenues—would deprive the SPLM of the means to support Sudanese rebels and lead to the collapse of the infant South Sudanese state. Just as power in South Sudan's ruling SPLM was not centred on one individual alone, Sudan's National Congress party was made up of factions ranging from the military, internal security and intelligence, the Muslim Brotherhood, and an influential business elite.[121] In 2012, a war of attrition sunk in between Sudan and South Sudan. Each side hoped the other would crumble under economic pressure and worked to support rebel groups operating within each other's territory.

Juba did not waste much time demonstrating who was in charge to the Asian national oil companies now operating within its borders. In the weeks following the oil shutdown, Stephen Dhieu Dau, the South Sudanese oil minister, announced that he had expelled Liu Yingcai, the Chinese President of the Petrodar consortium, claiming that Petrodar had assisted Khartoum in confiscating South Sudan oil shipments and was under-reporting the number of oil wells in its concessions.[122] On 13 January, Liu had written to Dau to report the first of several oil shipment confiscations by Khartoum. 'GOS (Government of Sudan) National Security is overseeing the loading and PDOC (Petrodar) full compliance is required.'[123] But the CNPC oilman was still thrown out of the country a month later by the oil minister.

The first confiscation took place on the same day that the high-level Chinese delegation arrived in Juba in hopes of supporting CNPC's position in talks over new oil contracts with South Sudan. The coincidental timing of the visit with Sudan's first oil confiscation was a demonstration of how the treacherous waters of Sudanese politics could not be navigated by Chinese oil diplomacy alone. The move to expel Liu was a wake-up call for CNPC, a lesson in the abrupt and unpredictable pace of Sudanese politics.[124] Although Beijing failed in its diplomatic efforts to protect CNPC's interests and stop the shutdown, its increased engagement in AU-mediated negotiations between the Sudans did help to redefine its role in the international community as a partner in helping to find a solution to outstanding oil issues. In contrast, as the crisis unfolded, India stood flatfooted, only reacting after the damage was done.

Well before South Sudan's separation, Bhaskar Balakrishnan, a former Indian Ambassador to Sudan, had sounded the alarm bell for trouble to come involving oil. 'The birth of the new nation may give rise to numerous thorny issues,' he warned in *The Hindu*.[125] But there was little response from New Delhi. Indian commentators criticised New Delhi's slow reaction to developments in the Sudans, including the delayed action to upgrade the Indian consulate in Juba to an embassy, despite the fact that OVL's South Sudan operation was one of India's largest investments overseas.[126]

In March 2012, two months after South Sudan's oil shutdown, India named Amarendra Khatua, an additional secretary in charge of the passport division at the Ministry of External Affairs, as Special Envoy to Sudan and South Sudan. It also extended an invitation to Salva Kiir to visit New Delhi and looked to ramp up relations with South Sudan through aid and investment in a mini oil refinery, a solar panel electrification programme, and other projects.[127] In the Indian press, the expulsion of the Chinese president of the Petrodar consortium, of which OVL was not a member, was seen as an opportunity for New Delhi to assert its position in South Sudan at the expense of China.[128] But a long history of China threatening India's interests at home and abroad was masking the reality that New Delhi and its national oil company were firmly attached to the fortunes and misfortunes of its Chinese counterpart. Much like Chevron trying to keep up with fast-paced Sudanese politics thirty years earlier, CNPC and OVL found themselves on shaky ground in South Sudan.

Mistakes of the past

In a short amount of time, South Sudan had begun to lay the foundation for governing its oil industry. The transitional agreements signed by CNPC, OVL and Petronas with the South Sudanese government in January 2012 established the Asian national oil companies as the major players in South Sudan. But the three oil consortia of which the companies had been part in Sudan in the past received a facelift: the Greater Nile Petroleum Operating Company became the Greater Pioneer Operating Company, Petrodar was renamed the Dar Petroleum Operating Company, and WNPOC was now the SUDD Petroleum Operating Company.

South Sudan also signed a new Petroleum Act into law in September 2012, which established principles for governing the oil industry in a more transparent and accountable manner. On paper, this legislation was vastly different from those under which the Asian national oil companies had worked in Sudan in the past.[129] These new rules and regulations were certainly very different from comparable laws at home, too. At a workshop conducted by the Ministry of Petroleum and Mining, Dr Sun Xiansheng, a CNPC manager appointed as President of Dar Petroleum, argued against strong local content provisions in South Sudan's Petroleum Act. He explained that in China there was no petroleum legislation, nor even an oil ministry, which would only entangle the industry in red tape; rather, Sun said, CNPC ran the oil industry.[130]

With CNPC subsidiaries, such as CPECC, and others opening up shop alongside their parent company in Juba, it appeared the Chinese oil industry might have the same overwhelming influence in South Sudan as in Sudan.[131] While the Petroleum Act was passed, in practice the question was left hanging whether the South Sudanese government would fully implement the new system.[132] There were a number of noticeable rifts about oil within the new government that suggested the industry's future management would be highly contested. If the oil industry was not managed in an equitable manner, the SPLM risked internalising the same grievances around oil in its own country that stirred its own rebellion when it was part of a united Sudan.

Political events concerning oil in Unity state in the lead-up to South Sudan's independence provide a good example of the impact of the old two-state issues upon the post-independence oil industry. Taban Deng Gai, the Governor of Unity state, requested that his state receive a 15 per cent stake in oil revenue when South Sudan separated, as opposed to the 2 per cent allocated under the CPA. He argued that the increased funding was needed to correct the environmental damage caused by the oil industry in the past.[133] After South Sudan became independent, Deng would not get what he was looking for. A draft of South Sudan's Petroleum Revenue Management Act maintained the 2 per cent allowance to oil-producing states, but did add 3 per cent for communities in those states.[134] Deng's demand was one issue among others that revealed friction around the oil industry within South Sudan, similar to that between southern Sudan and the Sudanese government before 2011.

President Jaafar Nimeiri had denied the southern Sudanese the opportunity to have a refinery built at Bentiu in Unity state in the early 1980s. Three decades later, the South Sudanese government pushed the idea of constructing several small refineries within its borders before and after independence, to meet domestic demand and capitalise on commercial opportunities in neighbouring states. President Kiir laid the foundation stone for the construction of a refinery at Thiangrial in Melut country of Upper Nile state in November 2012, promising locals that his government would provide roads, health, education and clean drinking water.[135] In an attempt to dispel the grievances of the past, an agreement was also signed to build an oil refinery in Bentiu.[136] But animosities were growing between states over where potential refineries should be located.[137]

The ripe grievances of local populations in oil-bearing communities carried over from the civil war were yet another threat presented by oil in South Sudan. The complaints of local commissioners on environmental issues have often gone unanswered by state governors and SPLM leaders.[138] There were few opportunities for local communities to mitigate their grievances regarding the oil industry in South Sudan. If left unregulated, the sensitive Sudd marshland of South Sudan may evolve into a protracted Niger Delta-esque scenario where local communities are pitted against negligent oil companies. If the internal political and social threats to South Sudan's stability from oil did not warrant enough concern for the future, the ongoing dispute with Sudan did. As the two sides went back to the negotiating table after the shutdown in 2012, they also returned to the battlefield.

The border regions between Sudan and South Sudan heated up in early 2012. In March, Sudanese planes bombed the El Nar oil field and later came dangerously close to hitting facilities at Unity oil fields operated by GNPOC near Rubkona outside Bentiu town, where Chevron oilmen had been killed by southern Sudanese rebels in February 1984. Now CNPC and its Asian partners were under fire, but this time from the Sudanese army. 'The warplanes are hovering everywhere .... One bomb actually just missed Unity base camp but anywhere else so far there is no information,' said Chom Juaj, GNPOC Vice-President.[139] 'It is a very dangerous game, because Sudan's (only) oil field is not that far from where they dropped the bomb,' he added, fearing that the fighting between the two Sudans would reach the nearby Heglig field.[140] 'If the South decides to retaliate, then the two countries will lose.'

South Sudan did retaliate. In early April the South Sudanese army moved against the disputed oil and garrison town of Heglig, which southerners knew as Panthou, in a major escalation of the fighting. South Sudan claimed that Heglig was being used by Sudan as a base for cross-border attacks.[141] To stem the ongoing assaults, South Sudan sent thousands of troops up the road to Heglig to battle the Sudanese army. The southern forces were joined by fighters of the Darfuri rebel group JEM.[142] JEM and other Darfur rebels had formed an alliance with the SPLM-North in Southern Kordofan and Blue Nile, known as the Sudan Revolutionary Front, to overthrow the NCP in Khartoum. All the troubles facing Sudan's long-time rulers came together in the battle for Heglig, which ended in a decisive southern victory. The SPLA then took control of Heglig.

Even though South Sudan still claimed the territory as its own, it faced strong international condemnation for attacking Heglig. The response from the United States, a long-time ally, was particularly harsh because President Kiir had earlier told his American counterpart, Barack Obama, that he would not go forward with the attack, and then went ahead anyway.[143] Facing international pressure from all sides after making this decision, including calls for restraint form China, Kiir halted the military advance and pulled back his troops after ten days.

The Sudanese celebrated the southern withdrawal as a liberation, but soon found that their former countrymen had not left the Heglig oil

facilities untouched. Sudan's oil minister Awad Al-Jaz claimed that southern forces had sabotaged the oil field's main electrical system and other
infrastructure with explosives. South Sudan's President vehemently denied
this. 'One day, if there is law in the world, Panthou will come back to us
by law.... That's why this talk about us damaging [the oil field] is a lie,'
he said.[144] Regardless of how the destruction of Heglig's oil infrastructure took place, it put Sudan in a tough spot. Repairs began soon after
Sudan reclaimed Heglig, but the damage would cut Sudan's remaining
115,000 bpd oil production almost in half at a time when its economy
was already in a tailspin.[145]

Those keen on a full-fledged military confrontation in both Sudan and
South Sudan would not get their wish in 2012. In September, the African Union mediated talks between the two Sudans and managed to
achieve a breakthrough. An agreement on oil fees was reached as well as
a resolution to nine other contentious issues. Thabo Mbeki, head of the
AU mediation team, had wisely kept the rejected oil agreement under
wraps in hopes that South Sudan would return to the table later on down
the road and accept the same agreement; if it became public knowledge,
South Sudan would have been pressured to demand new terms to save
face. 'If we remain silent, then they can come back later and accept it,
maybe in six months,' said Mbeki in January 2012.[146] As he predicted, in
early August, the same oil package, with some very minor changes, was
accepted by South Sudan. The death of Ethiopian President Meles
Zenawi delayed its official signing, but the agreement went ahead the
following month. The oil agreement amounted to South Sudan paying
Sudan $11 per barrel for oil travelling through the GNPOC pipeline
and $9 per barrel for oil passing through the PDOC pipeline. The total
per barrel payment was broken down into processing, transportation, and
transit fees. South Sudan also agreed to pay Sudan $3.028 billion to help
cope with the financial gap left by the loss of oil revenue.[147] Additional
oil fees would also be charged by Sudan to the Asian national oil companies in the new agreement. India's oil ministry openly criticised the
imposition of new transit fees on the operating companies, on the grounds
that OVL had 'invested in a united Sudan' and should not be penalised
for its division.[148]

The post-independence years demonstrated that while Sudan and
South Sudan managed to reach an oil agreement, albeit with difficulty,
implementing it from start to finish would be a much bigger challenge.

Khartoum insisted that South Sudan cut its support to its former allies in the SPLM-North before the oil agreement could be implemented. The multiple agreements signed also failed to address disputes over borders, Abyei, and security issues. In 2012, oil production stayed at zero for South Sudan. The shine of the Sudans was fading for Asia's oil giants.

11

THE REFORM YEARS

April 2012: Salva Kiir did not get what he wanted on his first trip to China as President of the Republic of South Sudan. Kiir had shut down his country's oil production in January, and in the process had brought a multi-billion Chinese-led oil project to a standstill. But Kiir was still hoping that China's President Hu Jintao would offer South Sudan financial support to build a new oil pipeline. He arrived in Beijing only days after ordering the withdrawal of his South Sudanese troops from the captured Heglig oil field near the disputed border with Sudan. 'Our neighbor in Khartoum has declared war on the Republic of South Sudan,' Kiir told the Chinese president. Hu was welcoming, but he was not ready to give Kiir what he wanted most.

'China sincerely hopes that South Sudan and Sudan can become good neighbors who coexist in amity and good partners who develop together,' Hu told Kiir.[1] China wanted to balance its relations between Khartoum and Juba. It was not prepared to throw its full political and economic weight behind a new pipeline that would undermine Sudan's position as the only transit route available to South Sudan to export its oil. During Kiir's visit Li Keqiang, China's premier-in-waiting at the time, asked the South Sudanese President to improve the security of Chinese workers and companies in the future and guarantee the stability of oil cooperation between the two countries.[2] Kiir did not have the same impact in China this time as he had had after his previous visit in 2007. Then, after Kiir as President of the Government of South Sudan had candidly told Hu that the south was going to secede from Sudan and take the major-

239

ity of its oil, China's relations with the region steadily grew. Five years later, as president of the independent South Sudan, Kiir left China without the promise of a new pipeline.

Asian national oil companies were now embroiled in not one but two unstable and insecure countries on the Nile. Sudan's economy went into steep decline after losing the majority of its oil to South Sudan's secession. But South Sudan was also facing economic catastrophe after it shut down its oil production. President Kiir was seeking the construction of a new pipeline from South Sudan to Kenya in order to break the hold that Sudan held over his country's fledgling economy. But the prospects for such a pipeline were stymied by both political reluctance in Beijing and a lack of investor confidence that there was enough oil left in South Sudan to justify a multi-billion dollar initiative. The evolving political situation in the Sudans was forcing both Chinese and Indian national oil companies to rethink their corporate economic and political strategies for international expansion in what remained a politically volatile environment.

CNPC was not the same company it had been when it first entered Sudan. It now sported a large international portfolio, some of which would in the future be likely to dwarf the size of its investment in the Sudans. It was still a risk-taker in the international oil industry, but had become more averse to betting high when the potential payoff was low. And over the years, the jarring violence and political instability in the Sudans only provided leverage for reformers within CNPC to call for a change in the company's overseas approach.

India's OVL was also looking to change its international strategy in the face of political turmoil in its host countries. Company managers watched as their profits dwindled in the Sudans and tried to diversify their overseas investments in response. But the company's main competitive advantage when investing abroad—support from the Indian government—was in jeopardy, as criticism of its floundering overseas ventures grew at home.

Life without oil

Kiir was not the only president who received a lukewarm reception in Beijing. In June 2011, Sudan's President Omar al-Bashir travelled there to meet Hu Jintao to discuss the approaching separation of South Sudan. Upon his arrival in Beijing, Bashir and President Hu repeated the political slogans of traditional friendship between their two countries.[3] 'When the American companies refused to work in the oil fields and when restrictions were imposed on the Western companies' operation in Sudan, we found in China the real partner,' said Bashir.[4] But while the verbal input was still there, a change in the economic output of Sudan-China relations was discernible. Bashir did not receive the backing he needed.[5]

China was certainly not going to abandon Sudan. In recent years, it had become more involved with the efforts of the US, the European Union, and the rest of the international community in the search for a solution to the oil dispute between Sudan and South Sudan, and for ways to help Sudan's economy after the loss of three-quarters of its oil production. But if Bashir hoped that the Chinese president would offer to bail out the Sudanese economy and protect his political future in the process, he was disappointed.

The economic spark of oil that had forged a partnership between China and Sudan in the past was no more. As Sudan's oil output stagnated, China's oil consumption continued to grow, decreasing the importance of Sudanese imports to just 3 per cent of total Chinese foreign crude imports in 2011.[6] At a meeting at CNPC headquarters with President Jiang Jiemin, Bashir and his delegation were told that the company would seek to increase output in the remaining Sudanese oil fields, but gave no details of new investments.[7] The meeting seemed to be a political formality rather than a genuine effort to pursue hard economic investments by CNPC. In the coming months, the Sudanese government would direct CNPC and its Asian partners to sell their share of crude oil from their production in remaining oil fields in Sudan to the domestic refinery in Khartoum, rather than on international markets. Between January and June 2012, 3.3 million barrels were sold to the Sudanese government, but Khartoum delayed payment of hundreds of millions of dollars to the Asian national oil companies.[8] The move was indicative of wider Chinese and Indian relations with Sudan.

China's and India's state-owned banks had begun to view Sudan as a risky bet after South Sudan's separation in 2011. In March 2012, the China EXIM Bank cancelled a loan to support agricultural development in Sudan after the financing could no longer be backed by oil shipments.[9] A senior Indian diplomat in Khartoum remarked that the Sudanese government's inability to repay its lines of credit with the India EXIM Bank was discouraging further Indian engagement.[10] Clearly, the political turmoil in Sudan was unnerving its Asian investors. Without a replacement for the lost three-quarters of its oil production, Sudan's economy fell into an immediate and steep decline. Bashir and his ruling NCP were beginning to feel enormous political pressure to turn the economy around.

After the south seceded, the Sudanese economy seemed to do a complete reversal back to its poor state in the late 1980s when President Bashir first seized power. His NCP had little to show in terms of economic and social development for the Sudanese people after more than twenty years of rule. The loss of oil led to a 70 per cent hole in the budget, and heavy spending on security and defence to fight the SPLA-North in South Kordofan and Blue Nile states promised to drag down the government's finances further. In 2012, inflation doubled and unemployment soared, the political opposition called for significant reform, and infighting within the NCP surfaced.[11] Hardliners in the Sudanese military blamed Bashir for letting the south go and were in no mood to compromise by negotiating with Juba over pipeline transit fees and the north-south border. Amid such political division, in the summer of 2012 student-led demonstrations in Khartoum and other northern towns hoped to repeat the recent Arab Spring protests in Tunisia and Egypt. Sudanese security forces brutally crushed the protests, but as the economy continued to sour, the possibility of popular uprising and political dissension within the NCP remained imminent.

In a move reminiscent of Nimeiri's efforts to revive a downtrodden economy in the early 1980s, the NCP sought to combine harsh austerity measures with a new surge in northern oil, gold, and agriculture exports that might save the Sudanese economy from complete disaster. But each industry faced a similar set of challenges. In May 2012, Awad Al-Jaz, the oil minister, travelled to Heglig to reopen the oil taps after the Sudanese army had been routed by the SPLA a month earlier. Trying to play the part, Al-Jaz wore a hard hat and military fatigues. But the sight of the ageing oil minister turning a rusty valve failed to inspire the economy. If the border with South Sudan remained a dangerous place to operate, the hundreds of millions of dollars in investment needed to bolster Sudan's oil fields would not come any time soon.

Other industries in Sudan also needed to attract investors if the government was to generate the revenue needed to begin to fill the gap left by oil. The NCP was hoping to profit from a gold rush in the country's northern region to generate billions in exports.[12] But substantial investment in new technology needed to dig deeper mines was required to sustain growth in gold output.[13] In its most ambitious drive to diversify the economy, the NCP sank billions of dollars of past oil earnings and accumulated foreign loans from Chinese and Arab banks in development of the Merowe dam and other hydroelectric dams on the Nile. The aim was to revive the breadbasket dream of boosting agriculture and increasing export revenue through cash crops. But it would take years to determine whether these colossal investments would pay off.[14] And the NCP had little time to waste. Life without oil was a painful one for the political elite in Khartoum. But they were not suffering alone.

The devil in the pipeline

Sudan and South Sudan may have been politically separated, but the economies of the two countries were still attached by over 3,000 kilometres of corrugated steel pipelines. These pipelines stretched from the southern oil fields to the Port Sudan export terminal on the Red Sea. But under the control of South Sudan's long-time enemies in Khartoum, the pipelines might as well have been wrapped tightly around the throat of South Sudan's economy.

Born as one of the poorest countries on earth, South Sudan had rampant poverty, insecurity, and corruption. Since the 2005 signing of the CPA the south's capital of Juba had gradually transformed from a backwater to a boomtown as the petrodollars rolled in.[15] But most South Sudanese saw little benefit from oil revenue; only a narrow political and business elite enjoyed the new restaurants and hotels sprouting up in Juba. Yet thanks to oil, there was some promise for the future. Spending from oil revenue drove growth in South Sudan's economy. If directed towards the country's potential in agriculture and other industries, the petro-dollars could lead to wider development. But that hope immediately dissipated when oil production dried up.

In May 2012, the Sudan Tribune, an independent media outlet based in Paris, published a leaked World Bank assessment forecasting the devastating consequences of the oil shutdown for South Sudan's economy. The World Bank feared that the poverty rate in South Sudan would rise to 83 per cent by the following year as the value of the South Sudanese pound plummeted and prices on goods from fuel to food—virtually all imported in the first place—rose sharply. At a briefing to international

donors, a World Bank official cautioned that the pending economic collapse 'could result in social and political fragmentation, unrest and instability'.[16] Most alarming to the World Bank was that neither President
Salva Kiir nor senior officials seemed to be aware of the economic implications of turning off oil production in the first place. When the Sudanese military got a hold of a copy, it used the information to argue for
delaying the reopening of the pipeline with the aim that the longer South
Sudan was not receiving petro-dollars, the sooner it would be unable to
support the SPLM-North and the greater the chance that it may fall
apart completely.[17]

South Sudan hoped to bankroll its oil reserves as future collateral and
sell off new oil concessions to help cover the gap. 'We should approach
a number of friends, a number of creditors, a number of people with good
hearts. Because up the road we have our oil in the ground,' said Marial
Awou Yol, South Sudan's Deputy Minister for Finance and Economic
Planning. 'We can mortgage it to get loans. What is wrong about that?'[18]
But selling the future to pay for the present was hardly a sustainable solution. World oil prices in the long run would have to remain at high enough
levels to repay any loans taken on, or else South Sudan would fall into a
cycle of debt.[19] Juba also looked towards its mining and agriculture potential as revenue generators to cushion the blow, but these industries would
require years of investment and development to produce sizeable government revenue.[20] In the meantime, economic decline only threatened
to fuel violence in South Sudan from Khartoum-supported South Sudanese rebel groups.

In February 2012, President Kiir travelled to the Kenyan port town of
Lamu to attempt to reverse instability at home. He met the leaders of
Kenya and Ethiopia to sign an agreement to develop the Lamu Port
South Sudan Ethiopia Transport (LAPSSET) corridor. The plan was to
construct a regional railway and road network, as well as oil pipelines and
deep-water port facilities, between the three countries at a price tag of
between $15 and $25 billion.[21] 'I have no doubt that this day will go
down in history as one of the defining moments—when we made a major
stride to connect our people to the many socio-economic opportunities
that lie ahead,' said then Kenyan President Mwai Kibaki.[22] South Sudan
had already signed memoranda of understanding with Kenya, Ethiopia
and Djibouti to build alternative pipelines from the existing routes
through Sudan.[23] LAPSSET would bring all the plans together in one

of the largest infrastructure projects ever planned on the African continent. The obvious benefit of the massive project for South Sudan was that a new pipeline running through Kenya would break Juba's dependence upon Sudan's pipeline.

But it was a plan fraught with challenges; the new pipeline would require substantial investment. Whereas the GNPOC and PDOC pipelines measure some 1,500 and 1,400 kilometres respectively, the new pipeline would need to be around 2,000 kilometres, depending on its route. Unlike the largely flat desert over which Sudan's existing pipelines run, South Sudan's pipeline may have to travel over diverse terrain through Kenya to its final destination at Lamu. Owing to the inclines and declines of the topography, more pumping and heating stations than the six stations along the existing pipelines' route would be necessary in order to keep the highly-acidic and congealing Sudanese Dar-blend crude moving.

The final major issue facing the new pipeline was one of security. Even before the pipeline left South Sudan it would possibly be vulnerable to South Sudanese rebel groups. In January 2012, the South Sudan Liberation Army, the SSLA, issued a statement saying that it would 'never allow the construction of the new pipeline'.[24] In order to bypass the unruly regions of north-eastern Kenya, where secessionist Somali groups reside, and avoid possible disruption by the Al-Shabaab Islamist group linked to Al-Qaeda and operating out of southern Somalia, South Sudan's pipeline would need to head due south through Kenya before going east to the coast.[25] To guard against potential sabotage, considerable time and due diligence would be necessary.

Because of these technical and security challenges it was likely that the proposed pipeline for South Sudan would take several years to construct, and its final price tag would probably be in the billions. South Sudanese officials remained bullish that the tremendous cost of the pipeline for the poor country would not be a problem. 'We don't need to have the money right now, we have the reserves,' said South Sudan's Finance Minister Kosti Manibe.[26] The South Sudanese oil minister Stephen Dhieu Dau claimed that the country held 7 billion barrels in proven oil reserves. But Dau was taking a cue from his former countryman and fellow oil minister Awad Al-Jaz in Sudan: in order to attract possible investors, his figures were based on speculation rather than hard evidence. Dau's own oil ministry released figures showing that only 1.7 billion barrels of proven oil reserves, mainly in Blocks 3 and 7 in Upper Nile state, were left; this would put production at less than 100,000 bpd by 2020.[27] Enhanced recovery techniques would increase this level, but the oil minister needed new discoveries to strengthen South Sudan's ability to pay for the new pipeline.

Virtually all oil companies operating in the Sudans faced an uncertain regulatory environment and persistent security issues caused by the fluid political environment surrounding South Sudan's independence. The French oil major, Total, managed to lose the tiresome intervention of White Nile in its Block B concession, but insecurity in Jonglei in the coming years delayed exploration operations,[28] and the exit of White Nile did not mean that the concession was safe from division by South Sudanese officials. At 120,000 square kilometres, the concession was regarded as too large to be explored efficiently by one company alone.[29] 'Definitely Block B will not be any longer continuing as Block B, it will be blocks of Block Bs, it will be many Bs,' said South Sudan's oil minister Dau.[30] The very likely division of the highly touted concession might open up access for CNPC, Petronas and OVL to find new stakes in South Sudan, but the uncertain business environment was doing little to encourage these companies to invest in the large-scale exploration efforts South Sudan needed to ensure the future growth of its oil industry.

Despite these challenges, a growing East African oil boom could make the South Sudan pipeline more feasible in the future. Beginning in 2006, the discovery of 3.5 billion barrels in oil reserves along Lake Albert in Uganda and successful exploration work underway in Kenya in 2012 have opened up the possibility of a regional pipeline network.[31] Total's CEO Christophe de Margerie has suggested that, in principle, a pipeline from Ugandan oil fields to Kenya could be linked with South Sudan.[32] But Uganda's plans to construct a large refinery to cater to East Africa's fuel needs were seen as a possible threat by redirecting needed investment away from the pipeline network.[33]

The position of the Chinese government and Chinese state-owned banks may also make or break the future possibilities for South Sudan's oil industry. In what appeared to be an abrupt change in Beijing's approach, shortly after Kiir returned to Juba in April 2012 Barnaba Marial Benjamin, then South Sudan's information minister, announced that China had offered an $8 billion loan to develop infrastructure across a number of industries.[34] 'Very few people these days give you money. And

China has been known for this,' remarked Benjamin.[35] But China did not make such an offer. A framework for a financial cooperation agreement was signed with the China EXIM Bank and South Sudan in 2012,[36] but only a fraction of the figure Benjamin alluded to was made available by Beijing, and the alternative pipeline to break Sudan's monopoly over the transportation of oil was not part of the package. 'At the moment what has been concluded and signed is in the region of $170 (million),' said Kornelio Koriom Mayik, the Governor of the Central Bank of South Sudan. 'The Chinese didn't agree to build a new pipeline; they said 'we built one (in the north already); you use it'.'[37]

South Sudan was certainly a prime candidate for Chinese loans. It needed help to meet its immense infrastructure needs, and Chinese companies were eager to construct new government ministries, roads, hospitals, and schools. The Chinese foreign ministry was keen to benefit from the political capital that such a large loan would entail; the commerce ministry wished to see an expansion of economic ties. But in the absence of oil production the actual lender, China's EXIM Bank, whose money was on the line, was less optimistic.[38]

A number of other Asian players announced their interest in taking part in the construction of South Sudan's new pipeline. In fact, Japan's Toyota produced feasibility studies for such an investment in 2012 and put the cost of a Juba-Lamu pipeline at $5 billion.[39] But South Sudan was in a bind without China's full support. If South Sudan wanted Beijing's blessing, it would need to make a deal with its long-time enemy in Khartoum.

The Chinese government saw political problems with the proposed pipeline. Its construction would not only signal China's abandonment of Khartoum, an outcome Chinese leadership was looking to avoid, but also make existing Chinese-built pipelines through Sudan obsolete. CNPC and its Asian partners had still not recouped their investments in both the GNPOC and PDOC pipelines.[40] However, this was not a deal breaker; CNPC was not totally against the idea. It was willing to provide technical support and help construct the pipeline if someone could guarantee it would be paid.[41] For its part, OVL hinted that it would rather see new oil from South Sudan continue to head north. 'Yes, we agree we need to build additional pipeline capacity for evacuation of crude oil,' said one OVL executive. 'However, we think this could be done by adding an additional pipeline (to) the existing one. This would be better economics and better politics.'[42]

In March 2013, Sudan and South Sudan once again announced that oil would be piped through the existing pipeline in Sudan. The two sides agreed to create a security buffer zone along their disputed border, which restarted production that had been stalled because of security problems after an oil agreement was signed but not implemented in September 2012.[43] Whether security and production could be maintained in the long run remained questionable, as the border was still undefined, Abyei was still in dispute, and a civil war with the SPLM-North and the Sudanese government was still ongoing. Sudan will receive a financial boost if production is maintained over the three and a half years' duration of the oil agreement, but the Sudanese government would never be able to cover the loss of oil to South Sudan completely.

For its part, South Sudan looked to enjoy billions in revenue by turning on oil production again. But the challenge of developing other sectors of its economy with the incoming petrodollars will be immense in the future, especially if much of the revenue is lost to corruption. If South Sudan is unsuccessful in diversifying its economy away from oil, volatile international oil prices disturbing its government's main revenue source will remain a danger to stability. Sudan's ability to threaten the lifeblood of South Sudan's economy by closing off or confiscating oil production through its pipelines also remains; the three and a half years' duration of the oil agreement signed between the Sudans in September 2012 is hardly a long time in the oil business. But if new discoveries are not made, the most distressing threat is that within a decade South Sudan's oil reserves could be significantly diminished.

Just as oil, the purported economic foundation of South Sudan, was unlikely to hold consistently, deep-seated political fissures in the ruling SPLM would become exposed over time. In July 2013, the different centres of power within the SPLM collided. South Sudan's Vice-President Riek Machar, and Pagan Amum, the SPLM's General Secretary, both came out publicly and criticised the leadership of Salva Kiir. Machar, who had spilt from the SPLM during the civil war and sided with Khartoum during some of the most violent years of the conflict, went as far to challenge Kiir for SPLM chairmanship and president of South Sudan in the upcoming 2015 elections. 'To avoid authoritarianism and dictatorship, it is better to change,' said Machar.[44]

Kiir was swift in his response. He first relieved Machar's former ally Taban Deng Gai from his governorship of Unity state.[45] Soon after, he removed Machar from the Vice-President post and sacked his entire Cabinet in order to form a new government. Amum, who had voiced his concern over what he saw as politically motivated dismissals by the president, was also suspended as SPLM General Secretary.[46] Kiir named new ministers by the end of the month, but the political upheaval added to already existing concerns over stability in South Sudan. For CNPC and OVL, a functioning oil agreement between the two Sudans would certainly boost international revenue. But if the hesitation shown by the companies in 2012 towards the proposed pipeline for South Sudan demonstrated anything, it was their deeper appreciation of the risks of operating in politically unstable and insecure environments.

Portfolio management

Unlike when it first entered Sudan in the mid-1990s, CNPC was no longer placing such a high value on gaining experience in managing large projects overseas. It was more concerned with its bottom line. Working in the Sudans was no longer seen as a ripe opportunity, but rather as an example of the sort of politically volatile environment that the company was seeking to avoid in the future as it expanded its global portfolio.

In 2012, CNPC had over $350 billion in revenue and ranked 6th on the Fortune Global 500 list of the largest global corporations. This put the Chinese national oil company alongside the oil majors Royal Dutch Shell, Exxon Mobil, BP and Chevron.[47] CNPC was still lagging behind in profits; Beijing's ceilings on fuel prices in China racked up billions in losses for the company each year.[48] Its excessive work force of 1.6 million, mostly in non-essential social services—a legacy of the company's ministry days when the government and not the company was in control of the oil industry—also prevented high levels of efficiency. But CNPC was no small player, and it never had been.

CNPC's home production still dwarfed its overseas output. In 2011, the company churned out over four times more oil in China alone than Sudan's total oil production at its peak.[49] While Sudan and South Sudan still provided 25 per cent of CNPC's total international production before the shutdown, the company also had impressive levels of production in Kazakhstan and Venezuela.[50] Sudan had been an important strategic investment during CNPC's first decade of international expansion, but it was far from the only game in town for the company. It now had a growing international portfolio with investments in the Middle East, Central Asia, and North and South America. If CNPC was going to take on significant risk in the future, it was now going to aim for a larger reward.

CNPC's operations in Sudan had proved to be a valuable training ground for its overseas staff. Many employees with Sudan experience were sent to the company's next big play in Iraq in 2008. Wang Shali, an old Sudan hand, otherwise known as 'Madame Wang' as one of the few women in the company to rise to the executive level, was a central planner in CNPC's investments in Iraq after the US occupation ended.[51] But Iraq also demonstrated that the days when Sudan dominated the company's international portfolio were over. Although constrained by Baghdad's service contracts, CNPC entered into a $15 billion partnership with BP to develop Iraq's Rumaila oil field. As the second largest oil field in the world, with between 17 to 20 billion barrels in reserves,[52] Rumaila makes South Sudan's oil holdings look rather insignificant.

There were also calls from within CNPC to diversify risk by investing in more stable, developed countries, such as the US, Canada, and Australia.[53] Investment in countries which many Western companies avoided during CNPC's initial international strategy were not made out of burning desire to do so, but by the necessity to avoid heavy competition. In 2009, out of the forty-four countries where CNPC was invested, close to half were regarded as high risk.[54] Sudan, Kazakhstan and Venezuela, where the majority of the company's international production and reserves was located, were part of this group. While China's supply security was ensured by shifting between suppliers on international markets when South Sudan shut off its oil production, it was CNPC's international operations that faced the brunt of the damage. The Asian national oil companies, not their home governments, were the ones facing oil supply insecurity due to their heavy investment in politically risky countries.

In 2011, GWDC, CNPC's subsidiary, terminated six drilling projects worth nearly $200 million as a result of insecurity due to the Arab Spring uprisings and civil wars in North Africa and the Middle East. This amounted to 16 per cent of the subsidiary's overseas operations.[55] US and European oil majors certainly have investments in high-risk countries, but they have been better diversified with a large variety of international oil assets to fall back on if trouble spots heated up. CNPC sought to expand into more stable countries not only diversify its overseas investments away from politically risky countries, but also to serve a wider company objective.

CNPC and its fellow Chinese national oil companies were hunting oil and gas companies in Western markets not only to access new markets and revenue streams, but also, more importantly, to acquire new technologies and expertise needed to extract deep water and shale oil and gas. Their long-term plan was to bring technical knowhow back home to unlock China's own huge potential in unconventional oil and gas assets. In 2012, CNPC purchased a 49.9 per cent stake in the Canadian oil company Encana for $2.2 billion.[56] CNPC's acquisition of a sizeable share in Encana's Alberta shale oil and gas operations rang national security alarm bells in Ottawa. Sharing US opinions south of the border, Canadian politicians worried about the influence of the Chinese government on a national oil company investing in Canada.[57] But the Canadian government ultimately approved the deal, since CNPC was not taking a controlling interest in Encana.

CNPC was actually falling behind its Chinese counterparts Sinopec and CNOOC in gaining access to the North American oil and gas industry. In 2012, CNOOC made a groundbreaking $15.1 billion purchase of the Canadian oil company Nexen in its bid to acquire oil and gas assets around the world.[58] After the landmark purchase, Canada's Prime Minister Stephen Harper said he would limit future investment from Chinese national oil companies, and the US government told CNOOC that it was not permitted to be the main operator of Nexen's stakes in the Gulf of Mexico.[59] It was clear that while the Chinese national oil companies were still facing plenty of political opposition in North America, they were gradually breaking into markets there. Acquiring Western oil and gas companies was so important to Chinese national oil companies that they stalled their work in Iran to avoid penalties from US sanctions that might upset their activities in the US.[60] As in Sudan, CNPC and its Chinese counterparts looked to profit from the lack of Western competition in Iran. But along with Tehran's stringent contract terms, losing the opportunity to enter US markets by advancing too quickly in Iran changed the company's calculus.

The same reassessment of objectives and strategies was also gaining traction in the boardroom of India's OVL, which had also capitalised on investments in Sudan, in part because of the absence of US and European competition. But now, along with CNPC, it was looking to enter the US, Canada and Australia, in pursuit of more politically-secure oil and gas assets. In order to enter the shale oil and gas boom in the US, ONGC Chairman Subhir Vasudeva commented in 2012 that needed to find a way to 'circumvent' any complications arising from its investments in Sudan and Iran, which were both under US sanctions. 'For any opportunity in the USA, we will have to address the law of the land,' he told a group of reporters.[61] This was a noticeable shift from the company's stance ten years earlier when OVL Managing Director Atul Chandra dismissively wrote off US sanctions on Sudan as demonstrating a 'double-standard'.

In 2002, when the former ONGC Chairman Subir Raha first defended the company's move to invest in Sudan during the civil war, he said that OVL acted on 'the advice of the external affairs ministry' with 'diplomatic equations' steering its decision-making on risk.[62] The comment may have been intended to shield the company from any criticism should things go wrong. But it also underlined OVL's general lack of attention to political risk at the time. A senior Indian government adviser said that while private firms were increasingly engaged in political risk assessments, OVL did not pay sufficient attention to its own ability to manage risk and at times relied too heavily on unreliable Indian diplomats to advise it.[63]

The Sudan gamble did initially pay off for OVL. Thanks to high international oil prices, the company recouped its original investment and made a handsome profit over the years. But after the signing of Sudan's peace agreement, Sudanese oil production started to fall and OVL's gains dwindled. New production from Vietnam, Russia and South America was rounding out OVL's portfolio, but falling production and South Sudan's subsequent oil shutdown dealt a major blow to the company's overseas oil ambitions. Sudanese oil production dropped from 54 per cent of OVL's total at the start of Sudan's peace agreement in 2005 to 17 per cent by the end of 2011.[64] After President Kiir turned off the oil taps in January 2012, OVL began to slip behind its long-term target of reaching 400,000 bpd in overseas production by 2020.[65] Already in 2011, total company production was only slightly over 175,000 bpd and was forecast to decrease further in the coming year.[66]

OVL had a growing list of troubles overseas. The unfolding civil war and imposition of European Union sanctions slowed its production in Syria, tightening international sanctions in response to Tehran's nuclear programme stalled exploration and production work in Iran, and the company was caught in a territorial dispute between Vietnam and China in a concession in the South China Sea. Its national counterparts now had a rare moment to outshine India's flagship oil company. 'We too had options to get into countries like Libya, Sudan, and other troubled waters, but we stayed away,' said R.K. Singh, Chairman of Bharat Petroleum.[67] There were similarities in the strategic responses of CNPC and OVL to insecurity and instability in international operations by diversifying their overseas investments. But there were also noticeable differences in their responses, based on the political conditions they respectively faced in China and India.

Friends and enemies

Mao Zedong wrote in 1926 that central to building the revolution was asking: who are our enemies and who are our friends?[68] The 10.18 Incident in 2008, where five Chinese oilmen lost their lives, and the ongoing insecurity in the Sudans was the writing on the wall that CNPC needed to re-evaluate its friends and enemies. In response to growing risks overseas, the company established the Global Resources and Strategy Research Department in 2009 to think strategically about its overseas political and security conditions. It also began to engage more intensively with outside actors, such as international private security companies and Chinese think-tanks, to provide political risk analysis. In some ways CNPC was adapting to new rules and regulations, and the cultures of the foreign countries it invested in, and trying to catch up with international oil companies by mitigating risk through public relations and corporate social responsibility. But in other ways, CNPC was seeking to internationalise the political power it had in China to its overseas operations.

Oil executives in Chinese national oil companies were at times dismissed or demoted by the Communist Party leadership for upsetting social stability in China through industrial environmental disasters. But the close relationship between the national oil companies and the Party, along with their high-level bureaucratic standing, financial clout, and technical expertise, gave the companies tremendous political power to shape policy in the oil industry at home. CNPC took this line of thinking with it when it went overseas. It assumed that close relations with the host government would essentially allow it to avoid political risk.

But political privilege at home did not translate into the same influence overseas. Many foreign governments were seriously weak compared to the strong hand of the Party in China. Even if they wanted to, these governments could not protect CNPC's interests within their own borders. At the same time, the Party leadership and the Chinese government did not have the same power overseas to ensure the sustainability of CNPC's investments as they had at home. After two decades of operating overseas, CNPC began to realise that it needed to develop its own capabilities to manage its political affairs abroad.

In the wake of instability in Sudan and other foreign countries, the International Department at CNPC began in the late 2000s to rethink and reform the way the company approached political risk overseas. The department recommended continuing to maintain close relations with a host country's government, military, police and local authorities, but also called for CNPC to go beyond a government-only approach by establishing ties with local communities, major political opposition groups, and religious leaders. The objective was to 'plant the seed of CNPC deep into the political soil of host countries.'[69] While it was in stark contrast to China's official policy of non-interference in the domestic affairs of other countries, the new strategy certainly reflected the reality of CNPC's position on the ground. It reflected the conclusions of a report on security in Sudan carried out by a Chinese think-tank, which found that the company had failed in the past to balance relations with the Sudanese government and the southern Sudanese authorities, state and country officials, and local populations.[70]

At first glance, dealing with the complex political and social dynamics of a host country was seen as a time-consuming and costly task by many at CNPC.[71] But the International Department insisted that CNPC workers should stop isolating themselves from the communities in which they worked, and instead embrace the local language, culture and customs.[72] It would take time for the word from headquarters to change the behaviour of the men on the ground, but hints of progress could be seen. One Sudanese doctor working to set up mobile clinics in the concession areas of GNPOC in Sudan noted that following the 10.18 Incident in 2008, the Chinese president of the consortium began to attend some meetings on its community development work, which he had never attended before.[73] Certainly, CNPC hoped that the end result of enhancing its community development work would give the company a better public image and translate into a more secure operational environment.

The political reorientation of the International Department also suggested enhancing relations with the national media in host countries. The company wanted local populations to know about the jobs it was generating and its community development work. CNPC was also hoping that closer ties with both national and international media would give it enough influence to keep a tight lid on reporting of attacks and kidnappings.[74]

But the company was generally not very savvy when it came to dealing with independent media. Its history as China's leading oil producer had created a company ethic that included an arrogant attitude towards outside opinion. CNPC executives, who ran the company in a military style, saw themselves as the backbone of the Chinese economy. State-run media rarely criticised national oil companies. Instead, CNPC could easily get a story run in the *China Daily* or *Xinhua* to tout the company's activities in China.[75]

At home, the company's politically privileged position still allowed it to avoid strong reprimands for environmental negligence. The aftermath of a massive oil spill caused by a pipeline explosion at CNPC facilities in the northern coastal city of Dalian in 2010 demonstrated the company's domineering behaviour. 'After the Dalian spill, [CNPC President] Jiang Jiemin addressed the media once,' said a Chinese journalist.[76] 'He said that CNPC would cover the costs, but that the Dalian municipality would have to do the clean-up. He did not apologize, he did not follow up, and that was that.' Although the Dalian spill was not nearly as severe as the Gulf of Mexico oil spill in the US that same year, it was the worst in China's history, spreading scores of kilometres of oil around the city's coastline.[77]

CNPC was not sheltered from public anger. State media were no longer the only source of news in China. The rise of social media platforms such as Sina Weibo, China's version of Twitter, quickly spread unfiltered news across the country.[78] The social backlash from Dalian caused the Party leadership to step in and give the CNPC boss Jiang Jiemin a disciplinary warning.[79] In response to the consequences of industrial environmental disasters at home, CNPC began to provide its executives with media and public relations training provided by international political risk consultancies and public relations firms.[80] But the company's troubles in China were far from over.

In 2011, the Party leadership demonstrated its continued influence over Chinese national oil companies by swapping oil executives between the three oil giants.[81] CNPC boss Jiang Jiemin was the only top executive to retain his position. He was also the only leader among the Chinese national oil companies to be selected as a full member of the Central Committee of the Communist Party.[82] But after China went through its once-in-a-decade leadership transition in 2012, and Xi Jinping took the reins of the Party and Chinese government from Hu Jintao, Jiang's political stock plummeted.

In 2013, Jiang was named head of the State-owned Assets Supervision and Administration Commission (SASAC), the government body that oversees CNPC and China's other large national companies. As head of SASAC, Jiang was in a position to help steer government regulations in favour of the national oil companies. But it was also an indication that he was being sidelined by the new Party leadership as he was not promoted to a high-level political posting, such as provincial governor. Nonetheless, Jiang hardly had time to get comfortable in his new posting at SASAC before he was sacked in September 2013. Along with four CNPC senior managers, Jiang faced a corruption probe from the Party's Central Commission for Discipline Inspection. It was an investigation that threatened to reach all the way to former CNPC boss Zhou Yongkang.

Zhou, the former security and energy tsar in China's outgoing Politburo Standing Committee, had supported Jiang's rise in the oil industry and was also closely linked to the other CNPC oilmen in the probe. But more significantly, Zhou was on the wrong side of one of the largest political scandals in modern China's history: the purging of Chongqing Party secretary Bo Xilai. A close ally, Zhou initially tried to deflect pressure to remove Bo from the Party. For his efforts, Zhou was later stripped of his right to choose his successor and handed over the security responsibilities of his position early, before his retirement.[83] Moves against past and present CNPC executives demonstrated that the new Chinese President Xi was consolidating his power by undermining Zhou's political influence while at the same time pushing forward an anti-corruption campaign. 'They're getting closer and closer to him,' said one former Chinese official about Zhou. 'One step at a time.'[84]

Whether the corruption probe facing CNPC will temper the power of Chinese national oil companies in the future, or if it is just a surgical removal of political opponents by Xi Jinping, is uncertain. The rise of other oilmen in Chinese politics, such as former Sinopec boss Su Shulin, showed that Chinese national oil companies may still have some friends in the Party leadership.[85] Nonetheless, just as the architects of CNPC's Sudan venture were facing troubles at home, the company's ability to manage political instability was also being tested abroad.

CNPC was also increasingly under the spotlight in China for its overseas operations. But in contrast to the critical public response CNPC received for the environmental consequences of its home operations, the reaction of many Chinese to the company's troubles in Sudan and elsewhere overseas followed a more nationalist line. After twenty-nine Chinese construction workers were kidnapped in Sudan in January 2012, one posting on Sina Weibo read, 'if it was the United States or Russia, they would have air dropped in special commandos by now'.[86] The kidnapping, and others like it, put pressure on CNPC and the Chinese government to respond to increasing levels of overseas insecurity. But neither was capable of doing so.

If the 10.18 Incident in Sudan was a wake-up call for CNPC about company security overseas, the uprising in Libya against Colonel Muammar Gaddafi's regime in February 2011 was a call to action for the Chinese government. Beijing moved to come to the aid of thousands of Chinese workers as civil strife and war grew in the North African country. Pictures of distraught Chinese construction workers fleeing armed robbery of their facilities flooded social media in China.[87] The Chinese government tried to show a strong face to the public that it was protecting citizens abroad. Along with chartered flights, the Chinese military, for the first time on a large scale, worked to evacuate over 30,000 Chinese citizens from Libya.

CNPC and other Chinese national oil companies generally relied on government-to-government ties to smooth out political risk in their host countries. But at the end of the 2000s, the Chinese Ministry of Foreign Affairs was hard pressed to keep up with the sheer amount of Chinese investment overseas.[88] There was a noticeable lack of confidence in CNPC about the Chinese government's ability to shield the company from harm overseas. 'It's not like the American embassy,' said one company official, believing that the US and other Western countries had better plans in place to protect and evacuate their citizens from hotspots around the world.[89] But the company was at the same time eager for 'powerful departments' in the Chinese government, such as the People's Liberation Army, to follow in the footsteps of Chinese companies and 'go global' to deter attacks and respond to kidnappings of Chinese workers overseas.[90] The PLA Special Forces, and Chinese private security firms such as the Shandong Huawei Security Group, were trying to improve their ability to protect Chinese interests around the world, but were still limited in their capacity to do so.[91] The issue of overseas security was part of an increasingly complex relationship between Chinese national oil companies and Beijing.

Similarly to other large international companies around the world, Chinese national oil companies have close relations with government officials. Chinese executives in strategic national companies participate in official Party working group deliberations on issues such as energy and food security and provide input on foreign policy. CNPC co-authored a major policy report with the Chinese government in 2000, and in recent years Chinese diplomats have been seconded to CNPC offices overseas.[92] In response to the growing number of international security incidents involving Chinese companies, the ministries of foreign affairs and commerce, along with SASAC, began to discuss the risks of operating in unstable countries and to publish guidelines on foreign investment and corporate social responsibility.[93] Foreign affairs officials were still frustrated that Chinese national oil companies seldom consulted them before investing overseas.[94] On occasion, the Chinese media have also suggested that the financial losses suffered overseas by national oil companies were a waste of state funds.[95] But what impact the Chinese government and media could have on the national oil companies without the support of the top level Party leadership remained questionable.

CNPC would certainly look to benefit from the increased government engagement where it could, but by the late 2000s it was also carving its own political path overseas. The 2007 Guidelines for Investment in Overseas Countries' Industries, published by the ministries of foreign affairs and commerce and the National Development and Reform Commission, removed Sudan as a destination where Chinese companies would receive government support, but CNPC pressed on undeterred.[96] That year, it invested in Block 13 on Sudan's Red Sea coast.[97] When Fu Chengyu, the current Chairman of Sinopec, had an overseas investment rejected through formal government procedures in 2009, he indicated that informal channels were the more efficient means for gaining government approval to invest overseas.[98] Chinese oil giants were still superseding formal regulation to invest abroad through their Party connections. These machinations were noticeably different from what Indian national oil companies were experiencing in relation to their government.

Losing Nirvana

After ten years of rapid expansion overseas, OVL's relations with the Indian government were facing some strain. Different views of OVL were developing in New Delhi. Although it experienced tensions with ONGC, its corporate parent, the Ministry of Petroleum and Natural Gas was a staunch ally of OVL's international ventures; the growth of the company's portfolio only added to the ministry's own clout. But the Ministry of External Affairs (MEA) was trying to balance India's wider foreign policy with its energy security interests. In late January 2006, the aggressive line of the oil minister Mani Shankar Aiyar in supporting international investments of India's oil industry came to an end after Prime Minister Manmohan Singh reshuffled his cabinet.

In less than two years in office, Aiyar had made quite a name for himself. As part of the energy security package, he wanted India to invest $25 billion in equity oil deals abroad,[99] which would be a potential major boon for OVL. But Aiyar ventured too far from his profile. Some in the MEA felt he had overstepped his boundaries by 'playing foreign minister' and operated an 'independent foreign policy'.[100] By engaging closely with Sudan, Myanmar and Iran from his oil minister post, Aiyar was seen by many to have usurped the MEA and its objective of balancing the new energy-driven foreign relations with India's wider foreign policy. In particular, Indian diplomats worried about American opposition to the idea of India increasing its energy cooperation with Iran. At the time, India was working on a nuclear cooperation agreement with Washington.[101] The MEA went to Prime Minister Manmohan Singh demanding his personal intervention to bring the oil minister into line. Singh gave Aiyar a warning to back down on pushing Indian overseas oil ventures too aggressively, but Aiyar proved defiant and was removed from his post in the 2006 cabinet reshuffle as a result. While oil diplomacy remained an important component of Indian foreign policy, Aiyar's approach had stepped on too many toes in New Delhi.

Even after South Sudan's oil shutdown, the Indian government still largely supported OVL acquiring overseas oil and gas assets. New Delhi generally continued to approve the company's requests, including several billion-dollar deals in Brazil, Venezuela and Azerbaijan.[102] 'OVL is now investing from the Caribbean to the South China Sea,' said one senior Indian diplomat.[103] The Indian Cabinet has tried to improve coordination between government ministries to support OVL's investments abroad. P.S. Raghavan became special envoy to the Sudans in early 2013. As the head of the MEA's Development Partnership Administration, a new body responsible for managing India's international development projects, Raghavan was well placed to support OVL and pursue India's wider interests in the Sudans.[104] But New Delhi still intervenes when it is deemed necessary. On the basis of its own assessment of financial, security and political risks, the Indian Cabinet has refused to approve sizeable investments in Nigeria, Ecuador, and elsewhere over the past decade.[105]

OVL was still trying to loosen the financial leash of the government on its overseas activities. It pushed New Delhi to lower its demands on the internal rate of return for projects and raise its investment ceiling to roughly $500 million without the condition of seeking government approval.[106] But OVL was also increasingly under the microscope in New Delhi. A 2011 Comptroller and Auditor General report found that OVL had failed to properly carry out due diligence in the evaluation of some of its international investments.[107] Much of the blame was placed on the company's $2.1 billion purchase of the British oil company Imperial Energy in 2009, an acquisition made to reap production from oil fields located in the Tomsk region of Western Siberia and to acquire Imperial's exploration know-how and technology, areas where OVL was highly deficient.[108] But Imperial was unable to turn a profit in the years after the Indian company took control, because of technical challenges that halved expected production levels.[109] The oil was under the ground; the trouble was how to get it out. And the revenue generated from the minimal crude produced was sucked away by the Russian government's changing tax regime for the oil fields.

Before the oil shutdown in South Sudan, the Indian Auditor General's report also scrutinised OVL's investments in Sudan. Failure to find oil in Block 5B was blamed on OVL's unwillingness to heed the warning of international consultants, who at the time of purchase in 2004 cautioned OVL that there were limited data available on the highly insecure concession.[110] The company countered the Auditor General's report by arguing that exploration risk was a natural part of the business.[111]

OVL's overseas problems were adding up. One senior adviser to the Indian government worried that ONGC, the corporate parent, was deliberately shovelling funds into its foreign arm in order to prevent New Delhi from 'sponging' more of its income towards subsidy provisions for

Indian oil refiners to keep fuel prices artificially low. 'It doesn't make sense beyond profit for Indian companies to do equity deals,' said the adviser.[112]

India only had to look to another Asian giant to see the possible repercussions of too many failed overseas investments by its national oil companies. Following the Middle East oil shocks of the 1970s, Japan began to subsidise the exploration investments of the Japan National Oil Corporation (JNOC). But after it had spent $9.7 billion on debts and investment in equity oil deals, JNOC investments were operating at a loss and making little contribution to Japanese energy security.[113] In contrast to JNOC's ventures abroad, the launch of major overseas investments by OVL in the early 2000s was well timed with a sharp rise in international oil prices helping the company earn ample profits. Whether fortune would continue to shine on the Indian national oil company in the long run was another matter.

OVL was also faced with critics outside its government. There has been considerable debate over time among Indian scholars about whether or not engaging in equity oil deals was beneficial to energy security.[114] In 2012, questions also began to surface in the media about whether or not the company was actually enhancing India's energy security.[115] There was also speculation that OVL was exploiting the government's concern for energy security in order to win support overseas.[116] S.P. Garg, OVL's Director of Finance, defended the practice of equity oil deals by saying that 'one must realize that as a company, we have control over the quantity of oil that we produce and in case of an emergency, that quantity can be imported to India.'[117] But unlike CNPC in Beijing, OVL had far less political clout in New Delhi to help it operate outside the government's oversight. It would have to continue to vigorously defend its position that it was contributing to India's energy security by investing overseas. Its success or failure in the Sudanese and other major overseas ventures would go a long way towards dictating the Indian government's support for OVL in the future.

Both CNPC and OVL had reached a watershed moment. Business as usual of concentrating their major overseas investments in politically risky and insecure countries would need to change, and their capacity to mitigate risk would have to improve. The reform years for the Asian national oil companies, generated by both internal and external sources, had begun.

CONCLUSION

THE SUDANESE FACTOR

This book demonstrates how the experiences of Chinese and Indian national oil companies in Sudan, and later South Sudan, both empowered and restricted their wider international expansion. While much attention is paid to the ways in which renewed Chinese and Indian engagement has impacted Africa, the book examines how the politics, civil wars, and foreign relations of two African countries influenced China and India as rising powers in the world. It illustrates the need to disaggregate the actors and relationships that constitute China and India in Africa more fully, in order to understand the role they play in their African engagements.

Informal and non-state actors are important in understanding Africa's relations with the rest of the world.[1] However, the recent re-emergence of China and India in Africa, concurrent with their rise as economic and political powers in the world, underscores the significance of formal and interstate aspects of African international relations, as trade and investment by Chinese and Indian national companies and state-owned banks has grown on the continent.[2] But this book's examination of Chinese and Indian national oil companies in Sudan and South Sudan demonstrates how what externally appear to be formal national-owned companies are not necessarily following instructions from their home governments, but rather have their own unique internal dynamics that in turn heavily influence the direction of China's and India's relations with Africa.

Chinese and Indian national oil companies have individual histories that define their relationships with their home governments. But although they may be nationally owned, they are, to a large extent, highly autonomous actors. Rather than simply acting on foreign policy directives from Beijing or New Delhi, these companies play a role in defining Chinese and Indian foreign policy through their overseas investments. But besides the relations between these companies and their home governments, they—like US and European oil companies—are also influenced by the political environments they enter when investing abroad.

It should come as no surprise that Sudanese agency was instrumental in both empowering and restricting the investments of Chinese and Indian national oil companies in Sudan and South Sudan. African political elites have long exploited their relations with external actors to acquire resources that cement their own domestic authority.[3] Chinese and Indian actors have mostly fallen into these long-established patterns between African and foreign actors from Europe and the US, rather than changing them.[4] But as the cases of Sudan and South Sudan demonstrate, African actors, whether political elites, rebels, civil society groups or corporations, can influence the interests and behaviour of external actors outside the continent and even in their home countries. Sudan and South Sudan are examples of Africa shaping China's and India's rise in the world through their influence on the international expansion of Chinese and Indian national oil companies.[5]

Sudan's confrontational foreign relations with the US initially served to empower the entry of CNPC and OVL into its oil industry, where both companies were able to exploit Sudanese oil as a major profit generator for their international operations. For CNPC in particular, Sudan was a strategic investment providing the company with crucial management and technical experience in operating a large overseas project and launching its various oil service subsidiaries into the international marketplace.

But as CNPC and OVL looked to move up the ladder in the international oil industry by exploiting deep-water and unconventional oil and gas assets around the world, Sudan's foreign relations with the US became problematic. In particular, the investments of CNPC in Sudan fed wider political opposition to Chinese national oil companies investing in the US. Their investments in Sudan limited the potential of Chinese and Indian national oil companies to acquire more advanced technology and expertise in the international oil industry which was available in the US and other Western markets.

The exploitative mode of governance of Sudan's ruling NCP in Khartoum also came to impact the international expansion of Chinese and Indian national oil companies in other ways. Even after Sudan's long-running civil war between the Sudanese government and the SPLA ended in 2005, local armed militias that once fought for the government in the civil war, and rebels from Sudan's other civil war in Darfur, targeted the oil industry. They opposed the work of CNPC and OVL because of the lack of development in oil regions and the revenue the oil industry was generating for Khartoum. Armed attacks on both CNPC and OVL dissuaded much needed investment in Sudan's ageing oil fields, lowering Sudan's oil output and decreasing its importance as a profit generator for the Asian national oil companies. When South Sudan became an independent country in 2011, and shut down its oil production after a dispute with Sudan the following year, both CNPC and OVL began to recognise the extent of their exposure to political instability and the limits to their home governments' ability to ensure sustainability of their investments through diplomacy.

The cumulative impact of Sudanese politics and civil wars on CNPC and OVL empowered the companies to begin to explore how they could avoid the consequences of political and security risk in their wider overseas investments. The instability of the Sudans was an important reason why both CNPC and OVL sought to diversify their international activities towards more politically stable countries. With its extensive operations in the Sudans, CNPC was particularly exposed to the consequences of security and political risk. These experiences galvanised strategic thinking in CNPC, which became more active in seeking ways to manage political affairs overseas without relying on the host government alone.

Both CNPC and OVL faced criticism at home that their operations in Sudan upset wider Chinese and Indian foreign relations, particularly with the US. But whereas CNPC continues to demonstrate its political power to influence government policy in China, OVL has been more susceptible to non-energy interests in India's foreign relations restricting its international expansion.

The business and politics of oil in China and India

Since they first arrived in Sudan, Chinese and Indian national oil companies have expanded throughout Africa, Central Asia, the Americas and the Middle East. Chinese national oil companies have received most of the international attention by investing tens of billions of dollars through mergers and acquisitions around the world. But their Indian counterparts have also been trying to keep pace and have acquired their own overseas oil and gas assets.

When Chinese national oil companies emerged on the international scene, they were quickly labelled as instruments of Beijing, 'locking-up' oil and gas resources around the world at the behest of their home government and for the exclusive use of their burgeoning domestic economy. Access to preferential loans from state-owned banks in China and offers of development assistance from Beijing to oil-rich countries were regarded by many as giving Chinese national oil companies a competitive advantage over their rivals in the US and Europe.

But this is an overly simplistic view of the nature of Chinese overseas oil investments and their Indian counterparts. Government ownership of the oil companies should not be confused with government control. Like all governments, both the Chinese and Indian governments are eager to promote the expansion of their national and private companies overseas. Asian national oil companies fall under the larger government system in China and India, are influenced by the policy decisions of their governments, particularly domestically, and ultimately are answerable to their political leaders. But while often supporting Chinese and Indian foreign policies, at the same time companies are very autonomous, and relatively free of the political dictates of Beijing and New Delhi when they invest overseas.[6] Asian national oil companies are not 'locking-up' oil for their home economies. Instead, they began to invest overseas in the 1990s to ensure their own long-term survival by replenishing their stagnating oil reserves and production at home with foreign assets. They follow their corporate strategies in a similar fashion to US and European oil companies, selling their foreign-produced oil to the highest bidder on international markets. Since most of the growth in new energy demand in the world is coming from China and India, Asian national oil companies may very well end up selling much of their foreign crude back home, but they remain largely profit-seeking corporations.

The Chinese and Indian governments are certainly eager to bolster their energy security through oil diplomacy and have offered state support through soft loans to their national oil companies. In Sudan, both CNPC and OVL received such diplomatic backing from their home governments in order to start up their initial investments. Chinese and Indian policy banks have continued to offer the companies loans for their overseas investments. But such support from home does not guarantee on its own the success of international bids, and detracts from the importance of how the companies themselves have built up cash reserves since the deregulation of domestic crude oil prices in China and India, and used them to leverage their international expansion.

During the 1990s, the Chinese government and Indian governments began to rationalise domestic crude oil prices to international levels. These domestic reforms were crucial for national oil companies to generate the funds needed to pursue their international strategies. The reforms influenced the size and scope of CNPC and OVL going abroad and subsequent high international oil prices have provided the companies with substantial profits to invest further overseas. This change in domestic policies was critical to empowering the Chinese and Indian national oil companies to invest overseas. In turn, the oil companies generated diplomatic support from Beijing and New Delhi for Sudan and other oil-rich countries, rather than passively waiting for the foreign policy of their home governments to determine their overseas objectives. But there is a notable difference in how the Chinese and Indian national oil companies derived their autonomy in their home countries, which demonstrates the extent to which Beijing and New Delhi have exerted leverage over them.

In China, the political power of oil executives was influential in leading Chinese national oil companies overseas on the basis of the oil industry's historical importance for the Party. The oil industry was a key generator of revenue for the Chinese government for decades after the discovery of the giant Daqing oil field in 1959. After China's main oil fields began to stagnate in the 1980s, CNPC began its international expansion. Before its Chinese counterparts were making large overseas investments, CNPC's Zhou Yongkang leveraged his close political connections with Communist Party leadership to receive government backing for the company to enter Sudan in 1995. This political power of CNPC and other Chinese national oil companies has been maintained through the continued emphasis of the Party on bringing the economic and managerial expertise of corporate executives, in oil and other strategic sectors, into key political and bureaucratic posts. American and European oil executives at ExxonMobil, Royal Dutch Shell, and Total certainly hold political influence in their home countries. But oil executives in

China are hardwired to the political system. Not only do they enjoy the benefits of high-level access to political leadership to advance their corporate strategies and influence government policy, they are also key candidates for positions in the upper echelons of the Party, where they can support their former national oil companies from within.

In India, it was not the political power of ONGC, and its foreign subsidiary OVL, that brought the company to Sudan. ONGC had struggled for years to find adequate oil reserves at home to keep pace with India's rising consumption levels. But close to a decade after CNPC started investing overseas, it was the growing concern in the Indian government about the country's energy security that gave OVL the policy room to invest more freely overseas. Tight government controls on overseas investments by Indian national oil companies were relaxed at the turn of the century and New Delhi became willing and able to provide high-level diplomatic support to OVL's overseas ventures.

CNPC leveraged its historic political power in China to launch its investment in Sudan, while OVL was empowered by favourable national policy in India. This is noteworthy when considering the level of control the Chinese and Indian government have over their national oil companies. Chinese national oil companies have at times heavily influenced government policy and circumvented bureaucratic procedures by gaining approval informally through their high-level access to the Party leadership. Indian national oil companies, while also part of the policy-making process on energy issues, are not an intimate part of the political establishment, and have faced government controls on their overseas investments more often than their Chinese counterparts.

Altogether, the shifts in the business and politics of oil in China and India should not be discounted in understanding the international expansion of Asian national oil companies. They demonstrate how and why 'state actors' from China and India often pursue strategies that diverge from, or may later come to conflict with, official Chinese and Indian foreign policy. But at the same time, it is vital to take into consideration how the experiences of Asian national oil companies in host countries such as Sudan and South Sudan influence their international expansion.

The global impact of Sudan and South Sudan on Asia's oil giants

From the moment oil exploration began in the early 1970s in Sudan, oil became ensnared in the country's divisive politics and only served to aggravate tensions between the government in Khartoum and the Southern Sudan Autonomous Region. For the next thirty-three years, oil remained a major point of contention between consecutive Sudanese governments and rebel groups in southern Sudan, and later Sudan and independent South Sudan. Oil was a major grievance that brought Sudan back to civil war after the policies of President Jaafar Nimeiri had undermined southern Sudanese political and economic rights in the early 1980s. Consequently, Nimeiri's politics and the civil war upset budding relations with the US government and led Chevron to suspend its operations. The seizure of power by the National Islamic Front in 1989 came to damage relations with Washington further and Chevron left Sudan in 1992.

After Sudan was placed on the US government's list of state sponsors of terrorism in 1993 and Washington imposed unilateral economic sanctions on it in 1997, the possibility that other US oil companies might invest in Sudan ended. CNPC was able to capitalise on the American exodus; now Sudan offered not only proven oil reserves, but also a dearth of US and European competition. Later, the Sudanese government's scorched earth campaign in and around southern Sudanese oil fields led to pressure from human rights activists in North America and Europe to push out most of the remaining Western oil companies in Sudan, making room for OVL to invest. If any foreign government had an influence on Chinese and Indian national oil companies investing in Sudan, it was not Beijing or New Delhi, it was Washington.

Chinese and Indian national oil companies have been depicted as taking advantage of overseas investments in politically unstable and insecure countries that US and European oil companies were reluctant to enter. But many Western oil companies invest in the trouble spots of the world; the nature of the business demands that oil companies go where the oil is. CNPC and OVL may be heavily invested in unstable countries, but dealing with political risk is more a trait of the entire international oil industry than an approach unique to Asian companies.

Even after Chevron left Sudan, US oil companies sought to enter the country despite the ongoing civil war; Canadian and European oil companies actually invested alongside their Asian counterparts. Only later were these Western oil companies pushed out by human rights activists and the US government, subjected to divestment pressures through their capital positions and consumer reputations in home markets (and in spite of the international pressure, some European companies, such as Schlumberger, one of the world's leading oil service companies, have remained engaged in Sudan throughout the decades). By contrast, their nationally-owned Asian counterparts faced virtually no civil society pressure in China and India.

In addition, the picture of Asian national oil companies simply arriving on the scene to replace Chevron and other Western oil companies departing Sudan does not do justice to the importance of Sudanese politics in directing these movements. Sudan has not been a passive recipient of Chinese and Indian oil investments; its government actively sought replacements for Chevron around the world. From President Nimeiri in the 1970s to President Bashir in the 1990s, Sudan sought to attract Chinese investment. When the timing was right with CNPC's corporate strategy to invest abroad, a match was finally made. Later, the Sudanese government would turn the tables on the Chinese national oil company when new Asian investors came on the scene.

Sudanese politics also played a key role in the arrival of India's OVL. In the shadow of its larger Chinese counterpart in Sudan, OVL's role may seem to be minimal. But the Indian oil company was significant for the purposes of Sudanese leaders governing the oil industry. CNPC and Malaysia's Petronas sought to purchase the oil stake of the departing Canadian oil company Talisman in 2003. But the Sudanese government wanted to balance the dominance of CNPC in the oil industry by bringing in the Indians. Khartoum exercised its political determination over the contractual rights of the Chinese and Malaysian national oil companies. In turn, OVL was awarded its most successful international investment to date and reaped the rewards of the Sudan venture along with its Asian peers.

In the late 1990s and early 2000s, Sudan gave both CNPC and OVL the opportunity to earn billions of dollars in profits, gain critical managerial and technical experience in operating large overseas projects, and garner further support from Beijing and New Delhi for their international expansion. It was by far the largest overseas oil producing venture and revenue generator for both companies during the first decade of their international operations. When CNPC first entered Sudan in the mid-1990s, and expanded its operations soon after, the investment of hundreds of millions of dollars in a foreign country was virtually unheard of in China. 'CNPC was taking a risk,' said one Chinese oil expert.[7] 'If it lost out in Sudan, we might not see the same oil industry in China as we do today.'

But CNPC succeeded. Sudan provided the company with critical experience in managing a large overseas project and a platform from which to launch its various oil service companies into the international scene. Sudan was also instrumental in elevating the careers of Chinese oilmen who served in the early years of the venture, including CNPC's current CEO Zhou Jiping. Company managers and executives are now taking their Sudan experience with them as they move on to further projects in the Middle East, Central Asia, and North and South America. Sudan also earned CNPC political clout at home. During their visits to Africa, high-level Party and Chinese government officials made Sudan and the CNPC-built oil refinery outside Khartoum a frequent stop to demonstrate China's 'mutual benefit' in Africa.

But over the years in Sudan, Asian national oil companies would experience negative influences from Sudan on their international expansion. The escalation of the Darfur civil war in 2003 may have been remote from the main operations of Asian national oil companies in Sudan compared with the fighting in the second civil war, but Darfur had far-reaching consequences for CNPC's and OVL's international operations. A divestment campaign originating on university and college campuses across the US targeted both Chinese and Indian national oil companies because of their investments in Sudan. The campaign was part of a larger civil society movement in the US that put unprecedented focus on Darfur and reinforced the imposition of the US government's longstanding sanctions on Sudan. Civil society attention to Sudan fed wider political opposition to Chinese national oil companies investing in US markets. In this way, the violent politics of the Sudanese government came to affect the international expansion of Asian national oil companies.

The ongoing exploitation and manipulation of populations in Sudan's periphery by the Sudanese government were also instrumental in altering the way CNPC viewed overseas security and its political relations with host governments. After local armed groups killed five of its workers in the 10.18 Incident in 2008, CNPC began to reform its security practices and expand its political relations when investing overseas beyond engaging the host government alone. The 10.18 Incident demonstrated how not only Sudan's political elite, but also local armed groups and political factions in oil regions could influence the oil companies. In 1984,

Chevron's close relationship with the Sudanese government led southern Sudanese rebels to attack its base camp at Rubkona. Twenty years later, CNPC was also regarded as an economic arm of Khartoum and was the target of numerous attacks by armed rebels.

The independence of South Sudan in 2011 also influenced the international expansion of CNPC and OVL. South Sudan's oil shutdown in January 2012 handed Chinese and Indian national oil companies their largest loss of revenue since they began their major overseas operations in the early 1990s. Not all oil companies have to face the immense political consequences of operating in a divided country, particularly one in which the oil fields are located right on the fault line. But South Sudan's separation did demonstrate the limits of the Chinese and Indian governments' ability to assist their national oil companies when facing political risk overseas. Along with diplomatic efforts of the wider international community, the Chinese government was unable to use its political and economic relations with the two Sudans to prevent South Sudan from shutting down its oil production in 2012. The Indian government only responded to the shutdown after it was too late. This lack of political influence indicated that Beijing and New Delhi were more adept at supporting the initial investments of Asian national oil companies in foreign countries than at sustaining their investments in the long term.

Hostilities between the two Sudans played a large role in pushing both CNPC and OVL to diversify their international portfolios towards investments in more politically stable countries. Both Beijing and New Delhi have begun to try to improve coordination between government ministries and national oil companies to mitigate and manage the consequences of political and security risk overseas. CNPC's political strength at home has sheltered it from any major reprimand for investing dangerously abroad. The company will look to take advantage of government support overseas where possible, but its exposure to instability and insecurity in Sudan and South Sudan has also pushed CNPC to seek more autonomy in conducting its political affairs abroad.

For OVL, the Sudan venture at first lifted its political standing at home. It demonstrated that the Indian national oil companies could compete for overseas oil, and even take on fierce Chinese competition. But the political instability in Sudan and South Sudan added another question mark to the company's inconsistent record overseas. The Indian government has been largely supportive of OVL, but it has restricted overseas investments when it deems the risk too great or when such investments upset the balance of wider Indian foreign policy.

A fragmented future

The overseas investments of CNPC and OVL in Sudan and South Sudan over the past two decades demonstrate important characteristics of China and India as rising powers. China and India are both large and diverse societies undergoing tremendous internal change as their economies continue to grow.[8] The political and economic influence of China and India in the world is a product of both traditional actors, such as political leaders and government ministries, and non-traditional actors, such as large corporations, which also shape foreign policies, international investments, and more.

But the world is also talking back to Chinese and Indian actors and influencing how they think and act. In the process of riding the highs and lows of changing Sudanese politics, diverging and conflicting interests that exist between actors in China and India were internationalised. Rather than simply a coordinated and well-executed plan drawn up by Chinese and Indian governments to expand their interests abroad, there was plenty of circumstance and chance at work, guided in part by the individuals, corporations and organisations that are at the forefront of Chinese and Indian engagement overseas. The idea of China and India as straightforward rising powers often paints over a complexity that lies behind.

National oil companies and their foreign ministries back home have feuded over how the companies upset China's and India's wider diplomatic relations by investing in Sudan. Conversely, Asian national oil companies discovered that their home governments could do very little to protect their interests in the face of political turmoil overseas. Complicating further the turbulent politics of Sudan and South Sudan, Chinese arms manufacturers, along with other arms suppliers, indirectly obstructed the overseas investment of Chinese national oil companies as Chinese-made weapons that fell into the hands of Sudanese rebel groups led to further insecurity and instability. There was also friction within the national oil companies. CNPC subsidiaries interested in drilling oil wells, regardless if they strike oil, to increase their own revenue, can upset relations between the wider CNPC group and the Sudanese government.

Even individuals in China and India played a large role in defining the foreign relations of China and India: Zhou Yongkang and Atul Chandra were instrumental in advancing the overseas strategies of CNPC and OVL respectively.[9] While this fragmentation of interests is certainly not unique to China and India, and separate interests can exist within a common goal, the national character of the national oil companies as part of the wider Chinese and Indian governments often betrays the diversity within. Moving away from seeing China and India as monolithic actors is critical to understanding the variety of ways in which they shape and are shaped by the Sudans, Africa, and the world.

The story of Chinese and Indian national oil companies in Sudan and South Sudan is far from finished. Sudan still represents the largest overseas achievement for CNPC and OVL. Future operations in the two Sudans will be a test case for the companies in managing political and security risk overseas. Despite having restarted oil production in April 2013, Sudan and South Sudan have a history of consistent political bickering and armed conflict that will continue to threaten the steady flow of crude. Multiple civil wars continue in Sudan and South Sudan faces its own threats of insecurity and rebellion. If production is unimpeded by Sudanese politics in the future, Chinese and Indian national oil companies will again enjoy handsome profits. But they will not serve their own long-term interests of international expansion by forgetting their experiences in the Sudans.

Whether or not future instability may cause Chinese and Indian national oil companies to leave the Sudans, as their US and European counterparts did in the past, is yet to be seen. If history tells us anything, it is that the turbulent politics and conflict surrounding oil will not go away until the last barrel of crude is pumped from beneath Sudanese soil. 'We couldn't see any indication that the situation would improve,' said former Chevron Vice-President Allan Martini, over twenty years after the US oil major left Sudan.[10] 'As far as I'm concerned, the situation still hasn't sorted itself out.'

NOTES

INTRODUCTION: THREE MINUTES IN FEBRUARY

1. The description of the Rubkona attack was related to the author in telephone interviews and personal communication with former Chevron employees in Sudan, 25 November 2008 and 9 December 2010.
2. Robert O. Collins, 'Letter to Dr. and Mrs. David Killingray', 10 February 1984; retrieved from the personal correspondence and diaries of Collins in the Sudan Archive at Durham University.
3. Personal communication, former Chevron country manager, 25 November 2008.
4. Robert O. Collins, *A History of Modern Sudan*, Cambridge: Cambridge University Press, 2008, p. 144.
5. Interview, former senior Sudanese oil official, Khartoum, 28 October 2007.
6. Notable academic and popular books on Sudan discuss the impact of oil on the country's politics and economy, but only give it chapter- or section-length treatment: J. Millard and Robert O. Collins, *Revolutionary Sudan: Hasan al-Turabi and the Islamist State, 1989–2000*, Leiden: Brill, 2000; Douglas H. Johnson, *The Root Causes of Sudan's Civil Wars*, Oxford: James Currey, 2003; Deborah Scroggins, *Emma's War: Love, Betrayal and Death in the Sudan*, London: Harper Perennial, 2004; Robert O. Collins, *A History of Modern Sudan*, Cambridge: Cambridge University Press, 2008; Matthew LeRiche and Matthew Arnold, *South Sudan: From Revolution to Independence*, London: C. Hurst & Co., 2012.
7. For a broader overview on China and India in Africa, see Chris Alden, Daniel Large and Ricardo Soares de Oliveira (eds), *China Returns to Africa: A Rising Power and a Continent Embrace*, London: C. Hurst & Co., 2008; Deborah Brautigam, *The Dragon's Gift: The Real Story of China in Africa*, Oxford: Oxford University Press, 2009; Emma Mawdsley and Gerard McCann (eds), *India in Africa: Changing Geographies of Power*, Oxford: Pambazuka Press, 2011.
8. One exception is literature on the implications of Chinese national oil companies' overseas investments in Sudan and Africa for Chinese foreign policy debates on non-interference, see Bates Gill and James Reilly, 'The Tenuous Hold of China Inc. in Africa', *Washington Quarterly*, Vol. 30, No. 3, 2007; Daniel Large, 'China's

Sudan Engagement: Changing Northern and Southern Political Trajectories in Peace and War', *China Quarterly*, Vol. 199, 2009; Linda Jakobson, 'China's Diplomacy toward Africa: Drivers and Constraints', *International Relations of the Asia-Pacific*, Vol. 9, 2009. There is also literature on the influence of African traders and communities in China, see Adams Bodomo, 'The African Trading Community in Guangzhou: An Emerging Bridge for Africa–China Relations', *China Quarterly*, Vol. 203, 2010. On the influence of African oil on American and European economic and political systems, see Nicholas Shaxson, *Poisoned Wells: The Dirty Politics of African Oil*, New York: Palgrave, 2007.

9. The following authors also consider how politics in host countries influences Asian national oil companies, but discuss only briefly the variety of strategic implications and responses: Tanvi Madan, 'India's Global Search for Energy', in Michael Kugelman (ed.), *Foreign Addiction: Assessing India's Energy Security Strategy*, Asia Program Special Report, No. 142, Washington, DC: Woodrow Wilson International Center for Scholars, 2008; Alex Vines, Lillian Wong, Markus Weimer and Indira Campos, 'Thirst for African Oil: Asian National Oil Companies in Nigeria and Angola', London: Royal Institute of International Affairs, 2009; Erica S. Downs, 'Who's Afraid of China's Oil Companies?', in Carlos Pascual and Jonathan Elkind (eds), *Energy Security: Economics, Politics, Strategies and Implications*, Washington, DC: Brookings Institution, 2010; Bo Kong, *China's International Petroleum Policy*, Santa Barbara: ABC-CLIO, 2010; Philip Andrews-Speed and Roland Dannreuther, *China, Oil, and Global Politics*, New York: Routledge, 2011.

10. On the role of China in Sudan, and Sudan in China's wider African and international relations, see Daniel Large, 'China's Sudan Engagement: Changing Northern and Southern Political Trajectories in Peace and War', *China Quarterly*, Vol. 199, 2009. For a broader look at China and India in Sudan and South Sudan, see Daniel Large and Luke A. Patey (eds), *Sudan Looks East: China, India and the Politics of Asian Alternatives*, Oxford: James Currey, 2011.

11. Petronas was arguably the second most important player in Sudan's oil industry after CNPC. Its story deserves greater attention than this book provides, but because Malaysia lacks broader significance as a rising power, focus is placed here on Chinese and Indian national oil companies.

12. Johnson, op. cit.

13. Ibid.

14. Collins, *A History*, pp. 109–11.

15. Gerald Prunier, *Darfur: The Ambiguous Genocide*, London: C. Hurst & Co., 2005; Julie Flint and Alex de Waal, *Darfur: A New History of a Long War*, London: Zed Books, 2008.

16. 'UN officials say Darfur conflict is worsening', *New York Times*, 23 April 2008.

1. AMERICAN DREAMING

1. Mia Farrow, 'China can do more on Darfur', *Wall Street Journal*, 7 October 2007; Nicholas D. Kristof, 'China's Genocide Olympics', *New York Times*, 24 January 2008.
2. John Darnton, 'Diplomatic realignment in Africa makes Americans welcome in Sudan', *New York Times*, 27 June 1977.
3. Personal communication, Brian Kay, 20 August 2011.
4. Telephone interview, John Sutherland, 23 September 2011.
5. John B. Miller, 'Landsat-1 Image Studies as Applied to Petroleum Exploration in Kenya', in P.W. Woll and W.A. Fischer (eds), *William T. Pecora Memorial Symposium*, Geological Survey Professional Paper 1015, 1977; John B. Miller and J. Vandenakker, 'Sudan Interior Exploration Mapping Project—Planimetry and Geology', Chevron Overseas Petroleum Inc., San Francisco, 1977.
6. Allan V. Martini with James L. Payne, 'Beyond Khartoum: Petroleum Exploration and Discovery', in Allen G. Hatley, Jr. (ed.), *The Oil Finders: A Collection of Stories about Exploration*, Utopia, TX: Centex Press, 1995, pp. 159–62.
7. Martini, op. cit., p. 169.
8. Nimeiri revealed the terms of the contract in a speech: 'Chevron will bear all costs of exploration, which is to be completed within two years. If oil is found, GOS (Government of Sudan) will receive as taxes 12.5 per cent of gross value plus 50 per cent of new profits': 'Nimeiri's 'Face the Nation' Speech', US Department of State, Electronic Telegrams, 1/1/1974—12/31/1974 November 1974, http://aad.archives.gov/aad/createpdf?dt=2474&rid=192153&dl=1345, accessed 10 March 2013.
9. 'Chevron Oil Exploration in Sudan', US Department of State, Electronic Telegrams, 1/1/1974—12/31/1974, December 1974, http://aad.archives.gov/aad/createpdf?dt=2474&rid=192153&dl=1345, accessed 10 March 2013.
10. Martini, op. cit., pp. 172–3.
11. Interview, Khartoum, 26 January 2007.
12. Personal communication, Brian Kay, 21 November 2008.
13. Martini, op. cit., p. 173.
14. Thomas J. Schull, 'Rift Basins of Interior Sudan: Petroleum Exploration and Discovery', *The American Association of Petroleum Geologists Bulletin*, Vol. 72, No. 10, 1988, p. 1131.
15. Martini, op. cit., p. 183.
16. Ibid., p. 184.
17. Ibid., p. 176.
18. Personal communication, Brian Kay, 27 August 2011.
19. Personal communication, Brian Kay, 21 & 26 November 2008.
20. Martini, op. cit., p. 183.
21. Personal communication, Brian Kay, 20 August 2011.
22. L.C. Lawyer and B.V. Kay, 'The Challenge of the Sudan', *Geophysics: The Leading Edge*, February 1984.

23. L.C. Lawyer, 'From the Other Side', *Geophysics: The Leading Edge*, 18, 10, December 1999.

24. Personal communication, Brian Kay, 21 November 2008.

25. Thomas J. Schull, 'Rift Basins of Interior Sudan: Petroleum Exploration and Discovery', *The American Association of Petroleum Geologists Bulletin*, Vol. 72, No. 10, 1988, pp. 1128–30; 'Reserves are Remote, Territory is Dangerous; Chevron Gave up Hope,' *Platt's Oilgram News*, Vol. 71, No. 16, 25 January 1993.

26. Schull, op. cit., p. 1131.

27. Personal communication, Brian Kay, 20 August 2011.

28. 'George M. Keller, Former Chevron Chairman and CEO, Remembered as "a True Leader and Visionary"', Press Release, Chevron, 17 October 2008.

29. Brian O'Reilly, 'The Biggest Bosses', *Fortune Magazine*, 3 August 1987.

30. Douglas Martin, 'George M. Keller, whose wager created Chevron, is dead at 84', *New York Times*, 18 October 2008.

31. Personal communication, Brian Kay, 21 November 2008.

32. Martini, op. cit., p. 171.

33. Ibid., p. 172.

34. Now common in the international oil industry, a production sharing agreement provides governments which cannot afford expensive exploration projects with a means to search for oil and gas by placing the risk with the company. If a company does not discover oil, it bears all the costs. But if it does find oil, the company can recover its costs from the proceeds of oil production and split the profit at an agreed rate with the government.

35. Sherief El Tuhami, 'Oil in Sudan: Its Discovery and Industrial Development', in Peter Gwynvay Hopkins (ed.), *The Kenana Handbook of Sudan*, London: Kegan Paul, 2007, pp. 661–2.

36. Martini, op. cit., p. 169.

37. El Tuhami, op. cit., p. 657.

38. Gregory Jaynes, 'In vast Sudan, money and skills are always missing', *New York Times*, 2 December 1980.

39. Richard Brown, 'International Responses to Sudan's Economic Crisis: 1978 to the April 1985 Coup d'Etat', *Development and Change*, Vol. 17, 1986, p. 488.

40. El Tuhami, op. cit., pp. 662–3.

41. Martini, op. cit., p. 183.

42. *Sudan, Quarterly Economic Review*, No. 1, 1982, Economist Intelligence Unit, p. 12.

43. El Tuhami, op. cit., pp. 662–3.

44. Peter Verney, *Raising the Stakes: Oil and Conflict in Sudan*, Hebden Bridge: Sudan Update, 1999, p. 31.

45. Telephone interview, former Chevron executive, 11 March 2013.

46. 'Standard Oil will aid new oil pipeline', *Spokane Chronicle*, 10 January 1983.

47. Charles Gurdon, *Sudan at the Crossroads*, Wisbech, Cambridgeshire: Middle East and North African Studies Press, 1984, pp. 85–6.

48. 'Sudan—The Role of Chevron', *APS Review Oil Market Trends*, Vol. 40, No. 22, 7 June 1993.

49. *Sudan, Country Report*, No. 4, 1983, Economist Intelligence Unit, 1983, p. 12.

50. Barbara Bush, *Barbara Bush: A Memoir*, New York: Scribner, 1994, pp. 90–91.

51. Mansour Khalid, *Nimeiri and the Revolution of Dis-May*, London: KPI, 1985, p. 305.

52. George H.W. Bush, *All The Best, George Bush: My Life in Letters and Other Writings*, New York: Touchstone, 1999, p. 158.

53. Tim Naftali, *Blind Spot: The Secret History of American Counterterrorism*, New York: Basic Books, 2005, p. 69.

54. Khalid, *Nimeiri*, p. 305; Mansour Khalid, *The Government They Deserve: The Role of the Elite in Sudan's Political Evolution*, London: Kegan Paul, 1990, p. 297, n. 59.

55. Robert O. Collins, *A History*, p. 95; Dennis Hevesi, 'Gaafar al-Nimeiry, a Sudan leader with shifting politics, dies at 79', *New York Times*, 11 June 2009.

56. Johnson, op. cit., p. 55.

57. Collins, *A History*, p. 117.

58. Khalid, *The Government*; Khalid, *Nimeiri*, p. 304.

59. G. Norman Anderson, *Sudan in Crisis: The Failure of Democracy*, Gainesville: University Press of Florida, 1999, p. 17.

60. 'The killers of Khartoum', *Time*, 12 March 1973.

61. Anderson, op. cit., p. 18.

62. David A. Korn, *Assassination in Khartoum*, Bloomington: Indiana University Press, 1993.

63. 'Security Help to Sudan', Memorandum of Conversation, Department of State, 6 March 1973; 'The Seizure of the Saudi Arabian Embassy in Khartoum', Intelligence Memorandum, US Department of State, Khartoum Embassy, June 1973.

64. Khalid, *Nimeiri*, p. 306.

65. 'U.S. Reaction to Sudanese Decision re Eight Palestinian Terrorists', Briefing Memorandum, US Department of State, 1 July 1974.

66. 'Return of Amb. Brewer to Khartoum', Telegram, US Department of State, 26 October 1974.

67. 'Further US Policy towards Sudan', Telegram, US Department of State, 11 September 1974.

68. 'Future Sudan/USG Relations', Telegram, US Department of State, 18 April 1975.

69. Sudan was the fourth largest trading partner of the US in Africa at the time; 'Sudan's Growing Importance as US Trading Partner', Telegram, US Department of State, December 1975.

70. Gurdon, op. cit., pp. 50–51.

71. Alex de Waal, 'Sudan: International Dimensions to the State and its Crisis', Occasional Paper no. 3, Crisis States Research Centre LSE, April 2007, pp. 4–5.

72. The US State Department also provided funds to the IMF to prevent Sudan from defaulting on its loan obligations; Richard Brown, 'International Responses

to Sudan's Economic Crisis: 1978 to the April 1985 Coup d'Etat', *Development and Change*, Vol. 17, 1986, pp. 505–6.

73. Darnton, op. cit.
74. Anderson, op. cit., p. 52.
75. Ibid., pp. 18–19.
76. 'Sudan (10/09)', Previous Editions of Sudan Background Note, US Department of State, http://www.state.gov/outofdate/bgn/sudan/129311.htm, accessed 20 December 2012.
77. 'Sudan: hearts, minds and helicopters', *Time*, 23 January 1984.
78. Johnson, op. cit., p. 67.
79. William R. Doerner and Philip Finnegan, 'Sudan threatened with disaster', *Time*, 4 February 1985.
80. Martini, op. cit., p. 161.
81. Peter Woodward, *US Foreign Policy and the Horn of Africa*, Aldershot: Ashgate, 2006, pp. 113–14.
82. 'Chevron Oil Exploration in Sudan', Telegram, US Department of State, 10 December 1974.
83. 'Sudan since the Coup Attempt—Implications for US', Telegram, US Department of State, 21 September 1976.
84. Personal communication, John Sutherland, 31 August 2011.
85. Telephone interview, James Payne, 3 January 2013.
86. 'Remarks of President Reagan and President Gaafar Mohamed Nimeiri of the Sudan Following Their Meetings', Ronald Reagan Presidential Library Archives, 21 November 1983, http://www.reagan.utexas.edu/archives/speeches/1983/112183a.htm, accessed 20 December 2012.
87. *Sudan*, *Quarterly Economic Review* No. 1, 1984, Economist Intelligence Unit, p. 10.
88. El Tuhami, op. cit., p. 664.

2. THE LONG GOODBYE

1. Telephone interview, Lillian Skander, 9 December 2010.
2. 'Sudan rebels raid Chevron complex', *The Register-Guard*, 3 February 1984; 'Sudanese rebels attack American firm killing 3', *The Afro American*, 11 February 1984.
3. 'Paratroops flown to U.S. Chevron complex', *Times Daily*, 4 February 1984.
4. Allan V. Martini with James L. Payne, 'Beyond Khartoum: Petroleum Exploration and Discovery', in Allen G. Hatley, Jr. (ed.), *The Oil Finders: A Collection of Stories about Exploration*, Utopia, TX: Centex Press, 1995, pp. 170–71.
5. Telephone interview, John Sutherland, 23 September 2011.
6. Martini, op. cit., p. 171.
7. Abel Alier, *Southern Sudan: Too Many Agreements Dishonoured*, Exeter: Ithaca Press, 1990, p. 215.

8. Only signs of oil had been found by Chevron in 1978 and discussion of the pipe-line project was premature; Alier, op. cit., p. 217.

9. Captain Salva Kiir Mayardrit, who led the southern forces at Bentiu, went on to become second-in-command of the SPLA under John Garang during the civil war and later the first President of South Sudan in 2011; Robert O. Collins, *A History of Modern Sudan*, Cambridge: Cambridge University Press, 2008, pp. 122–3.

10. Ibid., p. 155.

11. The Sudanese Constitution signed after the first civil war in 1973 protected freedom of religion in Sudan; Douglas H. Johnson, *The Root Causes of Sudan's Civil Wars*, Oxford: James Currey, 2003, p. 56.

12. Peter Nyot Kok, 'Adding Fuel to the Conflict: Oil, War and Peace in the Sudan', in Martin Doornbos, Lionel Cliffe, Abdel Ghaffar M. Ahmed and John Marka-kis (eds), *Beyond Conflict in the Horn: Prospects for Peace, Recovery and Development in Ethiopia, Somalia, and the Sudan*, London: James Currey, 1992, pp. 106–7.

13. Telephone interview, William Doh, 3 September 2008.

14. Personal communication, William Doh, 21 September 2008.

15. Personal communication, Brian Kay, 21 November 2008.

16. Leben Moro, 'Oil Development Induced Displacement in the Sudan', Working Paper, University of Durham, 2009, pp. 3–4.

17. Robert O. Collins, 'Letter to John Winder', 10 February 1984; retrieved from Collins personal correspondence and diaries in the Sudan Archive at Durham University.

18. Telephone interview, Jim Payne, 3 January 2013.

19. 'South Sudan: Compounding Instability in Unity State', International Crisis Group *Africa Report* No. 179, 2011, p. 2.

20. Kok, op. cit., p. 109.

21. Collins, *A History*, p. 123.

22. Johnson, op. cit., pp. 60–2.

23. The Marxist military junta of Mengistu Haile Mariam allowed the rebels to stay within Ethiopia's borders, but knowing the secessionist intentions of the Anyanya II, he offered little more support, so as not to encourage his own rebels. Sharon E. Hutchinson, 'A Curse from God? Religious and Political Dimensions of the Post-1991 Rise of Ethnic Violence in South Sudan', *Journal of Modern African Studies*, Vol. 39, No. 2, June 2001, pp. 310–1.

24. Personal communication, William Doh, 21 September 2008.

25. Collins, op. cit., p. 136; Kok, op. cit., p. 107.

26. Former Anyanya leaders seeking independence included Akwot Atem, Samuel Gai Tut, and William Abdullah Chuol. Collins, op. cit., pp. 140–43.

27. Peter Verney, *Raising the Stakes: Oil and Conflict in Sudan*, Hebden Bridge: Sudan Update, 1999, p. 18.

28. *Sudan, Oil and Human Rights*, New York: Human Rights Watch, 2003, pp. 145–6.

29. Charles Gurdon, *Sudan at the Crossroads*, Wisbech, Cambridgeshire: Middle East and North African Studies Press, 1984, p. 98.

30. *Sudan, Quarterly Economic Review* No. 1, 1984, Economist Intelligence Unit, p. 10.

31. 'Sudan oil search to start', *Globe and Mail*, 17 December 1983.

32. 'Sudan—The Role of Total', *APS*, Vol. 40, No. 22, 7 June 1993.

33. Interview, Khartoum, 30 October 2007.

34. *Force majeure* is a contractual clause that provides the right to suspend company operations without contractual penalty in the face of an Act of God or, in the cases of Chevron and Total, a state of war. Interview, Total representatives, Juba, South Sudan, 3 November 2007; 'Briton's murder link with Sudan emergency', *Glasgow Herald*, 1 May 1984.

35. Collins, op. cit., p. 144.

36. '3 Workers die, 7 wounded in raid on Sudanese camp', *The Palm Beach Post*, 3 February 1984.

37. Robert O. Collins, 'Letter to Dr. and Mrs. David Killingray', 10 February 1984; retrieved from the Collins personal correspondence and diaries in the Sudan Archive at Durham University.

38. Raphael K. Badal, 'Oil and Regional Sentiment in Southern Sudan', Discussion Paper, Syracuse University, No. 80, June 1983.

39. Telephone interview, Allan Martini, 19 February 2013.

40. Robert O. Collins, undated letter (1980–82); retrieved from Collins personal correspondence and diaries in the Sudan Archive at Durham University.

41. 'Paratroops flown to U.S. Chevron complex', *Times Daily*, 4 February 1984.

42. Telephone interview, 17 December 2010.

43. Steven K. Hindly, 'Chevron Oil's huge gamble in Sudan', *The Day*, 2 October 1982.

44. *Sudan, Oil and Human Rights*, New York: Human Rights Watch, 2003, p. 145.

45. 'Still no word on nine being held by Sudanese rebels', *Lakeland Ledger*, 19 November 1983.

46. *Sudan, Oil and Human Rights*, op. cit., p. 145.

47. Standard Oil of California, '1982 Supplement to the Annual Report', San Francisco, SOCAL, 1983, p. 35; Standard Oil of California, '1983 Supplement to the Annual Report', San Francisco, SOCAL, 1984, p. 38.

48. Verney, op. cit., p. 18.

49. Robert O. Collins, 'Letter to Dr. and Mrs. David Killingray', 10 February 1984; retrieved from Collins personal correspondence and diaries in the Sudan Archive at Durham University.

50. Telephone interview, Allan Martini, 11 March 2013.

51. Telephone interview, Allan Martini, 19 February 2013.

52. 'Paratroops flown to U.S. Chevron complex', *Times Daily*, 4 February 1984.

53. 'Sudanese troops guard U.S. oil installations', *The Telegraph*, 4 February 1984.

54. Personal communication, Brian Kay, 25 November 2008.

55. 'Sudan accord with Saudi financier puts pressure on Chevron to develop oil fields', *Wall Street Journal*, 1 November 1984.

56. Robert O. Collins, 'Letter to John Winder', 10 February 1984; retrieved from the Collins personal correspondence and diaries in the Sudan Archive at Durham University.

57. Telephone interview, Allan Martini, 19 February 2013.

58. Deborah Scroggins, *Emma's War: Love, Betrayal and Death in the Sudan'*, London: Harper Perennial, 2004, pp. 87–8.

59. Robert O. Collins, 'Letter to Dr. and Mrs. David Killingray', 10 February 1984; retrieved from the Collins personal correspondence and diaries in the Sudan Archive at Durham University.

60. Robert O. Collins, *Civil Wars and Revolution in the Sudan: Essays on the Sudan, Southern Sudan and Darfur 1962–2004*, Hollywood: Tsehai, 2005, p. 139.

61. Johnson, op. cit., p. 68.

62. Telephone interview, John Sutherland, 23 September 2011; Collins, op. cit., p. 143.

63. 'Sudan accord with Saudi financier puts pressure on Chevron to develop oil fields', *Wall Street Journal*, 1 November 1984.

64. Gurdon, op. cit., pp. 85–6.

65. *Sudan, Quarterly Economic Review*, No. 3, 1984, Economist Intelligence Unit, p. 20.

66. 'Sudan: hearts, minds and helicopters', *Time*, 23 January 1984.

67. *Sudan, Quarterly Economic Review*, No. 2, 1984, Economist Intelligence Unit, p. 14.

68. Collins, op. cit., pp. 151–5.

69. Gregory Jaynes, 'In vast Sudan, money and skills are always missing', *New York Times*, 2 December 1980.

70. Collins, op. cit., p. 155.

71. Jack Anderson, 'US training Sudanese to protect Chevron investments', *Kentucky New Era*, 19 October 1983.

72. Jack Anderson, 'U.S.'s involvement in Sudan's civil war tied to oil interest?', *The Dispatch*, 21 October 1983.

73. Ibid.

74. Telephone interview, Allan Martini, 19 February 2012.

75. Peter Woodward, 'External Relations after Nimeiri', in Peter Woodward (ed.), *Sudan after Nimeiri*, London: Routledge, 1991, p. 210.

76. 'U.S. said set to send arms to Sudan', *Record-Journal*, 6 March 1984.

77. Stephan Hindy, 'Civil war threatened in debt-ridden Sudan', *Williamson Daily News*, 2 April 1984.

78. 'Oil plants guarded', *Times-News*, 4 February 1984.

79. Carol Berger, 'Who dropped the bombs in Omdurman?', *Globe and Mail*, 31 March 1984.

80. William R. Doerner, 'Sudan threatened with disaster', *Time*, 4 February 1985.

81. See Alex de Waal, *Famine that Kills*, New York: Oxford University Press, 1989.

82. *Sudan, Quarterly Economic Review* No. 2, 1985, Economist Intelligence Unit, p. 9; Khalid, *The Government*, pp. 342–3.

83. Alex de Waal, 'Sudan: International Dimensions to the State and its Crisis', Occasional Paper no. 3, Crisis States Research Centre, London School of Economics and Political Science, April 2007, p. 5.

84. 'Reagan frees $67 million in aid to troubled Sudan', *Chicago Tribune*, 2 April 1985.

85. Gurdon, op. cit., pp. 85–6.

86. Hunter R. Clark and Philip Finnegan, 'Sudan toppling an unpopular regime', *Time*, 15 April 1985.

87. G. Norman Anderson, *Sudan in Crisis: The Failure of Democracy*, Gainesville: University Press of Florida, 1999, pp. 19–20.

88. Collins, op. cit., p. 156.

89. 'Sudan Gov't Suggests Oil Export Plan be Ended, White Nile be Abolished', *Platt's Oilgram News*, Vol. 64, No. 173, 8 September 1986.

90. Interview, Khartoum, 9 February 2007.

91. Collins, op. cit., p. 184.

92. Sadiq chose to follow an ambiguous foreign policy of non-alignment, staying closer to Libya than the US would have liked. After Libyan terrorists began to target Americans in Sudan during the late 1980s, Washington pulled out much of its diplomatic personnel from Khartoum. Peter Woodward, *US Foreign Policy and the Horn of Africa*, Aldershot: Ashgate, 2006, pp. 32–3.

93. Meghan L. O'Sullivan, *Shrewd Sanctions: Statecraft and State Sponsors of Terrorism*, Washington, DC: Brookings Institution, 2003, pp. 237–8.

94. Omar al-Bashir also received military training in Malaysia; Anderson, op. cit., pp. 3–4.

95. The NIF had faired poorly in the 1986 national elections that brought Sadiq to power. J. Millard Burr and Robert O. Collins, 'The Islamist Revolution', in *Revolutionary Sudan: Hasan al-Turabi and the Islamist State, 1989–2000*, Leiden: Brill, 2000, pp. 1–24.

96. Personal communication, Brian Kay, 21 November 2008.

97. Personal communication, Brian Kay, 10 November 2012.

98. 'Sudan—The Role of Chevron', *APS*, Vol. 40, No. 22, 7 June 1993.

99. '*Sudan, Quarterly Economic Review* No. 3, 1988, Economist Intelligence Unit, p. 17.

100. J. Millard Burr and Robert O. Collins, *Revolutionary Sudan: Hasan al-Turabi and the Islamist State, 1989–2000*, Leiden: Brill, 2000, pp. 234–5.

101. Interviews, former Sudanese oil officials, Khartoum, 9 February 2007 and 12 October 2010.

102. 'Chevron Pulls Out', *Middle East Economic Digest*, 26 June 1992.

103. *Soil and Oil: Dirty Business in Sudan*, Washington, DC: Coalition for International Justice, 2006, p. 9.

104. 'Sudan—Reserves and Production', *APS*, Vol. 40, No. 22, 7 June 1993.

105. Lawrence M. Fisher, 'New chief at Chevron sees greater expansion', *New York Times*, 23 August 1988; 'The Scramble for Oil's Last Frontier', *Businessweek*, 11 January 1993.

106. David Brown, 'Crash of '86 Left Permanent Scars', *Explorer*, January 2006.

107. 'Can the E&P Industry Avoid Future Shock?', *Oil and Gas Journal*, Vol. 95, No. 36, 8 September 1997.

108. Patrick Lee, 'Pumping life into Chevron', *Los Angeles Times*, 4 December 1989.

109. 'Chevron sues Pennzoil in bid to bar takeover', *Los Angeles Times*, 8 December 1989.

110. Tom Bower, *The Squeeze: Oil, Money and Greed in the Twenty-First Century*, London: HarperPress, pp. 76–7.

111. Marshall Loeb, 'Getting Pushed Out of America', *Fortune*, Vol. 130, Issue 5, 9 May 1994.

112. Ibid.

113. 'The Scramble for Oil's Last Frontier', *Businessweek*, 11 January 1993.

114. Bower, op. cit., p. 82.

115. Marshall Loeb, 'Getting Pushed Out of America', *Fortune*, Vol. 130, Issue 5, 9 May 1994.

116. Interview, Sudanese oil official, Khartoum, 28 October 2007.

117. BP, *Statistical Review of World Energy June 2010*, London: BP, 2010.

118. Personal communication, Brian Kay, 21 November 2008.

119. Ricardo Soares de Oliveira, *Oil and Politics in the Gulf of Guinea*, London: C. Hurst & Co., 2007, p. 194.

120. Personal communication, 22 February 2013.

121. 'Chevron Pulls Out', *Middle East Economic Digest*, 26 June 1992.

122. Telephone interview, Jim Payne, 3 January 2013.

123. 56,000 tons of pipe manufactured for the Sudan pipeline were sitting in storage in Italy after the Rubkona attack. Standard Oil of California, '1984 Supplement to the Annual Report', SOCAL, San Francisco, 1985, p. 39.

124. BP, '*Statistical Review of World Energy June 2010* London: BP, 2010; Gurdon, op. cit., p. 82.

125. US Department of State, 'Section 8, Sudan Peace Act Report', 21 April 2003, http://www.state.gov/p/af/rls/rpt/2003/19790.htm, accessed 9 March 2013.

126. Telephone interview, Allan Martini, 19 February 2013.

127. Personal communication, John Silcox, 22 February 2013.

128. Peter Woodward, *US Foreign Policy and the Horn of Africa*, Aldershot: Ashgate, 2006, p. 53.

129. J. Millard Burr and Robert O. Collins, op. cit., p. 56.

130. Ken Silverstein, 'Official pariah Sudan valuable to America's War on Terrorism', *Los Angeles Times*, 29 April 2005.

131. Madelaine Drohan, 'Into Africa', *Globe and Mail*, 24 September 1999; interview,

Sudanese oil official, Khartoum, 9 February 2007; *Malik v. State Petroleum Corporation*, 2008 British Columbia Supreme Court 1600, p. 15.

132. Marshall Loeb, 'Getting Pushed Out of America', *Fortune*, Vol. 130, Issue 5, 9 May 1994.

133. Personal communication, Brian Kay, 21 November 2008.

134. Telephone interview, Brian Kay, 24 November 2008.

135. Telephone interview, Allan Martini, 19 February 2013.

136. Robert O. Collins, 'Letter to Paul Howall', 29 March 1984; retrieved from Collins personal correspondence and diaries in the Sudan Archive at Durham University.

137. Personal communication, 20 August 2011.

3. BOARDROOMS AND BATTLEFIELDS

1. Interview, Sudanese oil official, Khartoum, 9 February 2007.

2. *Soil and Oil: Dirty Business in Sudan*, Washington, DC: Coalition for International Justice, 2006, pp. 9–11.

3. *Malik v. State Petroleum Corporation*, 2008 British Columbia Supreme Court, 1600, p. 15.

4. 'Canadians Trumpet Oil Prospects in New Venture', *Middle East Economic Digest*, Vol. 37, No. 2, 1993.

5. *Malik v. State Petroleum Corporation*, 2008 British Columbia Supreme Court 1600, p. 41.

6. 'International Sudan', *Platt's Oilgram News*, Vol. 69, No. 172, 6 September 1991.

7. 'More Oil Concessions', *Sudan News & Views*, University of Pennsylvania, African Studies Center, No. 11, 31 August 1995.

8. 'Sudanese Guerilla Threaten Canadian Oil Operator', *APS Review Oil Market Trends*, Vol. 47, No. 19, 11 November 1996.

9. Years earlier, Anyanya II spilt from Garang for the same reason; the idea of unity in fact held little appeal for most southerners. Douglas H. Johnson, 'The SPLA Split: Surviving Factionalism', in *The Root Causes of Sudan's Civil Wars*, Oxford: James Currey, pp. 91–110.

10. John Young, 'Sudan: Liberation Movements, Regional Armies, Ethnic Militias and Peace', *Review of African Political Economy*, Vol. 30, No. 97, pp. 424–5.

11. *Sudan, Oil and Human Rights*, New York: Human Rights Watch, 2003, p. 159.

12. David Keen, 'The Economic Functions of Violence in Civil Wars', *The Adelphi Papers*, Vol. 38, Issue 320, 1998, p. 39.

13. John Harker, 'Human Security in Sudan: The Report of a Canadian Assessment Mission', Government of Canada, 2000, pp. 47–8.

14. 'Arakis Puts Little Stock in Rebel Threats', *Platt's Oilgram News*, Vol. 73, No. 156, 15 August 1995.

15. 'Arakis Has New Sudan Plan in Works', *Platt's Oilgram News*, Vol. 73, No. 181, 20 September 1995.

16. J. Millard Burr and Robert O. Collins, *Revolutionary Sudan: Hasan al-Turabi and the Islamist State, 1989–2000*, Leiden: Brill, 2000, pp. 240–5.

17. 'Arakis Energy: The Rest of the Story', *Stockwatch*, 14 June 2006.

18. 'Arab Group International Bails Out of Arakis Energy Sudanese Project', *The Oil Daily*, Vol. 45, No. 179, 19 September 1995.

19. 'Unrepentant Terry Alexander Blames Failure of Arakis' Plans on US State Department', *The Oil Daily*, Vol. 49, No. 38, 1999.

20. 'Arakis Energy, Once More', *Sudan: News and Views*, Issue 11, University of Pennsylvania, African Studies Center, 31 August 1995.

21. 'New Arakis Chief Sees Sudan Work with Several Firms', *Platt's Oilgram News*, Vol. 73, No. 247, 26 December 1995.

22. 'First Oil Transported out of Sudan Field', *Platt's Oilgram News*, Vol. 74, No. 124, 16 June 1996.

23. 'Sudan Deal Signed by Arakis, Govt & Partners', *Platt's Oilgram News*, Vol. 75, No. 43, 4 March 1997.

24. James Norman, 'Lundin Clan Takes 8.2% Stake in Arakis, Wants Place on Company's Board', *Platt's Oilgram News*, 26 March 1997.

25. Interview, senior Sudanese oil official, 12 October 2010.

26. Burr and Collins, op. cit., p. 245.

27. J. Millard Burr and Robert O. Collins, unpublished manuscript made available to author.

28. Arakis hired Dale Hunter, the former Occidental pipeline project manager in Yemen, and appointed James Taylor, a recently retired Occidental executive, to its board of directors. Peter Verney, *Raising the Stakes: Oil and Conflict in Sudan*, Hebden Bridge: Sudan Update, 1999, p. 89.

29. Interviews, current and former Sudanese oil officials, Khartoum, 9 February 2007 and 15 October 2010.

30. Interview, senior Sudanese official, 27 January and 9 February 2007.

31. Interview, Sudanese oil official, Khartoum, 15 October 2010.

32. Sudan and Syria were the only two countries on the terrorism sponsor list that were not already subject to comprehensive US sanctions.

33. Nathan E. Farge, Arakis's Senior Vice-President and general counsel, later explained that the company only 'sought guidance' from Washington, not special treatment. It was advised to wait until the US Treasury Department regulations were released. David B. Ottaway, 'U.S. eased law on terrorism to aid oil firm; exemption let Occidental seek major deal in Sudan', *Washington Post*, 23 January 1997; David B. Ottaway, 'GOP targets Sudan loophole', *Washington Post*, 7 February 1997.

34. In the following year, Occidental would briefly re-emerge as a possible partner of the International Petroleum Corporation in oil concessions south of the main blocks. However, Republicans in the US House of Representatives were pushing the Clinton administration to close the loophole in the Anti-Terrorism Act that allowed US companies to invest in Sudan's oil industry. This political pressure

proved overwhelming for Occidental. The company claimed it was because of the 'commercial terms' of the deal that it was not going ahead, but Lucas Lundin, the Swedish director of its potential partner, the International Petroleum Corporation, said that 'Washington told (Occidental) they couldn't sign'. David B. Ottaway, 'Wielding aid, U.S. targets Sudan; $20 million to be sent to neighbors who are backing rebel forces', *Washington Post*, 10 November 1996; David B. Ottaway, 'GOP targets Sudan loophole', *Washington Post*, 7 February 1997.

35. James Norman, 'Arakis Pulls in Two Hefty Partners for Sudan Work', *Platt's Oilgram News*, Vol. 74, No. 238, 9 December 1996.

36. 百年石油1878–2000, 北京, 石油工业出版社, 2009年 (Wen Houwen, Wang Zhu-jun, Zhang Jiangyi, and Guan Xiaohong (eds), *A History of Petroleum in China: 1878–2000*, Beijing: Petroleum Industry Press, 2009, p. 290).

37. 'Reserves are Remote, Territory is Dangerous, Chevron Gave up Hope', *Platt's Oilgram News*, Vol. 71, No. 16, 25 January 1993.

38. Awad al-Jaz, 'The Oil of Sudan: Challenges and Achievements', in Peter Gwyn-vay Hopkins (ed.), *The Kenana Handbook of Sudan*, London: Kegan Paul, 2007, p. 673.

39. Interview, Sudanese oil official, 7 February 2007.

40. Verney, op. cit., p. 88.

41. Interview, Sudanese oil official, Khartoum, 15 October 2010.

42. 'Malaysia and Sudan sign two pacts', *New Straits Times*, 7 June 1991.

43. 'Petronas steps out in national service', *New Straits Times*, 24 July 2000.

44. Zainal Aznam Yusof, 'The Developmental State: Malaysia', in Paul Collier and Anthony J. Venables (eds), *Plundered Nations?: Successes and Failures in Natural Resource Extraction*, New York: Palgrave Macmillan, 2011, pp. 205–6.

45. Interview, Sudanese oil official, Khartoum, 15 October 2010.

46. See Roland Marchal, 'Malaysia-Sudan: from Islamist Students to Rentier Bourgeois', in Daniel Large and Luke A. Patey (eds), *Sudan Looks East: China, India and the Politics of Asian Alternatives*, Oxford: James Currey, 2011.

47. 'Petronas steps out in national service', *New Straits Times*, 24 July 2000.

48. Wen et al., op. cit., p. 290.

49. Talisman, 'Annual Report 1998', Calgary: Talisman, 1999, p. 2.

50. 'Talisman to buy Arakis for stock at $175.7 million', *Wall Street Journal*, 18 August 1998.

51. Talisman, 'Annual Report 1998', Calgary: Talisman, 1999, p. 3.

52. On the basis of a peace charter signed the previous year, the Khartoum Peace Agreement granted southern Sudan 'rights to self-determination' through a southern referendum after a four-year interim period. It brought the Nuer-dominated splinter groups under the national army as the South Sudan Defence Forces (SSDF) to fight the SPLA. Johnson, op. cit., pp. 122–3.

53. Telephone interview, Reg Manhas, Talisman Vice-President of Corporate Affairs, 3 February 2009.

54. At the same time Paulino Matip, then a general in the Sudanese Army, drove

his forces against Machar's men and civilian populations to gain control of oil areas. The infighting between the Nuer factions pushed some of Matip's own commanders, such as Peter Gadet and his 1,000 armed men, back into the arms of the SPLA. Sharon E. Hutchinson, 'A Curse from God? Religious and Political Dimensions of the Post-1991 Rise of Ethnic Violence in South Sudan', *Journal of Modern African Studies*, Vol. 39, No. 2, June 2001, pp. 322–5.

55. *Global Trade, Local Impact: Arms Transfers to all Sides in the Civil War in Sudan*, New York: Human Rights Watch, 1998.
56. John Harker, 'Human Security in Sudan: The Report of a Canadian Assessment Mission', Government of Canada, 2000, pp. 47–8.
57. 'Sudan begins oil exports', BBC News, 30 August 1999.
58. Nhial Bol, 'Islamic regime begins to export oil', Inter Press Service, 30 August 1999.
59. Jeffrey Jones, 'Canadian church group blasts Arakis oil deal', Reuters, 4 March 1997.
60. Martin Regg Cohn, 'Oiling the wheels of revolution: two Canadian companies defy rebel threats to deal in Sudan's hinterland', *Toronto Star*, 20 April 1997.
61. Steve Chase, 'Talisman plays with fire in Sudan', *Globe and Mail*, 9 October 1999.
62. Harker, op. cit., p. 64.
63. *Sudan, Oil and Human Rights*, New York: Human Rights Watch, 2003, p. 398.
64. Nicholas Coghlan, *Far in the Waste Sudan: On Assignment in Africa*, Kingston: McGill-Queen's University Press, 2005, p. 56.
65. Madelaine Drohan, *Making a Killing: How and Why Corporations use Armed Force to do Business*, Guilford, CT: The Lyons Press, 2003, p. 249.
66. 'New constitution edges Sudan on to democratic road', *New Straits Times*, 13 July 1998.
67. Georgette Gagnon and John Ryle, *Report of an Investigation into Oil Development, Conflict and Displacement in Western Upper Nile, Sudan*, Canadian Auto Workers Union, 2001; *Documentation of the Impact of Oil on Sudan*, European Coalition on Oil in Sudan, 2001; *The Scorched Earth*, Christian Aid, 2003; *Sudan, Oil and Human Rights*, New York: Human Rights Watch, 2003.
68. Robert O. Matthews, 'Canadian Corporate Responsibility in Sudan: Why Canada Backed Down', in John J. Kirton and Michael J. Trebilcock (eds), *Hard Choices, Soft Law: Voluntary Standards in Global Trade, Environment and Social Governance*, Aldershot: Ashgate, 2004, pp. 244–5.
69. *Sudan, Oil and Human Rights*, New York: Human Rights Watch, 2003, p. 393.
70. Harker, op. cit., p. 15.
71. 'Business: fuelling a fire', *The Economist*, 2 September 2000.
72. Drohan, op. cit., p. 269–71.
73. Coghlan, op. cit., p. 33.
74. *Sudan, Oil and Human Rights*, New York: Human Rights Watch, 2003, pp. 645–50.
75. Paul Haavardsrud, 'Cheap Talisman getting cheaper: 'Sudan discount' grows', *Financial Post*, 26 September 2001.

76. Drohan, op. cit., pp. 280–82.

77. Talisman, 'Annual Report 1998', Calgary: Talisman, 1999, p. 26.

78. Talisman, 'Annual Report 2000', Calgary: Talisman, 2001, p. 19.

79. Talisman, 'Corporate Social Responsibility Report 2001', Calgary: Talisman, 2002, p. 17.

80. Drohan, op. cit., p. 276.

81. There was some speculation that this move was also intended to stem legislation brewing in the US Congress for wider sanctions on religious persecution that might have hit key US allies in the Middle East. Meghan L. O'Sullivan, 'Sanctioning Sudan', in *Shrewd Sanctions: Statecraft and State Sponsors of Terrorism*, Washington, DC: Brookings Institution, 2003, p. 242.

82. James Bennet, 'U.S. cruise missiles strike Sudan and Afghan targets tied to terrorist network', *New York Times*, 21 August 1998.

83. Peter Woodward, *US Foreign Policy and the Horn of Africa*, Aldershot: Ashgate, pp. 93–9.

84. Coghlan, op. cit., p. 31.

85. Allen D. Hertzke, 'Gentle as Doves, Wise as Serpents in the Sudan Battle', in *Freeing God's Children: The Unlikely Alliance for Global Human Rights*, Lanham: Rowman and Littlefield, 2004; Peter Woodward, 'Peacemaking in Sudan', *US Foreign Policy and the Horn of Africa*, Ashgate: Aldershot, 2006, pp. 113–33; Ivar A. Iversen, *Foreign Policy in God's Name: Evangelical Influence on US Policy towards Sudan*, Oslo: Norwegian Institute of Defence Studies, 2007.

86. Talisman also faced legal threats. In 2001, the Presbyterian Church of Sudan and Sudanese individuals displaced from the oil fields brought a class action lawsuit against Talisman and the Khartoum government in a US federal district court under the Aliens Tort Claims Act. The case would ultimately be dismissed in October 2009; *Sudan, Oil and Human Rights*, New York: Human Rights Watch, 2003, pp. 495–6; 'Ottawa aids firm in genocide case: Talisman sued in U.S. over Sudan role, Washington asked to intervene in court', *Toronto Star*, 6 July 2005.

87. Activists successfully pushed the US Securities and Exchange Commission to call upon foreign companies listed on US markets to disclose their activities and the associated risks of investment in countries facing US sanctions, including Sudan; Hertzke, op. cit., p. 282.

88. The Sudan Peace Act also sought to enhance humanitarian support and engage the US government in a concerted effort to bring about peace between the Sudanese government and the SPLA.

89. Campion Walsh, 'Bush Administration and Greenspan Oppose Tighter Sudan Sanctions', *Dow Jones News*, 24 July 2001.

90. Claudia Cattaneo, 'U.S. human rights legislation lessens pressure on Talisman', *Financial Post*, 14 July 2001.

91. Hertzke, op. cit., pp. 284–5.

92. Ken Silverstein, 'Official pariah Sudan valuable to America's War on Terrorism', *Los Angeles Times*, 29 April 2005.

93. Hertzke, op. cit., p. 285.

94. O'Sullivan, op. cit., p. 246.

95. Telephone interview, Reg Manhas, 3 February 2009.

96. Terry Macalister, 'Talisman may quit Sudan', *Guardian*, 17 October 2001.

97. 'The world according to Buckee', Canwest News Service, 6 November 2006.

98. Talisman, 'Annual Report 2002', Calgary: Talisman, 2003, p. 55.

99. *Whose Oil? Sudan's Oil Industry, Facts and Analysis*, European Coalition on Oil in Sudan, Utrecht, April 2008, p. 28.

100. Talisman, 'Annual Report 2002', Calgary: Talisman, 2003, pp. 2–4.

101. Telephone interview, Reg Manhas, 3 February 2009.

102. 'Talisman among top firms praised for ethical conduct', *Calgary Herald*, 29 April 2009.

103. Nicholas Köhler, 'Talisman? A responsible corporation?' *Macleans*, 15 June 2009.

104. 'The world according to Buckee', Canwest News Service, 6 November 2006.

105. The NIF government redivided Sudan into twenty-six states in 1994, creating Unity state out of an oil-rich region of the former western Upper Nile province. The International Petroleum Corporation merged with Sands Petroleum to form Lundin Oil in 1997, and when Talisman bought many of its assets in 2001, this became Lundin Petroleum with Sudan as its main asset. Interview, Christine Batruch, Vice-President of Corporate Responsibility, Lundin, Geneva, 6 November 2008; 'Upstream Development Proceeds despite Intensified Conflict', *Petroleum Economist*, Vol. 65, No. 1, 1998.

106. 'Sudan E&P Continues to Make Advances', *Oil and Gas Journal*, Vol. 95, No. 8, 24 February 1997.

107. Interview, Christine Batruch, 6 November 2008.

108. *Sudan, Oil and Human Rights*, New York: Human Rights Watch, 2003, pp. 589–90.

109. Interview, Christine Batruch, Geneva, 6 November 2008.

110. Christine Batruch, 'Oil and Conflict: Lundin Petroleum's experience in Sudan', in Alyson J.K. Bailes and Isabela Frommelt (eds), *Business and Security: Public–Private Sector Relationships in a New Security Environment*, Stockholm: Stockholm International Peace Research Institute, 2004, p. 13.

111. 'Statement by John Dor, Governor of Unity State, Sudan', May 2001, www.lundin-petroleum.com, accessed 2 June 2005.

112. Batruch, op. cit., p. 13.

113. *Sudan, Oil and Human Rights*, New York: Human Rights Watch, 2003, p. 583.

114. Ibid., p. 595.

115. Ibid., p. 600.

116. 'Petronas makes further inroads into Sudan's oil industry', *Business Times*, 29 April 2003; 'OMV/Sudan/Blocks: Sells Stakes in Blocks 5A, 5B', *Dow Jones*, 2 September 2003.

117. Lundin, 'Lundin Annual Report 2003', Stockholm: Lundin, 2004, p. 2.

118. Ibid., p. 5.

119. Lundin, 'Annual Report 2001', Stockholm: Lundin, 2001, p. 26; Lundin, 'Annual Report 2005', Stockholm: Lundin, 2005, p. 45.

120. OMV, 'Annual Report 2004', Vienna: OMV, 2004, p. 42.

121. OMV, 'Annual Report 2003', Vienna: OMV, 2003, p. 54: OMV, 'Annual Report 2005', Vienna: OMV, 2005, p. 67.

122. Petronas also found the stoppages due to insecurity to be one of the biggest challenges in Sudan, but the Malaysian company stayed on and bought out Lundin for its stake. Interviews, Petronas and Lundin company representatives, Khartoum, 12 September 2006 and 1 November 2007.

123. It was not until 2008 that Lundin abandoned the concession after the joint operator, WNPOC, drilled three dry wells. Sanjay Dutta, 'OVL to quit block in Sudan', *The Times of India*, 27 April 2009.

124. In 2001, Lundin delisted from the Nasdaq stock market in New York when Talisman bought most of its assets, taking the company out of the US government's domain of influence.

125. OMV, 'OMV signs Exploration and Production Sharing Agreement for the highly prospective Block 5B onshore Sudan', 3 May 2001, www.omv.com, accessed 2 June 2005; Lundin, 'EU Issues Resolution on Sudan', 9 November 2001, www.lundin-petroleum.com, accessed 2 June 2005.

126. Interview, Christine Batruch, 6 November 2008.

127. Lundin would not be able to easily wipe away the stain of operating in Sudan. The European Coalition on Oil in Sudan, a Holland-based NGO, continued to pressure the company after its exit, claiming Lundin and its partners may have been complicit in war crimes and crimes against humanity during the civil war; European Coalition on Oil in Sudan, 'Unpaid Debt: The Legacy of Lundin, Petronas and OMV in Sudan, 1997–2003', Utrecht: ECOS, June 2010.

128. Terry Macalister, 'Pressed Talisman quits Sudan', *The Guardian*, 1 November 2002.

129. Coghlan, op. cit., p. 33.

130. 'ONGC Videsh Sells Stake in Hell Hole Bayou to Oil India', *Rigzone*, 12 March 2003; 'OVL takes Oil India for a ride', *Indian Express*, 31 August 2003. Oil India abandoned its US stake a month later.

131. David B. Ottaway, 'Chinese fought on NYSE listing; groups cite oil firm's role in Sudan', *Washington Post*, 27 January 2000.

132. John Lebate and Stephen Fidler, 'Sudan ties jeopardize Chinese oil listing', *Financial Times*, 6 October 1999.

133. Stephan Diamond, 'PetroChina Syndrome: Regulating Capital Markets in the Anti-Globalization Era', *Journal of Corporation Law*, Vol. 29, Fall 2003, p. 47.

134. *Sudan, Oil and Human Rights*, New York: Human Rights Watch, 2003, pp. 614–15.

135. Wang Xiangwei, 'PetroChina sets out stall of sweeteners for investors,' *South China Morning Post*, 24 January 2000.

136. Stephan Diamond, 'PetroChina Syndrome: Regulating Capital Markets in the Anti-Globalization Era', *Journal of Corporation Law*, Vol. 29, Fall 2003, p. 48.

137. Hertzke, op. cit., p. 280.
138. Diamond, op. cit., pp. 61–2.

4. OIL FOR THE PARTY

1. The failed $18.5 billion bid by the China National Offshore Oil Corporation to purchase the US oil company Unocal in July 2005 was evidence of the fierce political opposition facing Chinese national oil companies in the US. Paul Blustein, 'Many oil experts unconcerned over China Unocal bid', *Washington Post*, 1 July 2005; Steven Lohr, 'The big tug of war over Unocal', *New York Times*, 6 July 2005.
2. Lim Tai Wei, *Oil in China: From Self-Reliance to Internationalization*, Singapore: World Scientific, 2010, pp. 43–4.
3. James Kynge, *China Shakes the World: A Titan's Rise and Troubled Future—and the Challenge for America*, New York: First Mariner Books, 2006, pp. 135–6.
4. Jin Zhang, *Catch-up and Competitiveness in China: The Case of Large Firms in the Oil Industry*, London: RoutledgeCurzon, 2004, pp. 73–4.
5. Bo Kong, *China's International Petroleum Policy*, Santa Barbara: ABC-CLIO, 2010, pp. 7–8.
6. Tatsu Kambara, 'The Petroleum Industry in China', *China Quarterly*, No. 60, December 1974, pp. 702–3.
7. Kenneth Lieberthal and Michel Oksenberg, 'The Case of Petroleum', in *Policy Making in China: Leaders, Structures, and Processes*, Princeton University Press, pp. 172–3.
8. Lim, op. cit., p. 12.
9. Interview, Chinese oil official, Beijing, 13 September 2011.
10. Lieberthal and Oksenberg, op. cit., pp. 177–8.
11. Tatsu Kambara and Christopher Howe, *China and the Global Energy Crisis: Development and Prospects for China's Oil and Natural Gas*, Cheltenham: Edward Elgar Publishing, 2007, p. 19.
12. Lieberthal and Oksenberg, op. cit., pp. 82–3.
13. Larry Chuen-ho Chow, 'The Changing Role of Oil in Chinese Exports, 1974–89', *China Quarterly*, No. 131, 1992, p. 753.
14. Zhang, op. cit., p. 75–6.
15. Lieberthal and Oksenberg, op. cit., pp. 185–6.
16. Ibid., pp. 187–9.
17. Lim, op. cit., p. 30.
18. Lieberthal and Oksenberg, op. cit., p. 46.
19. Jessica Leatrice Wolfe, 'Political Implications of the Petroleum Industry in China', *Asian Survey*, Vol. 16, No. 6, June 1976, pp. 525–39.
20. Richard Baum, *Burying Mao: Chinese Politics in the Age of Deng Xiaopeng*, Princeton University Press, 1994, p. 55.
21. Ibid., pp. 55–6.

22. Barry Naughton, *Growing Out of the Plan: Chinese Economic Reform, 1978–1993*, Cambridge: Cambridge University Press, 1996, pp. 69–72.

23. Lieberthal and Oksenberg, op. cit., p. 264.

24. Eventually, Yu returned to the PLA as head of its Political Department. Lieberthal and Oksenberg, op. cit., p. 227; Baum, op. cit., p. 406, n. 30.

25. Fox Butterfield, '70 are reported killed in collapse of Chinese oil rig', *New York Times*, 7 July 1980; James P. Sterba, 'China indicts four industry figures in oil rig accident that killed 72', *New York Times*, 28 August 1980.

26. Baum, op. cit., pp. 104–5.

27. Ibid., pp. 83–4.

28. BP, *Statistical Review of World Energy*, BP, 2011.

29. In terms of energy use per capita, however, China remains nowhere near the US. The average Chinese consumes five times less energy than the average American. In fact, if China were to consume the same per capita amount of oil as the US, it would use three times the total world consumption. Spencer Swartz and Shai Oster, 'China tops U.S. in energy use', *Wall Street Journal*, 18 July 2010; James Kynge, *China Shakes the World: A Titan's Rise and Troubled Future—and the Challenge for America*, New York: First Mariner Books, 2006, p. 134.

30. Nicholas Becquelin, 'Zhu Rongji's Oil Men: A Faction in the New Cabinet', *China Perspectives*, No. 16, March/April 1994.

31. Zhang, op. cit., p. 164.

32. BP, *Statistical Review of World Energy*, BP, 2011.

33. *China's Customs Statistics Yearbooks*, Beijing: China Customs Press, multiple years.

34. BP, *Statistical Review of World Energy*, BP, 2011.

35. *China's Customs Statistics Yearbooks*, Beijing: China Customs Press, multiple years.

36. During the 1990s, oil from the Asia-Pacific region, particularly from Indonesia, comprised on average 41 per cent of Chinese oil imports. This dropped to 9 per cent in the 2000s, after the Minas crude blend from Indonesia went into decline and China's oil demand continued to skyrocket. As a result, the proportion of Chinese oil imports coming from Africa rose from 9 to 27 per cent on average each year from one decade to the next. *China's Customs Statistics Yearbooks*, Beijing: China Customs Press, multiple years.

37. International Energy Agency, *World Energy Outlook 2011*, Paris: IEA, 2012.

38. Energy Information Administration, 'China', Country Analysis Brief, 4 September 2012, http://www.eia.gov/countries/cab.cfm?fips=CH, accessed 11 March 2013; International Energy Agency, *World Energy Outlook 2010*, Paris: IEA, 2011, pp. 107–8.

39. Erica S. Downs, 'Business Interest Groups in Chinese Politics: The Case of the Oil Companies', in Cheng Li (ed.), *China's Changing Political Landscape: Prospects for Democracy*, Washington, DC: Brookings Institution Press, 2008, pp. 125–8.

40. Erica S. Downs and Michal Meidan, 'Business and Politics in China: The Oil Executive Reshuffle of 2011', *China Security*, Issue 19, 2011.

41. Interview, Chinese journalist, Beijing, 17 November 2011.

42. Downs, op. cit., p. 134.

43. Downs and Meiden, op. cit., pp. 5–6.

44. Zhang, op. cit., p. 80.

45. Trist Saywell and Ahmed Rashid, 'Innocent Abroad: China's National Oil Company Joins the Big League', *Far Eastern Economic Review*, 26 February 1998.

46. Bo Kong, *China's International Petroleum Policy*, Santa Barbara: ABC-CLIO, 2010, pp. 32–3.

47. 'China's New Petroleum Structure Continues to Evolve under Reform (Part 2)', *Oil and Gas Journal*, Vol. 95, No. 40, 6 October 1997; Saywell and Rashid, op. cit.

48. Barry Naughton, 'Claiming Profit for the State: SASAC and the Capital Management Budget', *China Leadership Monitor*, No. 18, 2008.

49. Bo, op. cit., pp. 37–8.

50. Ibid., pp. 39–41.

51. 'Foreign partnerships being sought in oil industry', BBC News, 29 December 1995.

52. Zhao Shaoqin, 'China exploring overseas business', *China Daily*, 8 September 1997.

53. Giles Hewitt, 'Chinese oil industry shifts overseas strategy', AFP, 25 September 1997.

54. Zhang, op. cit., pp. 180–4.

55. Saywell and Rashid, op. cit.

56. 'China's New Petroleum Structure Continues to Evolve under Reform (Part 2)', *Oil and Gas Journal*, Vol. 95, No. 40, 6 October 1997.

57. Dianne Solis, 'Pumping for money: Once-aloof countries woo oil investors at conference', *Dallas Morning News*, 16 February 1998.

58. Like the US, China was politically interested in Sudan as a counterweight to Soviet-allied Ethiopia. *Sudan, Quarterly Economic Review*, No. 4, 1985, Economist Intelligence Unit pp. 20–21.

59. China and Sudan also share a history of colonial oppression. Charles Gordon, the British Governor General of Sudan in the 1880s, earlier served in China, where as a captain in the British forces he took part in the 1860 sacking of the Summer Palace in Beijing. He was later killed in Khartoum in the Mahdist uprising of 1885. Ali Abdalla Ali, *The Sudanese–Chinese Relations Before and After Oil*, Khartoum: Sudan Currency Printing Press, 2006, p. 26; Daniel Large, 'China's Sudan Engagement: Changing Northern and Southern Political Trajectories in Peace and War', *China Quarterly*, Vol. 199, 2009, p. 613.

60. 'Swedish LO Promises Support to Danish LO', US Department of State, Electronic Telegrams, 1/1/1973—12/31/1973, http://aad.archives.gov/aad/createpdf?dt=2472&rid=205&dl=1345, accessed 10 March 2013.

61. 'Oil in Sudan?', Electronic Telegrams, 1/1/1976—12/31/1976, http://aad.archives.gov/aad/createpdf?dt=2082&rid=56798&dl=1345, accessed 10 March 2013.

62. Ali, op. cit., p. 8.

63. Personal correspondence, Brian Kay, 25 November 2008.

64. Daniel Large, 'China and the Contradictions of 'Non-interference' in Sudan', *Review of African Political Economy*, Vol. 35, No. 115, p. 95.

65. 'Chinese FM Ends Visit', *Arab Press Service Organisaton*, Vol. 40, No. 3, 15 January 1994; Peter Verney, *Raising the Stakes: Oil and Conflict in Sudan*, Hebden Bridge: Sudan Update, 1999, p. 83.

66. In January 1986, Chinese and Sudanese government officials established the Sino-Sudanese Economic and Trade Joint Commission, which served as the basis for a host of bilateral agreements. Linda Jakobson and Zha Daojiong, 'China and the Worldwide Search for Oil Security', *Asia-Pacific Review*, Vol. 12, No. 2, 2006, p. 66.

67. Li Yan, 'MOFTEC lauds growing exchanges with Sudan', *China Daily*, 14 December 1994; 'Sudanese delegation boosts ties', *China Daily*, 16 December 1994.

68. Interview, CNPC senior geologist, Beijing, 30 September 2011.

69. J. Millard Burr and Robert O. Collins, *Revolutionary Sudan: Hasan al-Turabi and the Islamist State, 1989–2000*, Leiden: Brill, 2000, pp. 248–9.

70. John Garnaut, 'Up against the Great Wall of China', *Sydney Morning Herald*, 21 November 2009.

71. Alice Lyman Miller, 'The Central Committee Departments under Hu Jintao', *China Leadership Monitor*, No. 27, Winter 2009, p. 2.

72. 'Bashir meets Chinese President, says Sudan opposed to Taiwan joining UN', BBC News, 28 September 1995.

73. 查道炯,《中国在非洲的石油利益》,《国际政治研究》,2006年,第4期·(Zha Daojiong, 'China's Oil interest in Africa,' *International Politics Quarterly*, No. 4, 2006); 云宗国,《苏丹石油开发项目前景广阔》,《国际经济合作》, 22–23页, 1997年第5期 (Yun Zongguo, 'The Oil Projects in Sudan are Very Promising', *International Economic Cooperation*, No. 5, 1997, pp. 22–3).

74. Tong Ting, 'Soft loans to develop oil project in Sudan', *China Daily*, 9 December 1995.

75. Jakobson and Zha, op. cit., p. 66.

76. Tong Ting, 'Soft Loans to Develop Oil Project in Sudan', *China Daily*, 9 December 1995.

77. 云宗国,《苏丹石油开发项目前景广阔》,《国际经济合作》, 22–23页,1997年第5期 (Yun Zongguo, 'The Oil Projects in Sudan are Very Promising', *International Economic Cooperation*, No. 5, 1997, pp. 22–3).

78. Central Bank of Sudan, '49th Annual Report 2009', Khartoum: CBOS, 2010, p. 165.

79. Saywell and Rashid, op. cit.

80. Dan Morgan and David B. Ottaway, 'Azerbaijan's riches alter the chessboard', *Washington Post*, 4 October 1998.

81. Ahmed Rashid, 'Go East, Go West', *Far Eastern Economic Review*, 14 August 1997; Saywell and Rashid, op. cit.

82. Xin Ma andPhilip Andrews-Speed, 'The Overseas' Activities of China's National

Oil Companies: Rationale and Outlook', *Minerals and Energy*, Vol. 21, No. 1, 2006, pp. 24–5.

83. Chinese policy banks, awash in cash reserves, were not only seeking to attain national energy security objectives by making 'loan for oil' deals with oil-rich countries; they were also eager to profit themselves from involvement in the oil investments. Bo, op. cit., p. 69; Erica S. Downs, 'China Development Bank's Oil Loans: Pursuing Policy—and Profit', *China Economic Quarterly*, 2011.

84. When national oil comapnies did go to Chinese policy banks for financing, Chinese government controls on the banking sector actually prevented even lower interest rates if full liberalisation was implemented. Trevor Houser, 'The Roots of Chinese Oil Investment Abroad', *Asia Policy*, No. 5, January 2008, pp. 141–66.

85. Erica S. Downs, 'Who's Afraid of China's Oil Companies?', in Carlos Pascual and Jonathan Elkind (eds), *Energy Security: Economics, Politics, Strategies and Implications*, Washington, DC: Brookings Institution, 2010, p. 93.

86. Trevor Houser, 'The Roots of Chinese Oil Investment Abroad', *Asia Policy*, No. 5, January 2008, pp. 160–1.

87. Downs and Meidan, op. cit., p. 7.

88. Bruce Gilley, 'Slick Manoeuvres: China's Petroleum Shake-up Dashes Competition Hopes', *Far Eastern Economic Review*, 2 July 1998.

89. Bo, op. cit., pp. 22–3.

90. Interview, Chinese academic, Beijing, 7 November 2010.

91. Downs, 'Business Interest Groups', p. 134.

92. Erica S. Downs, 'China', The Brookings Foreign Policy Studies, Energy Security Series, Washington, DC: The Brookings Institution, 2006, p. 22.

93. Interview, former Chinese diplomat, Beijing, 26 September 2011.

94. Erica S. Downs, 'China's "New" Energy Administration', chinabusinessreview.com, November–December 2008, pp. 42–5.

95. Downs, 'China', p. 24.

96. Ibid., pp. 22–3.

97. Erica S. Downs, 'Business Interest Groups in Chinese Politics: The Case of the Oil Companies', in Cheng Li (ed.), *China's Changing Political Landscape: Prospects for Democracy*, Washington, DC: Brookings Institution, 2008, pp. 123–4.

98. Inappropriate safety measures to save time and money, common across many Chinese industries, were seen as the cause of the blowout. 'Tragedy of errors in gas blowout', *China Daily*, 12 January 2003; 'Oil boss Ma Fucai resigns', *Caijing*, 20 April 2004.

99. Ma was already under scrunity from Party leaders for his poor handling of massive labour protests at Daqing in 2002. Richard McGregor, 'CNPC president quits over gas explosion', *Financial Times*, 14 April 2004; Downs, 'Business Interest Groups', p. 124.

100. Richard McGregor, *The Party: The Secret World of China's Communist Rulers*, London: Penguin, 2010, pp. 63–4.

101. Bo, op. cit., pp. 45–7.

102. Downs, 'China', pp. 22–3; Downs, 'China's "New" Energy Administration', p. 43.

103. Downs, 'China', p. 24; Downs, 'Business Interest Groups', p. 129.

104. Interview, Chinese academic, 8 November 2010.

105. Barry Naughton, 'SASSAC and Rising Corporate Power in China', *China Leadership Monitor*, No. 18, 2008.

106. Interview, international energy journalist, Beijing, 17 October 2011.

107. Erica S. Downs, 'Who's Afraid', pp. 77–8.

5. A CHINESE MIRACLE

1. Wen et al., op. cit., p. 300.

2. 'Sudan inaugurates oil pipeline', Associated Press, 31 May 1999.

3. *Sudan, Oil and Human Rights*, New York: Human Rights Watch, 2003, pp. 172–5.

4. Wen et al., op. cit., p. 293.

5. Ibid., p. 289.

6. J. Millard Burr and Robert O. Collins, *Revolutionary Sudan: Hasan al-Turabi and the Islamist State, 1989–2000*, Leiden: Brill, 2000, pp. 248–9.

7. 'Beyond the Job', CNODC, http://www.cnpcint.com/workatconodc/beyondthe-job/peoplestories1.html, 2007, accessed 7 September 2011.

8. Wen et al., op. cit., p. 300.

9. Linda Jakobson and Zha Daojiong, 'China and the Worldwide Search for Oil Security', *Asia-Pacific Review*, Vol. 12, No. 2, p. 66; China National Petroleum Corporation, '2004 Annual Report', Beijing: CNPC, 2005, p. 36.

10. Interview, oil industry insider, Beijing, 23 October 2011.

11. Interview, CNPC international geologist, Beijing, 30 September 2011.

12. CNPC went on to discover the Fula oil field in 2000 and complete a 716-kilo-metre pipeline to Khartoum four years later. Wen *et al.*, op. cit., p. 289; China National Petroleum Corporation, '2004 Annual Report', Beijing: CNPC, 2005, p. 31.

13. Interview, CNPC international geologist, 30 September 2011.

14. Xu Yihe, 'China CNPC's Pursuit for Foreign Oil Fuels Competition', *Dow Jones*, 3 June 1999.

15. 'Talisman Focuses Growth Strategy on E&P outside Canadian Core', *Oil and Gas Journal*, 31 May 1999.

16. BP, *Statistical Review of World Energy*, BP, 2011.

17. Tong Xiaoguang and Shi Buqing, 'Changing Exploration Focus Paved Way for Success', *GEO ExPro*, May 2006.

18. *Malik v. State Petroleum Corporation*, 2008 British Columbia Supreme Court 1600, S015741, p. 12.

19. 'Talisman Focuses Growth Strategy on E&P outside Canadian Core', *Oil and Gas Journal*, 31 May 1999.

20. Interview, Sudanese oil official, Khartoum, 28 October 2007.

21. Wikileaks cable, 'Positives And Negatives In Sudan's Oil Industry', 12 March 2008, http://wikileaks.org/cable/2008/03/08KHARTOUM367.html, accessed 9 November 2012.

22. Peter Verney, *Raising the Stakes: Oil and Conflict in Sudan*, Hebden Bridge: Sudan Update, 1999, p. 55.

23. Wen et al., op. cit., p. 290.

24. 周吉平，《海外创业的标志工程—中国石油天然气集团公司苏丹石油项目》，《中国石油》2000年12月 (Zhou Jiping, 'The Symbolic Achievement in the Overseas Business: The Sudan Project of CNPC', *China Petroleum*, December 2000, pp. 15–6).

25. 'Garang: "oil firms are targets"', BBC News, 17 June 2001.

26. Interview, CNPC official, Beijing, 26 October 2011.

27. Interview, Chinese oil industry consultant, 18 October 2011.

28. Nicholas Coghlan, *Far in the Waste Sudan: On Assignment in Africa*, Montreal and Kingston: McGill-Queen's University Press, 2005.

29. Interview, Chinese oil industry consultant, Beijing, 26 September 2011.

30. Coghlan, op. cit., p. 46–9.

31. Ibid., p. 37.

32. Ibid., pp. 50–1.

33. *Sudan, Oil and Human Rights*, New York: Human Rights Watch, 2003, pp. 175–8.

34. Interview, CNPC official, Beijing, 26 October 2011.

35. Interview, oil industry consultant, Beijing, 26 September 2011.

36. Interview, CNPC official, Beijing, 26 October 2011.

37. Richard Cockett, *Sudan: Darfur and the Failure of an African State*, New Haven and London: Yale University Press, 2010, pp. 162–3.

38. Ken Silverstein, 'Official Pariah Sudan valuable to America's War on Terrorism', *Los Angeles Times*, 29 April 2005.

39. Interview, CNPC official, Beijing, 26 October 2011.

40. *Sudan, Oil and Human Rights*, New York: Human Rights Watch, 2003, p. 190.

41. Ibid., p. 191.

42. Interview, CNPC official, Beijing, 26 October 2011.

43. Wen et al., op. cit., p. 298.

44. Interview, general manager, international oil service company, Khartoum, 14 October 2010.

45. Wen et al., op. cit.

46. BP, *Statistical Review of World Energy*, BP, 2011.

47. Erica S. Downs, 'Who's Afraid of China's Oil Companies?', in Carlos Pascual and Jonathan Elkind (eds), *Energy Security: Economics, Politics, Strategies and Implications*, Washington, DC: Brookings Institution, 2010, p. 86.

48. The author's estimates are based on data from 'CNPC said Sudan project contributed nearly half total quity oil secured from abroad in 03', *China Business*

News, 25 February 2004; Winnie Lee, 'In Bid to Grow Overseas, PetroChina, CNPC Form JV', *Platts Oilgram News*, 13 June 2005; Erica S. Downs, 'The Fact and Fiction of Sino-Africa Energy Relations', *China Security*, Vol. 3, No. 3, Summer 2007; China National Petroleum Corporation, 'Annual Reports', Beijing: CNPC, 2004–08; Downs, 'Who's Afraid', p. 88.

49. Wen et al., op. cit., p. 292.
50. ZPEB was later transferred to Sinopec in China's 1998 oil sector reorganisation, but continued to operate in Sudan. Su Yongdi stayed with CNPC.
51. Wen et al., op. cit., p. 291.
52. Felix K. Chang, 'Chinese Energy and Asian Security', *ORBIS*, Vol. 45, Issue 2, 22 March 2001.
53. Interview, Sudanese ministry official, London, 2 July 2008.
54. Interview, Sudanese oil company manager, Khartoum, 14 October 2010.
55. Interview, Asian national oil company manager, Khartoum, 15 October 2010.
56. Wen et al., op. cit.
57. Deborah Brautigam, *The Dragon's Gift: The Real Story of China in Africa*, Oxford: Oxford University Press, 2009, p. 155.
58. Ian Johnson, 'China cuts Sudan a deal on Nile oil project—engineering firm sees know-how as profit enough', *Wall Street Journal*, 20 December 1999.
59. Brautigam, op. cit., pp. 155–7.
60. *Sudan, Oil and Human Rights*, New York: Human Rights Watch, 2003, p. 460.
61. Zhou, op. cit., pp. 15–6.
62. Ibid.
63. Wen et al., op. cit.
64. Daniel Large and Luke A. Patey, 'Introduction', in Daniel Large and Luke A. Patey (eds), *Sudan Looks East: China, India, and the Politics of Asian Alternatives*, Oxford: James Currey, 2011, pp. 20–4.
65. See Harry Verhoeven, '"Dams are Development": China, the Al-Ingaz Regime and the Political Economy of the Sudanese Nile', in Daniel Large and Luke A. Patey (eds) *Sudan Looks East: China, India, and the Politics of Asian Alternatives*, Oxford: James Currey, 2011.
66. Wikileaks cable, 'China in Sudan: Rising Dragon or Paper Tiger?', Khartoum to Washington, DC, 26 January 2007. http://wikileaks.org/cable/2007/01/07 KHARTOUM119.html, accessed 17 June 2012.
67. Interview, geologist, CNPC International Sudan, Khartoum, 15 October 2010.
68. Interview, geologist, CNPC International Sudan, Beijing, 7 November 2011.
69. Wen et al., op. cit., p. 297.
70. Zhao Shaoqin, 'China exploring overseas business', *China Daily*, 8 September 1997.
71. BP, *Statistical Review of World Energy*, BP, 2011.
72. Zhou, op. cit.
73. Wen et al., op. cit.
74. Zhou, op. cit.

75. Interview, oil industry consultant, Beijing, 18 October 2011.

76. 'Sudanese First Vice President visits Sichuan', *Xinhua*, 1 April 2001.

77. 'Chinese state councilor meets Sudanese guests', *Xinhua*, 13 December 2004.

78. 'China boosts domestic security spending by 11.5 pct', Reuters, 5 March 2012.

79. Interview, international energy journalist, Beijing, 6 October 2011.

80. Edward Wong, 'China locks down restive region after deadly clashes', *New York Times*, 6 July 2009; 'Senior leader calls to build "steel wall" in Xinjiang for stability', *Xinhua*, 11 July 2009.

81. 'CNPC in Sudan', China National Petroleum Corporation, 2009, p. 10.

82. Xie Ye, 'CNPC pumps money into Sudan', *China Daily*, 19 May 2003.

83. Wen et al., op. cit., p. 291.

84. Interview, Sudanese businessman, 13 October 2010, Khartoum.

85. Interview, CNPC senior geologist, Beijing, 30 September 2011.

86. *China's Customs Statistics Yearbooks*, Beijing: China Customs Press, multiple years; Energy Information Administration, 'Country Analysis Briefs: China, September 2012, http://www.eia.gov/countries/cab.cfm?fips=CH, accessed 9 November 2012.

87. Erica S. Downs, 'The Chinese Energy Security Debate', *China Quarterly*, No. 177, 2004, pp. 35–6.

88. Linda Jakobson and Dean Knox, 'New Foreign Policy Actors in China', Stockholm International Peace Research Institute Policy Paper 26, September 2012, p. 26.

89. Downs, 'The Fact and Fiction', pp. 46–7; Arthur Krober and G.A. Donovan, 'Sudan Oil: where Does it Go?', *China Economic Quarterly*, Q2, 2007, p. 18.

90. Downs, 'Who's Afraid', pp. 88–9.

91. Trevor Houser, 'The Roots of Chinese Oil Investment Abroad', *Asia Policy*, No. 5, January 2008, pp. 162–3.

92. Te Kan, 'CNPC in Sudan, Model of South-South Co-op', *China Daily*, 3 November 2006.

93. Zhou, op. cit.

94. 'Sudanese president receives special envoy Zhou Yongkang', BBC News, 6 July 1999.

95. Zhou, op. cit.

6. KEEPING THE LIGHTS ON

1. See H.N. Kaul, *K D Malaviya and the Evolution of India's Oil Policy*, New Delhi: South Asia Books, 1992.

2. 'ONGC: Coping with Competition', *Frontline*, Vol. 15, No. 8, 11 April 1998.

3. 'ONGC's Mumbai High output up 15%', *Economic Times*, 2 December 2002.

4. 'India goes it alone in its bid to find more oil', *Financial Times*, 9 November 1981; R.C. Murthy, 'Energy Review: India's oil and gas—A long haul to self-sufficiency', *Financial Times*, 17 February 1982.

5. 'India goes it alone in its bid to find more oil', *Financial Times*, 9 November 1981; R.C. Murthy, 'Energy Review: India's oil and gas'.

6. Ministry of Petroleum and Natural Gas (MPNG), 'Table—10 Production of Crude Oil and Natural Gas', *Basic Statistics on Indian Petroleum and Natural Gas 2008–09*, New Delhi: Government of India, 2009, p. 11.

7. 'India will be world's 3rd largest economy by 2030', *The Times of India*, 27 February 2012.

8. MPNG, *Basic Statistics on Indian Petroleum & Natural Gas*, New Delhi: Government of India, 2011, p. 3.

9. BP, *Quantifying Energy, BP Statistical Review of World Energy*, London: BP, 2012.

10. Ibid.

11. Energy Information Administration, Country Analysis Brief: India, http://www.eia.gov/cabs/india/Full.html, November 2011, accessed 15 February 2012; Planning Commission, *Integrated Energy Policy: Report of the Expert Committee*, New Delhi: Government of India, 2006, p. 45.

12. Energy Information Administration, Country Analysis Brief: India, http://www.eia.gov/countries/analysisbriefs/India/india.pdf, November 2013, accessed 8 July 2013.

13. Energy Information Administration, Country Analysis: India, www.eia.doe.gov, March 2009, accessed 20 April 2010.

14. Reserve Bank of India, *Table 129, India's Foreign Trade—US Dollars, Handbook of Statistics on the Indian Economy, 2007–08*, Mumbai: Rekha Misra, 2008, p. 197.

15. Sanjeev Sanyal, *The Indian Renaissance: India's Rise after a Thousand Years of Decline*, London: Viking/Penguin, 2008, pp. 47–9.

16. Reserve Bank of India, op. cit., p. 197.

17. Dilip Hiro, 'India: A Giant Rising, Thirsty for Oil', in *Blood of the Earth: The Global Battle for Vanishing Oil*, London: Politico's Publishing, 2007, p. 216.

18. Pradeep Puri, 'Administered price mechanism in oil sector: Bane or boon?' *Business Standard*, 20 May 1997.

19. 'India defends loan request', *New York Times*, 14 August 1981.

20. Reserve Bank of India, op. cit.

21. 'Discovery of oilfield in Arabian Sea raises India's hopes of becoming self-sufficient in fuel: 1986 is target year', *New York Times*, 18 July 1976; BP, *Quantifying Energy, BP Statistical Review of World Energy*, London: BP, 2008, p. 16; Reserve Bank of India, op. cit.

22. Daniel Yergin, 'Ensuring Energy Security', *Foreign Affairs*, Vol. 85, No. 2, March/April 2006, p. 72.

23. A.R. Sihag and A. Sen, 'Petroleum sector reforms: progress and prospects', *The Hindu*, 4 October 2001.

24. MPNG, 'Annual Report 2004–2005', New Delhi: Government of India, 2005, p. 82.

25. B.M., 'Repudiating Malaviya Legacy: Oil Multinationals' Return', *Economic and Political Weekly*, 2–9 January 1988.

26. Ibid.

27. Kannan Srinivasan, 'ONGC's Decline and What Should Be Done', *Economic and Political Weekly*, 22 February 1997.

28. NELP put government approval of oil and gas exploration licenses on a fast track, replacing the previous lengthy process; Tanvi Madan, 'India', The Brookings Foreign Policy Studies: Energy Security Series, The Brookings Institution, November 2006, pp. 38–9.

29. There was strong sentiment that India had limited prospects for commercial oil discovery and that the most attractive concessions were in the possession of ONGC and other national oil companies. Even under the new fast track system, delays in the awarding of contracts and an absence of geological data depressed international participation. Dednath Shaw, 'Securing India's Energy Needs: The Regional Dimension', Center for Strategic and International Studies, 2005, p. 40; 'After a long round, NELP-VII has no big names to show off', *Financial Express*, 1 July 2008.

30. Tanvi Madan, op. cit., p. 31.

31. 'India launches ninth edition of NELP', *Economic Times*, 15 October 2010.

32. The discoveries of natural gas in the Krishna-Godavari basin in eastern India by the Indian oil company Reliance Industries in May 2007 and multiple oil finds by the Edinburgh-based Cairn Energy in Rajasthan over the years brought much needed hope to the Indian oil industry. MPNG, *Basic Statistics on Indian Petroleum & Natural Gas*, Government of India, 2011, p. 11; Rajeev Jayaswal, 'Getting the giants to join the great Indian oil hunt', *Economic Times*, 24 May 2007.

33. On the technological side, ONGC set about to rejuvenate its main oil fields at Bombay High, now called Mumbai High, and petroleum resources in Assam. These efforts quickly produced results, with an increase in production of 15 per cent in Mumbai High by late 2002. ONGC also empowered its onsite geologists in individual oil fields in hopes of improving efficiency; in the past, basin managers had been in charge of multiple oil fields. 'ONGC's Mumbai High output up 15%', *Economic Times*, 2 December 2002; 'ONGC: Action and Reaction', *Oil and Gas Update India*, Vol. 23, No. 13, February 2006.

34. ONGC, 'Annual Report 2002–3' and 'Annual Report 2011–12', New Delhi: ONGC, 2003 and 2012.

35. 'Company Monitor: Oil and Natural Gas Corporation (ONGC), India Oil and Gas Report Q4 2008', *Business Monitor International*, 2008, p. 66.

36. Department of Commerce, Government of India, 'Export-Import Data Bank', http://commerce.nic.in/, 9 November 2012, accessed 20 November 2012.

37. *India, IMF Country Report*, No. 08/51, Washington, DC: IMF, 2008, p. 16.

38. Department of Commerce, Government of India, 'Export-Import Data Bank', http://commerce.nic.in/, 9 November 2012, accessed 20 November 2012.

39. Sumit Ganguly, 'The ONGC: Charting A New Course?' Austin: Baker Institute Energy Forum, 2007, p. 22; Madan, op. cit., p. 7.

40. Madan, op. cit., pp. 36–7.

41. 'No extension for ONGC Chairman Subir Raha', *The Hindu*, 26 May 2006.

42. Madan, op. cit., pp. 24–5.

43. 'ONGC, IOC conferred Maharatna status', *Business Standard*, 16 November 2010.

44. Sumit Ganguly, 'The ONGC: Charting A New Course?', Baker Institute Energy Forum, 2007, p. 29.

45. Madan, op. cit., p. 69.

46. Amy Kazmin, 'India cuts petrol subsidies', *Financial Times*, 25 June 2010.

47. 'Indian Politics: Unfinished Journey', *The Economist*, 24 March 2012.

48. ONGC, 'Annual Report 2003–4', New Delhi: ONGC 2004; 'Goldman Sachs Report—ONGC Response', Corporate Communications, www.ongcindia.com, 8 March 2009, accessed 20 January 2009; ONGC, 'Annual Report 2007–8', New Delhi: ONGC, 2008.

49. 'India upstream oil firms pay 40 pct of fuel subsidy', Reuters, 21 May 2012; ONGC, 'Annual Report 2011–12', New Delhi: ONGC, 2012.

50. ONGC, 'Annual Report 2011–12', New Delhi: ONGC, 2012.

51. 'ONGC not worried about subsidy burden', *Business Standard*, 17 May 2008.

52. 'Slump in Q2 profits due to subsidy burden: Sudhir Vasudeva, ONGC', *Economic Times*, 9 November 2012.

53. Indian refiners on the other hand had been devastated by government price ceilings on refined products, despite receiving billions in under-recovery payments each year. ONGC, 'Annual Report 2002–03' and 'Annual Report 2011–12', New Delhi: ONGC, 2003, and 2012.

54. 'ONGC Videsh on track in projects', *Indian Business Insight*, 27 January 2004.

55. 'Profile and Bibliography, Atul Chandra', *Businessweek*, http://investing.business-week.com/, accessed 26 November 2012.

56. David Knott, 'Do or Die Year for OVL', *Oil and Gas Journal*, Vol. 96, Issue 32, 10 August 1998.

57. Interview, former ONGC Videsh manager, New Delhi, 3 December 2008.

58. 'ONGC Videsh on track in projects', *Indian Business Insight*, 27 January 2004.

59. Interview, Indian diplomat, New Delhi, 12 December 2008.

60. 'ONGC Videsh on track in projects', *Indian Business Insight*, 27 January 2004.

61. 'Oil's well that ends well', *Business Standard*, 5 July 2003.

62. 'Oil hunt', *Business World*, 7 July 2003.

63. Interview, Indian oil analyst, New Delhi, 2 December 2008.

64. Interview, OVL executive, New Delhi, 11 December 2008.

65. 'ONGC Videsh on track in projects', *Indian Business Insight*, 27 January 2004.

66. Ibid.

67. David Knott, 'Do or Die Year for OVL', *Oil and Gas Journal*, Vol. 96, Issue 32, 10 August 1998.

68. 'ONGC: Coping with Competition', *Frontline*, Vol. 15, No. 8, 11 April 1998.

69. ONGC, 'Strategic vision: 2001–2020', www.ongcindia.com (accessed 20 January 2009).

70. Madan, op. cit., pp. 13–4.

71. Ibid., p. 26.

72. Dednath Shaw, 'Securing India's Energy Needs: The Regional Dimension', Center for Strategic and International Studies, 2005, pp. 6–10.

73. The policy was developed together by the ministers of petroleum, finance and external affairs, along with the deputy chairman of India's powerful Planning Commission. MPNG, 'Annual Report 2004–2005', New Delhi: Government of India, New Delhi, 2005, p. 2.

74. Planning Commission, 'India Hydrocarbon Vision—2025', Government of India, 2000.

75. Edward Luce, 'Head to head in the quest for national energy security: India's overseas competition with China has an effect on diplomacy', *Financial Times*, 17 November 2004.

76. Madan, op. cit., p. 17.

77. The bulky report detailed the needs, opportunities and threats facing the Indian energy sector and presented recommendations to efficiently manage the wide range of energy options including coal, oil and natural gas, hydropower electricity and other, renewable, sources.

78. Government of India Planning Commission, 'Integrated Energy Policy, Report of the Expert Committee', New Delhi: Government of India, 2006, pp. 54–5.

79. OVL, 'Annual Report 2006–07', New Delhi: OVL, 2007, p. 19.

80. 'Oil hunt', *Businessworld*, 7 July 2003.

81. Interview, ONGC Videsh executive, New Delhi, 11 December 2008.

82. 'ONGC Seeks to be Global Oil and Gas Player', *Oil and Gas Journal*, 17 March 2003.

83. OVL, 'Annual Report 2006–07', New Delhi: OVL, 2007, p. 20.

84. OVL and ONGC, 'Annual Report' for the years 2002–03 to 2006–07, New Delhi: OVL and ONGC, New Delhi, 2003–07.

85. 'Oil hunt', *Businessworld*, 7 July 2003.

86. T.S. Subramanian, 'The Sakhalin Venture', *Frontline*, Vol. 22, Issue 22, 22 October–4 November 2005.

87. T.S. Subramanian, 'Sakhalin Success', *Frontline*, Vol. 23, Issue 26, 30 December 2006–12 January 2007.

88. Interview, former Sudanese oil official, Khartoum, 15 October 2010.

89. Ninan Koshy, 'India joins Sudan's war'; C. Raja Mohan, 'Sakhalin to Sudan: India's energy diplomacy', *The Hindu*, 24 June 2002.

90. Tony Seskus and Claudia Cattaneo, 'Talisman's woes keep oilpatch on guard', *National Post*, 24 June 2002.

91. Edward Luce, *In Spite of the Gods: The Strange Rise of Modern India*, London: Little Brown Book Group, 2006, p. 314.

92. Narendra Taneja, 'Gift of the Nile', *Outlook*, 1 July 2002.

93. Ibid.

94. Taneja, op. cit.

95. 'Sudan's civil strife doesn't deter Indian oil explorer', *Calgary Herald*, 9 July 2002.

96. 'Profile of Atul Chandra', *Hindustan Times*, www.hindustantimes.com, accessed 16 December 2010.

97. Interview, Indian oil analyst, New Delhi, 2 December 2008.

98. Interview, former MEA official, New Delhi, 16 December 2008.

99. Interview, Indian political analyst, New Delhi, 3 December 2008.

100. The Cabinet Committee on Economic Affairs, whose acceptance OVL had to gain to follow through with the investment, insisted that it must secure insurance. Taneja, op. cit.

101. 'Sudan offers peace dividend to India', *Financial Express*, 4 June 2004.

102. Jyoti Malhotra, 'As Sudan oil map changes India works alongside China', *Business Standard*, 8 April 2011.

7. AN OIL TITAN REINCARNATED

1. Eric Watkins, 'Indian Refiner Receives Country's First Foreign Equity Crude', *Oil and Gas Journal*, 21 May 2003.

2. 'Sudan oil set to start flowing', *The Telegraph*, 8 May 2003.

3. 'ONGC Group's Venture Will Enhance India's Energy Security: Deputy PM', *ONGC News*, 16 May 2003, http://www.ongcindia.com/, accessed 23 March 2012.

4. 'ONGC pursues Sudan expansion', *Financial Times*, 16 September 2003.

5. Narendra Taneja, 'Gift of the Nile', *Outlook*, 1 July 2002.

6. 'ONGC Makes Progress in Sudan', *International Petroleum Finance*, Vol. 26, March 2003.

7. Raja C. Mohan, *Crossing the Rubicon: The Shaping of India's New Foreign Policy*, New York: Palgrave, 2003, pp. 142–3.

8. Chanakya Sen, 'Chou En-Lai's African Journey as Viewed by the Indian Press', *Asian Survey*, Vol. 4, No. 6, June 1964, pp. 880–9.

9. A.K. Dubey, 'Indo-African Economic Relations (1965–85): A Case of South-South Interaction', *Africa Quarterly*, Vol. 27, No. 3–4, 1987–88, p. 53.

10. Wang Xiaotian, 'Trade between China, Africa strengthening,' *China Daily*, 19 July 2012; 'India, Africa aim for $90 billion trade in three years,' *Economic Times*, 18 March 2012.

11. Somini Sengupta, 'India tiptoes in China's footsteps to compete but not offend', *New York Times*, 4 April 2008.

12. Anup Jayaram, 'Face-off', *Business World*, 16 August 2004.

13. John Larkin, 'Indian tortoise aims to be hare—New Delhi bets state oil firm can win race for energy security', *Wall Street Journal*, 19 May 2005; Tanvi Madan, 'India', The Brookings Foreign Policy Studies: Energy Security Series, The Brookings Institution, 2006, p. 43.

14. Interview, Indian MEA official, New Delhi, 19 February 2008.

15. 'The Effects of China–India Actions', *APS Review Oil Market Trends*, Vol. 65, Issue 26, 26 December 2005.

16. 'China and India: Bidding partners, at least on paper', *International Herald Tribune*, 20 January 2006.

17. 'ONGC, CNPC take Colombia stake (Latin America)', *The Oil Daily*, 7 August 2006.

18. Margaret McQuaile, 'Africa is Staging Ground for Push by China, India to Control More Output', *Platts Oilgram News*, 26 October 2004; Tanvi Madan, 'India's ONGC: Balancing Different Roles, Different Goals', Austin: The James Baker III Institute for Public Policy, Rice University, 2007.

19. *Sudan: Country Report*, 2012, Economist Intelligence Unit, pp. 10–12; Ministry of Commerce, Government of India, 'Export-Import Data Bank', http://commerce.nic.in/, 26 November 2012, accessed 27 November 2012.

20. 'India—Sudan Relations', Ministry of External Affairs, Government of India, January 2012, mea.gov.in/mystart.php?id=50044526, accessed 24 February 2012.

21. Sanjay Dutta, 'Diplomatic arm-twisting clears Sudan oil deal', *The Times of India*, 14 March 2003.

22. Veeramalla Anjaiah and Ivy Susanti, 'Sudan wants to strengthen ties with Indonesia', *Jakarta Post*, 25 February 2005.

23. 'Oil hunt', *Business World*, 7 July 2003.

24. 'Talisman Marks End of Era with Completion of Sudan Sale', *Oil and Gas Journal*, 4 July 2003.

25. 'Sudan chose ONGC as less open to censure', Reuters, 11 November 2002.

26. 'Petronas to hit ONGC's overseas investment plan', *The Times of India*, 18 December 2002; Chris Varcoe, 'Sudan sale to close in March', *Calgary Herald*, 1 February 2003.

27. 'OVL to acquire 11 pc stake in Sudan oil field', *The Times of India*, 21 January 2004.

28. Ibid.

29. 'India's share of equity oil in Sudan may go up by 1 MT', *Financial Express*, 19 January 2004.

30. Al Thani elected not to sell in the end. Anup Jayaram, 'Face-off', *Business World*, 16 August 2004; 'Sinopec buys Kazakh oil assets, returns to Sudan', Reuters, 22 October 2004; 'Kuwait's Kharafi buys 3 pct stake in Sudan oil co.', Reuters, 16 March 2008; 'Egypt Kuwait Hldg buys 5 pct of Sudan's Petrodar', Reuters, 25 March 2008; *Business World* incorrectly reported that CNPC had captured the block when it was Sinopec. In the end, Al-Thani would hold on to its stake, later selling to the Egyptian company Tri Ocean in March 2008 for $400 million. OVL's offer was only $68.4 million four years earlier.

31. Erica S. Downs, 'The Fact and Fiction of Sino-African Energy Relations', *China Security*, Vol. 3, No. 3, Summer 2007, p. 50; Bo Kong, *China's International Petroleum Policy*, Santa Barbara: ABC-CLIO, 2010, p. 139.

32. The Sinopec project was to construct a segment of a pipeline project of the larger Melut Basin undertaking, involving a host of companies from Asia and Europe.

33. 'Malaysian firms secure $900 mm in Sudan oil jobs', *Business Times*, 4 October 2004.

34. 'India—Sudan Relations', Ministry of External Affairs, Government of India, January 2012, mea.gov.in/mystart.php?id=50044526, accessed 24 February 2012.

35. Neena Vyas, 'Kalam calls for greater Indo-Sudan cooperation', *The Hindu*, 21 October 2003; 'India—Sudan, Joint Statement', Press Release, Ministry of External Affairs, Government of India, 22 October 2003.

36. 'India—Sudan, Joint Statement', Press Release, Ministry of External Affairs, Government of India, 22 October 2003.

37. Interview, international journalist, London, 30 January 2012.

38. 'Sudan India's Relations', Embassy of the Republic of the Sudan, New Delhi, India, www.sudanembassyindia.org/sudan_india_relations.html, accessed 10 May 2010; 'India and Sudan Partners in Development', Embassy of India in Khartoum, Sudan, www.indembsdn.com/eng/india_sdn_partners.htm, accessed 12 May 2010.

39. Priya Mutalik-Desai, 'Bilateral Trade Agreements The Indo-Sudan Experience', *Economic and Political Weekly*, Vol. 8, No. 19, 12 May 1973, pp. 880–84.

40. Department of Commerce, Government of India, 'Export-Import Data Bank', http://commerce.nic.in/, 9 November 2012, accessed 20 November 2012.

41. Deepak Nayyar, 'The Internationalization of Firms From India: Investment, Mergers and Acquisitions', *Oxford Development Studies*, Vol. 36, No. 1, 2008, p. 114.

42. 'Sudan plans more oil projects for India', *Hindustan Times*, 9 March 2006.

43. 'Operative Lines of Credit' (As of 7 February 2012), Exim Bank of India, http://www.eximbankindia.com/locstat07022012.doc, accessed 8 February 2012: A $50 million US line of credit (LoC) in January 2004 to finance exports of machinery and locomotives and other goods from India to Sudan; a $350 million LoC to Bharat Heavy Electricals Ltd. in January 2006 to construct the Kosti Combined Cycle Power Plant; a $41.9 million LoC to Sudan to finance the Singa-Gadaref transmission and a sub-station project, also in January 2006; a $48 million LoC to Sudan for agriculture, education and infrastructure projects in February 2007; a $52 million LoC in July 2007 for infrastructure and livestock projects; $25 million LoC for the Eldeum Sugar Project in White Nile state.

44. 'India–Sudan, Joint Statement', Press Release, Ministry of External Affairs, New Delhi, 8 June 2005.

45. ONGC Videsh, 'Indian Tri Colour Hoisted by ONG BV at Sudan's Heglig Base Camp, Heglig Base', *ONGC Videsh News*, 19 May 2003, www.ongcvidesh.com/News.aspx, accessed 20 January 2009.

46. 'OVL gets okay on Sudan oil blocks', *Financial Express*, 24 August 2003.

47. ONGC Videsh, 'Annual Report 2004–05', New Delhi: ONGC Videsh, p. 179.

48. 'IndianOil to train Sudanese pipeline engineers', *Hindustan Times*, 10 September 2005.

49. Vandana Hari, 'ONGC Jump Starts Plan to Build Sudan Products Line', *Platt's Oilgram News*, 22 June 2004.

50. 'No insurance for ONGC in Sudan', *Indian Express*, 25 June 2004.

51. 'ONGC to build $1.2bn oil refinery in Sudan', *The Times of India*, 3 February 2005.

52. The refinery investment nonetheless was included in wider analyses of India's Africa engagement for years to come, counted as one of the largest Indian investments on the continent despite the fact it was never built. Sanusha Naidu, 'India's Growing African Strategy', *Review of African Political Economy*, Vol. 35, No. 1, 2008, p. 119.

53. Archana Chaudhary and Rukmani Vishwanath, 'ONGC in loan talks for Sudan refinery deal', *The Hindu*, 8 January 2005. In a non-recourse loan, the lender can only use the project itself as collateral, not the wider assets of a company.

54. 'Costs delay Sudan refinery project eyed by Petronas', Reuters, 28 May 2005; Nesa Subrahmaniyan, 'Petronas Defers Sudan Oil Refinery Project on Rising Costs', Bloomberg, 9 June 2008.

55. 'ONGC Videsh on track in projects', *Asia Africa Intelligence Wire*, 27 January 2004.

56. Pratim Ranjan Bose, 'Hike in oil recovery boosts OVL's Sudan field earnings', *The Hindu*, 10 November 2004; interview, oil analyst, New Delhi, 12 December 2008.

57. ONGC Videsh, 'Annual Reports' for the years 2003–04 to 2011–12, ONGC Videsh, New Delhi, 2004–12.

58. ONGC Videsh, 'Annual Reports' 2002–03 and 2011–12, ONGC Videsh, New Delhi, 2003 and 2012.

59. 'India Eyes Oil Prospects in African Countries', *Alexander's Gas and Oil Connections*, 4 March 2005.

60. The 180,000 bpd refinery is located on India's west coast in Karnataka state.

61. 'Core Business or Core Competency', *Oil and Gas Update India*, Vol. 7, No. 9, September 2004.

62. Michael A. Hitt, R. Duane Ireland and Robert E. Hoskisson, 'ONGC's Growth Strategy', in *Strategic Management: Competitiveness and Globalization*, 7th edition, Mason: Thomson South-Western, 2005.

63. '3 mt Sudan crude—for OVL annually', *The Hindu*, 14 March 2003; ONGC, 'Annual Report 2002–03', New Delhi: ONGC, p. 191.

64. James Norman, 'Petrodollars', *Platt's Oilgram News*, 31 January 2005; 'Outlook bright for ONGC's overseas assets', *Hindustan Times*, 26 June 2006.

65. Interview, political analyst, New Delhi, 10 December 2008.

66. Ferris-Rotman, 'RPT—ONGC to cut Imperial capex after delisting—sources', Reuters, 3 March 2009.

67. 'ONGC takes control of Imperial Energy', *The Times of India*, 1 January 2009.
68. ONGC Videsh, 'Annual Reports 2010–11', New Delhi: ONGC Videsh, 2011, p. 5.
69. 'ONGC Videsh on track in projects', *Indian Business Insight*, 27 January 2004.
70. 'Govt asks OVL to hold on to Sudan crude', *Business Standard*, 22 September 2003.
71. 'ONGC Videsh in Sudan dream deal', *Asia Africa Intelligence Wire*, 4 November 2003.
72. ONGC Videsh, 'Annual Reports' for the years 2003–04 to 2011–12, New Delhi: ONGC Videsh, 2004–2012; BP, *Statistical Review of World Energy 2012*, BP, 2012.
73. ONGC Videsh, ibid.; BP, ibid.
74. 'UK's Trafigura to hawk ONGC's Sudan crude', *The Times of India*, 5 September 2003.
75. 'Integrated Energy Policy, Report of the Expert Committee', Planning Commission, New Delhi: Government of India, 2006, p. 59; ONGC Videsh, 'Annual Report 2004–05', New Delhi: ONGC Videsh, 2005.
76. 'Integrated Energy Policy, Report of the Expert Committee', Planning Commission, New Delhi: Government of India, 2006, p. 59.
77. The Mangalore refinery bought 10–12,000 bpd of OVL's share in 2008 and 2009. 'India's MRPL offers euro payment for Nile Blend', Reuters, 30 March 2009.
78. 'Integrated Energy Policy, Report of the Expert Committee', Planning Commission, New Delhi: Government of India, 2006, p. 62.
79. 'ONGC Videsh on track in projects', *Asia Africa Intelligence Wire*, 27 January 2004.
80. Nivedita Mukherjee, 'India hunts for oil', *India Today*, 2 October 2010.
81. Sujay Mehdudia, 'OVL, PDVSA of Venezuela to form joint venture', *The Hindu*, 10 April 2008.
82. 'New Division on Energy Security', Ministry of External Affairs, Government of India, http://pib.nic.in/newsite/erelease.aspx?relid=30972, 6 September 2007, accessed 28 March 2012.
83. Interview, Director of Energy Security, MEA, 11 December 2008.
84. 'International Cooperation Division', Ministry of Petroleum and Natural Gas, Government of India, http://petroleum.nic.in/aric.pdf, accessed 28 March 2012.
85. Madan, op. cit., p. 49.
86. Utpal Bhaskar, 'Race to ensure energy security', https://www.livemint.com/, 16 August 2012, accessed 23 August 2010.
87. Edward Luce, 'Head to head in the quest for national energy security: India's overseas competition with China has an effect on diplomacy', *Financial Times*, 17 November 2004.
88. Feroz Ahmed and Anup Jayaram, 'Oil's not well', *Business World*, 6 April 2009.
89. ONGC Videsh, 'Annual Report 2006–07', New Delhi: ONGC Videsh 2007, p. 19.

90. ONGC Videsh, 'Annual Reports 2011–12', New Delhi: ONGC Videsh 2012, p. 1.

8. THE RISE AND FALL OF AN ACTIVIST CAMPAIGN

1. See Julie Flint and Alex de Waal, *Darfur: A New History of a Long War*, London: Zed Books, 2008.

2. 'UN officials say Darfur conflict is worsening', *New York Times*, 23 April 2008.

3. Sections of this chapter draw on Luke A. Patey, 'Against the Asian Tide: the Sudan Divestment Campaign', *Journal of Modern African Studies*, Vol. 47, No. 4, 2009, pp. 551–73.

4. Rebecca Hamilton, 'Moving China', *Fighting for Darfur: Public Action and the Struggle to Stop Genocide*, New York: Palgrave Macmillan, 2011.

5. Save Darfur, www.savedarfur.org, accessed 11 January 2008.

6. Rebecca Hamilton and Chad Hazlett. '"Not on our Watch": the Emergence of the American Movement for Darfur', in Alex de Waal (ed.) *War in Darfur and the Search for Peace*, Cambridge, MA: Harvard University Press, 2007, pp. 337–66.

7. Sandy Siegel, 'Out of Africa', *UCLA Magazine*, 1 April 2009.

8. Telephone interview, Adam Sterling, 17 July 2008.

9. Beth Ford Roth, 'Vote on Sudan divestment expected from UCSD regents', *KPBS Public Broadcasting*, 16 Match 2006.

10. Daniel J. Hemel and Zachary M. Seward, 'Endowment tied to Sudan', *The Harvard Crimson*, 25 October 2004.

11. Philip Rocker, 'Student-driven Sudan divestment campaign grows', *New York Times*, 25 April 2006.

12. Sam Graham-Felsen, 'Divestment and Sudan', *The Nation*, 20 April 2006.

13. James Bowman, 'Darfur Now', http://www.jamesbowman.net/reviewDetail.asp?pubID=1869, accessed on 7 November 2012.

14. Nora Boustany, 'Sudan divestment effort gains momentum at state level', *Washington Post*, 7 October 2006.

15. Interview, Bennett Freeman, Senior Vice-President at Calvert Investments, Bethesda, 22 July 2010.

16. Interview, analyst, Conflict Risk Network, New York, 27 July 2012.

17. United to End Genocide, *Our History: Sudan Divestment Task Force* (video), https://endgenocide.org/who-we-are/our-history/, accessed 6 November 2012.

18. Sudan Divestment Task Force, 'Sudan Company Report, First Quarter', *Genocide Intervention Network*, Washington, DC, 2009.

19. Sudanese Petroleum Corporation, 'Statistics for Crude Oil and Productions', http://www.spc.sd/en/statics_crude.php, accessed 19 November 2010.

20. Sudan Divestment Task Force, 'PetroChina, CNPC, and Sudan: Perpetuating Genocide', Sudan Divestment Task Force, Washington, DC, 2007, p. 24.

21. Interview, Sudan Divestment Task Force, senior member, Copenhagen, 29 November 2007.

22. Nick Timiraos, 'Sudan-Divestment activists get act together', *Wall Street Journal*, 19 July 2006.

23. Since the targeted model only amounted to a focus on a few dozen foreign companies, elimination of any financial holdings tied to a larger fund portfolio could be done without significantly threatening the value of the whole. Accordingly, a company such as PetroChina could easily be replaced by one of similar value in the same industry. Furthermore, if divestment amounted to more than 0.5 per cent of the total original value of the fund, the targeted model allowed restrictions to be relaxed. Telephone interview, Adam Sterling, co-founder, Sudan Divestment Task Force, 17 July 2008; personal communication, Divestment Senior Field Organiser, Sudan Divestment Task Force, 21 January 2008.

24. Sudan Divestment Task Force, www.sudandivestment.org, accessed 26 May 2009.

25. Jeremy Pelofsky, 'Activists say Sudan divestment campaign working', Reuters, 12 August 2007.

26. Ross Kerber, 'Fidelity shareholders lose bid for divestment', *Boston Globe*, 20 March 2008.

27. Martin Plaut, 'UBS urged to drop Chinese listing', BBC News, 19 October 2007.

28. AOL, 'Petro China Stock Quote' http://finance.aol.com/quotes/petrochina-company-limited/ptr/nys, accessed 10 June 2009.

29. Carol J. Loomis, 'Warren Buffett gives away his fortune', *Fortune Magazine*, June 2006; Berkshire Hathaway, 'Shareholder Proposal Regarding Berkshire's Investment in PetroChina', 21 May 2007.

30. Richard McGregor, 'Buffett sells PetroChina stake', *Financial Times*, 19 October 2007.

31. Sudan Divestment Task Force, op. cit., pp. 19–20.

32. Richard McGregor, 'Buffett sells PetroChina stake', *Financial Times*, 19 October 2007.

33. 'Buffet on investing and the markets', *Forbes*, 29 February 2008.

34. Normally the fiduciary duty of investment managers demands that they perform in the financial and legal interests of their clients, excluding social concerns.

35. Sheryl Gay Stolberg, 'Bush signs into law Sudan divestment measure', *New York Times*, 1 January 2008.

36. 'Testimony of Bennett Freeman', *United States Senate Committee on Banking, Housing, and Urban Affairs*, 3 October 2007.

37. Vivienne Walt, 'Khartoum is booming, courtesy of China', *Fortune Magazine*. 6 August 2007.

38. Interview, Sudanese oil official, Ministry of Energy and Mining, Khartoum, 21 January 2007.

39. The worst spikes of violence in Darfur came during periods in 2003 and 2004 before a low-intensity conflict set in. See Julie Flint and Alex de Waal, *Darfur: A New History of a Long War*, London: Zed Books, pp. 150–1.

40. *Sudan: Country Profile*, Economist Intelligence Unit, 2009, p. 20.

41. International Monetary Fund (IMF), 'Country Report No. 08/174', Washington, DC: IMF, 2008, p. 16.

42. Energy Information Administration, 'Country Analysis Briefs: Sudan', November 2010, http://www.eia.doe.gov/emeu/cabs/Sudan/Oil.html, accessed 30 November 2010.

43. Holly Hubbard Preston, 'Sudan divestment campaign gains momentum,' *New York Times*, 23 May 2008.

44. For example, CNPC was targeted through its publicly-traded subsidiary PetroChina, with listings in New York, Hong Kong and Shanghai. However, close to 90 per cent of the company is owned by the Chinese government. Petronas is nearly completely owned by the Malaysian government and three-quarters of OVL is the property of New Delhi, not counting cross-holdings by other national-owned companies. John Mitchell and Glada Lahn, 'Oil for Asia', London: Chatham House, 2007, p. 5.

45. Ali Abdallah Ali, 'Sudan-China relations; still on a high pitch', *Sudan Tribune* 29.4.2008, http://www.sudantribune.com/spip.php?article26933, accessed 29 May 2009.

46. Interview, Conflict Risk Network analyst, New York, 27 July 2012.

47. SDTF, 'What do we request of companies whose business operations in Sudan are of concern?', http://www.sudandivestment.org/engagement_principles.asp, accessed 29 May 2009.

48. Jeremy Pelofsky, 'Activists say Sudan divestment campaign working', 12 August 2007, 11 April 2008.

49. James Boxell and Andrew England, 'Rolls-Royce to quit Sudan over Darfur', *Financial Times*, 19 April 2007.

50. Interview, GNPOC procurement manager, Khartoum, 27 October 2007.

51. SDTF, 'Sudan Company Report (First Quarter 2009)', Washington, DC: Genocide Intervention Network, 2009, pp. 117–20.

52. Jedrzej George Frynas, 2005. 'The False Developmental Promise of Corporate Responsibility: Evidence from Multinational Corporations', *International Affairs*, Vol. 81, No. 3, pp. 581–98; Michael Blowfield, 'Reasons to be Cheerful? What we Know about CSR's Impact', *Third World Quarterly*, Vol. 28, No. 4, 2007, pp. 683–95.

53. Keynote presentation by Qin Anjiang attended by author, Khartoum, 12 September 2006.

54. Wikileaks, 'Pre/sudan: Chinese Oil Company Vp Discusses Sudan with Se Gration', 1 June 2009, http://wikileaks.org/cable/2009/06/09BEIJING1435.html, accessed 26 June 2012.

55. Interview, CNPC representative, Beijing, 26 February 2008.

56. Petronas, 'Sustainability Report 2007', Kuala Lumpur: Petronas, 2008, p. 26; Petronas, 'Sustainability Report 2009', Kuala Lumpur: Petronas, 2010, pp. 60–1.

57. Petronas, 'Annual Report 2008', Kuala Lumpur: Petronas, 2009, p. 35.

58. 'Spreading Smiles in Africa, A Partial List of CSR Success Stories of ONGC', www.ongcindia.com, accessed 5 January 2009.

59. Ashish Gupta, 'The greening of Sudan', *Outlook*, 5 April 2008.

60. Sandy Siegel, 'Out of Africa', *UCLA Magazine*, 1 April 2009.

61. Various interviews with international and local NGOs, Khartoum, September 2006 and November 2007.

62. European Coalition on Oil in Sudan, 'To divest from Sudan?', http://www.ecosonline.org/back/pdf_reports/To%20divest%20from%20Sudan%20final.pdf, 2006, accessed 9 May 2009.

63. Interview, former student activist, London, 4 July 2008.

64. Interview, former student activist, Washington, DC, 22 July 2010.

65. 'Testimony of Bennett Freeman', *United States Senate Committee on Banking, Housing, and Urban Affairs*, 3 October 2007.

66. Interview, Bennett Freeman, Bethesda, 22 July 2010.

67. Interview, CRN Analyst, New York, 27 July 2012.

68. Alexandra Cosima Budabin, 'Genocide Olympics: how Activists Linked China, Darfur and Beijing 2008', in Daniel Large and Luke A. Patey (eds), *Sudan Looks East: China, India, and the Politics of Asian Alternatives*, Oxford: James Currey, 2011, pp. 139–56.

69. Howard French, 'China in Africa: all trade, with no political baggage', *New York Times*, 8 August 2004.

70. Peter S. Goodman, 'China invests heavily in Sudan's oil industry', *Washington Post*, 23 December 2004.

71. Elizabeth C. Economy and Adam Segal, 'China's Olympic Nightmare: What the Games Mean for Beijing's Future', *Foreign Affairs*, July/August 2008.

72. Interview, Chinese academic, Beijing, 27 October 2010.

73. 'Darfur collides with Olympics, and China yields', *New York Times*, 13 April 2007.

74. Alexa Olesen, 'China appoints special envoy for Darfur', Associated Press, 11 May 2007.

75. Wang Suolao, 'Non-Interference and China's African Policy: The Case of Sudan', Symposium on Chinese-Sudanese Relations, 26 July 2007, http://www.cffpa.com/books/chinaweb.pdf, accessed 15 March 2013.

76. Daniel Large, 'China and the Contradictions of 'Non-interference' in Sudan', *Review of African Political Economy*, No. 115, 2008, p. 100.

77. Andrew S. Natsios, *Sudan, South Sudan, & Darfur: What Everyone Needs to Know*, Oxford: Oxford University Press, 2012, p. 159.

78. 'China's leader visits Sudan and focuses on growing economic ties', Reuters, 3 February 2007.

79. Interview, Chinese academic, Beijing, 27 October 2010.

80. Bates Gill, Chin-hao Huang and J. Stephen Morrison, 'Assessing China's Growing Influence in Africa', *China Security*, Vol. 3, No. 3, Summer 2007, p. 14.

81. Linda Jakobson, 'The Burden of "Non-interference"', *China Economic Quarterly*,

Q2, 2007; Daniel Large, 'China and the Contradictions of "Non-interference" in Sudan', *Review of African Political Economy*, No. 115, 2008, p. 100.

82. Wang Suolao, 'Non-Interference and China's African Policy: The Case of Sudan', Symposium on Chinese-Sudanese Relations, 26 July 2007, http://www.cffpa.com/books/chinaweb.pdf, accessed 15 March 2013.

83. 'Hu puts forward four-point principle on solving Darfur issue', *Xinhua*, 2 February 2007.

84. Alaa Shashine, 'China urges West to put pressure on Darfur rebels', *International Herald Tribune*. 28 February 2008.

85. Interview, former Chinese diplomat, Beijing, 3 March 2008.

86. *Sudan, Quarterly Economic Review*, No. 4, 1991, Economist Intelligence Unit, pp. 4–5.

87. Bill Varner, 'China threatens to veto UN Darfur resolution over oil sanctions', Bloomberg, 17 September 2004.

88. Interview, Beijing, 27 October 2011.

89. Maureen Fan, 'Arrival of Olympic Torch in China shines a light on politics, security', *Washington Post*, 1 April 2008.

90. John Garnaut, 'Up against the Great Wall of China', *Sydney Morning Herald*, 21 November 2009.

91. Linda Jakobson and Dean Knox, 'New Foreign Policy Actors in China', Stockholm International Peace Research Institute Policy Paper 26, September 2010.

92. Richard McGregor, *The Party: The Secret World of China's Communist Rulers*, London: Penguin, 2010, p. 62.

93. Beyond the Ministry of Foreign Affairs (MFA), there are several bodies across the Communist Party and government that shape Chinese foreign policy. At the top, the Foreign Affairs Leading Small Group of the Party is 'the brain' of China's foreign policy decision-making. The MFA and the International Department of the Party, often referred to as China's 'second foreign ministry', act as 'the arms and legs' of Chinese foreign policy; neither exercises much real power on its own. Interview, Chinese academic, Beijing, 27 October 2010; interview, Chinese academic, Copenhagen, 25 September 2012.

94. Trist Saywell and Ahmed Rashid, 'Innocent Abroad: China's National Oil Company Joins the Big League', *Far Eastern Economic Review*, 26 February 1998.

95. Interview, oil industry insider, Beijing, 18 October 2011.

96. Linda Jakobson and Zha Daojiong, 'China and the Worldwide Search for Oil Security', *Asia-Pacific Review*, Vol. 12, No. 2, pp. 67–8.

97. Bo Kong, *China's International Petroleum Policy*, Santa Barbara: ABC-CLIO, 2010, p. 55.

98. Leslie Wayne and David Barboza, 'UNOCAL deal: a lot more than money is at issue', *New York Times*, 24 June 2005.

99. James Kynge, *China Shakes the World: A Titan's Rise and Troubled Future—and the Challenge for America*, New York: First Mariner Books, 2007, p. 143.

100. Trevor Houser, 'The Roots of Chinese Oil Investment Abroad', *Asia Policy*, No. 5, January 2008, p. 158.

101. 'ONGC explores oil in Sudan amidst risks', *Sudan Tribune*, 2 February 2005.

102. ONGC, 'ONGC Distribution of Shareholding' www.ongcindia.com, 24 April 2009, accessed 20 January 2009; Joseph Lison, 'ONGC's Sudan deals come under attack', *Wall Street Journal*, LiveMint, 30 June 2008.

103. Sanjay Dutta, 'ONGC braces for jolt in Sudan', *The Times of India*, 15 December 2007.

104. 'A Company in a Hurry', *Middle East Economic Digest*, 19 September 2003.

105. Sudan supplies a significant amount of the world's gum arabic, a key ingredient in soda drinks and other food products. See 'Soda pop diplomacy', *Washington Post*, 8 November 1997.

106. Interview, Indian external affairs official, New Delhi, 11 December 2008.

107. Lison Joseph, 'ONGC's Sudan deals come under attack', *Wall Street Journal*, LiveMint, 30 June 2008.

108. Telephone interview, Colin Gonsalves, December 2008.

109. Personal communication, divestment senior field organiser, 3 February 2009.

110. Helene Cooper, 'Incentive in Sudan talks: normalized ties with US', *New York Times*, 17 April 2008; John Kerry, 'Diplomacy has chance in Sudan', *Boston Globe*, 27 April 2009.

111. Interview, Chinese oil analyst, Beijing, 27 September 2011.

112. Winnie Lee, 'In Bid to Grow Overseas, PetroChina, CNPC Form JV', *Platts Oilgram News*, 13 June 2005.

113. The following year, PetroChina admitted in its 2010 filing to the US Securities and Exchange Commission that it had purchased and refined a limited amount of Sudanese crude for cost-saving purposes, but later it indicated that this practice would stop even though the repercussions of the US restrictions were unclear. Chen Aizhu, 'PetroChina to retool new plant to avoid Sudan oil', Reuters, 3 August 2010; Chen Aizhu, 'PetroChina starts $2 bln new refinery in south China', *Reuters*, 9 September 2010; PetroChina, 'Form 20-F', The United States Securities and Exchange Commission, FY 2010, 11 May 2011.

114. Edward Alden and Richard McGregor, 'Why US-China links are in flux', *Financial Times*, 16 April 2006.

115. 'Taking the summit by strategy', *The Economist*, 8 April 2009; 'The dragon's teeth', *The Economist*, 7 April 2012.

116. Frank Wolf, 'Rep. Frank Wolf—Charles Freeman Orchestrated His Own Fall', *Washington Post*, 14 March 2009.

117. Charles Freeman, 'Rep. Wolf's assault on me was shoddy and inaccurate', *The Hill*, 29 March 2009.

9. WAR IN PEACE

1. 李向阳、刘泓波、李兵，《跨国营救：为了九位骨肉同胞—写在中国石油在苏丹遇害者骨灰和获救人员回国之际》，中国石油新闻中心，2008年11月6日 (Li Xiangyang,

Liu Hongbo, Li Bing, 'Rescue Work in Another Country for 9 Chinese compatriots', CNPC News Center, 6 November 2008). http://news.cnpc.com.cn/system/2008/11/06/001207678.shtm, accessed 13 December 2012).

2. Wikileaks cable, 'Further Information On Murder Of Chinese Oil Workers, New Security Measures', 7 November 2008, http://wikileaks.org/cable/2008/11/08KHARTOUM1625.html, accessed 27 June 2012.

3. Wikileaks cable, 'Chinese Embassy Official Discusses Hostage Negotiations', 13 November 2008, http://wikileaks.org/cable/2008/11/08KHARTOUM1653.htm, accessed 27 June 2012.

4. Interviews, CNPC official and Chinese oil industry insider, Beijing, 27 September and 26 October 2011.

5. BP, *Statistical Review of World Energy*, BP, 2009; Ministry of Finance and National Economy (Sudan), www.mof.gov.sd/, accessed 18 November 2009.

6. Based on a 2.15:1 average exchange rate between Sudanese pounds and American dollars over the period. *Sudan Country Report* No. 08/174, Washington, DC: International Monetary Fund, 2008; *Sudan Country Report* No. 12/299, International Monetary Fund, 2012.

7. 'The Road Towards Sustainable and Broad-Based Growth,' World Bank, 2009, p. 1.

8. Michael L. Ross, 'The Political Economy of the Resource Curse', *World Politics*, Vol. 51, No. 2, 1999.

9. United Nations Development Programme (Sudan), http://www.sd.undp.org/focus_poverty_reduction.htm, accessed 19 November 2009.

10. *Sudan Country Report* No. 08/174, Washington, DC: International Monetary Fund, 2008, p. 16; *Sudan Country Report* No. 12/298, International Monetary Fund, 2012, p. 30.

11. *Sudan Country Report* No. 08/174, Washington, DC: International Monetary Fund, 2008, p. 32.

12. Abda Yahia El Mahdi, 'Budget Analysis for Pro-poor Spending', Unicorns and UNDP Sudan, July 2008.

13. 'Sudan: Breaking the Abyei Deadlock', International Crisis Group Africa Briefing No. 47, 2007, p. 7.

14. Personal communication, international activist, 10 February 2009.

15. Interview, former government official, Ministry of Energy and Mining, 20 June 2011.

16. Wikileaks cable, 'Positives And Negatives In Sudan's Oil Industry', 12 March 2008, http://wikileaks.org/cable/2008/03/08KHARTOUM367.html, accessed 27 June 2012.

17. Wikileaks cable, 'China in Sudan: Rising Dragon or Paper Tiger?', Khartoum to Washington, DC, 26 January 2007, http://wikileaks.org/cable/2007/01/07KHARTOUM119.html, accessed 27 June 2012.

18. Daniel Large and Luke A. Patey, 'China, India and the Politics of Sudan's Asian

Alternatives', in Daniel Large and Luke A. Patey (eds), *Sudan Looks East: China, India and the Politics of Asian Alternatives*, Oxford: James Currey, 2011, p. 189.

19. Leben Moro, 'Oil Development Induced Displacement in the Sudan', Sir William Luce Fellowship Paper No. 10, Durham University, 2009, pp. 17–9.

20. 'Unity State MPs in South Sudan parliament lash back at Governor Deng', *Sudan Tribune*, 27 January 2008; 'Black Gold', *In Sudan Magazine*, Khartoum, UNMIS, July 2009, p. 6; 'Sudan, Whose Oil? Sudan's Oil Industry: Facts and Analysis', European Coalition on Oil in Sudan, 2008, p. 33.

21. Telephone interview, UN official in Sudan, 30 January 2009.

22. *Sudan Transitional Environment Program: Scoping Statement for a Programmatic Environmental Assessment of Oil Exploration and Production Activities in Southern Sudan*, US Agency for International Development Sudan, 2007, pp. 10–1.

23. Unpublished consultancy review of environmental measures in existing oil contracts obtained by author.

24. *Synthesis Report, Sudan: Post-conflict Environmental Assessment*, UN Environment Programme (UNEP), 2007, p. 149.

25. Interview, oil consultant, Khartoum, 2 September 2006.

26. *Sudan, Whose Oil? Sudan's Oil Industry: Facts and Analysis*, European Coalition on Oil in Sudan, 2008, pp. 32–3.

27. Ibid., p. 13.

28. Interview, CNPC geologist, Beijing, 7 November 2011.

29. Interview, former Chinese oil executive, Beijing, 11 December 2010.

30. Jeffrey Gettleman, 'Ethiopian rebels kill 70 at Chinese-run oil field', *New York Times*, 25 April 2007.

31. The Chinese were working for Zhongyuan Petroleum Engineering Co. Ltd., which, when it was formerly controlled by CNPC, was one of the first companies to enter Sudan during the civil war in the mid-1990s. Eric Watkins, 'Petronas Lets Ethiopian Seismic Contract', *Oil and Gas Journal*, 15 May 2006.

32. Shashank Bengali, 'A burning fire', *Mcclatchy*, 17 September 2007, http://blogs.mcclatchydc.com/nairobi/2007/09/a-burning-fire.html, accessed 28 June 2012.

33. Wikileaks cable, 'Black Gold: Petroleum Resources in Ethiopia', 27 February 2008, http://wikileaks.org/cable/2008/02/08ADDISABABA512.htm, accessed 27 June 2012.

34. Petronas, 'Annual Report 2011', Kuala Lumpur: Petronas, 2012, p. 42.

35. William Davison, 'Petrotrans may face attack in Ethiopia oil search, group says', Bloomberg, 9 August 2011.

36. 'Militants warn Chinese oil companies', *Xinhua*, 30 March 2006.

37. Karl Maier, 'Kidnapped Chinese workers freed in Nigeria, in good health', Bloomberg, 4 February 2007.

38. *A Strategy for Comprehensive Peace in Sudan*, International Crisis Group Africa Report No. 130, 2007, p. 12.

39. Sara Pantuliano, Omer Egemi, Babo Fadlalla and Mohammed Farah with Mohammed Elamin Abdelgadir, *Put out to Pasture: War, Oil and the Decline of*

Misseriya Humr Pastoralism in Sudan, Humanitarian Policy Group, Overseas Development Institute, March 2009, p. 23.

40. *Sudan's Southern Kordofan Problem: The Next Darfur?*, International Crisis Group Africa Report No. 145, 2008, p. 15.

41. Unpublished report from international organisation acquired by author.

42. Sara Pantuliano et al., op. cit., p. 19.

43. Edward Thomas, 'Against the Gathering Storm: Securing Sudan's Comprehensive Peace Agreement', Chatham House, 2009, p. 30.

44. Wikileak cable, 'Positives and Negatives in Sudan's Oil Industry', 12 March 2008, http://wikileaks.org/cable/2008/03/08KHARTOUM367.html, accessed 27 June 2012.

45. 'Two Chinese workers killed in Sudan', *Xinhua*, 31 March 2004.

46. Sara Pantuliano et al., op. cit., p. 11.

47. Victor Tanner and Jerome Tubiana, *Divided They Fall: The Fragmentation of Darfur's Rebel Groups*, Small Arms Survey HSBA Working Paper 6, Geneva: Small Arms Survey, July 2007, pp. 58–9.

48. Sara Pantuliano et al., op. cit., p. 23.

49. Alfred de Montesquiou, 'Darfur rebels conduct raid on oilfield', Associated Press, 27 November 2006.

50. Daniel Van Oudenaren, 'Safety lapses shown to be chronic at Chinese oil venture in Sudan', *Sudan Tribune*, 17 February 2010.

51. Wikileaks cable, 'Jem claims responsibility for Defra attack and continues to hold hostages', 29 October 2007, http://wikileaks.org/cable/2007/10/07KHARTOUM1670.htm, accessed 27 June 2012.

52. Sara Pantuliano et al., op. cit., p. 23.

53. *Sudan's Southern Kordofan Problem: The Next Darfur?*, International Crisis Group Africa Report No. 145, 2008, p. 16.

54. Andrew Heavens, 'Darfur rebels reject new Chinese peacekeepers', BBC News, 25 November 2007.

55. Wikileaks cable, 'Fear of Loss of International Credibility May Keep Jem on Course', 29 November 2007, http://wikileaks.org/cable/2007/11/07KHARTOUM1871.html, accessed 27 June 2012.

56. 'Sudanese army denies rebel attack oil field', *Sudan Tribune*, 12 December 2007.

57. 'Darfur rebels say they attacked Chinese-run oilfield in Sudan', AFP, 11 December 2007.

58. 'China seeks safety guarantees after Sudan oilfield attack', AFP, 13 December 2007.

59. Jeffrey Gettleman, 'Sudan's army beats back rebel attack on capital', *New York Times*, 11 May 2008.

60. Sara Pantuliano et al., op. cit., p. 23.

61. 'Four Indian oil workers kidnapped in Sudan's Abyei', AFP, 16 May 2008.

62. 'Four Indian oil workers kidnapped in Sudan', *Economic Times*, 15 May 2008.

63. 'Kidnappings: India calls Sudan envoy', *Indian Express*, 22 May 2008.

64. 'Indian oil worker kidnapped in Sudan returns home', AFP, 14 June 2008.

65. 'Kidnapped Indian oil worker escapes in Sudan', Reuters, 7 June 2008.

66. 'Kidnapped Indian oil worker released in Sudan', AFP, 27 July 2008.

67. 'Indian oil worker kidnapped in Sudan returns home', AFP, 14 June 2008.

68. 'Petronas steps out in national service', *New Straits Times*, 24 July 2000.

69. 李向阳、刘泓波、李兵,《跨国营救:为了九位骨肉同胞——写在中国石油在苏丹遇害者骨灰和获救人员回国之际》, 中国石油新闻中心, 2008年11月6日 (Li Xiangyang, (Liu Hongbo, Li Bing, 'Rescue Work in Another Country for 9 Chinese compatriots', CNPC News Center, 6 November 2008, http://news.cnpc.com.cn/system/2008/11/06/001207678.shtml, accessed 13 December 2012).

70. 'Sudan kidnappers want Chinese oil firms out: report', AFP, 24 October 2008.

71. 'Sudan: rebel says Chinese hostages moved to area government forces cannot reach,' *Al-Sharq al-Awsat*, 25 October 2008 (via BBC monitoring).

72. The Sudanese army denied the clash took place. 'Sudan: rebel says Chinese hostages moved to area government forces cannot reach,' *Al-Sharq al-Awsat*, 25 October 2008 (via BBC monitoring); 'Conflicting reports on fate of Chinese hostages in Sudan', *Sudan Tribune*, 28 October 2008.

73. 'Sudanese army denies military operation against Chinese kidnappers', *Sudan Tribune*, 26 October 2008; 李向阳、刘泓波、李兵,《跨国营救:为了九位骨肉同胞——写在中国石油在苏丹遇害者骨灰和获救人员回国之际》, 中国石油新闻中心, 2008年11月6日 (Li Xiangyang, Liu Hongbo, Li Bing, 'Rescue Work in Another Country for 9 Chinese compatriots', CNPC News Center, 6 November 2008, http://news.cnpc.com.cn/system/2008/11/06/001207678.shtml, accessed 13 December 2012).

74. Wikileaks cable, 'Further Information on Murder of Chinese Oil Workers, New Security Measures', 7 November 2008, http://wikileaks.org/cable/2008/11/08KHARTOUM1625.html, accessed 27 June 2012.

75. 李向阳、刘泓波、李兵,《跨国营救:为了九位骨肉同胞——写在中国石油在苏丹遇害者骨灰和获救人员回国之际》, 中国石油新闻中心, 2008年11月6日 (Li Xiangyang, (Liu Hongbo, Li Bing, 'Rescue Work in Another Country for 9 Chinese compatriots', CNPC News Center, 6 November 2008, http://news.cnpc.com.cn/system/2008/11/06/001207678.shtml, accessed 13 December 2012).

76. Interviews, CNPC official and Chinese oil industry insider, Beijing, 27 September and 26 October 2011.

77. Wikileaks cable, 'Further Information On Murder Of Chinese Oil Workers, New Security Measures', 7 November 2008, http://wikileaks.org/cable/2008/11/08KHARTOUM1625.html, accessed 27 June 2012; Wikileaks cable, 'Chinese Embassy Official Discusses Hostage Negotiations', 13 November 2008, http://wikileaks.org/cable/2008/11/08KHARTOUM1653.html, 27 June 2012.

78. Interview, 26 October 2011.

79. 'Sudan and China differ on hostage deaths', *New York Times*, 28 October 2008; 'Conflicting reports on the fate of Chinese hostages in Sudan', *Sudan Tribune*, 28 October 2008; Wikileaks cable, 'Govt Official Accuses NCP of Withholding

Oil', 3 November 2008, http://wikileaks.org/cable/2008/11/08KHARTOUM
1608.html, accessed 27 June 2012.

80. Wikileaks cable, 'Further Information on Murder of Chinese Oil Workers, New
Security Measures', 7 November 2008, http://wikileaks.org/cable/2008/11/
08KHARTOUM1625.html, accessed 27 June 2012.

81. 'China condemns Sudan killings', *Sudan Tribune*, 29 October 2008.

82. Victor Tanner and Jerome Tubiana, *Divided They Fall: The Fragmentation of Darfur's Rebel Groups*, Small Arms Survey HSBA Working Paper 6, Geneva: Small
Arms Survey, July 2007, p. 52.

83. Sara Pantuliano et al., op. cit., p. 24.

84. 'China condemns Sudan killings', *Sudan Tribune*, 29 October 2008.

85. 李向阳、刘泓波、李兵,《跨国营救：为了九位骨肉同胞—写在中国石油在苏丹遇
害者骨灰和获救人员回国之际》, 中国石油新闻中心, 2008年11月6日 (Li Xiang-
yang, Liu Hongbo, Li Bing, 'Rescue work in another country for 9 Chinese
compatriots', CNPC news center, 6 November 2008, http://news.cnpc.com.cn/
system/2008/11/06/001207678.shtml, accessed 13 December 2012).

86. Interview, former Chinese diplomat, Beijing, 25 October 2011.

87. Wikileaks cable, 'Chinese Embassy Official Discusses Hostage Negotiations',
13 November 2008, http://wikileaks.org/cable/2008/11/08KHARTOUM1653.
html, accessed 27 June 2012.

88. Ibid.

89. Matthew Arnold and Matthew LeRiche, *Neither 'Joint' nor 'Integrated': The Joint
Integrated Units and the Future of the CPA*, HSBA Small Arms Survey, Sudan
Issue Brief No. 10, March 2008.

90. Aly Verjee, 'Sudan's Aspirational Army: A History of the Joint Integrated Units',
The Center for International Governance Innovation, SSR Issue Paper No. 2,
May 2011, pp. 7–8.

91. UN Security Council, *Report of the Secretary-General on the Sudan*, 23 July 2008,
p. 1.

92. *Central Reserve Police*, Sudan Human Security Baseline Assessment, Small Arms
Survey, January 2011.

93. Wikileaks cable, 'Further Information on Murder of Chinese Oil Workers, New
Security Measures', 7 November 2008, http://wikileaks.org/cable/2008/11/08
KHARTOUM1625.html, accessed 27 June 2012.

94. *Armed Entities in Southern Kordofan*, Sudan Human Security Baseline Assessment, Small Arms Survey, June 2011.

95. 'Militarization in and around Abyei', HSBA Small Arms Survey, 2 June 2011.

96. *Sudan's Spreading Conflict (I): War in South Kordofan*, International Crisis Group
Africa Report No. 198, 2013, pp. 8–10.

97. 'China, Sudan agree on agriculture cooperation', *China Daily*, 19 November 2009;
'Chinese security chief Zhou Yongkang meets Sudan president 16 Nov', BBC
News, 20 November 2009.

98. John Garnaut, 'Up against the Great Wall of China', *Sydney Morning Herald*, 21 November 2009.

99. Genocide was added to charges against Bashir in February 2010. 'Omar Bashir indicted for genocide', Reuters, 12 July 2010.

100. 'Sudan FM goes public with his displeasure over receiving Iranian warships', *Sudan Tribune*, 5 November 2013.

101. Interview, Chinese academic, Beijing, 7 November 2010.

102. Interview, Chinese academic, Beijing, 8 November 2010.

103. Interview, CNPC manager, Beijing, 26 October 2011.

104. Talisman, 'Corporate Social Responsibility Report 2001', Calgary: Talisman, 2002, p. 17.

105. Nicholas Coghlan, *Far in the Waste Sudan: On Assignment in Africa*, Montreal and Kingston: McGill-Queen's University Press, 2005, p. 47.

106. 韩树举, 王洪涛, 张军, 贺红旭, 《中国石油天然气集团公司海外项目防恐安全管理探索与实践》, 《中国安全生产科学技术》, 2009年增刊. (Han Shuju, Wang Hongtao, Zhang Jun, He Hongxu, 'The Exploration and Practice of Anti-terrorism and Safety Management of CNPC Overseas Projects', *Journal of Safety Science and Technology*, 2009).

107. JIUs had both a Sudan Armed Forces commander and an SPLA commander, giving out two sets of orders to their forces and confusing the security environment as a result.

108. Interview, CNPC official, Beijing, 26 October 2011.

109. Interview, Chinese oil industry insider, Beijing, 18 October 2011.

110. Interview, Chinese oil industry insider, Beijing, 18 October 2010.

111. Interview, CNPC official, 26 October 2011.

112. 韩树举, 王洪涛, 张军, 贺红旭, 《中国石油天然气集团公司海外项目防恐安全管理探索与实践》, 《中国安全生产科学技术》, 2009年增刊. (Han Shuju, Wang Hongtao, Zhang Jun, He Hongxu, 'The Exploration and Practice of Anti-terrorism and Safety Management of CNPC Overseas Projects', *Journal of Safety Science and Technology*, 2009).

113. Ibid.

114. Coco Liu, 'Chinese seek anti-terrorism training for work abroad', *Global Post*, 10 August 2010.

115. Interview, Chinese oil industry insider, Beijing, 18 October 2011.

116. Interview, CNPC official, Beijing, 7 November 2011.

10. NEW COUNTRY, OLD PROBLEMS

1. Interview, Sudanese oil official, 12 November 2010.

2. This amount was determined after 2 per cent was given to the oil producing states from their share of production. A National Petroleum Commission was to be established with equal representation from the NCP and SPLM to formulate policies, monitor and manage the oil industry.

3. *Sudan's Comprehensive Peace Agreement: The Long Road Ahead*, International Crisis Group (ICG) Africa Report No. 106, p. 7.

4. It was not until mid-2009 that southern geologists were finally stationed with key operating companies. *Sudan's Comprehensive Peace Agreement: Beyond the Crisis*, Brussels: ICG, 2008, p. 13; 'Black Gold', *In Sudan Magazine*, United Nations Mission in Sudan, Khartoum, July 2009, p. 5.

5. To the SPLM's frustration, the NCP government also began to transfer oil revenue in Sudanese pounds rather than American dollars, putting at risk the southern government's foreign exchange reserves. Interview, former government official, Ministry of Energy and Mining, London, 25 January 2008; 'South Sudan refutes claims that oil revenues have been paid in hard currency', *Sudan Tribune*, 29 August 2010.

6. Global Witness, *Fuelling Mistrust: The Need for Transparency in Sudan's Oil Industry*, Global Witness, 2009.

7. Alan Boswell, 'South Sudan reacts angrily to report of possible oil fraud by North', *Voice of America*, 2 November 2009.

8. 'Sudan rejects accusations of manipulations in oil revenue figures', *Sudan Tribune*, 27 September 2009.

9. Interview, CNPC manager, Khartoum, 15 October 2010.

10. 'Sudan oil figures stoke suspicions: report', Reuters, 17 March 2010.

11. Interview, CNPC and OVL managers, Khartoum, 15 and 27 October 2010.

12. The 'Three Areas' witnessed some of the worst fighting of the civil war and were heavily contested in negotiations on account of their strategic natural resource wealth in oil, agriculture and water. The Nuba Mountains and Blue Nile were to hold popular consultations to determine their future political status in Sudan. Jason Gluck, *Why Sudan's Popular Consultation Matters*, United States Institute of Peace Special Report 260, 2010.

13. *Sudan: Breaking the Abyei Deadlock*, ICG Africa Briefing No. 47, 2007; Douglas H. Johnson, 'Why Abyei Matters: The Breaking Point of Sudan's Comprehensive Peace Agreement?', *African Affairs*, Vol. 107, No. 426, 2008.

14. Unlike the ABC, the PCA did not take oral and historical evidence into account. Douglas H. Johnson, 'The Heglig Oil Dispute between Sudan and South Sudan', *Journal of Eastern African Studies*, Vol. 6, No. 3, 2012, pp. 566–7.

15. In 2009 the Heglig and Bamboo oil fields, placed outside Abyei by the PCA, were set to produce six times more Nile blend crude than the Diffra oil field, which was inside the region. *Sudan: Breaking the Abyei Deadlock*, ICG Africa Briefing No. 47, 2007, p. 8.

16. Heglig was actually not included in the disputed areas under review by the Technical Ad Hoc Border Committee (Kafia Kingi, Bahr al Arab 14 miles, Kaka, Migeinis and Jodha), but was put forward as an additional 'claimed area' by the SPLM after independence; Personal communication, source close to African Union mediation team, 13 August 2013; 'Sudan's SPLM Threatens to Refer Abyei Row to Hague', *Platts Oilgram News*, 28 July 2009.

17. Sudan says 80% of North-South border demarcation complete', *Sudan Tribune*, 5 May 2010.

18. Sudan Petroleum Unit, Ministry of Finance and National Economy, 'Oil Production Monthly—year 2008', http://www.mof.gov.sd/topics_show_E.php?topic_id=1#, accessed 18 June 2010.

19. Ministry of Petroleum: Sudanese Petroleum Corporation, http://www.spc.sd/en/statics_crude.php, accessed 18 January 2013.

20. The estimates varied according to the assumed recovery factor of total 'oil in place' in a reservoir. S.M. Ali Abbas et al., 'Fiscal Adjustment in Sudan: Size, Speed, and Composition', IMF, 2010, p. 27.

21. Republic of Sudan, Ministry of Petroleum, Sudanese Petroleum Corporation, http://www.spc.sd/, accessed 15 June 2011.

22. In Block 5A, the low quality of oil from the Thar Jath and Mala fields forced WNPOC to make an agreement with GNPOC that it could only send 10 per cent of the crude into its pipeline, as a measure designed to ensure that the quality of Nile blend remained high, holding back the true potential of the concession; interview, political analyst and CNPC geologist, Khartoum, 11 and 15 October 2010.

23. Wikileaks cable, 'Oil Executives Doubt Minister's Claim of 2009 Production Increase', 24 November 2008, http://wikileaks.org/cable/2008/11/08KHARTOUM1702.html, accessed 24 January 2013.

24. Interview, former government oil official, London, 20 June 2011.

25. Telephone interview, international oil analyst, 28 January 2009.

26. Interview, Sudanese oil official, Khartoum, 15 October 2010.

27. *Sudan's Oil Industry on the Eve of the Referendum: Facts and Analysis IV*, European Coalition on Oil in Sudan (ECOS), 2010, p. 15.

28. Norwegian Petroleum Directorate, 'Sudan', 5 July 2011, http://www.npd.no/en/Publications/Reports/Oil-for-development-2010/OfD-projects-Core-countries/Sudan/, accessed 24 January 2013.

29. 'Sudan works with CNPC, Petronas on oil extraction', Reuters, 28 September 2010, http://uk.reuters.com/article/2010/09/28/sudan-sudapet-idUK-LDE68R1MA20100928, accessed 24 January 2013.

30. Interviews, CNPC geologist, Khartoum, 15 October 2010; CNPC official, Beijing, 30 September 2011.

31. Interview, oil service company manager, Khartoum, 14 October 2010.

32. 'OVL to quit in Sudan', *Times of India*, 27 April 2009.

33. Interview, former Sudanese oil company manager, 15 October 2010.

34. Wikileaks cable, 'Positives and Negatives in Sudan's Oil Industry', 12 March 2008, http://wikileaks.org/cable/2008/03/08KHARTOUM367.html, accessed 24 January 2013.

35. Interview, government official, Sudan Ministry of Energy and Mining, 2 November 2007.

36. 'Sudan police crack down on protests—witness', Reuters, 30 August 2006.

37. Interview, government official, Ministry of Energy and Mining, 2 November 2007.

38. The organisational challenge facing Chinese national oil companies is discussed in Jin Zhang, *Catch-up and Competitiveness in China: The Case of Large Firms in the Oil Industry*, London: RoutledgeCurzon, 2004.

39. 周吉平，《海外创业的标志工程—中国石油天然气集团公司苏丹石油项目》，《中国石油》，2000年12月 (Zhou Jiping, 'The Symbolic Achievement in the Overseas Business: The Sudan Project of CNPC', *China Petroleum*, December 2000, pp. 15–6).

40. Maggie Cox, 'CNPC reorganizes into eight integrated service companies, seeking international market', *Drilling Contractor*, http://www.drillingcontractor.org/cnpc-reorganizes-into-eight-integrated-service-companies-seeking-international-market-5388, accessed 25 January 2013.

41. Interview, Sudanese oil official, Khartoum, 2 November 2007.

42. Wikileaks cable, 'Oil Executives Doubt Minister's Claim of 2009 Production Increase', 24 November 2008, http://wikileaks.org/cable/2008/11/08KHARTOUM1702.html, accessed 24 January 2013; interview, international oil service company manager, Khartoum, 14 October 2010.

43. ONGC Videsh, 'Annual Report 2010–2011', New Delhi: ONGC Videsh, 2011, p. 11; Petronas, 'Annual Report 2011', Kuala Lumpur: Petronas, 2012, p. 41.

44. 'South Sudan's flag raised at independence ceremony', BBC News, 9 July 2011; Jeffrey Gettleman, 'After years of struggle, South Sudan becomes a new nation', *New York Times*, 9 July 2011.

45. Matthew LeRiche and Matthew Arnold, *South Sudan: From Revolution to Independence*, London: C. Hurst & Co., 2012, pp. 116–20.

46. 'MPM Marketing Report', Republic of South Sudan, Ministry of Petroleum and Mining, 2012, p. 18; *Approved Budget 2012/13*, Republic of South Sudan, 2012, p. 17.

47. Edward Thomas, 'Against the Gathering Storm: Securing Sudan's Comprehensive Peace Agreement', Chatham House, 2009, p. 27.

48. *Sudan Mirror*, Vol. 5, Issue 2, 24 December—5 January 2009.

49. 'South Sudan: billions lost in fake contracts, inflated payrolls', *Sudan Tribune*, 17 July 2012.

50. Hereward Holland, 'South Sudan officials have stolen $4 billion: president', Reuters, 4 June 2012.

51. Matip died of diabetes in a Nairobi hospital in August 2012.

52. LeRiche and Arnold, op. cit., pp. 159–62.

53. *South Sudan: Compounding Instability in Unity State*, ICG Africa Report No. 179, 2011, p. 10.

54. Peter Gadet, the cunning Nuer commander who changed allegiances from the Sudanese government to the SPLA during the civil war, defected from the SPLA in March 2011. Operating from a base north of the border and receiving arms

and logistical support from the Sudanese government, Gadet led a force of almost 2,000 under the banner of the South Sudan Liberation Army. While Gadet rejoined the SPLA later in the year, part of his rebel group did not. *South Sudan: Compounding Instability in Unity State*, ICG Africa Report No. 179, 2011, pp. 12–6.

55. The rebel leader David Yau Yau, from the Murle, linked his grievances to the intense ethnic fighting in Jonglei state in 2009. 'My Neighbour, My Enemy: Inter-tribal Violence in Jonglei,' Small Arms Survey, HSBA Issue Brief No. 21, 2012.

56. China was only one of several major arms suppliers to Sudan, along with Russia, Belarus and Iran. *China's Growing Role in African Peace and Security*, London: Saferworld, 2011, p. 49; *Reaching for the Gun: Arms Flows and Holdings in South Sudan*, Small Arms Survey HSBA Issue Brief No. 19, Geneva, Small Arms Survey, 2012.

57. *Sudan's Comprehensive Peace Agreement: The Long Road Ahead*, ICG Africa Report No. 106, 2006, pp. 8–9.

58. The US firm Jarch Capital also claimed rights to parts of Block B according to an agreement it signed in early 2004 with the SSDF southern militia: interview, international oil service company manager, Juba, 1 November 2006.

59. Interview, company managers, Khartoum, 4 November 2007.

60. 'Understanding White Nile acquisition of oil concession in S. Sudan', *Sudan Tribune*, 4 July 2006.

61. Interview, Philip Ward, Juba, 1 November 2006.

62. John Agou Wuoi, 'South Sudan Jonglei leaders endorse UK oil White Nile', *Sudan Tribune*, 8 May 2007.

63. A ruling by the National Petroleum Commission, which was established by the NCP and SPLM, also allocated a 10 per cent stake in Total's consortium to the southern Sudanese Nilepet. Philip Theon Aleu, 'French Total prepares to resume oil activities in Sudan's Jonglei', *Sudan Tribune*, 19 March 2008; 'The National Petroleum Commission', Note from Rapporteur's Office, NPC, Khartoum, June 2007.

64. 'Southern Leaders Compete for a New State', *Africa Confidential*, Vol. 51, No. 3, 5 February 2010.

65. Months after the dispute was settled, Kiir replaced Leek as Governor of Jonglei with Kuol Manyang. One oil company manager remarked that 'It is likely that Manyang was appointed to the position just to stand up to Riek Machar.'; Wikileaks cable, 'Positives and Negatives in Sudan's Oil Industry', 12 March 2008, http://wikileaks.org/cable/2008/03/08KHARTOUM367.html, accessed 9 November 2012.

66. Interview, former SPLM oil adviser, London, 20 June 2011.

67. ASCOM. www.ascom.md, accessed 29 November 2009; 'Sudan oil body endorses Ascom & discusses Total concession', *Sudan Tribune*, 26 August 2009.

68. Interview, former oil official, Khartoum, 15 October 2010.

69. OVL ended up spending close to $90 million as its share of exploration costs; 'Swedish Lundin fails to find oil in the third Sudanese well', *Sudan Tribune*, 30 October 2008; Sanjay Dutta, 'OVL to quit block in Sudan', *The Times of India*, 27 April 2009; 'Flop Sudan oil venture results in $89m loss', *The Telegraph* (Calcutta), 27 April 2009.

70. Daniel Large, 'China's Sudan Engagement: Changing Northern and Southern Political Trajectories in Peace and War', *China Quarterly*, Vol. 199, 2009, p. 622.

71. Peter S. Goodman, 'China invests heavily in Sudan's oil industry', *Washington Post*, 23 December 2004.

72. Daniel Large, 'Southern Sudan and China: 'Enemies into Friends'?', in Daniel Large and Luke A. Patey (eds), *Sudan Looks East: China, India and the Politics of Asian Alternatives*, Oxford: James Currey, 2011, pp. 167–70.

73. Wikileaks cable, 'Se Gration Meeting with Chinese Vfm Zhai', 3 February 2010, http://wikileaks.org/cable/2010/02/10ADDISABABA174.html, accessed 17 June 2012.

74. Andrew Higgins, 'Oil interests push China into Sudanese mire', *Washington Post*, 24 December 2011.

75. 'South Sudan and China commit to stronger ties', *Sudan Tribune*, 22 October 2011.

76. 'China confidence about prospect of co-op with Sudan: CPC official', *Xinhua*, 16 November 2005.

77. Andrew Higgins, 'Oil interests push China into Sudanese mire', *Washington Post*, 24 December 2011.

78. Interviews, oil industry consultant and CNPC geologist, Beijing, 18 October 2011 and 7 November 2011.

79. *China's New Courtship in South Sudan*, ICG Africa Report No. 186, 2012, p. 20.

80. Wikileaks, 'Pre/sudan: Chinese Oil Company Vp Discusses Sudan with Se Gration', 1 June 2009, http://wikileaks.org/cable/2009/06/09BEIJING1435.html, 27 June 2012.

81. Interview, CNPC manager, Beijing, 26 October 2011.

82. Interview, CNPC geologist, Beijing, 7 November 2011.

83. Andrew Higgins, 'Oil interests push China into Sudanese mire', *Washington Post*, 24 December 2011.

84. Indian diplomats also speak fondly of India's President Fakhruddin Ali Ahmed's December 1975 visit to Juba, where the whole town showed up to see him.

85. Interview, Khartoum, 12 October 2010.

86. Julius N. Uma, 'Envoy: S. Sudan to respect India's oil deals after independence', *Sudan Tribune*, 4 May 2011.

87. Amitav Ranjan, 'Sudan wants to redraw ONGC Videsh oil contracts', *Indian Express*, 11 October 2011.

88. Interview, OVL manager, Khartoum, 14 October 2010.

89. 'Sudan and South Sudan: Over a Barrel Again', *Oil Market Report*, International Energy Agency, Paris, 10 February 2012, p. 24.

90. In the run-up to independence, hundreds of northern Sudanese workers, who had become the backbone of the industry, were expelled or else opted to leave South Sudan because of insecurity. A small number of South Sudanese remained, but were unable to maintain previous production levels. Hereward Holland, 'Tensions running high after refugee camp bombing', Reuters, 18 November 2011.

91. Interview, CNPC official, Beijing, 30 September 2011; 'China trains petro-leum-related workers in South Sudan', *Xinhua*, 11 July 2011.

92. Interview, CNPC geologist, Beijing, 18 October 2011.

93. Hereward Holland, 'South Sudan could pump some oil by end-November—minister', Reuters, 3 November 2012.

94. Personal communication, source close to AU mediation team, 13 August 2013.

95. *China's New Courtship in South Sudan*, ICG Africa Report No. 186, 2012, p. 26.

96. Sudan was to receive fee payments in arrears from 9 July 2011 according to the terms of a possible future oil deal. Alan Boswell, 'South Sudan and Sudan at loggerheads over oil talks', *McClatchy*, 22 November 2011.

97. For an in-depth analysis of the negotiations, see *China's New Courtship in South Sudan*, ICG Africa Report No. 186, 2012, pp. 26–8.

98. Jeffrey Gettleman and Josh Korn, 'Warnings of all-out war in fight over Sudan town', *New York Times*, 22 May 2011; *Militarization in and around Abyei*, HSBA Small Arms Survey, 2 June 2011, http://www.smallarmssurveysudan.org, accessed 29 January 2013.

99. Louise Charbonneau, 'Residents in Sudan border states survive on roots, leaves—U.N.', Reuters, 8 January 2013.

100. The project of Sinohydro, which was building roads near Kordofan, was financed by the EXIM Bank of China, but the Sudanese rebels claimed the road was being built to facilitate Sudanese army movements. This was similar to the justification given by southern Sudanese rebels for its targeting of oil companies during the second civil war. Ulf Laessing and Sui-Lee Wee, 'Kidnapped Chinese workers freed in Sudan oil state', Reuters, 7 February 2012; Andrew Jacobs and Jeffrey Gettleman, 'Kidnappings of workers put pressure on China', *New York Times*, 31 January 2012.

101. 'ICRC intervenes to release Chinese hostages in Sudan', *Sudan Tribune*, 5 January 2012.

102. Wang Xiaocong, 'In Sudan, oil major CNPC may be over a barrel', *Caixin*, 29 August 2011.

103. Salma El Wardany and Jared Ferrie, 'China's envoy to Africa expresses concern over Sudan oil, border disputes', Bloomberg, 8 December 2011.

104. Interview, CNPC geologist, Beijing, 7 November 2011.

105. 'Pipeline Problems', *Africa-Asia Confidential*, Vol. 5, No. 2, 2011.

106. 'China expresses concern over stalled oil talks between Sudan, South Sudan', *Xinhua*, 5 December 2011.

107. 'China urges Sudan & South Sudan to break oil deadlock', *Sudan Tribune*, 12 December 2011.

108. 'Sudan's parliament authorizes confiscation of oil exports', *Sudan Tribune*, 9 December 2011; 'South Sudan threatens to suspend oil production if north imposes charges unilaterally', *Sudan Tribune*, 1 December 2011.

109. Interview, CNPC official, Khartoum, 15 October 2010.

110. *China's New Courtship in South Sudan*, ICG Africa Report No. 186, 2012, p. 28.

111. Ibid., p. 22.

112. Ibid., p. 23.

113. 'Statement by H.E. Salva Kiir Mayardit, President of the Republic of South Sudan to the National Legislature on the Current Oil Crisis', Government of the Republic of South Sudan, 23 January 2012.

114. Alexander Dziadosz, 'South Sudan's Chinese oil puzzle', Reuters, 14 November 2012.

115. *Approved Budget 2010*, Ministry of Finance and Economic Planning, GOSS, 2010.

116. 'Sudan Oil Talks Fail; Pipeline Shutdown Looms', Voice of America, 27 January 2012, http://m.voanews.com/a/151254.html, accessed 20 August 2013.

117. Personal communication, source close to AU mediation team, 12 August 2013.

118. 'Sudan Oil Talks Fail; Pipeline Shutdown Looms', Voice of America, 27 January 2012, http://m.voanews.com/a/151254.html, accessed 20 August 2013.

119. *China's New Courtship in South Sudan*, ICG Africa Report No. 186, 2012, p. 30.

120. Personal communication, source close to AU mediation team, 12 August 2013.

121. Armin Rosen, 'Sudan on the Brink: A Khartoum Spring?', *World Affairs*, July/August 2012.

122. Jared Ferrie, 'Oil brings new friction to Sudan and South Sudan', Inter Press Service, 14 February 2012.

123. Liu Yingcai, 'Letter to Hon. Stephen Dhieu Dau: MT Sea Sky Loading 650,000 bbls Dar Blend Crude Oil form Marsha Bashayer 2 Marine Terminal', PDOC/PRES/MPM/12-002, 13 January 2012.

124. Alexander Dziadosz, 'South Sudan's Chinese oil puzzle', Reuters, 14 November 2012.

125. Bhaskar Balakrishnan, 'Oil's not well in South Sudan', *The Hindu*, 10 February 2011.

126. Rohit Bansel, 'Our $3-bn war', *The Pioneer*, 4 April 2012.

127. 'India extends diplomatic overtures to South Sudan', *India Today*, 3 June 2012; Sachin Parashar, 'India names new special envoy to restart Sudan-S Sudan cross-border oil flow', *Times of India*, 3 January 2013.

128. Sachin Parashar, 'Indian envoy in South Sudan on oil mission', *Times of India*, 2 April 2012.

129. 'The Petroleum Act', Laws of South Sudan, Government of South Sudan, 2012.

130. 'The Petroleum Act 2012 and Draft Petroleum Regulations', Ministry of Petroleum and Mining, Government of South Sudan, Workshop Report, 2012, p. 5.

131. Soluxe International, 'Inaugural Ceremony of CNPC Logistic and Living Base in South Sudan', Company News, 30 August 2011, http://www.soluxeint.com/2011/0830/1780.html, accessed 14 February 2013.

132. *Blueprint for Prosperity: How South Sudan's Laws hold the key to a transparent and accountable oil sector*, Global Witness, 2012.

133. James Gatdet Dak, 'Sudan Unity State governor says more oil share post-2011', *Sudan Tribune*. 19 August 2009.

134. 'Petroleum Revenue Management Bill', 2012, Bill No. 61, Laws of South Sudan, p. 18.

135. Thomas Kenneth, 'South Sudan: President Kiir Visits PFPF and Lays Foundation Stone of Thiangrial Refinery', Government of South Sudan, 23 November 2012.

136. 'South Sudan embarks on building Bentiu oil refinery', *Sudan Tribune*, 14 December 2012.

137. *South Sudan: Compounding Instability in Unity State*, ICG Africa Report No. 179, 2011, p. 29.

138. In 2006, Vice-President Riek Machar had pleaded for villagers to allow Petrodar to continue its work in the face of protests. Compensation for damage to farms and infrastructure projects was promised, but did not materialise. Unpublished report from international organisation obtained by author.

139. 'Sudan says no desire for full-fledged war with south despite military escalation', *Sudan Tribune*, 28 March 2012.

140. 'Oil well bombing raises heat in Sudan oil dispute', Reuters, 6 March 2012.

141. 'Sudan troops' advance on Heglig oil field", BBC News, 13 April 2012.

142. Alan Boswell, 'Amid a trail of corpses, little doubt that Sudan, South Sudan are now at war', *McClatchy*, 16 April 2012.

143. Personal communication, source close to AU mediation team, 12 August 2013.

144. Yara Bayoumy, 'Kiir, back from China, says Heglig belongs to South Sudan', *Reuters*, 27 April 2012.

145. 'Sudan admits impact of Heglig crisis on economy', *Sudan Tribune*, 15 April 2012; 'Sudan says Juba owes $1 billion, says Heglig oil production to be boosted', *Sudan Tribune*, 9 May 2012.

146. Personal communication, source close to AU mediation team, 12 August 2013.

147. 'Agreement between The Government of the Republic of South Sudan and The Government of the Republic of Sudan on Oil and Related Economic Matters', Addis Ababa, 27 September 2012, pp. 6–7.

148. 'OVL seeks transit fee waiver to move crude oil from South Sudan to North', *The Hindu*, 16 October 2012.

11. THE REFORM YEARS

1. Sudarsan Raghavan, 'South Sudan's president visits China during crisis', *Financial Times*, 24 April 2012.

2. 'Chinese vice premier meets South Sudanese president', *Xinhua*, 26 April 2012.

3. Two months before his arrival, Bashir sent a close aide to Beijing to meet Zhou Yongkang, the former boss of CNPC and Sudan's ally on China's Politburo Standing Committee. Bashir wanted Zhou to ensure that he would be safe from the ICC warrant for his arrest on genocide charges in Darfur. There was little chance China would act on the warrant, as Beijing was not a signatory to the Rome statute that created the ICC, but Bashir was taking all precautions. When his plane had to be rerouted on the way to China, delaying his visit, the Sudanese media were quick to allege that NATO forces were seeking to intercept the Sudanese president if he ventured over Afghanistan. Andrew Higgins, 'Oil interests tie China to Sudan leader Bashir, even as he faces genocide charges', *Washington Post*, 22 June 2011; 'Sudan parliament slams Turkmenistan & Tajikistan over Bashir's flight', *Sudan Tribune*, 29 June 2011.

4. Barbara Demick, 'Confusion as Sudan president arrives day late in Beijing', *Los Angeles Times*, 28 June 2011.

5. Bashir's visit to China resembled his predecessor Jaafar Nimeiri's trip to Washington in 1985. Nimeiri was looking for US financial support for his crumbling, oil-deprived economy. After failing to get what he wanted, Nimeiri discovered on his way home that after sixteen years of military rule, he had been overthrown by popular protests.

6. *China's New Courtship in South Sudan*, ICG Africa Report No. 186, 2012, p. 25, n. 150.

7. 'China, Sudan deepen oil-sector ties', *Wall Street Journal*, 29 June 2011.

8. ONGC Videsh, 'Annual Report 2011–12', New Delhi: ONGC Videsh, 2012, p. 22.

9. 'China refused to find agricultural project in Sudan for lack of oil collateral: Bashir', *Sudan Tribune*, 10 March 2012.

10. Interview, senior Indian diplomat, 12 October 2010.

11. *Sudan: Major Reform or More War*, Africa Report No. 194, Brussels: ICG, 2012.

12. Guillaume Lavallee, 'Sudan gold miners vie for desert riches,' AFP, 23 August 2010.

13. Ulf Laessing, 'Gold last hope for Sudan to avert economic collapse', Reuters, 18 July 2012.

14. See Harry Verhoeven, '"Dams are Development": China, the Al-Ingaz Regime, and the Political Economy of the Sudanese Nile', in Daniel Large and Luke A. Patey (eds), *Sudan Looks East: China, India and the Politics of Asian Alternatives*, Oxford: James Currey, 2011.

15. Jeffrey Gettleman, 'The boom is drowned out by the boys on motorbikes', *New York Times*, 29 November 2007; Gregg Carlstrom, 'Juba: East Africa's economic boom town', *Al Jazeera*, 7 July 2011.

16. 'South Sudan economy on the verge of collapse, World Bank warns', *Sudan Tribune*, 6 May 2012.

17. Personal communication, source close to AU mediation team, 13 August 2013.

18. Jared Ferrie, 'South Sudan hunts for loans as oil-output halt dents economy', Bloomberg, 11 May 2012.

19. *Blueprint for Prosperity: How South Sudan's New Laws hold the Key to a Transparent and Accountable Oil Sector*, London: Global Witness, 2012, pp. 20–21.

20. Fred Oluoch, 'Farming, minerals to cushion South Sudan economy', *The East African*, 2 February 2013.

21. Jaindi Kisero, 'Lamu abuzz with construction as South Sudan seeks new pipeline', *The East African*, 11 February 2011.

22. 'Lamu port project launched for South Sudan and Ethiopia', BBC News, 2 March 2012.

23. 'South Sudan and Kenya sign memorandum on construction of oil pipeline', *Sudan Tribune*, 24 January 2012; 'South Sudan in Ethiopia-Djibouti oil pipeline deal', *BBC News*, 9 February 2012.

24. Toby Collins, 'South Sudanese rebels threaten proposed oil pipeline', *Sudan Tribune*, 27 January 2012.

25. Jon Termin and Raymond Gilpin, *The Politics of Oil and a Proposed Pipeline for South Sudan*, United States Institute of Peace, 27 January 2012, http://www.usip. org/publications/the-politics-oil-and-proposed-pipeline-south-sudan, accessed 11 February 2012.

26. 'South Sudan says oil pipeline via Kenya to cost $3 billion', Reuters, 10 August 2012.

27. 'MPM Marketing Report', Ministry of Petroleum and Mining, Republic of South Sudan, 2012, pp. 11–2.

28. Interviews, Total managers, Juba and Khartoum, 2 November 2006 and 30 October 2007.

29. Alexander Dziadosz, 'South Sudan to split Total oil block: officials', Reuters, 14 September 2012.

30. Hereward Holland, 'South Sudan could pump some oil by end-November—minister', Reuters, 3 November 2012.

31. Catherine Byaruhanga, 'Ugandans evicted to make way for oil refinery', *BBC News*, 14 November 2012; William Wallis and Orla Ryan, 'Kenya to lead strike on Somali militants', *Financial Times*, 9 August 2012.

32. 'Total eyeing South Sudan-Uganda oil pipeline', Reuters, 7 December 2011.

33. Adam Green, 'East Africa oil: smaller explorers hit hurdles', *Financial Times*, 22 November 2012.

34. Jared Ferrie, 'China to loan South Sudan $8 billion for infrastructure projects', Bloomberg, 28 April 2012.

35. Sudarsan Raghavan, 'South Sudan's president visits China during crisis', *Financial Times*, 24 April 2012.

36. Wayne Ma, 'South Sudan seeks oil-sector help from China', *Wall Street Journal*, 24 April 2012.

37. Katrina Manson, 'South Sudan faces finance crunch', *Financial Times*, 15 May 2012.

pp. [247–251]

38. *China's New Courtship in South Sudan*, ICG Africa Report No. 186, 2012, p. 11.
39. 'Toyota Tsusho puts a $5b bid for Lamu-Juba oil pipeline', *The Standard*, 15 August 2012.
40. *China's New Courtship in South Sudan*, ICG Africa Report No. 186, 2012, p. 25.
41. Interview, Chinese academic, Beijing, 25 October 2011; Jaindi Kisero, 'Lamu abuzz with construction as South Sudan seeks new pipeline', *The East African*, 11 February 2011.
42. Kabir Taneja, 'ONGC reluctant to support South Sudan pipeline offer', *Sunday Guardian*, 30 September 2012.
43. 'Sudan rivals 'to resume pumping oil', *BBC News*, 12 March 2013.
44. Simon Tisdall, 'South Sudan: two years old but nothing to celebrate', *The Guardian*, 4 July 2013.
45. 'South Sudan's Kiir relieves Unity state governor Taban Deng', *Sudan Tribune*, 8 July 2013.
46. Simon Tisdall, 'South Sudan president sacks cabinet in power struggle', *The Guardian*, 24 July 2013.
47. Fortune, 'Global 500', http://money.cnn.com/magazines/fortune/global500/2012/full_list/, accessed 15 August 2012.
48. Leslie Hook, 'PetroChina to Beijing: give us a break', *Financial Times*, 30 October 2012.
49. China National Petroleum Corporation, 'Annual Report 2011', Beijing: CNPC, 2012, p. 25.
50. Julie Jiang and Jonathan Sinton, *Overseas Investments by Chinese National Oil Companies: Assessing the Drivers and Impacts*, International Energy Agency, 2011, p. 18.
51. Chen Zhu, 'Clad in purple, Big Oil's iron lady in Iraq', *Caixin*, 25 February 2011.
52. Hassan Hafida, 'BP, CNPC win Iraq oil', *Wall Street Journal*, 9 October 2009.
53. Wang Xiaocong, 'More Chinese oil giants wearing a maple leaf', *Caixin*, 22 November 2011.
54. 韩树举, 王洪涛, 张军, 贺红旭 《中国石油天然气集团公司海外项目防恐安全管理探索与实践》, 《中国安全生产科学技术》, 2009年增刊 (Han Shuju, Wang Hongtao, Zhang Jun and He Hongxu, 'The Exploration and Practice of Anti-terrorism and Safety Management of CNPC Overseas Projects', *Journal of Safety Science and Technology*, supplement, 2009).
55. 'CNPC terminates 6 overseas projects, estimates losses of 1.2 bln yuan', *Xinhua*, 22 August 2011.
56. Leslie Hook, 'PetroChina in $2.2bn Canada gas deal', *Financial Times*, 14 December 2012.
57. Shawn McCarthy, 'PetroChina, Encana strike natural gas pact', *Globe and Mail*, 13 December 2012.
58. Roberta Rampton and Scott Hagget, 'CNOOC-Nexen deal wins U.S. approval its last hurdle', Reuters, 12 February 2012.

59. Nathan Vanerklippe, Shawn Vanderklippe, Shawn McCarthy and Jacquie McNish, 'Harper draws a line in the oil sands', *Globe and Mail*, 9 December 2012; Rebecca Penty and Sara Forden, 'Cnooc said to cede control of Nexen's U.S. Gulf assets', Bloomberg, 2 March 2013.

60. Chinese national oil companies also have technical and managerial limitations and along with their Indian counterparts have been frustrated by Iran's hard bargaining on contracts. Erica Downs, 'Cooperating with China on Iran', Policy Brief, The German Marshall Fund of the United States, 2012, p. 3.

61. 'India ONGC says presence in Iran, Sudan may affect US plans', Reuters, 4 September 2012.

62. Alam Srinivas, 'Oil is a secular sector', *The Outlook*, 25 November 2002.

63. Interview, Indian government adviser, New Delhi, 12 December 2008.

64. ONGC Videsh, 'Annual Reports' for the years 2005–6 to 2011–12, New Delhi: ONGC Videsh, 2006–12.

65. Ajay Modi, 'OVL output slides on unrest in Sudan, Syria', *Business Standard*, 26 March 2012.

66. ONGC Videsh, 'Annual Report 2011–12', op. cit., p. 2.

67. Anilesh S. Mahajan, 'ONGC Videsh's overseas woes: Could the problems have been avoided?', *Business Today*, 3 August 2012.

68. Mao Zedong, *Quotations from Chairman Mao Tsetung*, Peking: Foreign Language Press, 1972, pp. 12–3.

69. Han et al., op. cit.

70. Interview, Chinese academic, Beijing, 26 September 2011.

71. Interview, Chinese oil industry insider, Beijing, 18 October 2011.

72. Han et al., op. cit.

73. Interview, Sudanese doctor, Khartoum, 13 November 2010.

74. Han et al., op. cit.

75. Interview, international energy journalist, Beijing, 6 October 2011.

76. Interview, Chinese journalist, Beijing, 17 November 2011.

77. Michael Wines and Keith Bradsher, 'Workers question China's account of oil spill', *New York Times*, 4 August 2010.

78. Interview, Chinese energy journalist, Beijing, 17 November 2011.

79. 'China's CNPC oil chief rebuked for Dalian spill', BBC News, 25 November 2011.

80. Interview, oil industry consultant, 18 October 2011.

81. Erica Downs and Michal Meidan, 'Business and Politics in China: The Oil Executive Reshuffle of 2011', *China Security*, Issue 19, 2011, p. 16.

82. Aibing Guo, 'PetroChina's Jiang named head of state—Assets Supervisor', Bloomberg, 18 March 2013.

83. Jamil Anderlini, 'Bo Ally Gives up China Security Roles', *Financial Times*, 13 May 2012.

84. Chris Buckley and Jonathan Ansfield, 'Senior Chinese Official Falls Under Scrutiny as Some Point to Larger Inquiry', *New York Times*, 1 September 2013.

85. Zhang Gaoli, a member of the incoming Politburo Standing Committee in 2012, also has an oil background. Leslie Hook, 'Sinopec chief tipped for political post', *Financial Times*, 22 March 2011; Xiaofei Li, 'Chinese Political Transition Makes Change Possible in Energy Approach', *Oil and Gas Journal*, 4 February 2013.

86. Andrew Jacobs and Jeffrey Gettleman, 'Kidnappings of workers put pressure on China', *New York Times*, 31 January 2012.

87. CNPC had close to 400 workers in Libya, mainly working in construction; its facilities were attacked and ransacked. Interview, international journalist, Beijing, 6 October 2011; 'CNPC halts production in Libya, withdraws staff', Reuters, 28 February 2011.

88. Interview, oil analyst, Beijing, 27 September 2011.

89. Interview, CNPC official, Beijing, 26 October 2011.

90. Han et al., op. cit.

91. Daniel Houpt, 'Assessing China's Response Options to Kidnappings Abroad', *China Brief*, Vol. 12, Issue 10, 2012.

92. Linda Jakobson and Dean Knox, *New Foreign Policy Actors in China*, Stockholm International Peace Research Institute (SIPRI), Policy Paper 26, 2012, pp. 25–6.

93. Ma Liyao, 'Ministry aims to bolster safety abroad', *China Daily*, 23 November 2011; interviews, energy journalists, Beijing, 6 October and 17 November 2011.

94. Bo Kong, *China's International Petroleum Policy*, Santa Barbara: ABC-CLIO, 2010, p. 140.

95. Yu Hongyan, 'Oil majors see losses in overseas investment', *China Daily*, 19 July 2011.

96. Bo, op. cit., p 149.

97. 'Sudan assigns Chinese CNPC offshore oil block', Reuters, 27 July 2007.

98. Jakobson and Knox, op. cit., p. 25, n. 121.

99. 'India can invest $25b to buy oil fields abroad', *The Times of India*, 24 March 2005.

100. Tanvi Madan, 'India's ONGC: Balancing Different Roles, Different Goals', The James A. Baker III Institute for Public Policy of Rice University, 2007, p. 59.

101. Wikileaks cable, '"Upa Cabinet Shuffle Good for America", 30 January 2006, http://wikileaks.org/cable/2006/01/06NEWDELHI657.html, accessed 27 June 2012.

102. 'OVL's Asset buying Azerbaijan gets CCEA nod', *The Hindu*, 31 January 2013.

103. Interview, senior Indian diplomat, Khartoum, 12 October 2010.

104. Telephone interview, Indian oil analyst, 22 January 2013.

105. Interview, Indian oil analyst, New Delhi, 10 December 2008.

105. Amitav Ranjan, 'Chinese onslaught forces OVL to seek lower hurdle rates', *Indian Express*, 25 July 2007; Sanjay Dutta, 'OVL's financial powers may increase 10-folds', *The Times of India*, 9 May 2011.

107. Comptroller and Auditor General of India, 'ONGC Videsh Limited Joint Venture Operation', Report No. 28 of 2010–11, Government of India, 2011.

108. Varun Rai, 'Adapting to Shifting Government Priorities: An Assessment of the Performance and Strategy of India's ONGC', Working Paper #91, Stanford: Program on Energy and Sustainable Development, 2010, pp. 58–9.

109. Utpal Bhaskar, 'OVL's Imperial miscalculation', LiveMint, 17 June 2010; San-jay Dutta, 'OVL gets $2.5 bn Imperial blues', *The Times of India*, 8 December 2011.

110. Comptroller and Auditor General of India, 'ONGC Videsh Limited Joint Venture Operation', Report No. 28 of 2010–11, Government of India, 2011, p. 11.

111. Siddhartha P. Saikia, 'OVL counters CAG view on 'unfruitful' expenses', 5 April 2011, http://www.mydigitalfc.com/petroleum/ovl-counters-cag-view-unfruit-ful-expenses-803, accessed 15 February 2013.

112. Interview, Indian government adviser, New Delhi, 12 December 2008.

113. The Koizumi government in 2001–06 restructured JNOC under the Japan Oil, Gas, and Metals National Corporation (JOGMEC) and applied restrictions to subsidisation. But the New National Energy Strategy released by Tokyo in May 2006 pledged more support to upstream oil companies, indicating that Japan may repeat the same mistakes if the investments of JOGMEC do not pan out. Peter C. Evans, 'Japan', The Brookings Foreign Policy Studies: Energy Security Series, The Brookings Institution, December, 2006, pp. 20–1.

114. Sudha Mahalingam, 'India's Energy Security: The Strategic Versus Economic Dimensions', in Sebastian Morris (ed.), *Oil and Natural Gas, India Infrastructure Report 2004, Ensuring Value for Money*, New Delhi: Oxford University Press, 2004; Shebonti Ray Dadwal and Uttam Kumar Sinha, 'Equity Oil and India's Energy Security', *Strategic Analysis*, Vol. 29, No. 3, 2005, pp. 522–3; Tanvi Madan, 'India', The Brookings Foreign Policy Studies: Energy Security Series, The Brookings Institution, November 2006, pp. 40–44; Shebonti Ray Dadwal, 'India's Overseas Assets: Do they Contribute to Energy Security?', *Strategic Analysis*, Vol. 36, No. 1, January 2012.

115. Ajay Modi, 'Is OVL making the right acquisitions?', *Business Standard*, 7 December 2012.

116. Tanvi Madan, 'India's Global Search for Energy', in Michael Kugelman (ed.), *Foreign Addiction: Assessing India's Energy Security Strategy*, Asia Program Special Report, No. 142, Woodrow Wilson International Center for Scholars, 2008, p. 9.

117. Ajay Modi, 'Is OVL making the right acquisitions?', *Business Standard*, 7 December 2012.

CONCLUSION: THE SUDANESE FACTOR

1. Thomas Callaghy, Ronald Kassimir and Robert Latham (eds), *Intervention and Transnationalism in Africa: Global-local Networks of Power*, Cambridge: Cambridge University Press, 2011; Scarlett Cornelissen, Fantu Cheru and Timothy M. Shaw

(eds), *Africa and International Relations in the 21st Century*, New York: Palgrave, 2012.

2. Timothy M. Shaw, 'China, India and (South) Africa: What International Relations in the Second Decade of the Twenty-first Century?', in Fantu Cheru and Cyril Obi (eds), *The Rise of China and India in Africa*, New York: Zed Books, 2010, p. 13.

3. Jean-François Bayart, 'Africa in the World: A History of Extraversion', *African Affairs*, Vol. 99, No. 395, 2000.

4. Christopher Clapham, 'Fitting China In', in Chris Alden, Daniel Large and Ricardo Soares de Oliveira (eds), *China Returns to Africa: A Rising Power and a Continent Embrace*, London: C. Hurst & Co., 2008.

5. Sudan did not have an impact only on Chinese and Indian engagement. The experiences of Talisman in Sudan had a transformational impact on the company's approach to corporate responsibility and political risk. Sudan also demonstrated that it held tremendous sway in US politics by igniting civil society action over the civil war in Darfur.

6. See Tanvi Madan, 'India's Global Search for Energy', in Michael Kugelman (ed.), *Foreign Addiction: Assessing India's Energy Security Strategy*, Asia Program Special Report, No. 142, Woodrow Wilson International Center for Scholars, 2008; Erica S. Downs, 'Who's Afraid of China's Oil Companies?', in Carlos Pascual and Jonathan Elkind (eds), *Energy Security: Economics, Politics, Strategies and Implications*, Washington, DC: Brookings Institution, 2010; Bo Kong, *China's International Petroleum Policy*, Santa Barbara: ABC-CLIO, 2010; Philip Andrews-Speed and Roland Dannreuther, *China, Oil, and Global Politics*, New York: Routledge, 2011.

7. Interview, Chinese oil expert, Beijing, 11 November 2011.

8. This transformation is particularly noticeable in China's one-party political system where policy-making, traditionally a fragmented process within the Communist Party and Chinese government, is increasingly influenced by non-traditional actors such as corporations, the media, non-governmental organisations and netizens. Kenneth Lieberthal and Michel Oksenberg, *Policy Making in China: Leaders, Structures, and Processes*, Princeton, NJ: Princeton University Press, 1988; Andrew Mertha, 'Fragmented Authoritarianism 2.0': Political Pluralization in the Chinese Policy Process', *China Quarterly*, Vol. 200, 2009; Linda Jakobson and Dean Knox, 'New Foreign Policy Actors in China', SIPRI Policy Paper 26, September 2012.

9. If international production and reserves of both Chinese and Indian companies continue to grow larger in comparison to assets at home, the need to adapt to political and security risk in the future will only increase. This possibility seems particularly relevant to OVL and India, where oil production continues to stagnate. China's production, along with the US and other countries in the world, may benefit in future from new shale oil and gas reserves.

10. Telephone interview, Allan Martini, 19 February 2013.

INDEX

Abyei: 197, 200, 237, 248; Ngok
Dinka population of, 192–3;
Sudanese military presence in, 226
Abyei Boundaries Commission
(ABC): PCA ruling on (2009),
212
Adar-Yale oil fields: 106; reserve
levels of, 148
Advani, L.K.: Indian Deputy Prime
Minister, 140, 143
Afghanistan: 70, 109; Operation
Enduring Freedom (2001–), 110
African Union (AU): 175, 226, 232,
236; Addis Ababa Summit
(2012), 230–1; High Level
Implementation Panel, 225;
Mission in Sudan, 172
Afro-Asian Relations Conference
(1955): attendees of, 146
Aggar, Malik: leader of SPLA-
North, 227
AGIP: member of Iminoco, 132
Agordeed oil field: reserve levels of,
148
Aiyar, Mani Shankar: 130; Indian
Oil Minister, 129, 137, 259
Albright, Madeleine: US Secretary
of State, 70
Alexander, James Terence: CEO of

Arakis Energy, 60; resignation of
(1995), 61
Algeria: 146
Ali, Hassan: Secretary General of
Sudanese Ministry of Energy and
Mining, 65
Alier, Abdel: President of High
Executive Committee, 33–4
American Federation of Labor and
Congress of Industrial Organiza-
tions (AFL-CIO): 78
Amnesty International: 68, 163
Amum, Pagan: 224, 231; meeting
with Li Changchun (2011), 223;
SPLM Secretary-General, 211,
223, 230, 248
Angola: 51–2, 146, 187; oil exports
of, 88; oil reserves of, 111
Anyanya: founding of, 6; members
of, 38, 219
Anyanya II: 38; Bentiu kidnapping
(1982), 41; emergence of, 32, 37;
members of, 61; role in Rubkona
Incident (1984), 38–41, 43, 272
Arab Group International (AGI): 61
Arab Petroleum Investments
Corporation: 23
Arab Spring: Egyptian Revolution
(2011), 242; Libyan Civil War

339

Toyota: estimation of cost of Juba-Lamu pipeline, 247

Transparency International: 73

al-Tuhami, Sharif: Sudanese Minister of Energy and Mining, 2–3, 19–20, 34, 37

Tunisia: 132, 146; Revolution (2010–11), 242

al-Turabi, Hassan: 50; foreign policy of, 53; founder of Popular Congress, 195; imprisonment of, 45, 48, 102–3; meeting with Lutfur Khan (1992), 59; spokesperson for Muslim Brotherhood, 34

UBS: financial investments of, 167

Uganda: 64, 120, 217; oil reserves of, 246

Uyghur: language of, 90

Umma Party: members of, 22

Union Bank of Switzerland: 126

United Arab Emirates (UAE): Abu Dhabi, 12; Dubai, 12

United Kingdom (UK): London, 110, 140, 173, 177, 199

United Nations (UN): 23, 67, 150, 175; Development Programme (UNDP), 187; geographical surveys, 14; Global Compact, 73; Mission in Sudan (UNMIS), 151, 172; personnel of, 74; Security Council, 12, 23, 147, 174. 176, 202

United Progressive Alliance: members of, 152

United States of America (USA): 13, 15, 109, 140, 202, 250, 252, 257, 264; 9/11 Attacks, 71, 110; aid provision to Sudan 26–7, 29, 45–6; Anti-Terrorism and

Effective Death Penalty Act (1996), 63–4; Central Intelligence Agency (CIA), 27, 110; Congress, 45, 70–2, 78, 163, 179; Defense Department, 45; energy consumption rate of, 125–6; Freedom from Religious Persecution Act, 70; government of, 23, 47, 70, 93, 137, 162, 165, 167, 182, 251, 269–71; government of, 53, 58, 73, 82, 102; military of, 43, 46, 129; National Intelligence Council, 182; Pentagon, 46, 71; Republican Party, 52; State Department, 25–7, 47, 53; Sudan Accountability and Divestment Act (2007), 168; Sudan Peace Act, 71–2; Treasury Department, 27, 47, 64; Washington DC, 13, 23, 27–8, 32, 45–9, 52, 58, 64, 71–2, 110, 119, 165, 179, 181–2, 269

Unity (state): 74, 110, 112, 200, 219, 222; Bentiu, 234–5; infrastructure investment in, 189; oil concession blocks of, 213; Rubkona, 1–3, 30–1, 235; Thar Jath oil field, 75

Unity oil field: 16, 49, 59, 67, 104, 116, 235; discovery of (1980), 16, 36; production rate for, 22, 72, 209, 214; sale of (1992), 50

University of Khartoum: Confucius Institute, 201

Unocal: attempted purchase of by CNOOC (2005), 179; personnel of, 96

Upper Nile (state): 43, 59, 200, 215, 222, 225; Bentiu, 1, 16, 21, 34–5, 37, 60, 110, 213; Melut, 16, 106, 148–9, 234; oil concessions for, 148–9; oil reserves of, 60, 246; Thiangrial, 234

ents of, 19, 23; oil embargo during, 19, 126

Yu Qiulu: 86, 90; Chairman of State Planning Commission, 87; Chinese Minister of Petroleum Industry, 85

Zaghawa: 162

Zenawi, Meles: 191; Chair of IGAD, 230; death of, 230, 236

Zeng Qinghong: 90; background of, 88; patron of Zhou Yongkang, 88, 94

Zhang Lifu: death of, 111

Zhongyuan Petroleum Engineering Co. Ltd (ZPEB): 112; ONLF Attack (2009), 191

Zhou Enlai: African tour (1963–4), 145

Zhou Jiping: 107, 119–20; CEO of CNPC International, 114, 116, 271; President of GNPOC, 66, 105, 114

Zhou Wenzhong: Chinese Deputy Foreign Minister, 174

Zhou Yongkang: 91, 94, 102, 116, 154, 177, 202–3, 267, 274; background of, 89, 104; Chinese Minister of Land and Natural Resources, 97, 101; CNPC General Manager, 91–2, 101; political career of, 90, 94, 97, 116–17; relationship with Bo Xilai, 256; Vice-President of CNPC, 96; visit to Sudan (2009), 201

Zhu Rongji: State Council of, 88, 97

Zimbabwe: 175